Financial Inclusion in Asia and Beyond

The World Bank considers financial inclusion to be an enabler for at least 7 of the 17 United Nations' sustainable development goals (SDGs). Financial inclusion, with its associated policy implications, is an important issue for ASEAN. This book examines the economic effects of financial inclusion. It explores issues surrounding measurement and impact of financial inclusion.

The book looks at various, salient topics including measurement of financial inclusion, the impact of (various indicators of) financial inclusion on development outcomes and macroeconomic volatility using aggregate data, as well as the effects of financial inclusion on poverty and development outcomes using micro data.

Tony Cavoli is associate professor in economics at the University of South Australia Business School. His research interests span the areas of international macroeconomics and finance, and he has published widely on such topics as exchange rate regimes and monetary policies, capital flows, economic and financial integration, financial inclusion, and development policy. He is currently the deputy editor of the *Journal of International Commerce, Economics and Policy,* and is also on the executive board of the American Committee on Asian Economic Studies.

Rashesh Shrestha is an economist at the Economic Research Institute for ASEAN and East Asia (ERIA) based in Indonesia. He conducts research on trade, human capital, and labour markets, and leads various projects related to economic development and integration of Southeast Asian countries. Before joining ERIA, he was associate lecturer at the Australian National University. He obtained his PhD in applied economics from the University of Wisconsin-Madison.

Routledge-ERIA Studies in Development Economics

The Indonesian Economy
Trade and Industrial Policies
Edited by Lili Yan Ing, Gordon H. Hanson and Sri Mulyani Indrawati

Social Protection Goals in East Asia
Strategies and Methods to Generate Fiscal Space
Edited by Mukul G. Asher, Fauziah Zen and Astrid Dita

World Trade Evolution
Growth, Productivity and Employment
Edited by Lili Yan Ing and Miaojie Yu

Emerging Global Trade Governance
Mega Free Trade Agreements and Implications for ASEAN
Edited by Lurong Chen, Shujiro Urata, Junji Nakagawa and Masahito Ambashi

East Asian Integration
Goods, Services and Investment
Edited by Lili Yan Ing, Martin Richardson and Shujiro Urata

Developing the Digital Economy in ASEAN
Edited by Lurong Chen and Fukunari Kimura

The Effects of Globalisation on Firm and Labour Performance
Edited by Chin Hee Hahn, Dionisius Narjoko, Ha Thi Thanh Doan and Shujiro Urata

Financial Inclusion in Asia and Beyond
Measurement, Development Gaps, and Economic Consequences
Edited by Tony Cavoli and Rashesh Shrestha

For more information about this series, please visit: www.routledge.com/Routledge-ERIA-Studies-in-Development-Economics/book-series/ERIA

Financial Inclusion in Asia and Beyond

Measurement, Development Gaps, and Economic Consequences

Edited by
Tony Cavoli and Rashesh Shrestha

Routledge
Taylor & Francis Group
LONDON AND NEW YORK

ERIA

First published 2021
by Routledge
2 Park Square, Milton Park, Abingdon, Oxon OX14 4RN

and by Routledge
605 Third Avenue, New York, NY 10017

Routledge is an imprint of the Taylor & Francis Group, an informa business

British Library Cataloguing-in-Publication Data
A catalogue record for this book is available from the British Library

Library of Congress Cataloging-in-Publication Data
A catalog record has been requested for this book

ISBN: 978-0-367-47688-5 (hbk)
ISBN: 978-1-003-03591-6 (ebk)

Typeset in Galliard
by Newgen Publishing UK

Contents

Illustrations

Figures

Tables

Appendices

Contributors

Rajabrata Banerjee is associate professor of economics at the University of South Australia Business Unit. He is an applied macroeconomist with more than 15 years of research experience in the field of economic growth and development. He has published around 20 research articles in high-ranking international journals, book chapters, and professional reports. He has also won competitive research funding from a number of international think-tanks. His research identifies factors that improve firm-level productivity and economic performances of countries and contributes to framing policies at the national and international levels.

Tony Cavoli is associate professor in economics at the University of South Australia Business School. His research interests span the areas of international macroeconomics and finance. He has published widely on such topics as exchange rate regimes and monetary policies, capital flows, economic and financial integration, financial inclusion, and development policy. He is currently the deputy editor of the *Journal of International Commerce, Economics and Policy*, and is also on the executive board of the American Committee on Asian Economic Studies.

Firmin Doko Tchatoka is associate professor at the School of Economics at the University of Adelaide. He received his PhD in economics in 2010 from the University of Montreal (Canada). Prior to joining the University of Adelaide, he held positions at the University of Tasmania, the University of Sherbrooke, and McGill University. His research focuses mainly on identification issues in Econometrics, with strong emphasis on weak instruments issues and model selection in GMM models. He has published many peer-reviewed articles including in popular econometrics journals such as the *Journal of Econometrics and Econometric Theory*. His applied work covers various topics including network econometrics, treatment effect models, forecasting, housing market, financial inclusion, and applied development economics. He has received many research excellence awards including an Australian Research Council (ARC) grant in 2019. He has given seminar and conference presentations around the world including at Yale University and the University of Toronto.

He has served on the African region committees of the Econometric Society meetings since 2017.

Ronald Donato is senior lecturer in economics at the University of South Australia. His research is primarily in the area of health economics, with a focus on regulatory reform, economic development, and public policy. He has published papers in numerous international journals, as well as book chapters and governmental and non-governmental reports covering a range of health-related matters including health system reform, primary healthcare, and indigenous health. His most recent research activity centres on the economics of nutrition and obesity in developing countries, successful ageing in low-income countries, and the influence of financial inclusion on child health outcomes.

Sasidaran Gopalan is currently is an assistant professor in the Department of Innovation in Government and Society, College of Business and Economics at United Arab Emirates University (UAEU), Abu Dhabi. Prior to this, he was a senior research fellow at the Nanyang Business School (NBS), Nanyang Technological University (NTU) in Singapore where he led the applied economic policy research at the Nanyang Centre for Emerging Markets, attached to the Division of Strategy, International Business and Entrepreneurship at NBS. He also worked as an assistant professor at the Graduate School of Public Policy, Nazarbayev University in Kazakhstan (2018–2019); a research fellow at the Lee Kuan Yew School of Public Policy, National University of Singapore (2015–2018); and a post-doctoral fellow at the Hong Kong University of Science and Technology (2014–2015).

Admasu Afsaw Maruta is an economist with research interests in development economics including economic growth, income inequality, poverty, education, health, and financial inclusion. He has published on foreign aid, economic growth, energy efficiency, financial development, and trade in top-ranked journals. Admasu holds a BA in economics from Haramaya University, Ethiopia; an MSc in agriculture and resource economics from the University of Alberta, Canada; an MA in business economics from Unity University, Ethiopia; and a PhD in applied economics from the University of South Australia. He is a consultant at the World Bank Group, Nigeria Macroeconomics, Trade, and Investment (MTI) unit.

Rogelio V. Mercado, Jr. is an economist at the Regional Cooperation and Integration Division of the Economic Research and Regional Cooperation Department of Asian Development Bank (ADB). He contributes to various division publications and knowledge products. His research interests include capital flows, financial integration, financial stress, portfolio allocation, asset price discovery, financial inclusion, and economic convergence. Rogelio has published in various journals including *Journal of Banking and Finance*, *Journal of International Money and Finance*, *Journal of Futures Markets*, *Review of Income and Wealth*, and has co-authored several book chapters. Prior to joining the ADB in July 2020, he was a senior economist at the South

East Asian Central Banks Research and Training Centre. He earned his PhD in economics from Trinity College, Dublin.

Samuel Nursamsu is an economist at Australia-Indonesia Partnership for Economic Development (Prospera). He received his master's degree in economics at the University of Wisconsin-Madison. His research expertise includes, but not limited to, international trade, labour economics, and development economics. His latest works are related to regulatory burdens in trade and investment in Indonesia.

Ilke Onur is senior lecturer of economics at the University of South Australia Business School. Ilke earned his PhD in economics from the University of Texas at Austin. His general field of research is applied microeconomics with special focus on industrial organisation, auctions, health and development economics, economics of information systems, and electronic commerce. More recently, he was a visiting researcher at the University of Tübingen in Germany. He is currently the academic editor of *PLOS ONE*. Over the past two years he has also served as an external reviewer for the grants programme for the Global Development Network. Earlier, he has also acted as an external reviewer for the research grants programme of the Scientific and Technological Council of Turkey.

Cyn-Young Park is director of Regional Cooperation and Integration at the Asian Development Bank (ADB). In her current capacity, she manages a team of economists to examine economic and policy issues related to regional cooperation and integration. She has written and lectured extensively on Asian economy and financial markets. Her work has been published in the *Journal of Banking and Finance*, *Journal of Futures Markets*, *Review of Income and Wealth*, and *World Economy*. Prior to joining the ADB, she was an economist (1999–2002) at the Organisation for Economic Cooperation and Development (OECD), where she contributed to the OECD Economic Outlook. She received her PhD in economics from Columbia University.

Ramkishen S. Rajan is Yong Pung How Professor at the Lee Kuan Yew School of Public Policy, National University of Singapore. Prior to this, he was professor of economics at ESSEC Business School, Asia- Pacific (2016–2017) after spending a decade (2006–2016) as professor of international economic policy at George Mason University (GMU) in Virginia, USA. He was the founding editor of the *Journal of International Commerce, Economics and Policy*, associate editor of the *Singapore Economic Review* and serves on the editorial board of various other academic journals.

Kimty Seng is an economist at the Center for Strategy and Innovation Policy (CSIP), Cambodia. He is also associate professor of economics at Royal School of Administration, Cambodia. His articles have been published in peer-reviewed journals including Journal of Development Studies and Journal of International Development. His recent work engages with the themes of inclusive legal justice, inclusive economic growth and development, and financial inclusion. His recent article has been published in Review of Social Economy. He obtained PhD in development economics from Waseda University, Japan.

Aizhan Sharipova is teaching assistant at the Graduate School of Public Policy, Nazarbayev University (Kazakhstan). After obtaining her bachelors degree with a major in finance at Karaganda Economic University, she graduated with a masters degree in economics from the University of Illinois at Urbana-Champaign, USA. Her research fields are macroeconomics and monetary policy with an empirical emphasis on issues relating to exchange rates, trade, and investments in developing economies.

Rashesh Shrestha is an economist at the Economic Research Institute for ASEAN and East Asia (ERIA) based in Indonesia. He conducts research on trade, human capital, and labour markets, and leads various projects related to economic development and integration of Southeast Asian countries. Before joining ERIA, he was associate lecturer at the Australian National University. He obtained his PhD in applied economics from the University of Wisconsin-Madison.

Patricia Sourdin is a consultant economist working on international trade and econometrics. She has published numerous articles and prepared reports and trade policy working papers on aspects of trade and trade costs, trade policy options, and trade facilitation for Pacific island economies for clients such as Organisation for Economic Cooperation and Development (OECD), Asia-Pacific Economic Cooperation (APEC), Economic Research Institute for ASEAN and East Asia (ERIA), Asian Development Bank (ADB), and the World Bank Group. She teaches econometrics and is currently visiting lecturer at the University of Adelaide and has been adjunct professor at the Johns Hopkins University in Bologna, the University of South Australia, and at Sciences Po in Paris.

Ha Trang Vo is a research scholar at the University of Adelaide, Australia. Her research interest is in financial inclusion and applied development economics. She graduated from the University of Sydney with first class honours degree in economics. Prior to this, she worked as chief economist for the Vietnam Bank for Agriculture and Rural Development for 10 years.

Preface and introduction

This book is an edited volume comprising research papers from a project of the Research Institutions Network of the Economic Research Institute for ASEAN and East Asia on the economic effects of financial inclusion. In broad terms, financial inclusion refers to the ability of consumers and firms to utilise formal financial services. The World Bank adds an efficiency characteristic in defining it as '... access to useful and affordable financial products...'.[1]

In a relatively short period, financial inclusion has become a dominant issue in financial development, economic policy, and inclusive growth. The world has made some progress in enhancing access to formal financial institutions. Globally, in 2017, 69% of adults had a bank account, an increase from 51% in 2011. The number of automatic teller machines (ATMs) per 100,000 adults globally increased from 41.6 in 2011 to 53.5 in 2017. Despite substantial gains, barriers to complete financial inclusion exist. In 2017, a significant number of adults did not have access to a bank account because financial services were too expensive (18%) or because they were too far away (13%). Despite advances in the degree to which financial services were provided digitally, and through the Internet, only 25% of people aged 15 years and above used a mobile phone to access a bank account, 22% used the Internet to pay bills, and only 4% used for mobile money services.

The objective of promoting greater levels of financial inclusion has been embraced by many nations across the development spectrum. The World Bank considers financial inclusion as an enabler for at least 7 of the 17 United Nations' sustainable development goals (SDGs). Financial inclusion and its associated policy implications are an important issue for the Association of Southeast Asian Nations (ASEAN). They are explicitly presented as a key element (element A4) of the ASEAN Economic Community Blueprint 2025 and are also related to some of the strategic measures in the ASEAN Socio-Cultural Community (ASCC) Blueprint 2025. More than 60 countries have implemented or are seeking to implement national strategies for financial inclusion designed to expand opportunities for financial inclusion through policies and regulations that support financial development, the provision of digital financial services, and financial literacy whilst being mindful of issues around consumer protection and the stability of the finance sector.

In light of growing interest on the topic, there is a need to explore the issues surrounding the measurement and impact of financial inclusion as most of the current work has focused on its determinants. Owing to the wide availability of survey data, it is now possible to explore these issues quantitatively to inform policymakers. This volume thus contributes towards filling this knowledge gap.

The chapters in this volume examine many salient topics – including measurement of financial inclusion, the impact of (various indicators of) financial inclusion on development outcomes and macroeconomic volatility using aggregate data, as well as the effects of financial inclusion on poverty and development outcomes using microdata. Here we briefly summarise the content of the chapters to this volume.

Chapter 1, 'The nature and landscape of financial inclusion in Asia' by Tony Cavoli and Rashesh Shrestha, overviews the nature of financial inclusion in Asia. It provides a series of definitions of, and motivation for, financial inclusion that will be employed as a reference for many of the subsequent chapters. Further, it analyses the state of progress for Asian countries in developing and implementing national financial inclusion strategies. The chapter also summarises some of the main development gaps seen in many popular indicators of financial inclusion – namely, the existence of gaps in financial inclusion by gender, rural versus urban populations, poverty, and education.

Broadly, the chapter finds that financial inclusion is growing in most regions in Asia. The increased focus by regulators and policymakers relating to financial inclusion is on financial literacy and education, as well as in financial technologies. Moreover, several development gaps pertain to financial inclusion – the most pervasive being the gap between the poor and non-poor segments of society and that between rural and urban populations.

Chapter 2, 'The composition of financial inclusion in ASEAN and East Asia: a new hybrid index and some stylised facts' by Rajabrata Banerjee and Ronald Donato, analyses the existing measures of financial inclusion and critically evaluates the two widely used existing methodologies to measure the dimensions, namely, the principal component analysis (PCA) method and the Euclidean distance method, respectively. It subsequently proposes a new hybrid financial inclusion index, which draws on the strengths of the existing measures. Five key stylised facts are proposed by critically evaluating three dimensions of financial inclusion – access, usage, and quality – in 22 Asian countries during 2004–2015. Utilising PCA scores, the chapter identifies the top two indicators under each dimension and by country, which are directly relevant for policy perspectives.

Amongst the key findings is that the top five and the bottom five countries are the same under all three measures. Countries either possessing very high or very low levels of financial inclusion are robust to measurement methodologies. This absence of ambiguity should present regulators with some clarity over the possible direction of the financial inclusion policy. There is also a pattern across countries in adopting usage, access, and quality dimensions of financial inclusion over time. The top two indicators appear to play a significant role across all developing countries in the sample. Knowledge of the most influential measures of financial inclusion for each country should present important policy implications for the design of financial inclusion policy.

Chapter 3, by Rajabrata Banerjee, Ronald Donato, and Admasu Afsaw Maruta, is titled 'The effects of financial inclusion on development outcomes: new insights from ASEAN and East Asian countries'. This study empirically examines the effects of financial inclusion on particular development outcomes, namely, economic growth, education, health, and income inequality. The study extends the current literature in terms of the broader range of development outcomes incorporated into the analysis. Further, and in contrast to other studies, this study uses both aggregated and disaggregated approaches to measure financial inclusion for 22 Asian countries in the period 2004–2015. Specifically, it first considers financial inclusion at an aggregate level by using a hybrid methodology to establish a financial inclusion index and to empirically examine its relationship with particular development outcomes. It then disaggregates the index into the three main dimensions of financial inclusions – access, usage, and quality – to examine whether specific dimensions are more strongly associated with certain development outcomes than with others. Finally, the chapter disaggregates further to the individual indicator level of financial inclusion and examines the effect of the top two indicators from each dimension based on PCA scores on the various development outcomes. Also, as part of the analysis, attention is given to the importance of political risk, a measure of institutional quality, on the effectiveness of financial inclusion on each development outcome. Essentially, this study bridges the nexus between the financial inclusion index, dimensions, and indicators by analysing its differing effects on development outcomes; analysing the role that political risk has on the effectiveness of financial inclusion; and determining the significance of aggregate and disaggregate measures of financial inclusion for informing policy.

Chapter 4, 'Financial inclusion: new measurement and cross-country impact assessment' by Cyn-Young Park and Rogelio V. Mercado, Jr., introduces a new composite index of financial inclusion for 151 economies using the PCA to compute weights for aggregating nine indicators of access, availability, and usage. Using the index, this chapter also assesses the impact of financial inclusion on poverty, income inequality, entrepreneurship, and female borrowing. Using a cross-sectional approach, the results provide robust evidence that higher financial inclusion significantly lowers poverty rates and increases entrepreneurship and female borrowing. However, the impacts of financial inclusion on poverty and other social goals are heterogeneous across country income groups, with the unit increase in financial inclusion yielding the largest reduction in poverty for low-income countries.

Chapter 5, 'Financial inclusion and macroeconomic volatility in Asia' by Sasidaran Gopalan, Ramkishen S. Rajan, and Aizhan Sharipova, examines the nexus between financial inclusion and macroeconomic volatility for 16 Asian emerging market and developing economies (EMDEs) for over two decades, between 1995 and 2017. In doing so, the main contributions of the chapter to the literature are fourfold. First, we focus exclusively on the Asian EMDEs using all available data. Second, we test for the relationship between reckless financial inclusion in the form of excessive credit growth and output volatility. Third, we investigate the importance of macroprudential policies in moderating output volatility induced by such reckless financial inclusion. Finally, we go beyond conventional measures of financial inclusion to understand the relationship between digital financial inclusion ('fintech') and output volatility for a broader sample of EMDEs.

The chapter finds a strong and robust negative relationship between financial inclusion and output volatility, implying that greater financial inclusion promotes output stability. However, our results also highlight a cautionary note: the joint association of financial inclusion and excessive credit growth tends to amplify output volatility. Our empirical analysis further shows that macroprudential policies help moderate the impact of reckless financial inclusion on output fluctuations, highlighting the promise and potential of macroprudential policies as effective tools of macro stabilisation. Finally, our analysis also reveals that the output-stabilising effects of traditional financial inclusion measures do not extend to advancements in digital financial inclusion. In other words, we find that greater digital financial inclusion amplifies output volatility in EMDEs.

Chapter 6 is titled 'Empowering the powerless: financial inclusion in developing Africa and Asia' by Firmin Doko Tchatoka and Ha Trang Vo. Financial inclusion has captured an enormous literature recently in both developing and developed countries. Financial inclusion is now widely acknowledged as a building block for both poverty reduction and opportunities for economic growth. The World Bank Group fixed a goal of enabling 1 billion people around the world to gain access to a transaction account through targeted interventions by 2020. Despite this undeniable effort, about 1.7 billion adults remain unbanked around the globe (Demirgüç-Kunt et al., 2015), and more than half are women from the poorest 40% of households in their country (Demirgüç-Kunt et al., 2018). This chapter uses survey data from *Financial Inclusion Insights* and employs multiple correspondence analysis, along with clustering methods, to build financial inclusion user typology in eight African and Asian countries: Kenya, Nigeria, Tanzania, Uganda, Bangladesh, India, Indonesia, and Pakistan.

It is found that poverty, location, gender, and education are key factors that determine the typology of financial inclusion users in both African and Asian countries considered. Whilst financially excluded people in Africa differ from those in Asia, both are mostly the powerless people: rural, poor, female, with no formal education, and no basic literacy and numeration skills. Moreover, the financial inclusion process appears more successful in Asia where banks dominate the market whilst in Africa mobile money providers are more prevalent.

Chapter 7, 'The poverty-reducing effects of financial inclusion: evidence from Cambodia' by Kimty Seng, analyses the effects of financial inclusion on poverty in terms of household income per capita, taking financial literacy into account. To accomplish this objective, the analysis is conducted by way of the endogenous switching model by households' financial literacy status, using data from the global *FinScope* survey on Cambodia conducted in 2015. In the survey, 3,150 household representatives over 18 years of age in both rural and urban areas were selected as samples. A complementary analysis was also carried out to further investigate the effects on the household budget deficit with an endogenous switching probit model.

The chapter concludes that the use of financial services will very likely make a great contribution to poverty reduction by reducing household budget deficit if the users have at least basic financial knowledge. Evidence suggests that household income per capita increases (and the probability of household budget deficits decreases) with the use of financial services, especially where the household is headed by financially literate women. These findings provide some insights into how financial inclusion can promote the reduction of poverty, especially when one considers policies on financial literacy and gender access. Although over the two decades prior to 2017, Cambodia's finance sector has developed significantly and has made a material contribution to economic growth and household welfare enhancement, the empirical evidence is still limited. Also, this study contributes to the literature by quantifying the pro-poor effects of financial inclusion controlling for financial literacy and addressing endogeneity and other estimation issues.

Chapter 8, 'Financial inclusion and savings in Indonesia' by Rashesh Shrestha and Samuel Nursamsu, discusses the status of financial inclusion and examines the impact of financial inclusion – based on the availability of bank branches on household outcomes – for Indonesia. According to the analysis of the World Bank's Financial Inclusion Survey (Findex) data, Indonesia has made some progress on expanding financial inclusion. The share of individuals with bank accounts had risen from less than 20% to just under 50% in 2017. Interestingly, whilst the gain between 2011 and 2014 was greater for individuals in the upper 60 percentile of income, the gain between 2014 and 2017 was more pro-poor. This progress has been made possible due to a concerted government effort to expand financial inclusion. Indonesia adopted a national strategy on financial inclusion in 2016, which focused on the use of bank accounts and financial literacy. One key strategy has been to transform all welfare programmes into cash payments and distributing them through the bank accounts. This had encouraged many individuals to open bank accounts. The share of Findex respondents receiving a government transfer through bank account had doubled between 2014 and 2017. Over the two decades prior to 2017, Indonesia has also experienced rapid growth in gross domestic product. In our empirical analysis, we study how financial inclusion enables households with income gains into savings for assets and earnings. Using the Indonesian Family Life Survey data, this chapter finds that living in areas with a high density of bank branches helps poor households accumulate savings. The marginal effect of financial inclusion on savings is highest amongst households in the bottom quintile of per capita consumption distribution. Thus, access to formal financial institutions can lead to an improvement in household welfare.

Chapter 9 is titled 'Financial Inclusion, Active Bank Accounts, and Poverty Reduction in India' by Tony Cavoli, Ilke Onur, and Patricia Sourdin. India is an important case study not just because of the size of the country and the economy but also because of the targeted efforts by the Reserve Bank of India (RBI) and the Government of India. Financial inclusion was in the 2005–2006 annual policy statement of the RBI. In 2010, the RBI required both private and public banks to submit a 3-year financial inclusion plan. Furthermore, in 2014, the Pradhan Mantri Jan Dhan Yojana (PMJDY) campaign – aimed at making banking facilities (savings and deposit accounts, remittances, credit, insurance, and pension) available to citizens – was implemented. In 2015, the Jan Dhan-Aadhar-Mobile was introduced to integrate PMJDY with biometric ID initiative and mobile technology. In 2017, the Government of India also launched 'Cashless India', promoting cashless payment modes (banking cards, mobile wallets, digital banking, etc.). In addition to these targeted and direct efforts, financial inclusion in the country benefited from an indirect push through the deposit payments to bank accounts for the Mahatma Gandhi National Rural Employment Guarantee scheme and the demonetisation on 9 November 2016. Using the *Financial Inclusion Insights* data on India, the chapter indicates that all these direct and indirect effects have been successful in a broad measure of financial inclusion – bank account ownership. Close to 80% of adults in India owned a bank account in 2017. However, not the same level of success is observed for the active use of these bank accounts. Only around 50% of the bank account owners reported using their bank account in the past 90 days. This suggests the existence of a considerable number of dormant bank accounts in India. The empirical analysis also shows that not only bank account ownership but also active use of bank accounts matters for poverty alleviation in India. The chapter also presents an analysis of the impact of financial inclusion (through bank account ownership) on poverty using a probit model. It also shows that whilst simply owning a bank account does not statistically decrease the likelihood of being in poverty, having an active account (defined as having used it in the previous 90 days) lowers the propensity to be poor by around 4%. The chapter observes some differences amongst males and females. For example, the effect of education on poverty is considerably more for females compared to males.

We believe that this book has a wide readership, particularly in the academic community. Graduate students and researchers interested in the research or subject of financial inclusion are the likely readers; therefore, the students, lecturers, researchers, and university libraries are the main target markets of this book. The book could also attract the attention of policymakers because of the policy insights and the richness of the empirical findings it offers – both in terms of topics covered and country coverage. Should the book be used as suggestive or recommended reading material, it would be very useful in courses on economic development or perhaps courses that focus on the Asian economic and financial policy and development.

Hereby, we would like to thank the contributors to this volume for their time and patience in creating each chapter. Further, we would like to convey our gratitude to all the participants to this project and to the various workshops and meetings that were held as part of it. We thank the Economic Research Institute for ASEAN and East Asia (ERIA) and the ERIA Research Institutions Network (RIN) for approving the project and for their ongoing support. Very special thanks go to Professor Jenny Corbett for supporting the project as the RIN member for Australia at the time the project was approved.

Note

1 www.worldbank.org/en/topic/financialinclusion

References

Demirgüç-Kunt, A., L. Klapper, D. Singer, and P. van Oudheusden (2015), *The Global Findex Database 2014: Measuring Financial Inclusion around the World*, Washington, DC: World Bank.

Demirgüç-Kunt, A., L. Klapper, D. Singer, S. Ansar, and J. Hess (2018), *The Global Findex Database 2017: Measuring Financial Inclusion and the Fintech Revolution*, Washington, DC: World Bank.

1 The nature and landscape of financial inclusion in Asia

Tony Cavoli and Rashesh Shrestha

1.1 Introduction

In a relatively short period, financial inclusion has become a dominant issue in the areas of financial development, policy, and inclusive growth. Globally, in 2017, 69% of adults had a bank account, an increase from 51% in 2011. The number of automatic teller machines (ATMs) per 100,000 adults globally increased from 41.6 in 2011 to 53.5 in 2017.

Despite substantial gains, barriers to complete financial inclusion exist. Globally, in 2017, a significant number of adults did not have access to a bank account because financial services were too expensive (18%), or because they were too far away (13%). Despite the advances made in financial services digitally and through the Internet, only 25% of people aged 15 years and above used a mobile phone to access a bank account, 22% used the Internet to pay bills, and 4% utilised mobile money services (World Bank, 2017a).

The objective of promoting greater levels of financial inclusion has been embraced by a great many nations across the development spectrum. The World Bank considers financial inclusion as an enabler for at least 7 of the 17 United Nations' sustainable development goals (SDGs). These goals include ending extreme poverty (SDG 1), where access to financial services can assist with investment in education or business. If these investments are made part of planting and harvesting, higher yields may result – contributing to reducing hunger (SDG 2), which presumably would positively impact good health and well-being (SDG 3). Increasing financial inclusion would help achieve the SDG of gender equality (SDG 5) by offering women greater control over their financial arrangements. Greater access to credit may contribute to gains in business innovation (SDG 9), and evidence suggests that financial inclusion has reduced inequality within countries (SDG 10) (Park and Mercado, 2016). This chapter presents evidence on the impact of financial inclusion on economic growth (SDG 8).

A recent work by the Consultative Group to Assist the Poor (Klapper et al., 2016) indicates that more SDGs can be potentially impacted by financial inclusion. For example, SDG 4, relating to quality education, can be attained through improvements in savings behaviour brought about by the elevating levels of financial inclusion. Works by Prina (2015) and Chiapa et al. (2016) for Nepal support this view, as does the work of Karlan et al. (2014) for developing economies in Asia and Latin America. SDGs 6 and 7 – on water and sanitation and energy infrastructure – have become attainable because of developments in digital financial services. Digital financial services can lower transaction costs, increase flexibility, and facilitate payments that would otherwise be prohibitive. Finally, SDG 9 on promoting innovation is made achievable by easier access to credit, which can be brought about by higher levels of financial inclusion.

Financial inclusion and its associated policy implications are an important issue for the Association of Southeast Asian Nations (ASEAN). They are explicitly presented as a key element (element A4) of the ASEAN Economic Community Blueprint 2025 and are also related to some of the strategic measures of the ASEAN Socio-Cultural Community (ASCC) Blueprint 2025, namely, measure A2 (empowering people and strengthening institutions), measure B (inclusivity), B1 (reducing barriers to financial products), and B2 (equitable access to financial products).

A final indication of the importance of this topic is that, as of 2017, more than 60 countries had implemented or were seeking to implement national strategies for financial inclusion. These strategies were designed to expand opportunities for financial inclusion through policies and regulations that support financial development, and provision of digital financial services and financial literacy whilst being mindful of issues around consumer protection and the stability of the financial sector (World Bank, 2017c).

So, what is financial inclusion? Whilst a degree of consensus on the broad definitions of financial inclusion exists, the factors that constitute financial inclusion are not static. In broad terms, it refers to the ability of consumers and firms to utilise financial services (Allen et al., 2016). The World Bank adds an efficiency characteristic in defining it as '… access to useful and affordable financial products…'.[1] Gardeva (2010) mentions that financial inclusion should involve '…access to a full suite of quality financial services, … at affordable prices … convenient (provided with) respect and dignity'.

Financial inclusion covers many categories and a typology is perhaps required to help organise its multifaceted nature. Some literature studies have attempted this exercise, and what emerges is that several individual measures of financial inclusion (indicators) can be grouped into categories (dimensions). A commonly used grouping of indicators is that used by the Alliance for Financial Inclusion (AFI) and adopted by the G20 through the Global Partnership for Financial Inclusion.[2] The AFI categorises indicators into three main dimensions – access, usage, and quality. Access refers to the availability of financial services in terms of physical proximity and includes indicators such as number of ATMs per 100,000 adults, number of branches per 100,000 adults, and number of mobile agent outlets per 100,000 adults. Usage refers to the regularity, frequency, and duration of use of financial services, and includes the percentage of adults with a bank account and those who are likely to save (or borrow) from a financial institution. Quality refers to the design of financial services to the satisfaction of the customer. Indicators include the use of savings for emergency funds and barriers to financial inclusion (e.g., reasons for not having an account). Sarma (2012) grouped indicators into penetration, availability, and usage. Hall (2014) grouped individual measures into financial participation, financial capability, and financial well-being, whilst Camara and Tuesta (2014) employed usage, access, and barriers as dimensions.

This chapter then examines the key impacts of financial inclusion on economic prosperity and well-being and other development indicators, such as those pertaining to health, education, gender, and social capital. It attempts to answer specific questions such as: What are the main individual dimensions of financial inclusion? Which are more effective at capturing the salient characteristics of financial inclusion? Financial inclusion landscapes vary significantly across countries. Thus, focusing on relatively few indicators is problematic as useful information relating to specific countries may be missed. But using too many is also difficult as it undermines the effective interpretation of financial inclusion which hampers the researcher's ability to isolate dominant indicators, and those which may drive significant policy implications.

Other questions in this chapter relate to the possible impacts of financial inclusion. For instance, is there a link between financial inclusion and outcomes such as growth, income inequality, health, education, and gender? Does financial inclusion differ by gender, education, poverty, and other development outcomes (i.e., are there 'gaps'?)? What is the role of policy? Might there be particular policies relating to financial inclusion that are more effective than others in addressing development outcomes? The importance of examining the effects of financial inclusion is emphasised by Beck et al. (2018) who suggested the following questions for further research:

(i) As financial inclusion increases, what are the financial and real consequences?
(ii) Whilst the literature suggests gains from financial inclusion, there is yet no clear road map for policymakers. What are the priorities for policymakers to further promote financial inclusion and maximise its real effects?

This chapter is structured as follows. Section 1.2 presents an overview of recent important literature. Section 1.3 presents an analysis of the nature of financial inclusion in the region – by subregional categories. Section 1.4 examines the state of financial inclusion regulation and policy. Section 1.5 presents some key development gaps. Section 1.6 concludes the chapter.

1.2 Brief comments on the existing literature

In broad terms, the literature on financial inclusion has proceeded down three paths – measurement, determinants, and effects. The rest of this section provides a brief summary of the recent contributions.

The first strand of literature has examined measurement issues pertaining to financial inclusion. Kempson et al. (2004) suggested that a good measure should incorporate as many dimensions as are practical, be simple to calculate, and be applied broadly and comparably across countries. As such, many academic contributions have employed various techniques to try to reduce the dimensionality of financial inclusion. As mentioned earlier, Sarma (2012), Hall (2014), and Camara and Tuesta (2014) have attempted to group indicators by category. This helps add meaning to the derived 'indices' based on data reduction.

This has been done in many ways. Sarma (2008) used a wide range of indicators combined into single country/single year measures by applying normalised inverse Euclidean distances. Though Park and Mercado (2016) used this method, they (2018a) utilised principal component analysis to allow the weights attributed to each indicator to be determined endogenously. Mialou et al. (2017) used factor analysis (for the same reasons as Park and Mercado, 2016) to combine various indicators from the International Monetary Fund (IMF) Financial Access Survey to form the Financial Institutions Access Index.[3] Different combinations of measures are used in different studies: Wang and Guan (2018) used two measures – access and usage – but used coefficients of variation to derive the weights whilst Kim et al. (2018) used three measures (penetration, usage, and availability) and equal weights.

A second strand examines the determinants of financial inclusion. A series of studies have focused on macro/aggregate determinants. Sarma and Pais (2011), using Sarma's 2008 index, examined the determinants of financial inclusion for 49 countries. They found that per capita gross domestic product (GDP) and adult literacy levels increase financial inclusion whilst rural population and inequality reduce the level of financial inclusion. Infrastructure is also found to be important in increasing financial inclusion (e.g., paved roads, phones, the Internet). Wang and Guan (2018) presented an analysis using Findex aggregate data and spatial techniques. They found that income, education, and use of communications equipment are important factors that explain the level of financial inclusion, whilst financial depth and banking health status are the main determinants.

More recent work has examined the micro-level determinants. Fungacova and Weill (2015) and Zins and Weill (2016) examined the determinants of financial inclusion for China and a set of African countries (respectively) using the World Bank Findex data for 2011 (World Bank, 2011). Both studies reported similar results, namely, being male, older, educated, and having higher incomes are all associated with higher financial inclusion, using a range of indicators. Allen et al. (2016) examined factors underpinning a variety of inclusion indicators. They found that lower transaction costs, the existence of legal rights, political stability, and physical proximity to financial institutions all increase the level of financial inclusion. Chakravarty and Pal (2013) investigated policy factors that may serve as determinants of financial inclusion. They examined the effect of banking policies for India using a long time series. Whilst social banking policies have assisted in developing financial inclusion across states in India, pro-market financial sector reform has adversely affected its pace.

Several recent studies have examined the effects of financial inclusion. Beginning with macro-level work, Rasheed et al. (2016), using data for 97 countries for 2004–2012, examined the impact of the number of ATMs and branches on the development of the banking sector (specifically, domestic credit to GDP and stocks traded, turnover ratio (%)). The reported impacts were generally positive and significant. Kim et al. (2018) examined the impact of (five indicators of) financial inclusion on per capita GDP for 55 Organisation of Islamic Cooperation (OIC) countries for 2004–2012. Subject to country differences, the effects were generally positive and significant. Park and Mercado (2016) investigated the impact of their financial inclusion index on income inequality, and found that the index had impacted inequality negatively.

Cavoli et al. (2019a) examined the impact of financial inclusion (the IMF financial institutions access index composite measure, as well as individual measures) on output volatility. The effect is positive and significant regardless of the measure of inclusion employed and is stronger for countries with lower incomes and when interacted with credit. This shows that the impacts of financial inclusion are not all positive. On the policy side, Cavoli et al. (2019b) examined the effect of (different indicators of) financial inclusion on optimal interest rate–based monetary policy. Financial inclusion generally lowers the policy rate. The effect is stronger for access-based indicators and inflation-targeting regimes.

There is also a range of recent micro-based studies on the effects of financial inclusion. Chauvet and Jacolin (2017) assessed the effect of inclusion (loans, overdraft, and credit) on firm performance, controlling for bank concentration for over 55,000 firms in 79 countries. An increase in financial inclusion results in firm growth, especially when bank concentration is low. Ahamed and Mallick (2019), using 2,635 banks in 86 countries, found that higher financial inclusion (using principal components analysis) results in greater bank stability (z-score). In an important study using data from China, Zhang and Posso (2019) examined the effect of a multidimensional index of financial inclusion on household income using the least squares, quantile estimations, and propensity score–matching techniques. Employing household survey data (approximately 6,200 households) for China, this paper found that the effect is positive across all households. Swamy (2014) examined the effect of financial inclusion in poor Indian households for women compared to men. The paper found that men are favoured. Chiapa et al. (2016) examined the impact of poor women's access to a savings account on the educational attainment of children. Using data from a field experiment in Nepal, this paper found that access to savings can help overcome scarcity issues and help with educational expenditures. An important strand of the literature also examines the relationships amongst indicators of financial inclusion. This allows us to ask the important questions of whether being financially included is itself a precondition for households and firms for further financial inclusion. Does financial inclusion exist in stages or in types? Are there early stages or basic levels of financial inclusion which, if achieved, might contribute to the attainment of, and latter stages/more evolved and sophisticated, financial inclusion? Which indicators fall into these categories? This dichotomy can be viewed through the observation of differences between formal and informal finance. De Koker and Jentzsch (2013) examined the role of formal financial services in determining the level of engagement with both informal financial services and mobile financial services. The results indicated that increased levels of financial inclusion will not likely reduce the use of informal financial services – that is, people will continue to use informal services, despite being banked.

Whether or not to incorporate the informal sector into a formal financial system is an extremely important policy issue. Informal financial services are typically those that are less regulated or even unregulated where consumers conduct many of their financial transactions independently of the formal financial system. This might involve financial transactions being conducted by savings groups and cooperatives that have carved out a niche, catering to specific groups of consumers.

There are two main points of view as to whether trying to (formally) financially include informal financial services makes for good policy. On the one hand, it may bring about unintended negative consequences. The formal financial system is often heavily regulated, cumbersome, and inefficient such that policymakers risk introducing these inefficiencies into the informal sector and potentially driving consumers away completely (Swift Institute, 2019). On the other hand, through the existing networks and market knowledge gained by informal finance providers, linking the two may make the formal sector more efficient whilst being able to provide safety nets to vulnerable consumers (Sustainable and Inclusive DFS, 2018).

A related line of enquiry pertains to the possible existence of a causal relationship between developments in financial technology (fintech) and financial inclusion. Ouma et al. (2017) investigated the effect of access to mobile financial services on savings behaviour in Africa, using financial access survey data, and logit and least squares estimators. The effects were found to be positive. A similar, though more basic, study by the IMF (2018b) that examined the impact of a range of technology-related variables (e.g., Internet access and mobile phone activity) on basic financial inclusion indicators showed that a positive relationship generally exists between them. Interestingly, the effect of technology leapfrogging was also examined. Leapfrogging (measured by the ratio of mobile to fixed-line subscriptions) has a negative impact on traditional financial inclusion measures.

1.3 The nature and landscape of financial inclusion in Asia

Using the dimensions of the AFI (access, usage, and quality) as a framing reference, this section presents some key stylised facts about the nature of financial inclusion, and the important policy and development implications for financial inclusion for ASEAN and Asia broadly. Rather than examine each country individually, this section mostly examines financial inclusion for countries belonging to the following regional groupings: ASEAN5 (Indonesia, Malaysia, the Philippines, Singapore, Thailand); CLMV (Cambodia, Lao PDR, Myanmar, Vietnam); Plus3 (China, the Republic of Korea, Japan); ANZ (Australia, New Zealand), and South Asia (Bangladesh, India, Pakistan, Sri Lanka).

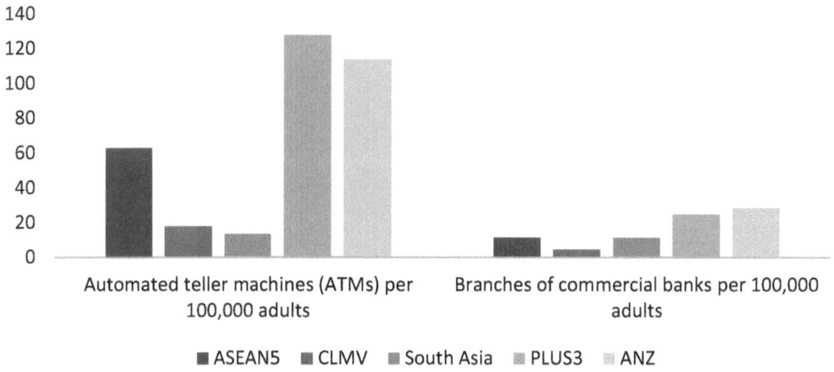

Figure 1.1 ATMs and branches, by region (2017).

ANZ = Australia and New Zealand; ASEAN5 = Indonesia, Malaysia, Philippines, Singapore, Thailand; CLMV = Cambodia, Lao PDR, Myanmar, Vietnam; Plus3 = China, Republic of Korea, Japan

Source: IMF (2018a).

1.3.1 Access

This section presents the two main access indicators – ATMs per 100,000 adults and branches of commercial banks per 100,000 adults. Both indicators are from the IMF Financial Access Survey (2018a).

Figure 1.1 shows that ATMs are more prominent generally. Further, the ASEAN Plus3 and ANZ present higher values – implying greater access – whilst South Asia and the CLMV have the lowest. Whilst expected, it is perhaps surprising to see just how low the ATM count is for South Asia and the CLMV, possibly indicating a lack of developed ATM infrastructure in those regions compared to a reliance on ATMs relative to branches for Plus3 and the ANZ.

Figure 1.2 shows the change in ATMs over the three time points – 2011, 2014, and 2017. For ASEAN5, the CLMV, and South Asia, the numbers grew whilst for the Plus3 and the ANZ, ATM numbers fell. This perhaps suggests that these regimes had reached a natural upper bound in ATMs as other forms of payments technology render the use of, and need for, cash less important.

1.3.2 Usage

This section presents the three main usage indicators from the World Bank Global Findex database. They are the percentages of (survey) respondents aged 15+ years who (i) have an account with a financial institution, (ii) have saved at a financial institution, or (iii) have borrowed from a financial institution.

Figure 1.3 shows that, as with Figure 1.1, the Plus3 and ANZ groups exhibit higher levels of usage generally. We also observe that saving is generally more

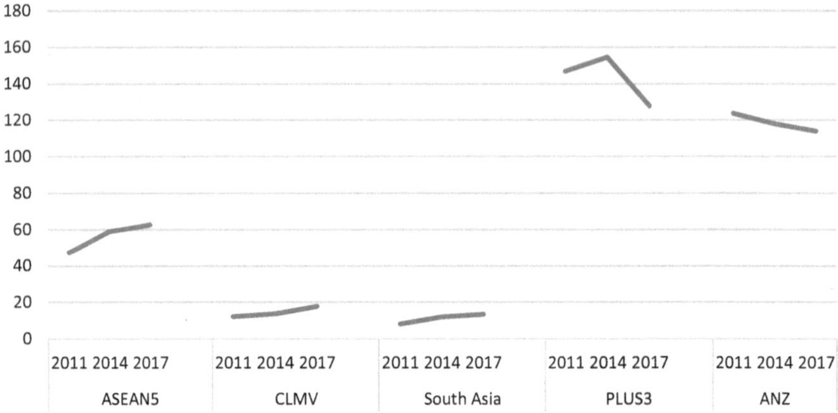

Figure 1.2 ATMs over time per region, per 100,000 adults.

ANZ = Australia and New Zealand; ASEAN5 = Indonesia, Malaysia, Philippines, Singapore, Thailand; ATM = automatic teller machine; CLMV = Cambodia, Lao PDR, Myanmar, Vietnam; Plus3 = China, Republic of Korea, Japan

Source: IMF (2018a).

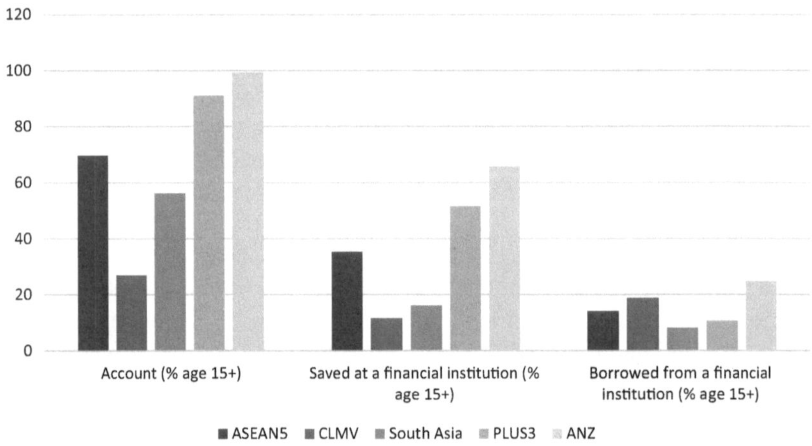

Figure 1.3 Financial inclusion usage indicators, by region (2017).

ANZ = Australia and New Zealand; ASEAN5 = Indonesia, Malaysia, Philippines, Singapore, Thailand; CLMV = Cambodia, Lao PDR, Myanmar, Vietnam; Plus3 = China, Republic of Korea, Japan

Source: World Bank (2017a).

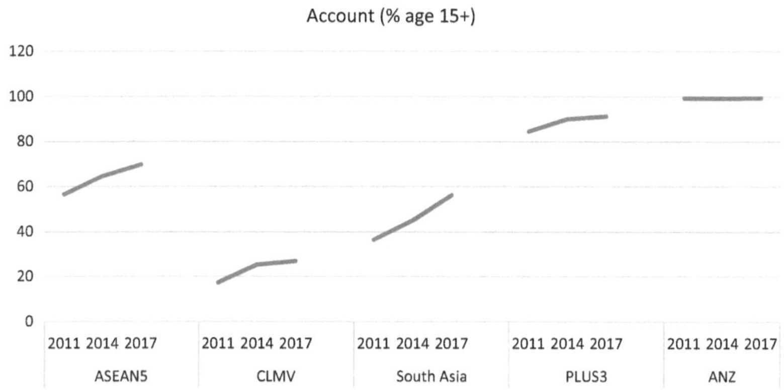

Figure 1.4 Possession of bank account over time, by region.

ANZ = Australia and New Zealand; ASEAN5 = Indonesia, Malaysia, Philippines, Singapore, Thailand; CLMV = Cambodia, Lao PDR, Myanmar, Vietnam; Plus3 = China, Republic of Korea, Japan

Source: World Bank (2011, 2014, 2017a).

prominent than borrowing, and that this is particularly acute for ASEAN5 and Plus3. The exception here is the CLMV where account ownership is relatively low, as is savings, but borrowing is relatively high.

If we observe the dynamics of the more prominent indicator, accounts, we see from Figure 1.4 that the number of accounts for ASEAN5, the CLMV, and South Asia is increasing over time, whereas those for the Plus3 and the ANZ have essentially plateaued, indicating a possible saturation point for accounts in those areas.

1.3.3 Quality

Here, we examine some indicators that pertain to the quality of financial inclusion. These indicators include any barriers to financial inclusion on the part of households and firms.

Figure 1.5 shows that the most likely reason consumers do not possess an account is the lack of funds. Interestingly, there do not appear to exist any significant regional disparities across the candidate reasons, except possibly for the CLMV and lack of funds. The high score for lack of funds for the CLMV highlights a possible desire to borrow and, therefore, might be related to the relatively high degree of borrowing taking place in that region (Figure 1.5). Figure 1.6 examines the issues of barriers to financial inclusion from a firm perspective, using data from the World Bank Enterprise Survey (World Bank, 2017b). Whilst collateral requirements remain the same for firms in East Asia and the Pacific as it does for South Asia, the proportion of firms believing that

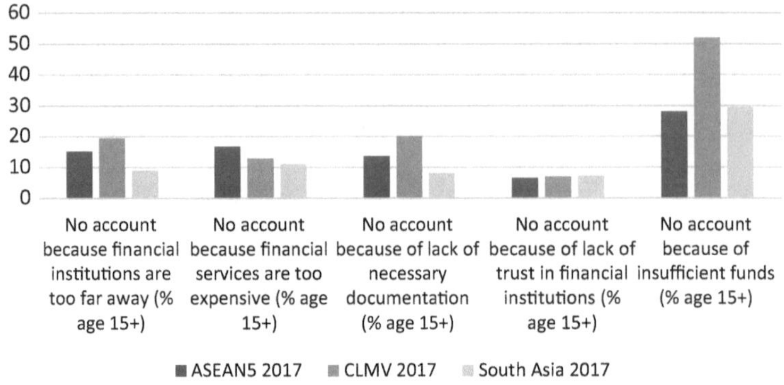

Figure 1.5 Reasons for not having an account, by region (2017).

ASEAN5 = Indonesia, Malaysia, Philippines, Singapore, Thailand; CLMV = Cambodia, Lao PDR, Myanmar, Vietnam

Source: World Bank (2017a).

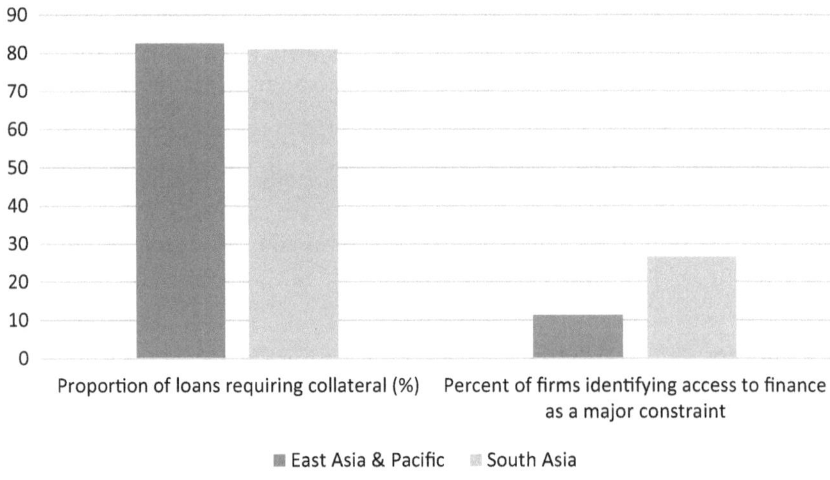

Figure 1.6 Barriers to financial inclusion for firms.

Source: World Bank (2017b).

access to finance is a significant constraint is materially higher for South Asia than for East Asia and the Pacific.

Figure 1.7 provides the same information as the right-hand side of Figure 1.6, the percentage of firms identifying access as a major constraint but for a selection of individual Asian nations. That South Asian nations occupy three of the top six positions here seems to confirm the notion that South Asian firms have greater difficulties with accessing finance.

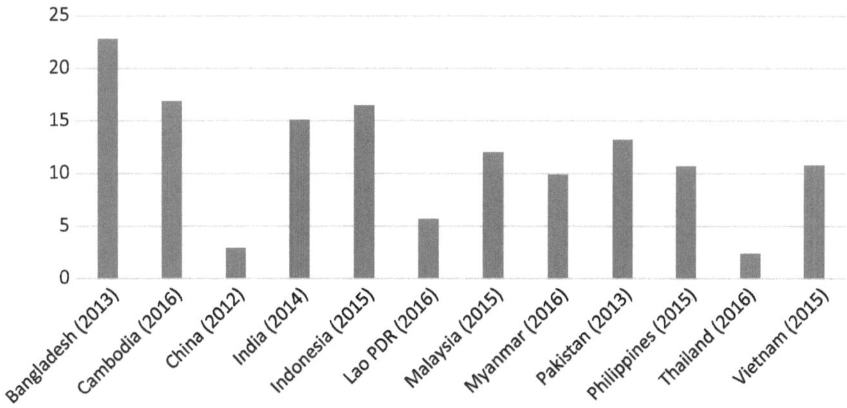

Figure 1.7 Percentage of firms identifying access to finance as a major constraint.
Source: World Bank (2017b).

1.4 Financial inclusion strategies and policies

An important way through which financial inclusion impacts development outcomes and development policies is how instruments such as national financial inclusion strategies (NFIS), policies, and regulations have affected the extent of financial inclusion in the region. This section briefly overviews the extent and nature of NFIS instruments, policies, and regulations for ASEAN and Asia.

The World Bank financial inclusion and consumer protection survey (World Bank, 2017c) collected data on the extent to which countries are implementing NFIS. Globally, 84% of the countries surveyed possess at least one of the following policy frameworks to support financial inclusion:

- A comprehensive NFIS. This is a stand-alone comprehensive policy that captures many facets of financial inclusion.
- A more general financial sector strategy that contains one or more components pertaining to financial inclusion.
- A national development strategy that contains one or more components relating to financial inclusion.
- Narrower strategies that target specific objectives such as financial capability or financial literacy/education.

The survey reported that, of those countries surveyed, 63 (51%) either have implemented a stand-alone NFIS or have one under development. Further, 45 (39%) countries have implemented or are implementing a financial sector strategy (development strategy with a financial inclusion component). There are 33 countries with a microfinance strategy and 71 nations which have policies relating to financial education or financial capability.

Table 1.1 documents the extent to which these types of strategies have either been implemented or are under development for Asia and the Pacific countries.

The clear objective of the national strategies as they relate to financial inclusion is to positively impact the enabling environment for financial inclusion in a way that supports growth in financial inclusion and development, whilst maintaining consumer protection and financial sector stability. The Economist Intelligence Unit (EIU) Global Microscope 2018 report (EIU, 2018) presented rankings for 55 countries on the enabling environment for financial inclusion. This ranking is based on factors across five broad categories: (i) government and policy support, (ii) stability and integrity, (iii) products and outlets, (iv) consumer protection, and (v) infrastructure (EIU, 2018, p.7). Colombia, Peru, and Uruguay occupy the first three positions, respectively. Table 1.2 reports the ranks of the Asian countries sampled.

A popular vehicle through which governments are involved in promoting financial inclusion is via financial education and financial literacy programmes. Tables 1.3 and 1.4 reveal the extent to which financial education and financial literacy programmes exist in Asian countries. Table 1.3 presents the degree to which any agency is responsible for leading and/or coordinating financial education policy and programmes. Mostly, at least one agency is involved in this process – the exceptions being Afghanistan, Bangladesh, Pakistan, and Vietnam.

Table 1.4 shows at which education levels financial education is included as a topic in public school curricula, either current or planned. Except for those countries for which no data is available, there is no country where some degree of financial education does not exist at some level within the public education system.

1.5 Gaps in financial inclusion

This section examines some of the key relationships between financial inclusion and important development considerations such as those pertaining to gender, education, poverty, health, and rural and urban populations. Particular attention will be paid to any 'gaps' that might exist in the level of financial inclusion based on those considerations. This is important for two reasons: First, it serves to motivate the work done on the effects of financial inclusion on income, education, health, and poverty outcomes. The second reason is that these gaps present opportunities for regulators and policymakers to employ strategies with financial inclusion that may impact development outcomes such that the SDGs of the United Nations can be adequately addressed.

We begin by examining the percentage of the adult population in possession of an account in a financial institution. Figure 1.8 shows account ownership for ASEAN5, the CLMV, and South Asia and displays whether any differences in account usage exist based on some of the development characteristics listed earlier. This figure and the others like it in this chapter are presented in a certain way and summarise a great deal of information. The dotted line is configured to represent the baseline – the percentage of all adults with an account – for each region. From this, we can assess the difference between this value and the proportion of account holders for any specific characteristics (women, rural, poor, low

Table 1.1 National financial inclusion strategies

	National financial inclusion strategy		*General financial sector development strategy with a financial inclusion component*		*National development strategy with a financial inclusion component*		*Microfinance strategy*		*Financial capability/ literacy/education strategy*	
	Existing	*In development*	*Existing*	*In development*	*Existing*	*In development*	*Existing*	*In development*	*Existing*	*In development*
Afghanistan	No	Yes	No	No	No	No	No	No	No	No
Australia	No	No	No	No	No	No	No	No	Yes	No
Bangladesh	No	Yes	Yes	No	Yes	No	No	Yes	No	Yes
Bhutan	No	Yes	Yes	No	No	No	No	No	No	Yes
Cambodia	No	Yes	Yes	No	No	No	Yes	No	No	No
China	Yes	No	No	Yes	Yes	No	No	No	No	Yes
Hong Kong SAR, China	No	No	No	No	No	No	No	No	Yes	No
India	No	Yes	No	No	No	No	No	No	Yes	No
Indonesia	Yes	No	Yes	No	Yes	No	No	Yes	Yes	No
Japan	No	No	Yes	No	No	No	No	No	Yes	No
Jordan	No	Yes	No	No	No	No	Yes	No	No	No
Korea, Republic of	Yes	No	No	No	No	No	Yes	No	Yes	No
Malaysia	Yes	No	Yes	No	Yes	No	Yes	No	Yes	No
Myanmar	No	Yes	No	Yes	No	Yes	No	No	No	Yes
New Zealand	No	No	No	No	No	No	No	No	Yes	No
Pakistan	Yes	No	No	No	No	No	No	No	No	No
Philippines	Yes	No	Yes	No	Yes	No	Yes	No	No	Yes
Sri Lanka	No	No	No	No	No	No	No	No	No	No
Thailand	Yes	No	Yes	No	Yes	No	Yes	No	No	Yes
Vietnam	No	Yes	No	No	Yes	No	Yes	No	No	No

Source: World Bank (2017c).

Table 1.2 Enabling environment for financial inclusion in Asia

Country	*Rank*
India	= 4
Philippines	= 4
Indonesia	7
China	13
Thailand	= 16
Pakistan	= 21
Sri Lanka	26
Vietnam	= 37
Bangladesh	= 40
Cambodia	= 43
Myanmar	= 51

Source: EIU 2018.

Note: These are ordered by rank.
The '=' refers to the fact that a county shares a ranking with another in the survey.

Table 1.3 Agencies involved in financial education programmes

	Institutional arrangements for leading and/or coordinating financial education			
	Single agency	*Multiple agencies*	*Other*	*No agency*
Afghanistan	No	No	No	Yes
Australia	Yes	No	No	No
Bangladesh	No	No	No	Yes
Bhutan	Yes	No	No	No
Cambodia	No	Yes	No	No
China	No	Yes	No	No
Hong Kong SAR, China	Yes	No	No	No
India	Yes	No	No	No
Indonesia	Yes	No	No	No
Japan	No	Yes	No	No
Jordan	Yes	No	No	No
Korea, Republic of	No	Yes	No	No
Malaysia	Yes	No	No	No
Myanmar	No	Yes	No	No
New Zealand	No	Yes	No	No
Pakistan	No	No	No	Yes
Philippines	No	Yes	No	No
Sri Lanka	Yes	No	No	No
Thailand	No	Yes	No	No
Vietnam	No	No	No	Yes

Source: World Bank (2017c).

Table 1.4 Financial education in schools and universities

	Education levels in which financial education is included in the curriculum			
	Primary	*Junior secondary*	*Senior secondary*	*University level*
Afghanistan				
Australia	Yes	Yes	Yes	No
Bangladesh	Yes	Yes	No	No
Bhutan				
Cambodia	Yes	No	No	No
China	Yes	Yes	Yes	Yes
Hong Kong SAR, China	Yes	Yes	Yes	No
India	No	Yes	Yes	No
Indonesia	Yes	Yes	Yes	Yes
Japan	Yes	Yes	Yes	No
Jordan	No	Yes	Yes	No
Korea, Republic of	Yes	Yes	Yes	Yes
Malaysia	Yes	Yes	Yes	No
Myanmar				
New Zealand	Yes	Yes	Yes	No
Pakistan				
Philippines	Yes	No	No	No
Sri Lanka	No	Yes	Yes	Yes
Thailand	Yes	Yes	Yes	Yes
Vietnam				

Source: World Bank (2017c).

education). We can also evaluate the account holders per specific characteristic across the three regional groups to allow for interregional comparison.

Account ownership for the CLMV is materially lower than for the other regions examined. This backs up the analysis conducted earlier. The regional gap does not appear to differ significantly across the different characteristics – an indication perhaps that not one specific issue warrants more concern from a development perspective than any of the others. However, when we examine the gaps that might exist within the region, we find that the percentage of account holders between males and females is quite even for ASEAN5 and the CLMV; however, a large gender gap exists in South Asia. As for the other characteristics, Figure 1.8 shows that a negligible rural gap for all regions exists and that the findings concerning the other characteristics seem to be what one might expect to find – that is, account holders are more likely to be older, wealthier, more educated, and employed.

We can also observe consumers' savings behaviour by examining the degree to which households saved for significant household considerations such as for old age or education, and whether any regional differences or gaps across specific demographics exist. Figure 1.9 shows the percentage of adults who saved

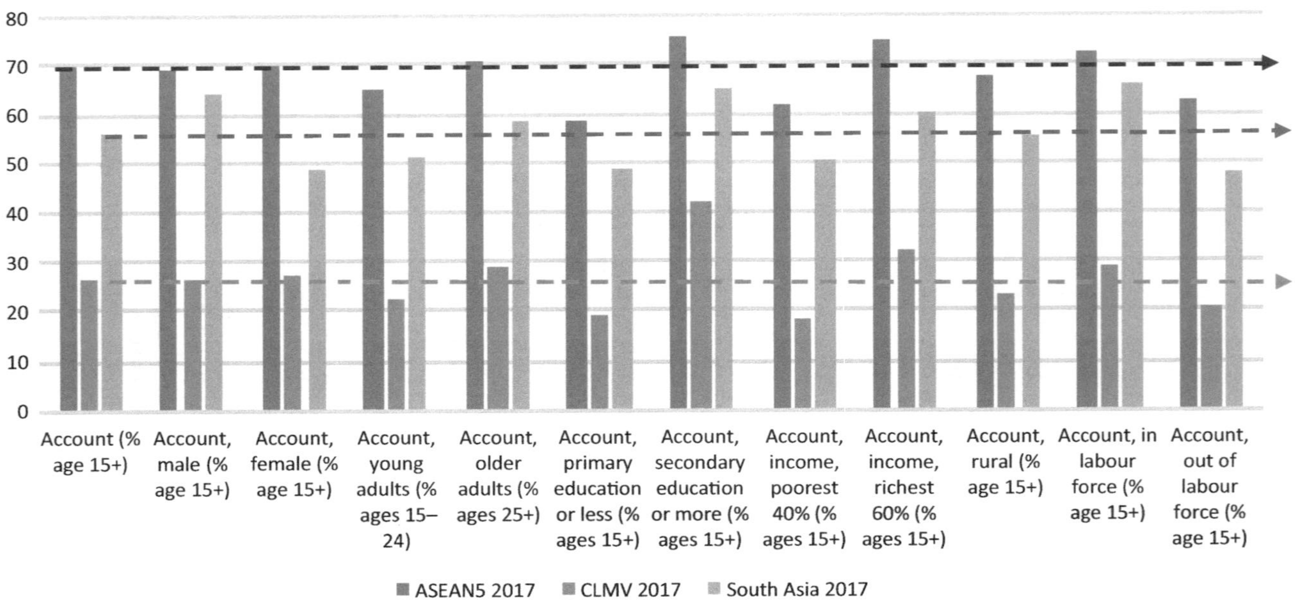

Figure 1.8 Account holders, by region (2017).

ASEAN5 = Indonesia, Malaysia, Philippines, Singapore, Thailand; CLMV = Cambodia, Lao PDR, Myanmar, Vietnam

Source: World Bank (2017a).

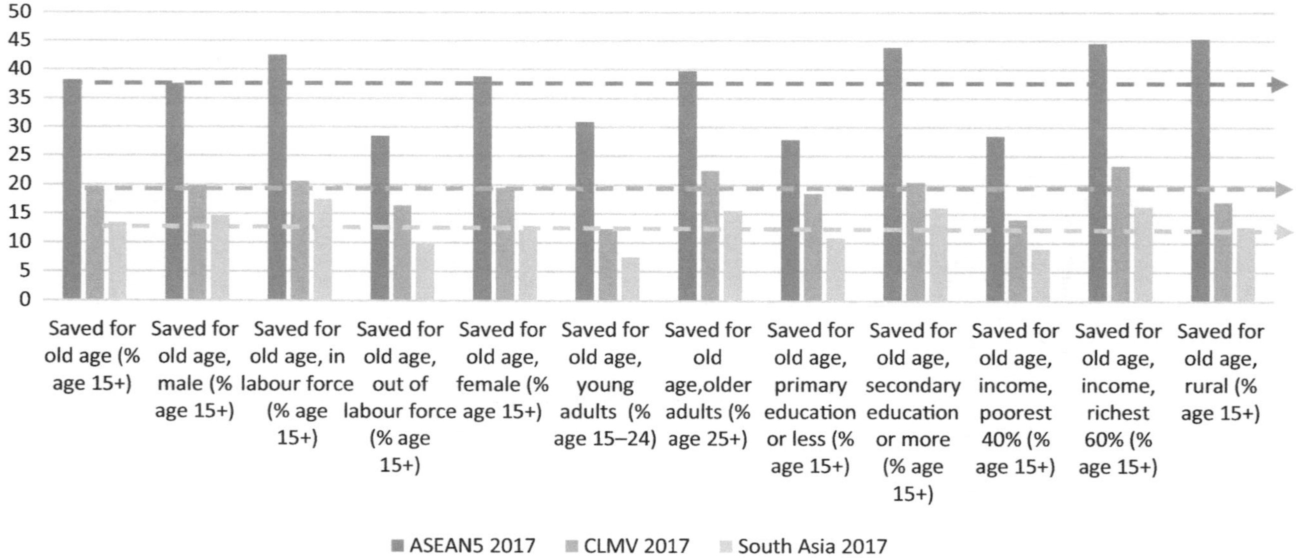

Figure 1.9 Saved for old age, by region (2017).

ASEAN5 = Indonesia, Malaysia, Philippines, Singapore, Thailand; CLMV = Cambodia, Lao PDR, Myanmar, Vietnam

Source: World Bank (2017a).

for old age. Whilst the ASEAN5 levels are considerably higher, as they are for account holders, it is South Asia rather than the CLMV that exhibits the lowest levels. Also, as with account holders, no gender gap appears for ASEAN5 and the CLMV, whilst a small gap exists for South Asia. Young adults across all regions are not saving for old age nor are the poorer segments of the communities surveyed, or those not working – a significant wealth gap in existence here. Interestingly, the rural gap is positive for ASEAN5 (i.e., it is higher than the average for all adults) whilst the rural gap is negative for the CLMV.

Figure 1.10 presents the percentage of households saving for education and shows broadly similar results but for two main differences. The first is that the CLMV nations are much closer to ASEAN, thus revealing a significant general gap to South Asia. The second is that the gap for those out of the labour force and for the poor, whilst still negative, is much lower than for saving for old age. This suggests a value being placed on education as a development outcome.

1.6 Fintech and financial inclusion

Fintech – digital technologies as applied to finance – is playing an increasingly significant role in providing financial services and, therefore, in the degree to which communities are financially included. Here, we briefly examine the relationship between fintech and financial inclusion, and what impact this nexus might have on development outcomes such as gender, poverty, and the rural–urban divide. Fintech should not be viewed as a measure of financial inclusion in and of itself but as a means through which greater financial inclusion might be achieved. Fintech initiatives, such as mobile payments and peer-to-peer borrowing and lending, have decreased the costs of providing financial services, thus allowing households and firms great capacity to access these services. In the same way as the Internet and mobile communications have facilitated the provision of digital financial services, these services should lead to higher levels of financial inclusion.

Figure 1.11 presents three indicators of the use of the Internet and mobile communications for the five regions that are analysed here. The indicators are broad measures of the extent to which financial technologies are supporting the access and use of financial services either for payments or for banking services. They are, respectively, the percentage of adults (15+ years) who used the Internet to buy something online in the past year, the percentage of adults who used a mobile phone to pay bills in the past year, and those who used a mobile phone or the Internet to access a bank account in the past year. The ANZ and Plus3 countries clearly have a greater capacity to provide digital financial services, whilst South Asia and the CLMV, the least. This is consistent with the earlier analysis of the more traditional inclusion indicators. Figure 1.12 focuses on ASEAN5, the CLMV, and South Asia and introduces a variable capturing what proportion of the population possesses mobile money accounts. Mobile money accounts are not tied to accounts with financial institutions but are accounts where funds are held in digital wallets as part of a mobile money application. Interestingly, mobile

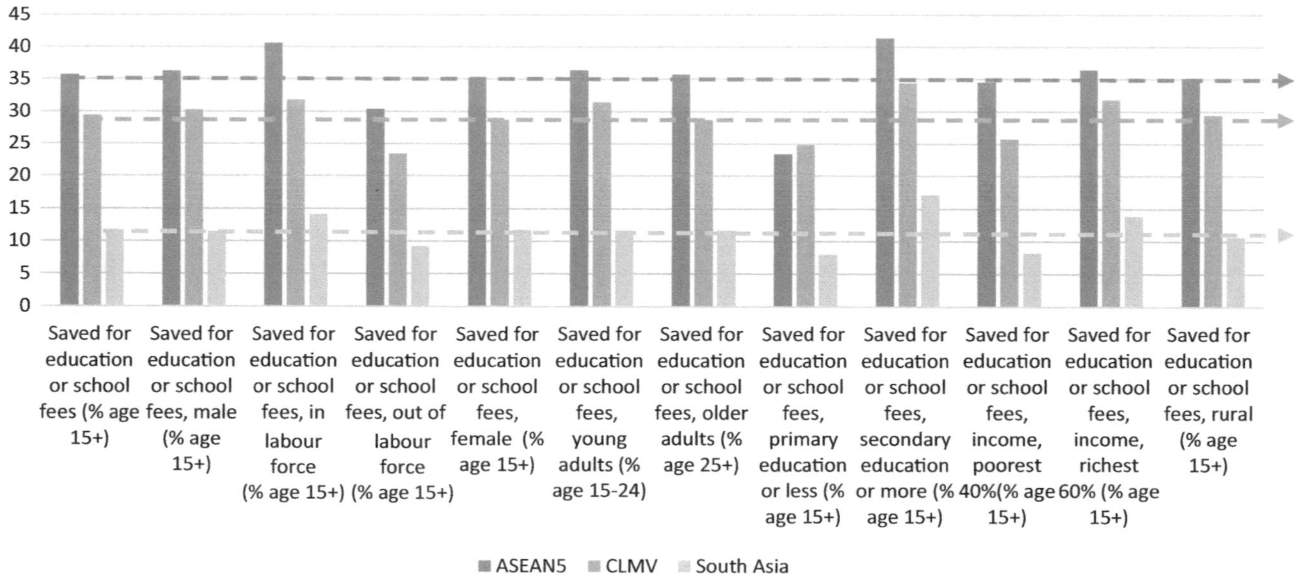

Figure 1.10 Saved for education, by region (2014).

ASEAN5 = Indonesia, Malaysia, Philippines, Singapore, Thailand; CLMV = Cambodia, Lao PDR, Myanmar, Vietnam

Source: World Bank (2017a).

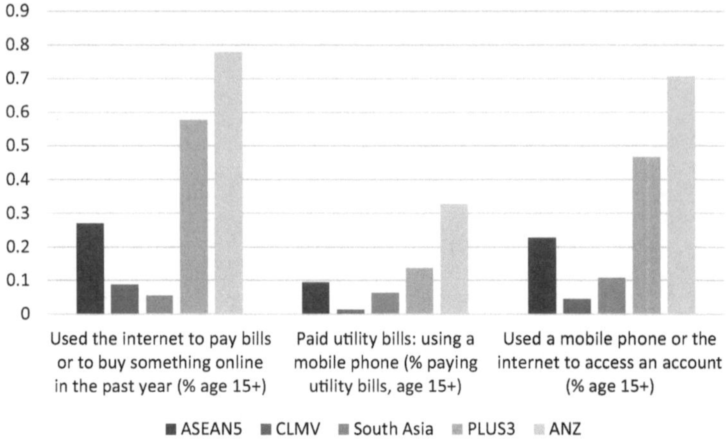

Figure 1.11 Internet use, by region (2017).

ANZ = Australia and New Zealand; ASEAN5 = Indonesia, Malaysia, Philippines, Singapore, Thailand; CLMV = Cambodia, Lao PDR, Myanmar, Vietnam; Plus3 = China, Republic of Korea, Japan

Source: World Bank (2017a).

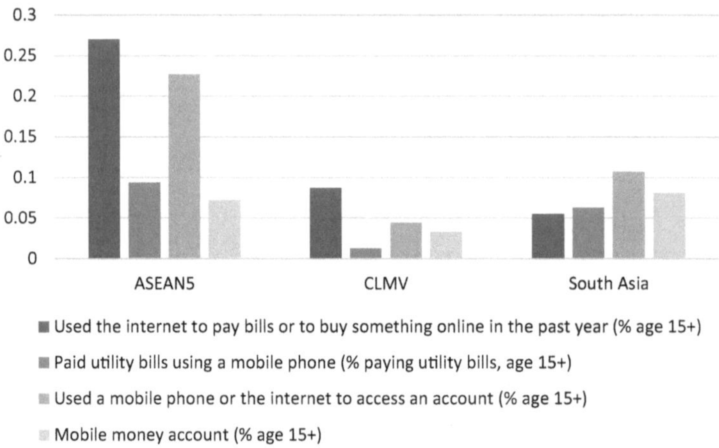

Figure 1.12 Internet use and mobile money, by region (2017).

ASEAN5 = Indonesia, Malaysia, Philippines, Singapore, Thailand; CLMV = Cambodia, Lao PDR, Myanmar, Vietnam

Source: World Bank (2017a).

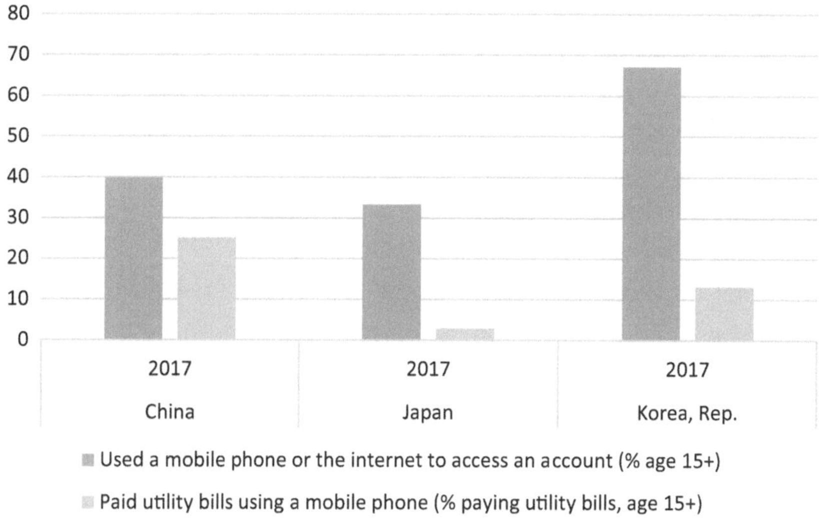

Figure 1.13 Use of mobile phones for banking and bills payment.
Source: World Bank (2017a).

money accounts are relatively more prominent in South Asia than in ASEAN5 and the CLMV.

Figure 1.13 provides another disconnect, in this instance, between the use of the Internet for banking versus for making payment. The Republic of Korea is higher in terms of the percentage of adults using the Internet to access existing accounts, whilst China leads (by double) the proportion of adults using the Internet to make purchases. This highlights China's leading position in the area of digital payments.

Figure 1.14 shows the rate of growth in mobile money accounts between 2014 and 2017. These have clearly increased in ASEAN5 and South Asia (albeit from a low base) but have curiously decreased in the CLMV.

Figure 1.15 reveals the mobile money account data for 2017 by country. The first panel reveals that Malaysia and Singapore possess a greater proportion of adult populations with mobile accounts. The second panel shows that the high level of mobile money account ownership (and indeed growth, though not shown here) in South Asia is being driven by Bangladesh. The third shows the mobile money accounts for the CLMV countries for which there is data. Cambodia records the highest proportions there.

Figures 1.16 and 1.17 present some useful analysis on the possible gaps as they pertain to Internet use and mobile money accounts. Some interesting results emerge. A material gender gap is absent regarding the use of mobile phones or the Internet for ASEAN5 and the CLMV but is pronounced for South Asia. A gender gap exists for ASEAN5 and South Asia for mobile money

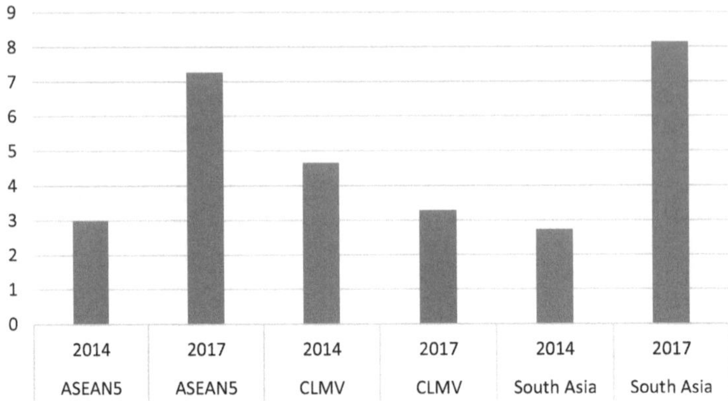

Figure 1.14 Mobile money account, by region (2014 and 2017).

ASEAN5 = Indonesia, Malaysia, Philippines, Singapore, Thailand; CLMV = Cambodia, Lao PDR, Myanmar, Vietnam

Source: World Bank (2014, 2017a).

accounts but not for the CLMV. The results for South Asia are consistent with the gender gaps that exist for traditional financial inclusion indicators, but the gap for ASEAN5 is quite unexpected when compared to those more traditional measures. Gaps exist for income and education levels in line with what would be expected. Finally, for ASEAN5, a positive rural gap exists for mobile phones and the Internet. This suggests that rural areas can be well serviced through digital financial services. However, a negative gap exists for mobile money – suggesting that those in rural areas favour the use of technologies to access existing financial services.

1.7 Concluding remarks

This chapter has presented some key patterns and stylised facts about the nature of financial inclusion, particularly at the regional level. Financial inclusion in ASEAN and East Asia has maintained steady growth in recent years as seen through the traditional indicators that measure the broader dimensions of financial inclusion, namely, access, usage, and quality. The growth has mainly occurred in South Asia, the CLMV, and ASEAN5. The more developed Plus3 and ANZ nations seem to exhibit saturation levels of financial inclusion, or perhaps a level of maturity, in the basic indicators such as ATMs, branches, and bank account ownership.

There is an increased focus on regulators to produce policies and regulations on financial inclusion. Most countries in the region now have an NFIS either in place or it is under development. Many also have policies attempting to increase levels of financial literacy and financial education as a way for households and firms to access their respective financial systems more effectively.

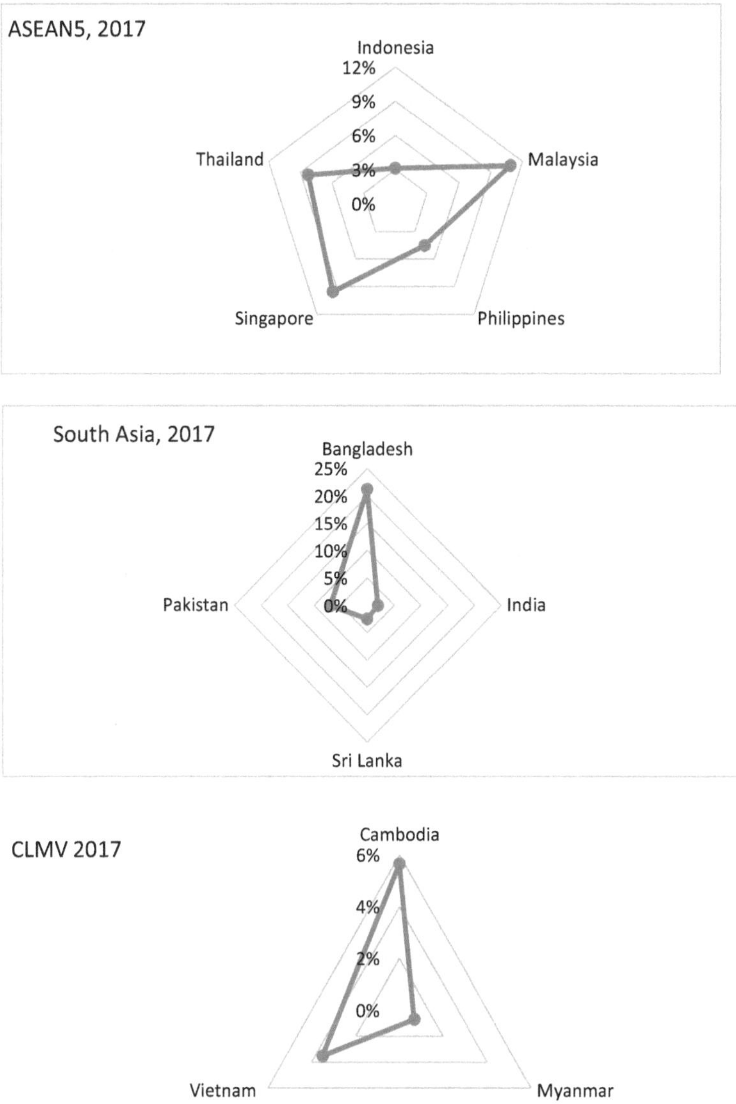

Figure 1.15 Mobile money account, by country and region (2017).

ASEAN5 = Indonesia, Malaysia, Philippines, Singapore, Thailand;CLMV = Cambodia, Lao PDR, Myanmar, Vietnam

Source: World Bank (2017a).

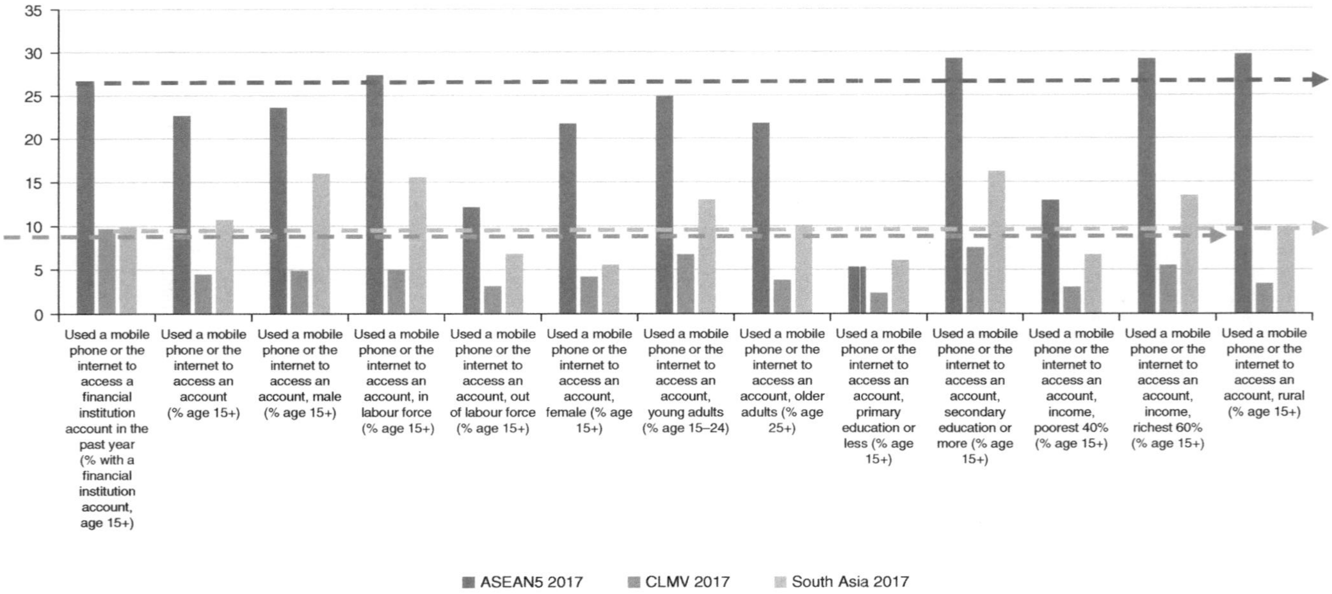

Figure 1.16 Use of mobile phone or Internet, by region (2017).

ASEAN5 = Indonesia, Malaysia, Philippines, Singapore, Thailand; CLMV = Cambodia, Lao PDR, Myanmar, Vietnam

Source: World Bank (2017a).

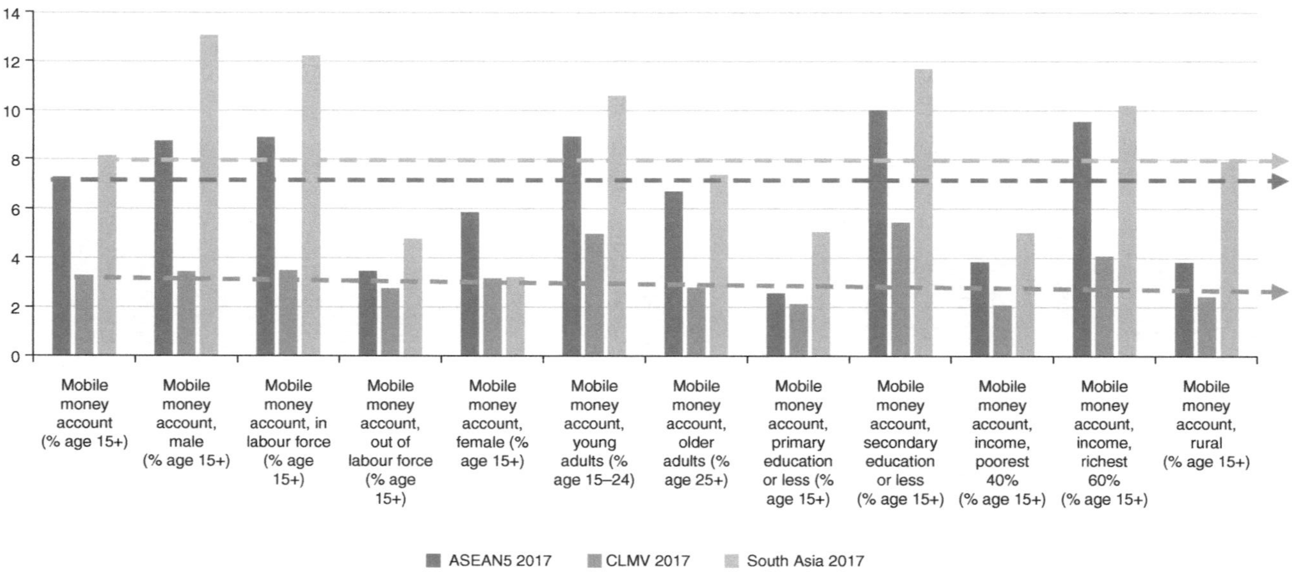

Figure 1.17 Mobile money account, by region (2017).

ASEAN5 = Indonesia, Malaysia, Philippines, Singapore, Thailand; CLMV = Cambodia, Lao PDR, Myanmar, Vietnam

Source: World Bank (2017a).

A major component of most countries' NFIS is related to fintech and digital finance. As with the more traditional indicators, the ANZ and Plus3 are significantly ahead in those measures that might imply a strong presence in digital finance. That said, the main sources of growth in those measures are in ASEAN5 and South Asia. Financial inclusion is one area where developing countries of ASEAN can adopt modern technologies to quickly leapfrog to an advanced stage rather than incrementally follow the footsteps of developed countries a few decades ago.

Many development gaps can be observed when analysing the various financial inclusion indicators. These gaps present opportunities for regulators and policymakers to employ strategies with financial inclusion that may impact development outcomes such that the United Nations' SDGs can be adequately addressed. Most pervasive are gaps relating to the poor versus the non-poor (where the poor reported lower levels of financial inclusion), education levels (where the less educated were less included), and rural and urban populations (where, generally, the rural communities reported lower levels of financial inclusion). The rural gap, however, was almost non-existent for some indicators pertaining to Internet use, suggesting that digital technologies may be used to help communities leapfrog more traditional ways of becoming more financially included.

Notes

1 www.worldbank.org/en/topic/financialinclusion
2 https://databank.worldbank.org/data/download/g20fidata/Indicators_note_formatted.pdf
3 www.data.imf.org/FAS

References

Ahamed, M.M. and S.K. Mallick (2019), 'Is Financial Inclusion Good for Bank Stability? International Evidence', *Journal of Economic Behavior & Organization*, 157(January), pp.403–427.

Allen, F., A. Demirguc-Kunt, L. Klapper, and M.M. Peria (2016), 'The Foundations of Financial Inclusion: Understanding Ownership and Use of Formal Accounts', *Journal of Financial Intermediation*, 27(1), pp.1–30.

Beck, T., M.S. Martinez-Peria, M. Obstfeld, and A. Presbitero (2018), 'Financial Inclusion: Drivers and Real Effects', *Voxeu*, 12 April 2018.

Camara, N. and D. Tuesta (2014), 'Measuring Financial Inclusion: A Multidimensional Index', *BBVA Research Paper*, 14(26).

Cavoli, T., S. Gopalan, and R.S. Rajan (2019a), 'Does Financial Inclusion Amplify Output Volatility in Emerging and Developing Economies?' Mimeo.

Cavoli, T., S. Gopalan, and R.S. Rajan (2019b), 'Financial Inclusion and the Optimal Interest Rate Rule'. Mimeo.

Chakravarty, S.R. and R. Pal (2013), 'Financial Inclusion in India: An Axiomatic Approach', *Journal of Policy Modeling*, 35(5), pp.813–837.

Chauvet, L. and L. Jacolin (2017), 'Financial Inclusion, Bank Concentration, and Firm Performance', *World Development*, 97, pp.1–13.

Chiapa, C., S. Prina, and A. Parker (2016), 'The Effects of Financial Inclusion on Children's Schooling, and Parental Aspirations and Expectations', *Journal of International Development*, 28(5), pp.683–696.

de Kocker, L. and N. Jentzsch (2013), 'Financial Inclusion and Financial Integrity: Aligned Incentives?', *World Development*, 44, pp.267–280. www.sciencedirect.com/science/article/abs/pii/S0305750X12002720

Economist Intelligence Unit (EIU) (2018), *Global Microscope 2018: The Enabling Environment for Financial Inclusion and the Expansion of Digital Financial Services.* New York: EIU.

Fungacova, Z. and L. Weill (2015), 'Understanding Financial Inclusion in China', *China Economic Review*, 34, pp.196–206. www.sciencedirect.com/science/article/abs/pii/S1043951X14001709

Gardeva, A. (2010). 'A Vision for Full Financial Inclusion'. Blog Post, 8 February 2010. Centre for Financial Inclusion.

Hall, T. (2014), *Measuring Financial Inclusion: Thinking 3 Dimensional.* Cambridge, MA: Citi Foundation.International Monetary Fund (IMF) (2018a), Financial Access Survey, https://data.imf.org/?sk=E5DCAB7E-A5CA-4892-A6EA-598B5463A34C (accessed 15 July 2018).

International Monetary Fund (IMF) (2018b), *Financial Inclusion in Asia-Pacific. Asia-Pacific Department Report 18/17.* Washington, DC: IMF.

Karlan, D., A. Ratan, and J. Zinman (2014), 'Savings by and for the Poor: A Research Review and Agenda', *Review of Income and Wealth*, 60(1), pp.36–78.

Kempson, E., A. Atkinson, and O. Pilley (2004), *Policy Level Response to Financial Exclusion in Developed Economies: Lessons for Developing Countries, Report of Personal Finance Research Centre.* Bristol: University of Bristol.

Kim, D.W., J.S. Yu, and M.K. Hassan (2018), 'Financial Inclusion and Economic Growth in OIC Countries', *Research in International Business and Finance*, 43, pp.1–14. www.sciencedirect.com/science/article/abs/pii/S0275531917304798

Klapper, L., M. El-Zoghbi, and J. Hess (2016), *Achieving the Sustainable Development Goals: The Role of Financial Inclusion.* Washington, DC: Consultative Group to Assist the Poor.

Mialou, A., G. Amidzic, and A. Massara (2017), 'Assessing Countries' Financial Inclusion Standing – A New Composite Index', *Journal of Banking and Financial Economics*, 2(8), pp.105–126.

Ouma, S.A., T.M. Odongo, and M. Were (2017), 'Mobile Financial Services and Financial Inclusion: Is It a Boon for Savings Mobilization?', *Review of Development Finance*, 7(1), pp.29–35.

Park, C.Y. and R. Mercado (2016), 'Does Financial Inclusion Reduce Poverty and Income Inequality in Developing Asia?', in S. Gopalan and T. Kikuchi (eds.), *Financial Inclusion in Asia: Issues and Policy Concerns.* London: Palgrave Macmillan, pp.61–92.

Park, C.Y. and R. Mercado (2018a), 'Financial Inclusion, Poverty, and Income Inequality', *The Singapore Economic Review*, 63(1), pp.185–206.

Prina, S. (2015), 'Banking the Poor via Savings Accounts: Evidence from a Field Experiment', *Journal of Development Economics*, 115, pp.16–31.

Rasheed, B., S.L. Law, L. Lee, and M.S. Habibullah (2016), 'The Role of Financial Inclusion in Financial Development: International Evidence', *Abasyn Journal of Social Sciences*, 9(2), pp 330–348.

Sarma, M. (2008), 'Index of Financial Inclusion', *Working Paper*, No. 215, New Delhi: Indian Council for Research on International Economic Relations (ICRIER).

Sarma, M. (2012), 'Index of Financial Inclusion: A Measure of Financial Sector Inclusiveness', *Berlin Working Papers on Money, Finance, Trade and Development*, July.

Sarma, M. and J. Pais (2011), 'Financial Inclusion and Development', *Journal of International Development*, 23(5), pp.613–628.

Sustainable and Inclusive DFS (2018), 'Banking the Underbanked: Formal vs Informal Financial Inclusion, Does It Matter?', https://medium.com/@SustainableDFS/banking-the-underbanked-formal-vs-informal-financial-inclusion-does-it-matter-1693974de449 (Accessed 25 February 2020)

Swamy, V. (2014), 'Financial Inclusion, Gender Dimension, and Economic Impact on Poor Households', *World Development*, 56, pp.1–15.

Swift Institute (2019), 'Financial Inclusion: Where the Formal and Informal Financial Systems Meet', https://swiftinstitute.org/newsletters/financial-inclusion-where-the-formal-and-informal-financial-systems-meet/ (Accessed 25 February 2020)

Wang, X. and J. Guan (2018), 'Financial Inclusion: Measurement, Spatial Effects and Influencing Factors', *Applied Economics*, 49(18), pp.1751–1762.

World Bank (2011), Global Findex, Database, https://globalfindex.worldbank.org/ (accessed 15 July 2018).

World Bank (2014), Global Findex, Database, https://globalfindex.worldbank.org/ (accessed 15 July 2018).

World Bank (2017a), Global Findex, Database, https://globalfindex.worldbank.org/ (accessed 15 July 2018).

World Bank (2017b), World Bank Enterprise Survey, https://datacatalog.worldbank.org/dataset/enterprise-surveys (accessed 28 June 2018).

World Bank (2017c), *The World Bank Financial Inclusion and Consumer Protection Survey – 2017 Report*. Washington, DC: World Bank.Zhang, Q. and A. Posso (2019), 'Thinking Inside the Box: A Closer Look at Financial Inclusion and Household Income', *The Journal of Development Studies*, 55(7):1616–1631.

Zins, A. and L. Weill (2016), 'The Determinants of Financial Inclusion in Africa', *Review of Development Finance*, 6(1), pp.46–57.

2 The composition of financial inclusion in ASEAN and East Asia

A new hybrid index and some stylised facts

Rajabrata Banerjee[1] *and Ronald Donato*[2]

2.1 Introduction

The Global Partnership for Financial Inclusion (GPFI) was launched by the G20 leaders at the Seoul Summit in 2010 to support financial inclusion amongst developing countries. Financial inclusion is broadly defined as a continuous development process for all members of an economy that provides greater ease of access, availability, and efficient usage of the formal financial system (Sarma, 2016). This definition shows three key characteristics or dimensions necessary for the successful realisation of financial inclusion: access, usage, and quality of available financial services. The same three dimensions were also identified by the GPFI at the St. Petersburg Summit in 2013 and later refined at the China Summit in 2016 (GPFI, 2016). Whilst access refers to how widely and what proportion of the population in an economy has access to financial services, usage refers to the volume and frequency of these financial services used by the population. On the other hand, quality refers to the level of financial knowledge and the quality of the products and the service delivery of these financial services.

The effect of financial inclusion on economic development has received ongoing attention from both academics and policymakers; however, a clear limitation to date is that there is no consistency in measuring financial inclusion. For instance, Sarma (2008) defined the dimensions of financial inclusion as comprising penetration, availability, and usage. In contrast, Camara and Tuesta (2014) defined them as usage, access, and barriers, respectively. Whilst usage is the common dimension in these studies, barriers are defined as financial exclusiveness where some sections of the population do not have access to financial services. Furthermore, there is no consistency regarding the definition of a dimension as studies used their preferred indicator to define a dimension. For example, Honohan (2008) measured access to financial inclusion by combining multiple sources of formal financial intermediation data, which is calculated by combining information on account numbers at banks and microfinance institutions with estimates from household surveys for a set of countries. Other studies considered statistics on financial service use to measure financial inclusion in general, such as accounts penetration measured by ATMs per 100,000 adults; bank branches per 100,000 adults; savings, credit, insurance, and life insurance premium volume to GDP (Van der Werff et al., 2013; Demirgüç-Kunt and Klapper, 2012; Kim et al., 2018). These differences in the measures adopted make it even more difficult to compare findings from studies that use a wide range of countries in their sample.

Another measurement issue is where studies use multiple indicators to create a dimension or an aggregate measure. There is an ongoing debate regarding the choice of methodology to calculate an aggregate financial inclusion index. Two prominent methodologies are widely used in the literature to calculate an aggregate financial inclusion index from a group of indicators. They are Euclidean distance–based measure introduced by Sarma (2008) and principal component analysis (PCA)–based measure used by Camara and Tuesta (2014) and Park and Mercado (2018b). Other similar methodologies used to calculate an aggregate financial inclusion index are factor analysis (Mialou et al., 2017) and multiple correspondence analysis (Dungey et al., 2018). These methodologies claim that they are superior to others and more comprehensively measure financial inclusion in developing countries.

An obvious concern amongst researchers is to find a reliable way of measuring financial inclusion that captures a wide variety of indicators. Unless we have a consistent approach to measuring financial inclusion that is widely applicable across countries, it would be difficult to assess its effect on various economic development outcomes – which is a priority for all policymakers at the macroeconomic level. In this context, our methodology performs two main tasks. First, based on the G20 report or the G20 Financial Inclusion Indicators (GPFI, 2016), we collected data on 22 Asian countries in the period 2004–2015 and, utilising the most comprehensive set of indicators to date, systematically constructed three dimensions of financial inclusion – access, usage, and quality, respectively. Second, we empirically analysed the two most prominent methodologies used, that is, the Euclidean distance–based and the PCA methods, to calculate an aggregate financial inclusion index. Subsequently, we constructed a hybrid financial inclusion index, which draws on the strengths of the two methodologies mentioned earlier. Third, we ranked all 22 countries under all three methodologies and compared their relative rankings. We also identified the two most prominent indicators by country and by year under each dimension of financial inclusion to highlight its policy importance.

On the basis of this analysis, we presented four stylised facts that showed various characteristics of the indicators and dimensions of financial inclusion. Our main finding is that the relative rankings of top and bottom financially inclusive countries do not vary significantly under all three methodologies, but they do differ to some degree concerning the middle-ranked countries. Several studies recognised that middle-income countries vary greatly in their institutional capacity to manage reforms and stimulate economic growth (Demetriades and Law, 2006; Subramanian et al., 2002). These countries face significant challenges to sustain higher economic growth and alleviate poverty and income inequality at the same time. Thus, in the context of financial inclusion, the implications are significant as their effect on various economic development may not be uniform across these middle income–ranked countries. The hybrid index of financial inclusion proposed here utilises a broad range of indicators across three dimensions of financial inclusion and draws on the strengths of the previously constructed indices in the literature. It is concluded that researchers go beyond competing methodologies by analysing the nexus between index, dimensions, and indicators of financial inclusion and their effect on particular development outcomes.

The chapter is organised as follows. The Section 2.2 briefly discusses the broad dimensions and indicators of financial inclusion typically used in the literature. Section 2.3 focuses on the Euclidean distance–based measure and the PCA method and constructs the hybrid index. Section 2.4 presents the rankings of 22 countries and compares them under all three methodologies. It also presents the top two indicators by country and by year based on the PCA scores used to construct the hybrid index. On the basis of the empirical findings, four stylised facts are presented. Finally, Section 2.5 provides a concluding discussion and identifies areas of future research.

2.2 Related literature

Most studies found that financial inclusion represents an important mechanism to reduce poverty and income inequality and promote economic development in poor countries (see Park and Mercado, 2016 for a broad overview). However, whilst measuring financial inclusion, the studies differed significantly regarding the type of indicators used, the definition of dimensions used to construct an aggregate index, and the methodology chosen to create such an index. At the country level, the Global Findex data set was the primary source to collect indicators on financial inclusion (Demirgüç-Kunt and Klapper, 2013). The data set considered multiple indicators covering three broad dimensions: a set of indicators showing the ownership and use of an account at a formal financial institution, a second set of indicators on saving patterns, and a final set of indicators showing their borrowing behaviours. Other studies that used similar indicators on penetration, savings, access to credit, loans, and insurance are Van der Werff et al. (2013), Allen et al. (2016), Zins and Weill (2016), and Kim et al. (2018). Some studies also defined a lack of financial inclusion as financial exclusion, which is a barrier to economic development for some groups and individuals when they are denied access to formal financial systems (Sinclair, 2001; Amidžić et al., 2014; Camara and Tuesta, 2014). Thus, the higher the extent of financial exclusiveness, the lower is the economic development in that country. In a multi-country study, Honohan (2008) considered household access to financial services as a single measure of financial inclusion and estimated what fraction of the adult population is using formal financial intermediaries in 160 countries. Similarly, at the industry level, Chauvet and Jacolin (2017) measured financial inclusion as the share of firms with access to credit, that is, having a loan from a financial institution.

Although these studies used a range of indicators, no attempt was made to combine these indicators into a single aggregate measure. Sarma (2008) argued that a robust and comprehensive measure that includes multiple dimensions of financial inclusion is helpful to demonstrate the current state of financial inclusion in an economy, to monitor the progress of the policy initiatives, and to compare its development with other countries over time. To create such a single index of financial inclusion, Sarma (2008) defined three dimensions of financial inclusion: banking penetration (dimension 1), availability of banking services (dimension 2), and usage (dimension 3). Banking penetration is defined as an inclusive financial system that has a wide range of users and penetrates widely amongst its users. The dimension is measured by the number of bank accounts as a proportion of the total population. Next, the availability of banking services is defined by an inclusive financial system that is easily available to its users. The dimension is measured by the number of bank branches per 1,000 population. Finally, following Kempson et al. (2004), usage dimension was defined by the notion of underbanked or marginally banked people.

Whilst these measures were comprehensive, except for measures defined by Demirgüç-Kunt and Klapper (2012), each dimension was based on a single indicator. In other words, three specific indicators were used to create the aggregate financial inclusion index. Sarma (2008) used a multivariate multidimensional approach of index construction like the approach of the United Nations Development Programme (UNDP) to calculate the human development index (HDI). However, unlike the UNDP that used simple arithmetic or geometric mean of all sub-indices to calculate the HDI, Sarma (2008) utilised a normalised inverse of the Euclidean distance method. The distance was computed from a reference ideal point and then normalised by the number of dimensions included in the aggregate index. However, whilst calculating the aggregate financial inclusion index, all dimensions were assigned equal weights due to the unavailability of data for all countries. A similar methodology was adopted by Yorulmaz (2013) in the context of financial inclusion in Turkey, and by Park and Mercado (2018a) to show the effect of financial inclusion on poverty and income inequality in 176 countries.

Amidžić et al. (2014) argued that when a composite index is computed using various indicators, some variables may possess attributes of multiple dimensions, thereby making it difficult to assign the weights adequately. Thus, assigning equal weights to all dimensions could potentially lead to measurement bias. Using factor analysis method to assign weights, the authors came up with three dimensions: (i) outreach (geographic and demographic penetration); (ii) usage (deposit and lending); and (iii) quality of financial services (disclosure requirement, dispute resolution, and cost of usage). In contrast, Camara and Tuesta (2014) and Park and Mercado (2018b) used two-stage PCA to calculate the aggregate financial index. In the first stage, the PCA was run on a group of indicators within each dimension to assign weights on indicators. Camara and Tuesta (2014) came up with three dimensions – usage, access, and barrier to financial inclusion. However, Park and Mercado (2018b) followed Sarma (2008) and defined the dimensions as access, availability, and usage, respectively. In the second stage, the PCA was run again to assign weights on all three dimensions. The advantage of using this kind of methodology is that the data using the PCA scores dictates the relative weights on each indicator and subsequently the weights on each dimension to calculate the aggregate index. Thus, unlike Sarma (2008), the methodology avoids assigning arbitrary weights to indicators and dimensions when calculating the aggregate index.

2.3 Construction of a hybrid index of financial inclusion

We constructed the hybrid index of aggregate financial inclusion by combining two existing methodologies, the Euclidean distance–based method of Sarma (2008) and the double PCA method of Camara and Tuesta (2014) and Park and Mercado (2018b). First, we discussed the strengths and weaknesses of these two methodologies and then explained the steps to construct the hybrid index.

2.3.1 Euclidean distance and double PCA methodologies

The Euclidean distance–based method is a multidimensional method which aggregates information on various forms of financial inclusion into a single index (Sarma, 2016). Sarma (2016) showed that it is important that the final index satisfies four mathematical properties, as follows:

(1) It must be a unit-free measure such that the values can be compared across countries and over time.
(2) The final index must be a bounded function, where the lower bound characterises the least financially inclusive system and the upper bound characterises the most financially inclusive system. In most common scenarios, this can be described as a value between 0 and 1.
(3) The value of the final index should be an increasing function of its dimensions. Thus, any improvements in financial inclusion indicators within each dimension appropriately reflect a higher value in the aggregate financial index. Mathematically, the index satisfies the monotonicity function.
(4) The index must also satisfy the homogeneity function. In other words, all dimensions are expressed as a constant return to scale to the aggregate index, where an equal increase in all dimensions will result in an equal change in the final number.

A normalised inverse of Euclidean distance method is used to aggregate the dimensions where the distance is computed as an average distance from the best and worst possible outcomes. A lower distance would indicate a higher value of the financial inclusion index and vice versa. Each dimension index, d_i, is computed as:

$$d_i = w_i \frac{A_i - m_i}{M_i - m_i} \tag{2.1}$$

where w_i refers to the weight attached to dimension i, A_i is the actual value, m_i is the lower bound value, and M_i is the upper bound value of dimension i, respectively. Although theoretically the value of w_i could range between 0 and 1, Sarma (2016) assigned equal weights to all three dimensions, arguing that all three dimensions are equally important for the aggregate index. Thus, w_i was set to 1. Regarding the choice of upper and lower-bound values, m_i was set to 0 and M_i was the observed 90th percentile of the distribution of dimension i. Sarma (2016) considered three dimensions: banking penetration (dimension 1), measured by the number of deposit bank accounts per 1,000 adult population; availability (dimension 2), measured by a combined index of the number of bank branches and the number of ATMs per 100,000 adults; and usage (dimension 3), measured by a combined value of credit volume to the private sector and deposit mobilised from the private sector as a proportion of the country's GDP.

Since all three dimensions were weighted equally, the aggregate financial inclusion index in a special form was calculated as follows:[3]

$$FI = \frac{1}{2}\left[\frac{\sqrt{d_1^2 + d_2^2 + \ldots + d_n^2}}{\sqrt{n}} + \left(1 - \frac{\sqrt{(1-d_1)^2 + (1-d_2)^2 + \cdots + (1-d_n)^2}}{\sqrt{n}}\right)\right] \tag{2.2}$$

where *FI* stands for financial inclusion index, and n is the total number of dimensions. Sarma (2016) assigned weight 1 to dimension 1 and 0.5 to dimensions 2 and 3, respectively. The study argued that the weights are based on the availability of data of each dimension for the countries in the sample and discussion with banking sector experts and other relevant researchers.

In contrast, Park and Mercado (2018b) criticised the methodology of Sarma (2008, 2016) on the ground of assigning arbitrary weights and, following Camara and Tuesta (2014), adopted a two-stage PCA method to assign weights to indicators and all dimensions, respectively.[4] In the first stage, all indicators were standardised following equation (2.1). It is important to note that Sarma (2016) had limited indicators and often considered a single indicator as a measure of a dimension; thus, a standardised value of a dimension would reflect the value of an indicator itself. In contrast, Park and Mercado (2018b) considered multiple indicators drawn from the Global Findex database and constructed three dimensions – access, availability, and usage, respectively. Consequently, in the first stage the PCA was used to derive weights for the standardised indicators within each dimension:

$$d_i = \frac{\Sigma_{j,k=1}^{p} \lambda_j P_k}{\Sigma_{j=1}^{p} \lambda_j} \tag{2.3}$$

where d_i stands for the index of dimension i derived from the PCA scores; $P_k = X\lambda_j$, where λ_j is the variance of the kth principal component representing their corresponding weights; and X is the number of indicator matrix. In the second stage, the PCA was again applied on all dimensions to assign weights:

$$FI = \frac{\Sigma_{j=1}^{p} \lambda_j P_{ki}}{\Sigma_{j=1}^{p} \lambda_j} \tag{2.4}$$

where similar to the previous stage, $P_k = X\lambda_\phi$, where λ_j is the variance of the kth principal component representing their corresponding weights, and X is the number of dimensions matrix. The advantage of this methodology is that it does not assign an arbitrary weight to indicators to create the dimension indices and to create the final financial inclusion index.

However, Sarma (2016) argued that the double PCA method may not be the best methodology to consider because of the following reasons. First, the PCA method works best to compute an index when the final index is based on a linear combination of the dimensions such that the weights reflect the variance–covariance structure of the dimensions. As a result, the final index would capture the first moments of the level data but not the second-order moments, which are more useful for this kind of analysis. Furthermore, unlike the Euclidean distance–based method, the PCA-based financial index would not satisfy all four necessary mathematical properties as mentioned earlier.

This discussion reveals the strengths and weaknesses of both methodologies. Whilst the Euclidean distance–based method is easy to compute and satisfies all mathematical properties of a robust and comprehensive financial inclusion index, it suffers from an arbitrary weighting scheme assigned to dimensions and indicators. On the contrary, the double PCA approach overcomes the arbitrary weighting issue by using the principal component scores as corresponding weights. The final index suffers from not satisfying all the four main properties required to compute a robust index. In this study, we constructed a hybrid index to overcome the limitations of both methodologies.

2.3.2 Construction of a hybrid index

We followed the latest update of the G20 report to define the dimensions and the corresponding indicators in each dimension (GPFI, 2016). We collected 23 indicators and grouped them into three dimensions of financial inclusion: usage, access, and quality, respectively. To our knowledge, this study incorporates the most extensive array of indicators to date. Multiple data sources were used to collect the indicators across 22 Asian countries in the period 2004–2015. Appendix 2.1 presents details of all indicators including the dimensions and corresponding data sources, and Appendix 2.2 presents the list of countries considered in this study. Usage is measured by 13 indicators, for example, use of mobile phones, use of the Internet, use of credit cards, use of deposit accounts, and nine other usage indicators. Similarly, access is measured by seven indicators, for example, the number of bank branches, number of ATMs, number of point of sale (POS) terminals, access to mobile phones, access to the Internet, and two other access indicators. Finally, the quality of financial services in these countries is measured by three indicators – emergency fund from savings, financial knowledge, and distance to the frontier of financial knowledge. Whilst financial knowledge measures the basic financial understandings of people in these countries – such as inflation, interest rate, money illusion, risk diversification, insurance premiums, and others – distance to the frontier of financial knowledge is a credit barrier measure, which measures the distance of each economy to the 'frontier' on the strength of their credit reporting systems and absolute level of regulatory performance (GPFI, 2016).

We implemented a two-stage procedure to construct the hybrid index. In the first stage, we considered all the indicators of financial inclusion and standardised them using Equation (2.1) following the method of Sarma (2008, 2016). All the standardised indicators are grouped under three dimensions. Next, following Equation (2.3) of Park and Mercado (2018b), we ran a PCA on all 13 indicators to assign weights on each indicator and constructed the usage dimension. Similarly, a PCA was run on all seven indicators to construct the access dimension and on three indicators to construct the quality dimension. Thus, instead of assigning arbitrary weights, we utilised the data to dictate the weights on each indicator to construct the dimension indices. However, in the second stage, instead of running the PCA method again, we used the Euclidean distance–based method of Sarma (2008, 2016) on all three dimensions to construct the final index of financial inclusion. The equal weighting scheme on each dimension was applied following equation (2.2) to construct the final index of financial inclusion.

The hybrid index is superior due to the following reasons: first, our hybrid index of financial inclusion uses many more indicators (23 indicators) than the previous studies of Sarma (2008, 2016), Camara and Tuesta (2014), and Park and Mercado (2018b). Thus, the hybrid index is comprehensive and captures a broad range of characteristics of the financial inclusion in developing countries in the period 2004–2015. Second, the construction of the hybrid index used the PCA to assign weights on dimensions but retained all four mathematical properties of the distance method in the final index. Thus, we drew on the strengths of both methodologies to create the hybrid index. It is also important to note that we could have followed the alternative method of adopting distance method in the first stage to create the dimension indices and then run the PCA in the second stage to create the final index. However, we considered this method inappropriate since there were 27 indicators in the first stage, and assigning equal weights to all of them would make the dimension indices biased and incorrectly reflect the importance of indicators in each dimension. After the dimension indices were settled using the PCA method and the error of arbitrary weighting scheme was minimised, adoption of the Euclidean distance–based method would consider the second-order moments of the dimensions to construct the final index and provided a more robust and comprehensive financial inclusion index. We followed the same procedure to create the hybrid financial inclusion index for all 22 Asian countries on an annual basis during the period 2004–2015. For comparison purposes, we also created two additional indices following the Euclidean distance–based method of Sarma (2008, 2016) and the double PCA method of Park and Mercado (2018b). The results are presented in the next section.

2.4 Empirical analysis and stylised facts

2.4.1 Rankings of countries

Table 2.1 presents the rankings on the financial inclusion of 22 Asian countries in 2004–2015 for all three methodologies: double PCA method of Park and Mercado (2018b), Euclidean distance–based method of Sarma (2008, 2016), and the hybrid index. Although all three indices are calculated for every year from 2004 to 2015 for all countries, due to paucity of space... Table 2.1 shows the rankings of all countries in 2004, 2011, and 2015, respectively.

In Table 2.1, the top rankings indicate more financially inclusive countries and lower rankings indicate those less financially inclusive. For 2004, we find that Japan ranked first and the Republic of Korea (henceforth Korea) second under all three methodologies. China ranked third in the PCA and the distance method but ranked fifth in the hybrid method whilst Hong Kong ranked fifth in the first two methodologies and ranked third in the hybrid method. However, we find

Table 2.1 Rankings on financial inclusion of countries

Country	*Double PCA method*			*Distance method*			*Hybrid method*		
	2004	*2011*	*2015*	*2004*	*2011*	*2015*	*2004*	*2011*	*2015*
Bangladesh	12	14	13	10	12	14	11	18	19
Brunei	20	20	21	19	18	21	20	21	21
Cambodia	17	18	18	17	17	18	15	13	18
China	3	5	5	3	3	3	4	5	5
Hong Kong	5	4	4	5	5	5	5	3	4
India	10	12	12	8	10	11	12	11	15
Indonesia	11	10	11	11	11	10	8	8	13
Japan	1	1	2	1	1	2	1	1	2
Korea, Rep. of	2	2	1	2	2	1	2	2	3
Lao PDR	22	21	22	22	22	22	22	22	22
Macau	21	22	20	21	21	20	19	19	12
Malaysia	7	9	9	7	7	9	7	9	8
Mongolia	8	8	7	12	8	7	9	6	7
Myanmar	19	19	19	20	20	19	21	20	20
Nepal	18	16	17	18	19	17	16	16	17
Pakistan	15	15	14	13	16	15	13	14	11
Philippines	14	13	16	14	14	16	14	12	16
Singapore	4	3	3	4	4	4	3	4	1
Sri Lanka	13	11	10	15	13	12	17	17	10
Taiwan	6	6	6	6	9	6	6	7	6
Thailand	9	7	8	9	6	8	10	10	9
Vietnam	16	17	15	16	15	13	18	15	14

Source: Authors' own calculation.

PCA = principal component analysis.

that the top five countries are the same under all three methodologies. They are Japan, Korea, China, Singapore, and Hong Kong. A similar pattern is observed for the five bottom-ranked countries under all three methodologies in 2004. They are the Lao PDR, Macau, Brunei, Myanmar, and Nepal. When we looked at the middle-ranked countries, the rankings differed on occasions based on the methodology chosen. For example, Vietnam ranked 16th and the Philippines ranked 14th under all three methodologies. However, whilst Thailand ranked 9th under the double PCA and distance-based measures, under the hybrid methodology the rank was marginally higher (10th). Similarly, India ranked 10th under double PCA and 8th under the distance-based measure but ranked 11th under the hybrid methodology in 2004.

We observed a similar pattern in the rankings of 2011 and 2015 in Table 2.1. The top five and the bottom five countries mostly had the same rank under all three methodologies. Interestingly, the same set of countries in 2004 that were in the top five were the same across the years, including in 2011 and 2015, respectively. As noted for 2015, these were Singapore, Korea, Japan, Hong Kong, and China. Bottom five countries – the Lao PDR, Nepal, Cambodia, Myanmar, and Brunei – consistently ranked in the lowest group of countries both over time, 2004–2015, and across the three methods. As for 2004, there were some occasional differences between the three methods in 2011 and 2015 amongst the middle-ranked countries as well as across time. For example, in 2015, Bangladesh ranked 19th under the hybrid method but 13th and 14th under the PCA and distance methods, respectively. Similarly, in 2015, Indonesia ranked 13th under the hybrid method and 11th and 10th under the PCA and distance methods, respectively. Also, India ranked 12th under the PCA method, 11th under the distance method, and 15th under the hybrid methodology. Thus, middle-ranked countries represented a source of interest in that not only was their rank ordering slightly sensitive to the methodological approach adopted but also their relative rankings tended to fluctuate more compared to the bottom-ranked countries. In this context, the hybrid method offered the opportunity to provide an additional lens for examining how middle-ranked countries performed.

Comparing the three methodologies, we find that they are consistent with the rankings of countries. Although the hybrid methodology is superior in the way it has been constructed by drawing on the strengths of the two previous methodologies and capturing a broad range of indicators, researchers should pay less attention to the debate on competing methodologies and focus more on the policy perspectives in respective countries. Thus, based on the observations, we formulated the following two stylised facts:

Stylised fact #1: The ranking of countries is broadly consistent under all three methodologies.

Stylised fact #2: The top- and bottom-ranked countries remain unchanged over time under all three methodologies, but some differences are observed with middle-ranked countries.

2.4.2 Distance from the frontier

To check if the gap between the middle-ranked, bottom-ranked, and the top-ranked countries is closing over time, based on the newly constructed hybrid index, we plotted the distance from the frontier of each country in the period 2004–2015. Since Japan ranked first in 2004 and ranked second in 2015, all countries were benchmarked against Japan, which was the frontier country in the sample.

Whilst panel (a) shows the distance from the frontier of the top seven countries, panels (b) and (c) show the same for middle-ranked and bottom seven–ranked countries, respectively. We find that amongst the top-ranked countries, although the relative position of countries such as Malaysia and Hong Kong have fluctuated since 2011, most countries are converging in recent years. Singapore's level of financial inclusion converged with Japan in 2012 and, by 2015, the country had exceeded the frontier level. However, there is no evidence of a convergence in the bottom-ranked countries in panel (c). All seven countries display a very flat pattern compared to the frontier level. Finally, there is mixed evidence of convergence amongst the middle-ranked countries in panel (b). Whilst there is clear evidence that for Thailand and Mongolia, the gap between their level of financial inclusion and the frontier level is closing, others do not show any significant level of convergence. It is also important to note that Figure 2.1 shows the relative ratio of financial inclusion between countries and not an absolute value. Thus, although financial inclusion may be increasing over time in the absolute sense, at an individual country level, for countries such as India and Bangladesh, this is not necessarily reflected in their relative ranks.

> ***Stylised fact #3***: Over 2004–2015, the top- and a few middle-ranked countries were converging to the frontier but there was no evidence of convergence amongst the bottom-ranked countries.

2.4.3 Top two indicators by country and year

Next, we utilised the PCA scores[5] from the first stage of the hybrid index construction to compare the frequencies of the indicators that received higher weightings for each country and year. Tables 2.2 and 2.3, respectively, present the top two indicators by country and by year.

Table 2.2 shows the top two indicators by country. For example, the top two indicators of Japan in the usage dimension (ranked first in 2004 and ranked second in 2015 in the hybrid method) are outstanding loans per 1,000 adults (with a 0.4094 weight) and percentage of adults who receive wages or government transfers into an account (with a 0.4078 weight). In the access dimension, the top indicators are the number of branches per 100,000 adults (with a 0.5836 weight) and percentage of adults with access to a mobile phone or device or the Internet in the home (with a 0.5412 weight). In contrast, for Korea (ranked second in 2004 and third in 2015 in hybrid method), the top two most effective

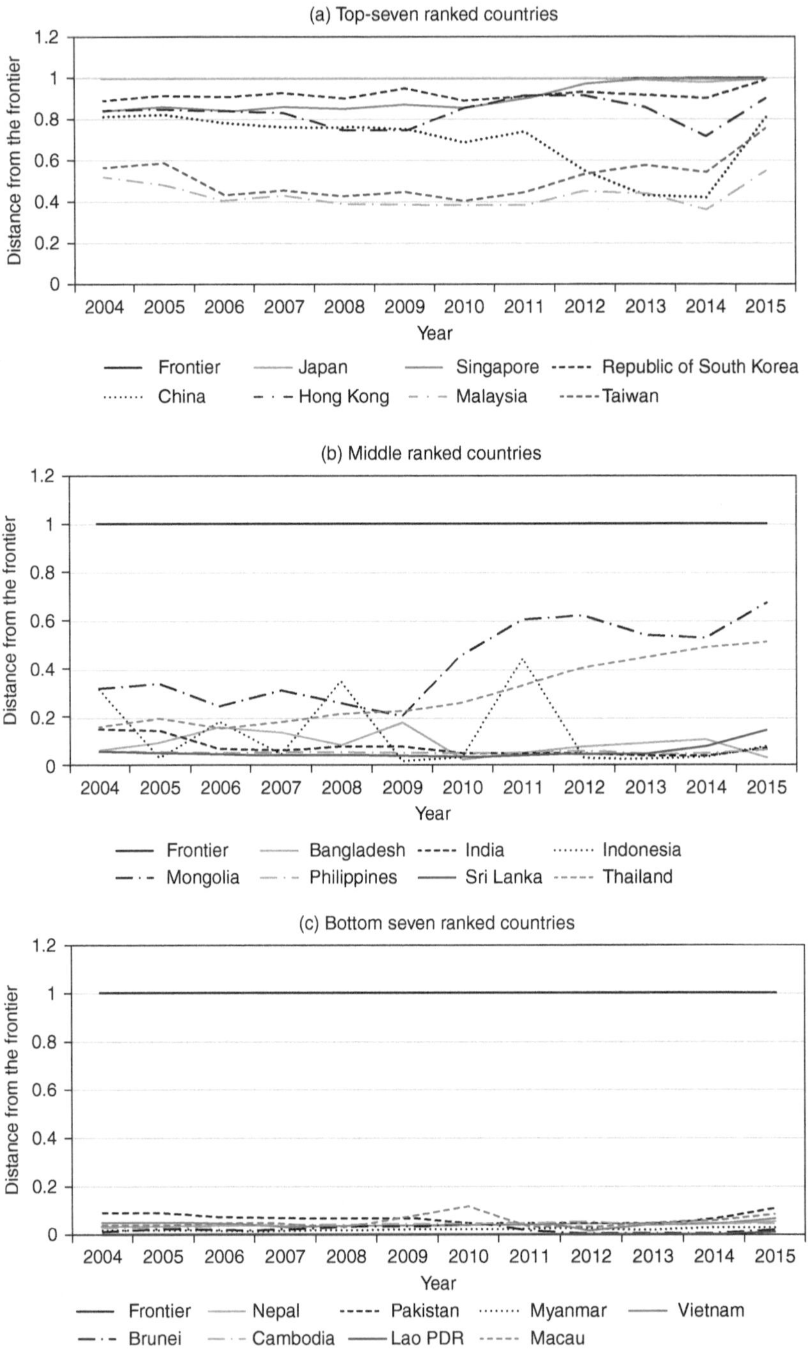

Figure 2.1 Distance from the frontier.

Source: Authors' own calculation. For data sources of individual indicators of financial inclusion, please refer to Appendix 2.1.

Table 2.2 Top two indicators of financial inclusion by country

Country	*Top two indicators*	*Weight*	*Frequency*
Panel A: Usage dimension			
Bangladesh	E-money accounts per 1,000 adults	0.4078	6
	Percentage of adults who report having an account (by themselves or with someone else) with a formal financial institution or a mobile money provider	0.3981	5
Brunei	Percentage of adults using a transaction account (with a bank or other formal financial institution or mobile money provider) to make or receive a digital financial payment	0.4375	1
	Outstanding loans per 1,000 adults	0.3345	8
Cambodia	Percentage of adults who receive wages or government transfers into an account	0.4348	6
	Percentage of adults using a debit card to directly make a payment from an account (with a bank or other formal financial institution)	0.4348	2
China	Retail cashless transactions per 1,000 adults	0.4097	5
	Percentage of adults who saved in a bank or other formal financial institution in the past year	0.3730	6
Hong Kong	Retail cashless transactions per 1,000 adults	0.4352	5
	Outstanding loans per 1,000 adults	0.4348	8
India	Percentage of adults who saved in a bank or other formal financial institution in the past year	0.3800	6
	Percentage of adults using the Internet to pay bills, make purchases, or send money online	0.3785	1
Indonesia	Outstanding loans per 1,000 adults	0.4679	8
	Percentage of adults who receive wages or government transfers into an account	0.4678	6
Japan	Outstanding loans per 1,000 adults	0.4094	8
	Percentage of adults who receive wages or government transfers into an account	0.4078	6
Lao PDR	E-money accounts per 1,000 adults	0.4460	6
	Retail cashless transactions per 1,000 adults	0.4455	5
Macau	Deposit accounts per 1,000 adults	0.5031	4
	E-money accounts per 1,000 adults	0.5028	6
Malaysia	Percentage of adults using a debit card to directly make a payment from an account (with a bank or other formal financial institution)	0.4304	2
	Percentage of adults who saved in a bank or other formal financial institution in the past year	0.4209	6

(*continued*)

Table 2.2 Cont.

Country	*Top two indicators*	*Weight*	*Frequency*
Mongolia	Percentage of adults who report having an account (by themselves or with someone else) with a formal financial institution or a mobile money provider	0.3954	5
	Deposit accounts per 1,000 adults	0.3857	4
Myanmar	Outstanding loans per 1,000 adults	0.4407	8
	Percentage of adults who receive wages or government transfers into an account	0.4407	6
Nepal	Deposit accounts per 1,000 adults	0.4473	4
	Percentage of adults who report having an account (by themselves or with someone else) with a formal financial institution or a mobile money provider	0.3862	5
Pakistan	Percentage of adults who saved in a bank or other formal financial institution in the past year	0.3899	6
	Percentage of adults who receive wages or government transfers into an account	0.3800	6
Philippines	Percentage of adults who saved in a bank or other formal financial institution in the past year	0.4040	6
	Outstanding loans per 1,000 adults	0.3793	8
Singapore	Percentage of adults who report having an account (by themselves or with someone else) with a formal financial institution or a mobile money provider	0.3656	5
	Outstanding loans per 1,000 adults	0.3579	8
South Korea	Percentage of adults who receive wages or government transfers into an account	0.4342	6
	Percentage of adults who saved in a bank or other formal financial institution in the past year	0.2758	6
Sri Lanka	Retail cashless transactions per 1,000 adults	0.4267	5
	Outstanding loans per 1,000 adults	0.4223	8
Taiwan	Percentage of adults who report having an account (by themselves or with someone else) with a formal financial institution or a mobile money provider	0.4147	5
	E-money accounts per 1,000 adults	0.3954	6
Thailand	Retail cashless transactions per 1,000 adults	0.4057	5
	E-money accounts per 1,000 adults	0.4050	6
Vietnam	E-money accounts per 1,000 adults	0.4439	6
	Deposit accounts per 1,000 adults	0.4332	4
Panel B: Access dimension			
Bangladesh	Number of ATMs per 100,000 adults	0.5296	6
	Number of branches per 100,000 adults	0.5290	16
Brunei	Number of branches per 100,000 adults	0.5226	16
	Number of POS terminals per 100,000 adults	0.5182	6

Table 2.2 Cont.

Country	*Top two indicators*	*Weight*	*Frequency*
Cambodia	Percentage of adults with access to a mobile phone or device or the Internet in the home	0.4932	15
	Number of branches per 100,000 adults	0.4899	16
China	Number of ATMs per 100,000 adults	0.4792	6
	Number of POS terminals per 100,000 adults	0.4723	6
Hong Kong	Number of branches per 100,000 adults	0.5263	16
	Percentage of adults with access to a mobile phone or device or the Internet in the home	0.5055	15
India	Percentage of adults with access to a mobile phone or device or the Internet in the home	0.4551	15
	Number of POS terminals per 100,000 adults	0.4371	6
Indonesia	Number of branches per 100,000 adults	0.4797	16
	Percentage of adults with access to a mobile phone or device or the Internet in the home	0.4680	15
Japan	Number of branches per 100,000 adults	0.5836	16
	Percentage of adults with access to a mobile phone or device or the Internet in the home	0.5412	15
Lao PDR	Percentage of adults with access to a mobile phone or device or the Internet in the home	0.5709	15
	Number of branches per 100,000 adults	0.5681	16
Macau	Number of branches per 100,000 adults	0.6138	16
	Number of ATMs per 100,000 adults	0.5715	6
Malaysia	Number of POS terminals per 100,000 adults	0.4836	6
	Percentage of adults with access to a mobile phone or device or the Internet in the home	0.4675	15
Mongolia	Number of branches per 100,000 adults	0.4847	16
	Number of POS terminals per 100,000 adults	0.4697	6
Myanmar	Number of ATMs per 100,000 adults	0.4934	6
	Percentage of adults with access to a mobile phone or device or the Internet in the home	0.4851	15
Nepal	Number of POS terminals per 100,000 adults	0.5066	6
	Percentage of adults with access to a mobile phone or device or the Internet in the home	0.4994	15
Pakistan	Percentage of adults with access to a mobile phone or device or the Internet in the home	0.4946	15
	Number of branches per 100,000 adults	0.4786	16

(*continued*)

Table 2.2 Cont.

Country	*Top two indicators*	*Weight*	*Frequency*
Philippines	Percentage of adults with access to a mobile phone or device or the Internet in the home	0.4714	15
	Number of ATMs per 100,000 adults	0.4643	6
Singapore	Number of branches per 100,000 adults	0.6028	16
	Percentage of adults with access to a mobile phone or device or the Internet in the home	0.5499	15
Korea, Rep. of	Number of branches per 100,000 adults	0.5275	16
	Number of mobile agent outlets per 100,000 adults	0.5153	1
Sri Lanka	Percentage of adults with access to a mobile phone or device or the Internet in the home	0.5306	15
	Number of branches per 100,000 adults	0.4874	16
Taiwan	Percentage of adults with access to a mobile phone or device or the Internet in the home	0.6562	15
	Number of branches per 100,000 adults	0.5920	16
Thailand	Percentage of adults with access to a mobile phone or device or the Internet in the home	0.5304	15
	Number of branches per 100,000 adults	0.4893	16
Vietnam	Number of branches per 100,000 adults	0.5487	16
	Number of ATMs per 100,000 adults	0.5067	6
Panel C: Quality dimension			
In all countries	Percentage of adults who responded 'savings' to the question: If you had an emergency that required [$10, or 1/25 of GDPPC] urgently, how would you get the money? (i) borrow from friends/relatives; (ii) work more; (iii) sell assets; (iv) take from savings; (v) take a loan from savings club; (vi) take a loan from bank; (vii) would not be able to find it	0.7071	1
	Getting credit: the strength of credit reporting systems and the effectiveness of collateral and bankruptcy laws in facilitating lending.	0.7071	1

Source: Authors' own calculation.

ATM = automatic teller machine; GDPPC = gross domestic product per capita; POS = point of sale

indicators in the usage dimension are the percentage of adults who receive wages or government transfers into an account (with 0.4342 weight) and percentage of adults who saved in a bank or other formal financial institution in the past year (with a 0.2758 weight). In the access dimension, the top indicators are the

Table 2.3 Top two indicators by years

Years	*Top two indicators*	*Weight*	*Frequency*
Panel A: Usage dimension			
2004	Percentage of adults who receive wages or government transfers into an account	0.3653	11
	Percentage of adults using a debit card to directly make a payment from an account (with a bank or other formal financial institution)	0.3609	5
2005	Percentage of adults who receive wages or government transfers into an account	0.3650	11
	Percentage of adults using a debit card to directly make a payment from an account (with a bank or other formal financial institution)	0.3606	5
2006	Percentage of adults who receive wages or government transfers into an account	0.3652	11
	Percentage of adults using a debit card to directly make a payment from an account (with a bank or other formal financial institution)	0.3607	5
2007	Percentage of adults who receive wages or government transfers into an account	0.3664	11
	Percentage of adults who saved in a bank or other formal financial institution in the past year	0.3557	2
2008	Percentage of adults who receive wages or government transfers into an account	0.3695	11
	Percentage of adults who report having an account (by themselves or with someone else) with a formal financial institution or a mobile money provider	0.3559	3
2009	Percentage of adults who receive wages or government transfers into an account	0.3726	11
	Percentage of adults who report having an account (by themselves or with someone else) with a formal financial institution or a mobile money provider	0.3559	3
2010	Percentage of adults who receive wages or government transfers into an account	0.3752	11
	Percentage of adults who report having an account (by themselves or with someone else) with a formal financial institution or a mobile money provider	0.3693	3
2011	Percentage of adults who receive wages or government transfers into an account	0.3731	11
	Outstanding loans per 1,000 adults	3124	1
2012	Percentage of adults who receive wages or government transfers into an account	0.3727	11
	Percentage of adults using a debit card to directly make a payment from an account (with a bank or other formal financial institution)	0.3655	5

(*continued*)

Table 2.3 Cont.

Years	*Top two indicators*	*Weight*	*Frequency*
2013	Percentage of adults who saved in a bank or other formal financial institution in the past year	0.3655	2
	Percentage of adults using a transaction account (with a bank or other formal financial institution or mobile money provider) to make or receive a digital financial payment	0.3631	2
2014	Percentage of adults who receive wages or government transfers into an account	0.3707	11
	Percentage of adults using a transaction account (with a bank or other formal financial institution or mobile money provider) to make or receive a digital financial payment	0.3624	2
2015	Percentage of adults using a debit card to directly make a payment from an account (with a bank or other formal financial institution)	0.3821	5
	Percentage of adults who receive wages or government transfers into an account	0.3784	11
Panel B: Access dimension			
2004	Number of debit cards per 1,000 adults	0.5477	6
	Percentage of adults with access to a mobile phone or device or the Internet in the home	0.5272	12
2005	Number of debit cards per 1,000 adults	0.5482	6
	Percentage of adults with access to a mobile phone or device or the Internet in the home	0.5248	12
2006	Percentage of adults with access to a mobile phone or device or the Internet in the home	0.5487	12
	Number of ATMs per 100,000 adults	0.3932	4
2007	Percentage of adults with access to a mobile phone or device or the Internet in the home	0.5540	12
	Number of ATMs per 100,000 adults	0.3827	4
2008	Percentage of adults with access to a mobile phone or device or the Internet in the home	0.5575	12
	Number of debit cards per 1,000 adults	0.5249	6
2009	Percentage of adults with access to a mobile phone or device or the Internet in the home	0.5607	12
	Number of debit cards per 1,000 adults	0.5252	6
2010	Percentage of adults with access to a mobile phone or device or the Internet in the home	0.5625	12
	Number of ATMs per 100,000 adults	0.4068	4
2011	Percentage of adults with access to a mobile phone or device or the Internet in the home	0.5423	12
	Number of ATMs per 100,000 adults	0.4998	4
2012	Percentage of adults with access to a mobile phone or device or the Internet in the home	0.5359	12
	Agents of payment service providers per 100,000 adults	0.4472	1

Table 2.3 Cont.

Years	*Top two indicators*	*Weight*	*Frequency*
2013	Percentage of adults with access to a mobile phone or device or the Internet in the home	0.5332	12
	Number of debit cards per 1,000 adults	0.4829	6
2014	Percentage of adults with access to a mobile phone or device or the Internet in the home	0.5654	12
	Number of debit cards per 1,000 adults	0.4467	6
2015	Percentage of adults with access to a mobile phone or device or the Internet in the home	0.5643	12
	Number of POS terminals per 100,000 adults	0.3630	1
Panel C: Quality dimension			
In all years	Getting credit: the strength of credit reporting systems and the effectiveness of collateral and bankruptcy laws in facilitating lending.	0.6491	1
	Financial knowledge score (i.e., arithmetic score which sums up correct responses to questions about basic financial concepts, such as: (i) inflation, (ii) interest rate, (iii) compound interest, (iv) money illusion, (v) risk diversification, (vi) main purpose of insurance)	0.5790	1

Source: Authors' own calculation.

ATM = automatic teller machine; POS = point of sale

number of branches per 100,000 adults (with a 0.5275 weight) and the number of mobile agent outlets per 100,000 adults (with a 0.5153 weight). The top two indicators are again different in the bottom five countries. Thus, the top two indicators in each dimension vary significantly across countries and provide important policy implications for individual countries.

Taken together, in the usage dimension, the top indicator is outstanding loans per 1,000 adults, which appear eight times as the top two indicators amongst the sample of countries. This is followed by three indicators in the second position, each appearing as the top two indicators six times in the sample (Table 2.2). They are (i) e-money accounts per 1,000 adults, (ii) percentage of adults who saved in a bank or other formal financial institution in the past year, and (iii) percentage of adults who receive wages or government transfers into an account. In the access dimension, we find the number of branches per 100,000 adults as the top indicator, which received the highest scoring 16 times from various countries in the sample. In the second position is the percentage of adults with access to a mobile phone or device or the Internet in the home, which received a high PCA score on 15 occasions. Amongst the three indicators in the quality dimension, the top-ranked indicator is the use of savings as a source of emergency funding followed by strength of credit reporting systems and the effectiveness of collateral and bankruptcy laws in facilitating lending.

In Table 2.3, we followed the same procedure of implementing the PCA scoring to find out the top indicators over time, keeping the country list fixed. For example, in 2004, the top two indicators in the usage dimension were the percentage of adults who receive wages or government transfers into an account (with a 0.3653 weight) and the percentage of adults using a debit card to directly make a payment from an account with a bank or other formal financial institution (with a 0.3609 weight). In contrast, in 2011, the top two indicators in the usage dimension were the percentage of adults who receive wages or government transfers into an account (with a 0.3731 weight) and outstanding loans per 1,000 adults (with a 0.3124 weight). In 2015, the top two indicators in the usage dimension were the percentage of adults using a debit card to directly make a payment from an account (with a bank or other formal financial institution) (with a 0.3821 weight) and percentage of adults who receive wages or government transfers into an account (with a 0.3784 weight). Thus, there is a significant variation amongst the top two weighted indicators over time. We found similar evidence for the top two indicators in access and quality dimension.

Again, taken together, the top two indicators in the usage dimension were (i) percentage of adults who receive wages or government transfers into an account, which appeared 11 times as one of the top two indicators, and (ii) percentage of adults using a debit card to directly make a payment from an account (with a bank or other formal financial institution), with a frequency of 6 times. Similarly, in the access dimension, the top two indicators were the percentage of adults with access to a mobile phone or device or the Internet in the home (frequency = 12) and the number of debit cards per 1,000 adults (frequency = 6), respectively. Finally, in the quality dimension, the top two indicators were the strength of credit reporting systems and the effectiveness of collateral and bankruptcy laws in facilitating lending and financial knowledge score, respectively.

When we compared the results of Tables 2.2 and 2.3, we observed a clear pattern amongst the top two indicators in each dimension across countries and over time. At least one common indicator appeared most frequently as one of the top two indicators based on the PCA scoring adjusted by country or year. In the usage dimension, we found the percentage of adults who receive wages or government transfers into an account as the most common indicator in both Tables 2.2 and 2.3 irrespective of whether the PCA scoring was by country or by year. Similarly, the percentage of adults with access to a mobile phone or device or the Internet at home was a common top indicator in the access dimension, and the strength of credit reporting systems and the effectiveness of collateral and bankruptcy laws in facilitating lending was a common top indicator in the quality dimension. Thus, these three indicators, each corresponding to a single dimension, appeared most frequently as one of the top two indicators for all countries and over time. From a policy perspective, these three indicators would be very important in promoting financial inclusion in Asia. On the basis of this observation, we formulated the following stylised fact:

Stylised fact #4: There are clear similarities across the developing countries in how each of the three dimensions of financial inclusion – access, usage, and quality – is adopted over time.

2.5 Conclusion and policy implications

The chapter overviews the existing dimensions of financial inclusion and critically evaluates the two widely used existing methodologies to measure these dimensions, the PCA, and the Euclidean distance methods, respectively. We subsequently proposed a new hybrid financial inclusion index, which draws on the strengths of existing measures and consistent with the ranking order of countries. Whilst the hybrid index overcomes the limitations of the previously constructed indices in the literature, it captures a broad range of indicators for developing countries in the sample. We proposed four key stylised facts by critically evaluating three dimensions of financial inclusion – access, usage, and quality – in 22 Asian countries in the period 2004–2015.

Under all three methodologies, we did not find significant differences in rankings amongst the set of top- and bottom-ordered countries. The top five and the bottom five countries under all three methodologies are virtually the same. Moreover, we found that the set of top- and bottom-tiered countries remain relatively unchanged over time. Related to this, a significant gap exists between the bottom-ranked countries and the distance to the frontier, and this gap has changed little over time. However, some occasional differences in rank orderings can be found across the three methodologies amongst middle-ranked countries. There are also greater fluctuations in ranking over time, including some countries demonstrating convergence with the top-ranked countries (Figure 2.1) but these tend to be sporadic and not uniform. More research focusing on these differences is required.

From a policy perspective, at least one indicator received the highest weighting (PCA scoring) under both country and time variations. We also showed the top two indicators of financial inclusion by each country and year. These indicators require more attention from policymakers for the successful realisation of financial inclusion in these countries. Also, notwithstanding the theoretically appealing nature in constructing a hybrid aggregate financial index, policymakers should give attention to the dimensions and indicators in respective countries and how they influence specific development outcomes. The next chapter examines these relationships in more detail by deploying the hybrid index measure and utilising the top two indicators and dimensions, separately, to test their relationship with certain development outcomes.

Acknowledgements

We sincerely thank Mr. Admasu Maruta for providing excellent research assistance to this project. We would like to acknowledge the funding from the Economic Research Institute for ASEAN and East Asia for the successful completion of this project.

Notes

1 Corresponding author. GPO Box 2471, Adelaide 5000, SA. Email: Rajabrata.Banerjee@unisa.edu.au
2 GPO Box 2471, Adelaide 5000, SA. Email: Ronal.Donato@unisa.edu.au
3 For detailed discussion on how the Euclidean distance method is applied using a normalised inverse of Euclidean distance, see Sarma (2016).
4 PCA is an empirical technique that helps researchers to reduce the dimensionality of large data sets and increases the interpretability of such dimensions without considerable reduction in information loss. This is an adaptive data analysis technique, which creates new uncorrelated variables that successively maximise variance (see Joliffe and Cadima, 2016).
5 All indicators were standardised before the PCA methodology was adopted. We utilised the data to dictate the weights on each indicator to construct the dimension indices. Since the PCA methodology avoids assigning arbitrary weights, we adopted the PCA scores to find the top two indicators.

References

Allen, F., A. Demirguc-Kunt, L. Klapper, and M.M. Peria (2016), 'The Foundations of Financial Inclusion: Understanding Ownership and Use of` Formal Accounts', *Journal of Financial Intermediation*, 27(1), pp.1–30.

Amidžic, G., A. Massara, and A. Mialou (2014), 'Assessing Countries' Financial Inclusion Standing: A New Composite Index', *IMF Working Paper*, No. 14/36. Washington, DC: International Monetary Fund.

Camara, N. and D. Tuesta (2014), 'Measuring Financial Inclusion: A Multidimensional Index', *BBVA Research Paper*, No. 14/26.

Chauvet, L. and L. Jacolin (2017), 'Financial Inclusion, Bank Concentration, and Firm Performance', *World Development*, 97, pp.1–13.

Demetriades, P. and S.H. Law (2006), 'Finance, Institutions and Economic Development', *International Journal of Finance & Economics*, 11(3), pp.245–60.

Demirgüç-Kunt, A. and L. Klapper (2012). *Measuring Financial Inclusion: The Global Findex Database*. Washington, DC: World Bank.

Demirgüç-Kunt, A. and L. Klapper (2013), 'Measuring Financial Inclusion: Explaining Variation in Use of Financial Services across and within Countries', *Brookings Papers on Economic Activity*, 2013(1), pp.279–340.

Dungey, M., F.D. Tchatoka, and M.B. Yanotti (2018), 'Using Multiple Correspondence Analysis for Finance: A Tool for Assessing Financial Inclusion', *International Review of Financial Analysis*, 59, pp.212–22.

Global Partnership for Financial Inclusion (2016), G20 Financial Inclusion Indicators, https://databank.worldbank.org/data/download/g20fidata/G20_Financial_Inclusion_Indicators.pdf (accessed 20 January 2019).

Honohan, P. (2008), 'Cross-Country Variation in Household Access to Financial Services', *Journal of Banking & Finance*, 32(11), pp.2493–2500.

Jolliffe, I.T. and J. Cadima (2016), 'Principal Component Analysis: A Review and Recent Developments', *Philosophical Transactions of the Royal Society A Mathematical, Physical and Engineering Sciences*, 374(2065), 20150202, April 2016.

Kempson, E., A. Atkinson, and O. Pilley (2004), 'Policy Level Response to Financial Exclusion in Developed Economies: Lessons for Developing Countries'. Report of Personal Finance Research Centre. Bristol: University of Bristol.

Kim, D.W., J.S. Yu, and M.K. Hassan (2018), 'Financial Inclusion and Economic Growth in OIC Countries', *Research in International Business and Finance*, 43, pp.1–14.

Mialou, A., G. Amidžić, and A. Massara (2017), 'Assessing Countries' Financial Inclusion Standing – A New Composite Index', *Journal of Banking and Financial Economics*, 2(8), pp.105–26.

Park, C.Y. and R. Mercado (2016), 'Does Financial Inclusion Reduce Poverty and Income Inequality in Developing Asia?', in S. Gopalan and T. Kikuchi (eds.), *Financial Inclusion in Asia: Issues and Policy Concerns*. London: Palgrave Macmillan, pp.61–92.

Park, C.Y. and R. Mercado (2018a), 'Financial Inclusion, Poverty, and Income Inequality', *The Singapore Economic Review*, 63(01), pp.185–206.

Park, C.Y. and R. Mercado (2018b), *Financial Inclusion: New Measurement and Cross-Country Impact Assessment*. Available at SSRN, http://dx.doi.org/10.2139/ssrn.3199427. (accessed 09 June 2020).

Sarma, M. (2008), 'Index of Financial Inclusion', *Working Paper*, No. 215, New Delhi: Indian Council for Research on International Economic Relations (ICRIER).

Sarma, M. (2016), 'Measuring Financial Inclusion for Asian Economies', in S. Gopalan and T. Kikuchi (eds.), *Financial Inclusion in Asia: Issues and Policy Concerns*. London: Palgrave Macmillan, pp.3–34.

Sinclair, S.P. (2001), *Financial Exclusion: An Introductory Survey*. Edinburgh: CRSIS College of Art/Heriot Watt University.

Subramanian, M.A., M.F. Trebbi, and M.D. Rodrik (2002), *Institutions Rule: The Primacy of Institutions over Integration and Geography in Economic Development (No. 2–189)*. Washington, DC: International Monetary Fund.

Van der Werff, A.D., J.M. Hogarth, and N.D. Peach (2013), 'A Cross-Country Analysis of Financial Inclusion within the OECD', *Consumer Interest Annual*, 59, pp.1–12.

Yorulmaz, R. (2013), 'Construction of a Regional Financial Inclusion Index in Turkey', *Journal of BRSA Banking and Financial Markets*, 7(1), pp.79–101.

Zins, A. and L. Weill (2016), 'The Determinants of Financial Inclusion in Africa', *Review of Development Finance*, 6(1), pp.46–57.

Appendix 2.1 Financial inclusion indicators and data sources

Indicators	*Sources*
Usage dimension	
Percentage of adults who report having an account (by themselves or with someone else) with a formal financial institution or a mobile money provider	WB Global Findex
Percentage of adults using a transaction account (with a bank or other formal financial institution or mobile money provider) to make or receive digital financial payment	WB Global Findex
deposit accounts per 1,000 adults	IMF Financial Access Surveys
E-money accounts per 1,000 adults	WB Global Payments Systems Survey
Retail cashless transactions per 1,000 adults	WB Global Payments Systems Survey
Outstanding loans per 1,000 adults	IMF Financial Access Surveys
Percentage of adults who receive wages or government transfers into an account (with a bank or other formal financial institution or mobile money provider)	WB Global Findex
Percentage of adults using a debit card to directly make a payment from an account (with a bank or other formal financial institution)	WB Global Findex
Payment using a mobile phone (from an account)	WB Global Findex
Payments using the Internet	WB Global Findex
Percentage of adults with at least one loan outstanding from a bank or other formal financial institution	WB Global Findex
Percentage of adults that saved at a bank or other formal financial institution in the past year	WB Global Findex
Number of mobile money transactions per 100,000 adults	IMF Financial Access Surveys
Access dimension	
Number of branches per 100,000 adults	IMF Financial Access Surveys
Number of ATMs per 100,000 adults	IMF Financial Access Surveys
Number of POS terminals per 100,000 adults	WB Global Payments Systems Survey
Number of mobile agent outlets per 100,000 adults	IMF Financial Access Surveys
Number of debit cards per 1,000 adults	WB Global Payments Systems Survey
Percentage of adults with access to a mobile phone or device or the Internet in the home	Gallup World Poll
Agents of payment service providers per 100,000 adults	WB Global Payments Systems Survey

Appendix 2.1 Cont.

Indicators	*Sources*
Quality dimension	
Financial knowledge score	WB Financial Capability Surveys and OECD National Financial Literacy and Inclusion Surveys
Use of savings for emergency funding	WB Global Findex
Distance to frontier	WBG Doing Business

Source: Authors' own calculation.

IMF = International Monetary Fund; OECD = Organisation for Economic Co-operation and Development; WB = World Bank; WBG = World Bank Group

Appendix 2.2 List of countries considered for financial inclusion rankings (in alphabetical order)

Bangladesh	Mongolia
Brunei	Myanmar
Cambodia	Nepal
China	Pakistan
Hong Kong	Philippines
India	Korea, Rep. of
Indonesia	Singapore
Japan	Sri Lanka
Lao PDR	Taiwan
Macau	Thailand
Malaysia	Vietnam

3 The effects of financial inclusion on development outcomes

New insights from ASEAN and East Asian countries

Rajabrata Banerjee,[1] *Ronald Donato, and Admasu Afsaw Maruta*

3.1 Introduction

Over the past decade, financial inclusion has received increasing attention amongst researchers and policymakers, and a growing body of empirical literature is emerging highlighting the potential benefits of increasing financial inclusion in developing countries (Demirgüç-Kunt et al., 2018; IEG, 2015; Allen et al., 2012). The Sustainable Development Goals (SDGs) proposed by the United Nations refer to financial inclusion as a mechanism for supporting inclusive economic growth (Jahan et al., 2019). In essence, financial inclusion is generally viewed as the extent of the population which has access to and use for formal financial services. In this context, research and policy attention have focused on those people who are socially excluded from the financial system and how strategies can be devised to enable the 'unbanked' segments of the population to enhance their engagement with the financial system. Expanding financial inclusion has the potential to benefit the poor through various channels, including the ability to accumulate savings and access credit that enable them to smoothen consumption patterns, better manage financial risk to deal with uncertainties, and invest in productive assets (Demirgüç-Kunt et al., 2018; IEG, 2015).

The study reported here considers a comprehensive data set on financial inclusion and development outcomes from 20 Asian countries over the period 2004–2015. This chapter builds on the previous chapter and contributes to the research enquiry on financial inclusion by filling several important research gaps in the literature. Specifically, they are (i) extending the array of development outcomes being analysed, (ii) using both aggregated and disaggregated measures of financial inclusion when determining its impact on development outcomes, (iii) giving greater attention to the role of political risk factors and its interaction effect when examining the impact of financial inclusion on development outcomes, and (iv) determining the broader policy implications that come with such closer examination. We briefly elaborate on these contributions in the pages that follow.

First, much of the empirical literature exploring the potential benefits of financial inclusion on development outcomes has focused on economic growth, poverty, and income inequality where research findings generally reveal the positive effects of financial inclusion on these outcomes (e.g., see Chapter 2). However, there is a dearth of empirical literature examining the effect of financial inclusion on other important development outcomes listed under SDGs and forming part of overall human development – specifically, health and education outcomes. This is surprising given the already-established positive nexus in the empirical literature between financial development and human capital and its impact on education and health outcomes. Accordingly, a key focus of this chapter is to extend the range of development outcomes under analysis by examining the impact of financial inclusion on economic growth, education, health, and income inequality. The aim is to offer greater insight and understanding into the extent to which financial inclusion impacts on particular development outcomes relative to others. This is particularly important from a policy perspective as the effect of financial inclusion on certain economic development outcomes may be stronger than others (e.g., health vs education vs poverty, etc.), which may vary across regions based on their demographic and institutional characteristics.

The second contribution of this chapter is that both aggregated and disaggregated measures of financial inclusion are incorporated into the analysis to discern a more nuanced understanding of how financial inclusion at a broader level and on an individual level impacts on development outcomes. Thus far, all empirical research on financial inclusion have either adopted an aggregate measure of financial inclusion by way of developing composite index measures (e.g., see Sarma, 2008; Park and Mercado, 2015, 2018) to analyse its impact, or studies have selected specific financial indicators (e.g., number of bank branches, number of automatic teller machines, deposit accounts), drawn from either an access or a usage component of the financial system, as a proxy measure of financial inclusion (e.g., Neaime and Gaysett, 2018; Demirgüç-Kunt and Klapper, 2012; Honohan, 2008). It is generally understood both in the construction of a composite financial index measure and in utilising individual indicators that financial inclusion, as noted in Chapter 2, is generally referred to as comprising three major dimensions or components – namely, usage, access, and quality (see Jahan et al., 2019). To date, the empirical literature has given very limited attention to the nexus between these three levels of aggregation, that is, composite index measure, dimensions, and indicators. Accordingly, and in contrast to other studies, this study uses both an aggregated and a disaggregated approach to measure and analyse financial inclusion. Specifically, we first consider financial inclusion at an aggregate level by using a hybrid methodology to establish a financial inclusion index (reported in Chapter 2) and to empirically examine its relationship with development outcomes. We then disaggregate the index into three dimensions of financial inclusions, specifically access, usage, and quality, to examine whether specific dimensions are more strongly associated with particular development outcomes than others. Finally, we disaggregate further to the individual indicator level of financial inclusion and examine the effect of the top two most influential indicators from each dimension, based on principal component analysis scores reported in the previous chapter, on the various development outcomes to see whether the impact of financial inclusion is sensitive to specific indicators. It is important to note here that we do not claim to establish all possible channels through which these indicators influence economic development, which would require a more rigorous empirical investigation at the country level and beyond the scope of this study. However, we show that the effect of financial inclusion is sensitive to the type of indicator chosen.

Related to this, as a third contribution, this study refers to the growing body of literature on institutional quality and examines how political factors mediate the effect of financial inclusion on economic growth, education, health, and income inequality. The importance of institutional quality for economic development is well established in the literature (see, e.g., Rodrik et al. 2004; Shleifer and Vishny, 1993; Gupta et al., 2001; Justino et al., 2013; Akresh et al., 2012). Also, a growing body of literature argues that if a country has lower political risk factors, the effect of financial inclusion is more immediate, such as ownership and usage of bank accounts and financial literacy (Allen et al., 2016; Grohmann et al., 2018). However, very little attention has been paid to how political factors moderate the effect of financial inclusion on various economic development outcomes.

The remainder of this chapter is structured as follows: Section 3.2 provides a brief overview of the literature on development outcomes. Section 3.3 describes the data, whilst Section 3.4 outlines the empirical methodology used in the analysis. Section 3.5 reports on the empirical findings and Section 3.6 concludes with discussion and policy implications.

3.2 Overview of the literature on development outcomes

The effect of financial inclusion on economic growth relates closely to the widely accepted evidence of the significant positive effect of financial development on long-run economic growth through the channel of more efficient use of capital stock (Goldsmith, 1969), and greater savings and thus higher volume of investment (McKinnon, 2010; Shaw, 1973). Financial inclusion itself connects people with banks; thus, access to a well-functioning financial system enables economically and socially excluded people to integrate better into the economy and actively contribute to its development. Financial inclusion plays a key role in building a strong foundation of a country's financial infrastructure and more effectively and extensively facilitates a more efficient flow of funds channelling savings to investment activities, thus promoting economic growth (Sharma, 2016). Several studies found empirical support to financial inclusion on economic growth. For example, Andrianaivo and Kpodar (2011) and Inoue and Hamouri (2016) showed the positive effects of financial inclusion on economic growth in African countries. Kim et al. (2018) demonstrated the same amongst countries of the Organisation of Islamic Cooperation (OIC) and Rasheed et al. (2016) and Demirgüç-Kunt and Kappler (2012) for a large sample of developing countries. Sarma (2008) reported similar findings for financial inclusion in India.

Several studies also demonstrated empirically how financial inclusion contributes significantly to reducing income inequality and poverty. As noted, expanding financial inclusion to those previously excluded from the financial system enhances the ability to access credit and accumulate savings, thus enabling individuals and households to smoothen consumption patterns, better manage financial risk to deal with uncertainties, and invest in productive assets (Demirgüç-Kunt et al., 2018; IEG, 2015). Agyemang-Badu et al. (2018) found that financial inclusion is inversely related to both poverty and income inequality in a study of African countries, whilst Park and Mercado (2015, 2018) demonstrated similar findings in developing Asian countries. Further, Neaime and Gaysset (2018) found that financial inclusion decreases income inequality in Middle Eastern and North African countries, and Honohan (2008) reported that financial access significantly reduced income inequality for 160 countries. Also, country-level studies showed that financial inclusion significantly reduces income inequality and poverty. For example, Huang and Zhang (2020), using Chinese provincial data, showed a gap reduction between urban and rural income. Burgess and Pande (2005) demonstrated the effects of state-led credit and savings facilities expansion on poverty reduction in India. Brune et al. (2011) and Allen et al. (2013) showed that greater access to savings/financial accounts can improve the well-being of poor households in Malawi and Kenya, respectively.

As highlighted before, there is very limited empirical literature exploring the nexus between financial inclusion and other development outcomes, specifically health and education. This is surprising given the already-established positive nexus in the empirical literature between financial development and human capital and its impact on education and health outcomes, and the high positive correlation between financial development with financial inclusion (Mor and Ananth, 2014; Ang, 2008; Mishkin, 2007). Dwyfor Evans et al. (2002) found evidence of complementarity between financial development and human capital. Cheston and Kuhn (2002) argued that financial inclusion offers the opportunity to potentially help women overcome exploitation, create confidence for economic reliance, and help carry out income-generating activities and thus invest more in children's schooling, nutrition, and health. Financial inclusion can ostensibly play an important role in expanding access of low-income households to education finance and lower barriers to accessing education. Similarly, financial inclusion can make important contributions to health outcomes, such as reduced child and infant mortality rates. This is through providing credit, savings, and insurance and thus assisting the financing of healthcare by smoothing income and consumption in the face of health shocks. Further, both education and health outcomes can be mediated through the higher wealth effects stemming from higher returns on savings and investment balances due to lower costs of accessing financial services through formal channels and the higher economic growth fostered by financial inclusion through the enhanced use of capital stock (Hakeem, 2010; Pritchett and Summers, 1996).[2]

As noted, much of the empirical literature on the impact of financial inclusion on development outcomes has focused mostly on economic growth and the related development outcomes of poverty and income inequality. Little to no attention has been given to other development outcomes that focus on social well-being. Accordingly, this study fills an important research gap by extending the range of development outcomes under investigation to encompass the effects of financial inclusion not only on economic growth and income inequality but also on education and health outcomes.

3.3 Data

This section overviews the development outcomes, the key independent variables, and other control variables used in each model. A summary of the description and the data sources of the outcome variables and all independent variables are presented in Appendix 3.1.

3.3.1 Development outcomes

In this study, we consider four development outcomes: economic growth, education, health, and income inequality. Following the standard literature, economic growth is measured by the annual percentage change in the real gross domestic product (GDP) per capita in $US purchasing power parity (PPP). Education outcome is measured by expected years of schooling. Several studies have argued that expected years of schooling is a better measure of educational attainment of children than other education indicators, such as literacy rates and enrolment rates (see Behrman and Deolalikar, 1991; Gylfason, 2001; Gakidou et al., 2010). As per the United Nations Development Programme (UNDP),[3] expected years of schooling show the number of years of schooling that a school-aged child can expect to experience if prevailing patterns of age-specific enrolment rates remain throughout the child's life. Higher financial inclusion is expected to generate higher expected years of schooling through credit, savings, and insurance.

Similarly, health outcome is proxied by child mortality rates (Gakidou et al., 2010). Child mortality rate shows the death rate of children under the age of 5. Since financial constraints are more prevalent in less-developed countries, better financial inclusion is expected to have a positive effect on maternal health through credit and insurance, thereby reducing child mortality rates. Finally, following the standard literature, we measure income inequality by the Gini index (Beck et al., 2007; Sarma and Pais, 2011; Park and Mercado, 2018). As noted, all definitions and corresponding data sources are provided in Appendix 3.1.

3.3.2 Financial inclusion index and disaggregated measures

The financial inclusion index is constructed using a hybrid index of aggregate financial inclusion by combining two existing methodologies: (i) the Euclidean distance–based method of Sarma (2008) and (ii) the double PCA method of Camara and Tuesta (2014) and Park and Mercado (2018). As noted, the hybrid index comprises three dimensions: usage, access, and quality of financial services, which we analyse separately. Further, each dimension has its indicators, which we derived from PCA scores, and we examined the effect of the top two most influential indicators from each dimension. Chapter 2 provides a detailed discussion on the construction of the financial inclusion index, the three dimensions comprising the index, and the top two most important indicators associated with each dimension. A unique feature of this study is that financial inclusion is analysed both at the aggregate level, using the hybrid index measure, as well as at the disaggregated level where the effects of financial inclusion are examined at the dimension and indicator level(s) for each development outcome. Specific details of the data set and the 20 Asian countries used in the analysis are elaborated in Chapter 2.

3.3.3 Political risk

Political risk is a measure of institutional quality which can have a direct impact on development outcomes, as well as an indirect impact by enhancing the effectiveness of financial inclusion on development outcomes. The importance of institutional quality on economic growth and development is well established (Scully, 1982; LaPorta et al., 1998; Acemoglu et al., 2005). Weak institutional quality – particularly political factors that lead to higher levels of corruption, internal conflicts, and insecure property rights (Levin and Satarov, 2000) – negatively impacts investment in productive activities (Chong and Calderon, 2000). Chong and Calderon (2000) presented cross-country evidence linking higher institutional quality with improved income inequality over time. In addition, lower political risks encourage investments in the education and health sectors (Glaeser et al., 2004). For instance, Justino et al. (2013) showed that civil conflict deteriorates educational systems by reducing government expenditures in the education sector. Corruption can also significantly reduce government revenue through tax evasion and drive up the price and reduce the level of human capital investment and government services in health (Shleifer and Vishny, 1993; Gupta et al., 2001).

Empirical studies have highlighted the importance of political risk factors, such as strengths of legal rights (Grohmann et al., 2018); efficient enforcement of rule of law (Park and Mercado, 2015, 2018); government stability (Claessens and Leaven, 2003); and lower corruption in supporting financial inclusion and financial development (Rojas-Suarez and Amado, 2014; Allen et al., 2016). Accordingly, this study incorporates political risk not only as a separate control variable but also as an interaction term to ascertain whether the effects of financial inclusion is enhanced in the presence of lower political risk. We use political risk ratings taken from the Political Risk Services group data set.[4] Here, political risk captures uncertainties related to government stability, internal conflict, corruption, religious tensions, law and order, as well as several other social and political attributes. Given the level of financial inclusion in a country, all these risk variables could, directly and indirectly, impact the level of economic development. The measurement unit takes a value between 0 (highest risk) and 12 (lowest risk).

3.3.4 Other control variables

The set of control variables used for each development outcome is drawn from the empirical development literature, and a summary description of each control variable is provided in Appendix 3.1.

Concerning economic growth (i.e., per capita real GDP growth) as the dependent variable in the regression model(s), we include initial per capita income, trade openness, life expectancy, inflation, domestic credit to the private sector (percent of GDP), growth of population, average years of schooling, and female labour force participation (percentage of the total labour force) as additional controls. It is standard in the empirical growth literature that the convergence effect is captured by including the real per capita GDP at the beginning of the period. Following Fischer (1993), we include inflation to measure the effect of monetary policies. Trade openness facilitates the use of advanced technologies and promotes investments in new inputs thereby increasing economic growth (Banerjee and Roy, 2014; Yanikkaya, 2003). Our models, therefore, include trade openness as measured by the ratio of the sum of exports and imports to the value of GDP (in US dollars). Life expectancy has a positive effect on economic growth by increasing the number of the working-age population (De la Croix and Licandro, 1999). Financial sector development can also increase the pool of savings and in turn a greater investment in productive activities (Ang, 2008). We use domestic credit to the private sector (percent of GDP) as a proxy for financial development. Becker et al. (1999) stated that in poorer, mainly agricultural, economies with limited human capital and rudimentary technology, a higher population significantly reduces economic growth. Accordingly, we include the growth of the population of the sampled countries. Krueger and Lindahl (2001) argued that the education sector positively contributes to economic growth through various mechanisms including the skills to adopt new technologies, and greater investment in human capital. Accordingly, we include average years of schooling in the growth regressions. Finally, a growing body of literature suggests that increasing women's participation in development can improve economic growth by improving overall family health and, thus, increase household productivity (World Bank, 1994). To capture this relationship, our growth models include female labour participation as a percentage of the total labour force.

In the regressions with education as the outcome variable, we include population under age 15, growth of per capita GDP, government expenditure on education, life expectancy at birth years, and pupil–teacher ratio at primary schools as control variables. Simon and Pilarski (1979) argued that an increasing population size reduces the amount of education that children receive. Hence, to capture this relationship, we include the population under age 15 in the education regressions. Public education expenditure provides an assessment of a government's priorities in education and a commitment to invest in human capital (Jung and Thorbecke, 2003) and, thus, government expenditure on education captures this effect in our models. The links between health and education are well established in the literature. For example, healthy children can learn better and thus positively contribute to long-run economic growth. To capture this effect, we include life expectancy in the education regression. Finally, following Dearden et al. (2002), we include pupil–teacher ratio at primary schools to capture the effect of better learning and teaching environments on educational attainment.

In the regressions with health as the outcome variable, we include growth of per capita GDP, adult female literacy rate, the prevalence of undernourishment, births attended by skilled health staff, government expenditure on the health sector, and expected years of schooling as control variables as all these variables have significant effects on child mortality rate (Galiani et al., 2005). For example, adult female literacy reduces child mortality rates because literate women can seek information for the betterment of health, nutrition, and education of their household members than illiterate women. In other words, higher levels of female illiteracy might be associated with poor levels of child health. Well-nourished children grow into healthy adults and, in turn, give their children a better start in life. Further, well-nourished women face fewer risks during pregnancy and childbirth, and their children set off on a firmer developmental path, both physically and mentally (Feeny and Ouattara, 2013).

Finally, in the regressions with income inequality as the dependent variable, we include growth of per capita GDP, trade openness, inflation, female labour force participation (percent of the total labour force), growth of population, life expectancy at birth, total and average years of schooling as additional controls. The extant literature suggests that these variables have a significant effect on income inequality. Hence, following Bjørnskov (2010), we include per capita income to test the Kuznets curve, which shows an inverted U-shape relationship between per capita income and income inequality. We also include population growth, following Ram (1984) who argued that population growth has a significantly negative effect on income distribution, as poor households could be affected by high fertility rates and temporary economic declines. Lin and Fu (2016) suggested that trade liberalisation promotes smooth distribution of income in developing countries as trade may increase the real return to the factor that is relatively abundant, including low-skilled workers. Trade openness is therefore included in the income inequality regressions.

3.4 Empirical methodology

This study considers a system of moment equations using the generalised method of moments (GMM) proposed by Blundell and Bond (1998) to tackle the possible issue of reverse causality that may exist between financial inclusion and economic development.[5] For example, countries with increasing economic growth may experience increasing financial inclusion. Higher economic growth leads to a higher standard of living, lower poverty, greater access and usage of financial products, and thus may significantly determine the level of financial inclusion. Also, other development outcomes, for example, education, can impact the level of financial inclusion of an economy. Educated people can understand the various financial products in the market, make informed decisions, and hence can improve their access to these products. Pena et al. (2014) stated that education is a way of measuring knowledge, skill sets, and the capacity to make decisions in formal financial markets. This indicates a positive association between financial inclusion and education. Similarly, better health outcomes can influence financial inclusion positively. A healthy economy signals more productive workers, better access to health-related financial products, such as credit and health insurance. This may in turn influence higher financial inclusion. Finally, income inequality can also influence financial inclusion in a less-developed country. Lower income inequality implies a higher standard of living. This could lead to higher financial development and a greater proportion of the population being able to access banking services, secure credit, insurance, and other financial products.

To address the reverse causality issues, the following equation is estimated in a system-GMM specification (Blundell and Bond, 2000):

$$DO_{it} = C_0 + C_1 DO_{it-1} + C_2 FI_{it-1} + C_3 \left(FI_{it-1} * PR_{it-1}\right) + C_4 PR_{it-1} + C_5 X_{it-1} + \lambda_t + \mu_i + \varepsilon_{it}$$

where i denotes the country (i = 1, …, 22) and t denotes the time (t = 2004, …, 2015). DO_{it} shows development outcomes, which take the following measures: economic growth, education (expected years of schooling), health (under-5 child mortality rate), and income inequality (Gini coefficient), respectively. DO_{it-1} captures the previous year's realisations of a particular development outcome. Similarly, FI_{it-1} denotes the level of financial inclusion, PR_{it-1} refers to political risk rating, and X_{it-1} is a vector of control variables specific to a development outcome.[6] *Also*, λ_t denotes the time-fixed effect, μ denotes country fixed effects and ε_{it} shows the idiosyncratic error term. In addition, all variables including the outcomes variables are transformed into their logarithmic form. The main reason is that the log–log specification smooths the data and allows for the interpretation of the coefficients as elasticities (Mishra and Newhouse, 2009). The most important coefficient of interest of this study is C_2. If C_2 is statistically significant and positive, financial inclusion, therefore, makes an important contribution to promoting development outcomes in Asian countries.

The GMM approach allows estimating a regression equation in differences and a regression equation in levels simultaneously, with each equation using its own set of instrumental variables (i.e., see Block, 2002; Narayan et al., 2011; Hasan et al., 2009). The plausibility of the instruments potentially depends on the consistency of the lagged values of the independent variables. Arellano and Bond (1991) and Arellano and Bover (1995) proposed two tests of specifications to verify the consistency of the instruments. The first one is the Sargan test of overidentifying restrictions which tests the overall validity of the instruments by analysing the sample analogue of the moment conditions used in the estimation process. Failure to reject the null hypothesis (which states overidentifying restrictions are valid) gives support to the model. The second test examines the presence of autocorrelation in the error process. Our findings from the study pass both the overidentifying restrictions and autocorrelation in the error process. Moreover, one major drawback of system-GMM estimation is the inclusion of too many instruments, which may introduce a bias in the coefficient estimates. Following Roodman (2009), we also control this by using the collapse option in all system-GMM specifications. Thus, our empirical specification shows that the basic identification assumptions of the system-GMM are robust.

3.5 Empirical results

This section reports on the empirical results for each of the development outcome specifications, namely, economic growth, education, health, and inequality.[7] The results for each development outcome are first reported at the aggregate level using the hybrid FI index and at the dimension level of financial inclusion, specifically usage, access, and quality, and presented in a single table (i.e., Tables 3.1, 3.3, 3.5, and 3.7). Consequently, we present the results for each development outcome showing the impact for the highest and second-highest ranked indicators for each dimension of financial inclusion (i.e., Tables 3.2, 3.4, 3.6, and 3.8). At each level of analysis (i.e., aggregate index, dimension, and indicators), particular attention is given to the effect of political risks, not only in terms of its direct effect on development outcomes but also indirectly through its interaction effect with financial inclusion. Further, a particular set of control variables is included for each development outcome based on our discussion in the previous section. We discuss the results here based on each development outcome.

3.5.1 Economic growth and financial inclusion

Table 3.1 presents the results at the index level (specifications 1 and 2) and the dimension level (specifications 3–6) concerning per capita economic growth. All model specifications incorporate political risk ratings, whilst an interaction term between political risk and financial inclusion is added in specification 2 at the index level, and in specifications 4–6 at the dimension level. At the index level, specifications 1 and 2 (before and after interaction, respectively) in Table 3.1 reveal that the financial inclusion index has a strong positive and significant relationship with economic growth, as do several other covariates including initial income per capita, life expectancy, financial deepening (i.e., domestic private credit as a percentage of GDP), and population growth. Further, the signs for all the coefficients for all the parameter estimates are in the expected directions. Political risk as a stand-alone control variable exerts a statistically significant positive relationship with economic growth across both specifications. However, we do not find statistical significance as an interaction term.

Unpacking financial inclusion to its individual dimensions, results for specification 3 (without political risk interaction) and specifications 4–6 (with interaction) reveal that usage represents the only financial inclusion dimension that has a positive relationship with economic growth under all four specifications (i.e., specifications 3–6).[8] Results reveal that neither access nor quality dimension

Table 3.1 Economic growth and financial inclusion at index and dimension(s) levels

Variables	*[1] Index No interaction*	*[2] Index With interaction*	*[3] Dimension No interaction*	*[4] Dimension With interaction (U)*	*[5] Dimension With interaction (A)*	*[6] Dimension With interaction (Q)*
Financial inclusion – index	0.023***	0.030**				
	(4.72)	(2.04)				
(Financial inclusion) x (Political risk rating)		−0.001				
		(−0.57)				
Political risk rating	0.171***	0.190***	0.128*	0.325	0.256	0.117*
	(3.44)	(2.89)	(1.98)	(0.90)	(1.42)	(1.81)
Financial inclusion dimension – Usage (U)			0.038*	0.123**	0.080**	0.042***
			(1.97)	(2.25)	(2.30)	(2.73)
Financial inclusion dimension – Access (A)			0.034	0.011	0.054	0.025
			(1.56)	(0.33)	(1.00)	(0.93)
Financial inclusion dimension – Quality (Q)			0.014	0.107	0.032	0.031
			(0.36)	(1.57)	(0.69)	(0.45)
(U) × (Political risk ratings)				0.049*		
				(1.65)		
(A) × (Political risk ratings)					0.028	
					(1.19)	
(Q) × (Political risk ratings)						0.001
						(1.12)
Initial per capita income	−0.051***	−0.050***	−0.070*	−0.136**	−0.063	−0.072*
	(−5.22)	(−5.13)	(−1.70)	(−2.09)	(−0.89)	(−1.93)
Trade openness	0.003	0.002	0.039	0.141	0.032	0.036
	(0.12)	(0.11)	(0.95)	(1.58)	(0.79)	(0.88)
Life expectancy	0.342**	0.406**	0.583***	0.358**	0.546	0.559***
	(2.51)	(2.06)	(5.53)	(2.47)	(1.46)	(4.82)

Inflation	–0.007	–0.007	–0.009	–0.027*	0.006	–0.007
	(–0.89)	(–0.81)	(–1.48)	(–1.94)	(0.41)	(–0.98)
Domestic credit to private sector (% of GDP)	0.071***	0.076***	0.107***	0.062**	0.187**	0.099***
	(6.01)	(4.40)	(3.92)	(2.38)	(2.41)	(3.30)
Growth of population	–0.020**	–0.021**	–0.031*	–0.032	–0.091*	–0.039**
	(–2.35)	(–2.21)	(–1.86)	(–1.01)	(–1.82)	(–2.36)
Average years of schooling	0.005	0.005	0.242	0.371	0.462	–0.232
	(0.07)	(0.08)	(1.46)	(1.14)	(1.22)	(–1.45)
Labour force, female (% of total labour force)	0.048	0.048	0.055	0.007***	0.010***	0.001
	(0.86)	(0.87)	(0.59)	(2.90)	(4.16)	(0.54)

Source: Authors' own calculation.

Notes: The dependent variable is growth of per capita income. The key independent variable is the financial inclusion index derived from the hybrid method and the dimensions of financial inclusion. All variables are expressed in logarithmic form. An unrestricted number of lags of endogenous variables is used. We, however, checked the consistency of the results by taking different lags of the endogenous variables and found that the qualitative nature of the results remains intact. ***, **, and * denote significance at the 1%, 5%, and 10% levels, respectively. Heteroscedasticity and autocorrelation robust t-statistics are in parentheses. Constant and country and time-fixed effects, which are not reported in the table, are included. The regressions include 178 observations and 20 Asian countries. Both Hansen test of overidentification restrictions and AR (2) test for serial correlation align with the conventional levels.

of financial inclusion has a statistically significant relationship with economic growth across any of the model specifications. Political risk as a stand-alone variable is statistically significant at 10% (i.e., specification 3 and 6). We also find a positive interaction effect when interacted with usage (i.e., specification 4) at 10%, implying the effect of usage is enhanced in the presence of lower political risks. The statistical significance of control variables remains consistent across all model specifications. The important observation made here is that whilst financial inclusion represents an important variable at the aggregate level, when disaggregated, however, the extent of its influence is not uniform across the three separate dimensions. In the case of economic growth, the 'driver' of financial inclusion is confined to the usage dimension only. We return to the issue of the relative importance of dimensions when reviewing other development outcomes.

Focusing on the indicators level in Table 3.2, we can find that specifications 1–4 contain the highest-ranked indicator(s) identified for each dimension, whilst specifications 5–8 represent results for the second-highest-ranked indicators of each dimension. Results are both before and after the inclusion of the political risk interaction term for each set of indicators. A notable observation from Table 3.2 is the far stronger relationship of the first-ranked indicators with respect to economic growth compared to the second-ranked indicators. In particular, the first-ranked indicators for both the usage indicator – the percentage of adults who receive wages into an account – and the quality indicator – the strength of the credit reporting system – yielded a strong positive relationship with economic growth across nearly all model specifications (1–4) whilst access indicator percentage of adults with access to mobile banking at home was significant (at 10%) under only one model specification (specification 1). In contrast, amongst the second-ranked indicators, only the usage indicator revealed a positive statistically significant relationship with per capita economic growth (specifications 5–8). Political risk as a stand-alone variable generated a statistically significant relationship with economic growth across the majority of model specifications. However, as an interaction effect, we find that only the quality indicator interaction term was statistically significant (i.e., specification 4). This implies that the impact of the particular financial indicator is enhanced in the presence of lower political risk factors. The statistical significance of the particular control variables is consistent with Table 3.1. The results at the indicator level are consistent with those presented in Table 3.1 at the dimension level, where usage tends to be the most relevant financial inclusion dimension impacting on economic growth. Importantly also, results from Table 3.2 demonstrate that indicators themselves matter, and the influence and importance of financial inclusion on a development outcome can pivot on specific indicators.

3.5.2 Education and financial inclusion

Table 3.3 presents the results at the index level (specifications 1 and 2) and the dimension level (specifications 3–6) concerning education outcomes (as measured by average years of schooling) after controlling for an array of control

Table 3.2 Economic growth and financial inclusion at indicators levels

Dimension	*Variables*	*Top indicators for each dimension (With interaction – specifications 2–4)*				*Second-ranked indicators for each dimension (With interaction – specification 6–8)*			
		[1]	*[2]*	*[3]*	*[4]*	*[5]*	*[6]*	*[7]*	*[8]*
Usage (U)	Percentage of adults who receive wages into an account	0.439*** (3.54)	0.315 (1.50)	0.430*** (4.20)	0.446*** (3.88)				
Access (A)	Percentage of adults with access to mobile banking at home	0.654* (1.75)	0.665 (1.57)	0.436 (1.07)	0.524 (1.35)				
Quality (Q)	The strength of credit reporting systems	0.592*** (3.32)	0.648*** (3.27)	0.565*** (3.58)	0.711 (1.35)				
Interaction: U	(Percentage of adults who receive wages into an account) * Political risk rating	0.064** (2.01)							
Interaction: A	(Percentage of adults with access to mobile banking at home) * Political risk ratings			0.147 (1.15)					
Interaction: Q	(The strength of credit reporting systems) * Political risk ratings				0.510*** (2.61)				
Usage (U)	Percentage of adults using the Internet to payments					0.046*** (3.82)	0.042*** (3.28)	0.049*** (3.81)	0.047*** (3.74)
Access (A)	Number of debit cards per 1,000 adults					0.008 (0.37)	0.002 (0.10)	0.044 (1.23)	0.016 (0.65)

(*continued*)

Table 3.2 Cont.

Dimension	*Variables*	*Top indicators for each dimension (With interaction – specifications 2–4)*				*Second-ranked indicators for each dimension (With interaction – specification 6–8)*			
		[1]	*[2]*	*[3]*	*[4]*	*[5]*	*[6]*	*[7]*	*[8]*
Quality (Q)	Financial knowledge					0.001	0.001	0.001	0.001
						(0.01)	(0.12)	(0.11)	(0.22)
Interaction: U	(Percentage of adults using the Internet to make payments) * Political risk ratings						0.021*		
							(1.72)		
Interaction: A	(Number of debit cards per 1,000 adults) * Political risk ratings							0.021	
								(0.69)	
Interaction: Q	(Financial knowledge) * Political risk ratings								0.002
									(1.16)
	Political risk ratings	0.064**	0.135	0.177***	0.515***	0.176*	0.130	0.148*	0.025
		(2.01)	(0.94)	(3.01)	(3.02)	(1.68)	(1.20)	(1.77)	(0.14)
	Initial per capita income	–0.099***	–0.109***	–0.102***	–0.100***	–0.083***	–0.093***	–0.080***	–0.097***
		(–4.25)	(–4.03)	(–4.89)	(–4.00)	(–5.53)	(–7.57)	(–5.59)	(–4.11)
	Trade openness	0.018	0.030	–0.004	–0.018	0.038	0.034	0.047*	0.035
		(0.51)	(0.85)	(–0.09)	(–0.60)	(1.48)	(1.27)	(1.66)	(1.40)
	Life expectancy	0.278	0.258	0.392	0.401*	0.275	0.327	0.204	0.243
		(1.22)	(1.12)	(1.29)	(1.75)	(0.80)	(0.98)	(0.63)	(0.78)
	Inflation	0.001	0.001	–0.001	–0.001	–0.003	–0.001	–0.004	–0.005
		(0.04)	(0.09)	(–0.08)	(–0.01)	(–0.23)	(–0.09)	(–0.29)	(–0.36)

Domestic credit to private	0.106***	0.099***	0.140***	0.106***	0.085***	0.074***	0.090***	0.091***
sector (% of GDP)	(3.49)	(3.48)	(4.32)	(3.55)	(3.34)	(2.52)	(3.21)	(3.22)
Growth of population	–0.027*	–0.017	–0.033*	–0.024	–0.036*	–0.031	–0.045**	–0.027*
	(–1.92)	(–1.04)	(–1.87)	(–1.23)	(–1.95)	(–1.33)	(–2.12)	(–1.75)
Average years of schooling	–0.071	0.030	0.056	0.067	0.029	0.051	0.024	0.078
	(–0.55)	(0.21)	(0.40)	(0.55)	(0.37)	(0.70)	(0.28)	(0.71)
Labour force, female (% of	0.003	0.004*	0.002	0.002	–0.001	0.001	0.001	0.016
total labour force)	(1.32)	(1.79)	(0.93)	(1.28)	(–0.20)	(0.12)	(0.31)	(0.23)

Source: Authors' own calculation.

Notes: The dependent variable is growth of per capita income. The key independent variables are the top two indicators from each dimension of financial inclusion. All variables are expressed in logarithmic form. Unrestricted number of lags of endogenous variables is used. We, however, checked the consistency of the results by taking different lags of the endogenous variables and the qualitative nature of the results remains intact. ***, **, and * denote significance at the 1%, 5%, and 10% levels, respectively. Heteroscedasticity and autocorrelation robust t-statistics are in parentheses. Constant and country and time-fixed effects, which are not reported in the table, are included. The regressions include 178 observations and 20 Asian countries. Both Hansen test of overidentification restrictions and AR (2) test for serial correlation align with the conventional levels.

Table 3.3 Education (average years of schooling) and financial inclusion at index and dimension(s) levels

Variables	*[1] Index No interaction*	*[2] Index With interaction*	*[3] Dimension No interaction*	*[4] Dimension With interaction (U)*	*[5] Dimension With interaction (A)*	*[6] Dimension With interaction (Q)*
Financial inclusion	0.003**	0.004*				
	(2.08)	(1.82)				
(Financial inclusion) × (Political risk ratings)		0.001*				
		(1.80)				
Political risk ratings	0.045**	0.044**	0.024*	0.031*	0.038*	0.035
	(2.34)	(2.30)	(1.71)	(1.70)	(1.88)	(1.51)
Financial inclusion dimension – Usage (U)			0.013***	0.011**	0.023**	0.012**
			(2.97)	(2.31)	(2.45)	(2.53)
Financial Inclusion dimension – Access (A)			0.001**	0.001*	0.009*	0.002
			(2.00)	(1.68)	(1.70)	(0.34)
Financial Inclusion dimension – Quality (Q)			0.011	0.011	0.011	0.031
			(1.22)	(1.24)	(1.10)	(1.56)
(Usage) × (Political risk ratings)				0.004**		
				(2.22)		
(Access) × (Political risk ratings)					0.003	
					(0.77)	
(Quality) × (Political risk ratings)						0.001
						(1.11)
Population under 15 years	–0.007**	–0.002**	–0.004**	–0.004**	–0.017***	–0.004*
	(–2.12)	(–2.26)	(–2.12)	(–2.25)	(–4.64)	(–1.93)
Growth, per capita GDP	0.002**	0.006*	0.004	0.003	0.011	0.005
	(2.27)	(1.76)	(0.82)	(0.47)	(0.87)	(1.03)

Government expenditure on education expenditure (% of GDP)	0.005**	0.004	−0.001	−0.002	0.029***	0.004
	(2.00)	(0.77)	(−0.11)	(−0.35)	(2.81)	(0.59)
Life expectancy at birth years	0.010	0.005	0.115*	0.104*	0.140	0.111*
	(0.28)	(0.14)	(1.90)	(1.69)	(1.20)	(1.85)
Pupil–teacher ratio, primary	−0.004	−0.003	−0.034***	−0.030***	−0.016	−0.026*
	(−0.62)	(−0.43)	(−3.60)	(−2.88)	(−0.88)	(−1.99)

Source: Authors' own calculation

Notes: The dependent variable is average years of schooling. The key independent variable is the financial inclusion index derived from the hybrid method and the dimensions of financial inclusion. All variables are expressed in logarithmic form. Unrestricted number of lags of endogenous variables is used. We, however, checked the consistency of the results by taking different lags of the endogenous variables and the qualitative nature of the results remains intact. ***, **, and * denote significance at the 1%, 5%, and 10%, levels respectively. Heteroscedasticity and autocorrelation robust t-statistics are in parentheses. Constant and country and time-fixed effects, which are not reported in the table, are included. The regressions include 101 observations and 20 Asian countries. Both Hansen test of overidentification restrictions and AR (2) test for serial correlation align with the conventional levels.

variables, including political risk. At the index level, Table 3.3 reveals that financial inclusion yields a statistically significant and positive relationship on education outcomes both before and after interaction effects (i.e., specifications 1 and 2).[9] Political risk rating yields a positive relationship in educational outcomes. Also, when interacted with financial inclusion, political risk exerts a statistically significant positive relationship (at 10%), implying that the influence of financial inclusion on educational outcomes is enhanced in the presence of lower political risks. The results for the array of statistically significant control variables, such as population under 15 years, per capita GDP growth, and government education expenditure as a percentage of GDP, have coefficient signs that are in concord with a priori expectations.

When disaggregating to the dimension level, specifications 3–6 in Table 3.3 reveal that usage is the dominant financial inclusion dimension influencing educational outcomes across all four specifications whilst, to a lesser extent, access also has some positive influence on educational outcomes of which two specifications were statistically significant at 10% (i.e., specifications 4 and 5). Results show no positive association for the quality indicator. We find political risk as a standalone variable to be significant (at 10%) for three out of the four specifications (i.e., specifications 3–5) whilst the influence of the usage dimension is enhanced in the presence of lower political risk factors (i.e., specification 4) as reflected in the strong statistically significant association of the interaction effect of political risk (i.e., specification 4). The statistical significance for the control variables used in the analysis remains mostly consistent across model specifications and the respective signs of the coefficients are in accordance with expectations.

When financial inclusion is disaggregated to the indicator level, Table 3.4 reveals that only the first-ranked indicators are statistically relevant, whilst no second-ranked indicators under any model specifications yield a positive relationship to education outcomes. Amongst the first-ranked indicators, we find that the financial inclusion indicator relating to usage represents the most important indicator influencing educational outcomes across all four specifications (three of these specifications were significant at 10%) whilst the quality indicator was significant for three of the four specifications (specifications 1–4). We do not find any statistical significance for the access indicator. In terms of institutional quality, we find that political risk yields a positive relationship across all model specifications. As an interaction effect, the influence of the usage indicator on educational outcomes is enhanced when interacted with political risk (i.e., specification 2). Again, the results reveal the sensitivity of the influence of financial inclusion on specific indicators that are dependent on the particular development outcomes.

3.5.3 Health and financial inclusion

Turning to health outcomes as measured by under-5 child mortality rates, results in specifications 1 and 2 in Table 3.5 reveal that financial inclusion as an index measure has a statistically significant positive effect on health outcomes.[10] Results

Table 3.4 Education (average years of schooling) and indicators of financial inclusion

Dimension	*Variables*	*Top indicators for each dimension (With interaction – specifications 2–4)*				*Second-ranked indicators for each dimension (With interaction – specifications 6–8)*			
		[1]	*[2]*	*[3]*	*[4]*	*[5]*	*[6]*	*[7]*	*[8]*
Usage (U)	Percentage of adults who receive wages into an account	0.079** (2.03)	0.159* (1.72)	0.075* (1.75)	0.071* (1.67)				
Access (A)	Percentage of adults with access to mobile banking at home	0.034 (0.55)	0.001 (0.01)	–0.012 (–0.10)	0.042 (0.65)				
Quality (Q)	The strength of credit reporting systems	0.123** (2.21)	0.118** (2.09)	0.120** (2.10)	0.051 (0.32)				
Interaction: U	(Percentage of adults who receive wages into an account) * Political risk rating		0.001** (2.00)						
Interaction: A	(Percentage of adults with access to mobile banking at home) * Political risk ratings			0.011 (0.21)					
Interaction: Q	(The strength of credit reporting systems) * Political risk ratings				0.027 (0.48)				
Usage (U)	Percentage of adults using the Internet to payments					0.001 (0.46)	0.001 (0.28)	–0.001 (–0.20)	0.001 (0.26)

(*continued*)

Table 3.4 Cont.

Dimension	*Variables*	*Top indicators for each dimension (With interaction – specifications 2–4)*				*Second-ranked indicators for each dimension (With interaction – specifications 6–8)*			
		[1]	*[2]*	*[3]*	*[4]*	*[5]*	*[6]*	*[7]*	*[8]*
Access (A)	Number of debit cards per 1,000 adults					0.001	0.002	–0.005	0.001
						(0.16)	(0.39)	(–0.67)	(0.04)
Quality (Q)	Financial knowledge					0.002	0.003	0.004	0.005
						(0.41)	(0.21)	(0.44)	(0.40)
Interaction: U	(Percentage of adults using the Internet to make payments) * Political risk ratings						0.005		
							(0.59)		
Interaction: A	(Number of debit cards per 1,000 adults) * Political risk ratings							0.017	
								(1.06)	
Interaction: Q	(Financial knowledge) * Political risk ratings								0.019
									(0.92)
	Political risk ratings	0.115***	0.099**	0.122**	0.132**	0.039**	0.054**	0.039**	0.059**
		(3.05)	(2.39)	(2.38)	(2.56)	(2.05)	(2.06)	(2.06)	(2.06)
	Growth per capita GDP	0.007	0.004	0.006	0.006	0.005*	0.003	0.005*	0.004**
		(1.15)	(0.60)	(1.03)	(0.92)	(1.98)	(0.06)	(1.77)	(2.04)
	Population under 15 years	–0.005***	–0.005***	–0.005**	–0.005**	–0.003*	–0.004*	–0.003*	–0.002**
		(–2.64)	(–2.62)	(–2.56)	(–2.50)	(–1.74)	(–1.93)	(–1.85)	(–2.58)

Government expenditure on education expenditure (% of GDP)	0.003	0.005	0.003	0.004	0.006	0.009	0.007	0.002
	(0.38)	(0.64)	(0.38)	(0.47)	(0.74)	(0.96)	(0.85)	(0.28)
Life expectancy at birth years	0.007	−0.037	0.008	0.009	−0.006	−0.030	−0.011	0.005
	(0.13)	(−0.54)	(0.16)	(0.18)	(−0.14)	(−0.52)	(−0.24)	(0.11)
Pupil–teacher ratio, primary	−0.022**	−0.029**	−0.022*	−0.021*	−0.005**	−0.003*	−0.009*	−0.012*
	(−2.30)	(−2.20)	(−1.94)	(−1.88)	(−2.00)	(−1.68)	(−1.91)	(−1.98)

Source: Authors' own calculation

Notes: The dependent variable is the average years of schooling. The key independent variables are the top two indicators from each dimension of financial inclusion. All variables are expressed in logarithmic form. An unrestricted number of lags of endogenous variables is used. We, however, checked the consistency of the results by taking different lags of the endogenous variables and the qualitative nature of the results remains intact. ***, **, and * denote significance at the 1%, 5%, and 10% levels, respectively. Heteroscedasticity and autocorrelation robust t-statistics are in parentheses. Constant and country and time fixed effects, which are not reported in the table, are included. The regressions include 128 observations and 20 Asian countries. Both Hansen test of overidentification restrictions and AR (2) test for serial correlation align with the conventional levels.

Table 3.5 Health (child mortality rate) and financial inclusion at the index and dimension(s) levels

Variables	*[1] Index No interaction*	*[2] Index With interaction*	*[3] Dimension No interaction*	*[4] Dimension With interaction (U)*	*[5] Dimension With interaction (A)*	*[6] Dimension With interaction (Q)*
Financial inclusion	–0.315***	–0.132***				
	(–2.68)	(–3.84)				
(Financial inclusion) x (Political risk ratings)		–0.187***				
		(–6.12)				
Political risk ratings	–0.056**	–0.046***	–0.047*	–0.056**	–0.026*	–0.049*
	(–2.30)	(–6.84)	(–1.71)	(–2.06)	(–1.78)	(–1.73)
Financial inclusion dimension – Usage (U)			0.090	0.323	0.183	0.108
			(0.40)	(1.29)	(0.83)	(0.47)
Financial inclusion dimension – Access (A)			–0.784***	–0.591*	–0.132**	–0.761**
			(–2.64)	(–1.93)	(–2.04)	(–2.48)
Financial inclusion dimension – Quality (Q)			0.010	0.061	0.242	0.924
			(0.02)	(0.10)	(0.39)	(0.28)
(Usage) × (Political risk ratings)				–0.008*		
				(–1.88)		
(Access) × (Political risk ratings)					–0.019**	
					(–2.39)	
(Quality) × (Political risk ratings)						–0.014
						(–0.28)
Growth, per capita GDP	–0.212***	–0.139***	–0.235***	–0.205***	–0.255***	–0.225***
	(–5.30)	(–12.60)	(–5.08)	(–4.31)	(–5.57)	(3.78)
Literacy rate, adult female (% of females 15 years and above)	0.004	–0.034***	–0.010	–0.001	–0.025	–0.008
	(0.32)	(–10.63)	(–0.66)	(–0.06)	(–1.56)	(–0.51)

Prevalence of undernourishment (% of population)	0.088*	0.082***	0.141**	0.112*	0.127**	0.142**
	(1.68)	(5.60)	(2.38)	(1.87)	(2.18)	(2.39)
Births attended by skilled health staff (% of total)	–0.010	0.001	–0.017	–0.011	–0.020*	–0.017
	(–0.81)	(0.18)	(–1.12)	(–0.73)	(–1.73)	(–1.08)
Government expenditure on health expenditure (% of GDP)	–0.107***	–0.218***	–0.393***	–0.339***	–0.396***	–0.393***
	(–5.49)	(–12.10)	(–4.60)	(–3.86)	(–4.75)	(–4.59)
Expected years of schooling	–0.593***	–0.722***	–0.603***	–0.533**	–0.716***	–0.624***
	(–2.77)	(–12.66)	(–2.82)	(–2.53)	(–3.36)	(–2.75)

Source: Authors' own calculation.

Notes: The dependent variable is child mortality rate, under-5 (per 1,000 live births). The key independent variable is the financial inclusion index derived from the hybrid method and the dimensions of financial inclusion. All variables are expressed in logarithmic form. Unrestricted number of lags of endogenous variables is used. We, however, checked the consistency of the results by taking different lags of the endogenous variables and the qualitative nature of the results remains intact. ***, **, and * denote significance at the 1%, 5%, and 10% levels, respectively. Heteroscedasticity and autocorrelation robust t-statistics are in parentheses. Constant and country and time-fixed effects, which are not reported in the table, are included. The regressions include 132 observations and 20 Asian countries. Both Hansen test of overidentification restrictions and AR (2) test for serial correlation align with the conventional levels.

also show that political risk is significant both before interaction (specification 1) and when interacted with the financial inclusion index (specification 2). This implies that the influence of financial inclusion is enhanced in the presence of lower political risk factors. The statistical significance and the sign of parameter coefficients for the array of other control variables – such as economic growth, literacy rates, the prevalence of undernourishment, government health expenditure as a percentage of GDP, and expected years of schooling – appear to be consistent with a priori expectations under both model specifications.

At the dimension level (i.e., specifications 3–6), Table 3.5 results reveal that access represents the only financial inclusion dimension that has a statistically positive influence on health outcomes. Neither usage nor quality dimensions had any statistical association with the dependent variable. Political risk yields a significant relationship with health outcomes across all the model specifications; and as an interaction term, the effectiveness of access dimension was enhanced in the presence of lower political risk factors (i.e., specification 5). As with other development outcomes, whilst higher financial inclusion reduces child mortality, this did not translate into a uniform influence at the dimension level, as results show that only access represented the only dimension that exerted a statistically significant influence on health outcomes.

Disaggregating at the indicator level, Table 3.6 shows that, after allowing for control variables, both first- and second-ranked financial inclusion indicators yielded statistically significant positive relationships on health outcomes across most model specifications (i.e., specifications 1–8). Specifically, across both sets of indicators, both usage and quality represented the two most influential dimensions on health outcomes. Political risk also exerted a statistically significant influence on health outcomes across all model specifications. In the case of the highest-ranked indicators, the political interaction effects were significant for all three indicators, suggesting that the influence of these indicators on health outcomes was enhanced in the presence of lower political risk factors (i.e., specifications 2–4). We do not find the political interaction effects to be statistically significant for second-ranked indicators. Again, all other control variables have coefficient signs that are consistent with expectations.

3.5.4 Income inequality and financial inclusion

Finally, turning to income inequality, as measured by the Gini coefficient, results presented in Table 3.7 reveal that at the aggregate level, financial inclusion exerts a positive influence in improving income inequality (i.e., specification 1). However, when introducing the interaction effect (specification 2), the financial inclusion index is statistically significant only as an interaction term and not as a stand-alone variable, implying that financial inclusion becomes relevant only in the presence of institutional quality. The signs for the coefficient estimate for the other control variables – specifically per capita growth, female labour force participation, life expectancy, and average years of schooling – are consistent with expectations.

Table 3.6 Health (child mortality rate) and indicators of financial inclusion

Dimension	*Variables*	*Top indicators for each dimension (With interaction – specifications 2–4)*				*Second-ranked indicators for each dimension (With interaction – specifications 6–8)*			
		[1]	*[2]*	*[3]*	*[4]*	*[5]*	*[6]*	*[7]*	*[8]*
Usage (U)	Percentage of adults who receive wages into an account	–0.242*** (–2.93)	–0.958*** (–5.12)	–0.270*** (–3.63)	–0.251*** (–3.43)				
Access (A)	Percentage of adults with access to mobile banking at home	–0.024 (–0.23)	–0.039 (–0.41)	–0.490*** (–3.38)	–0.016 (–0.17)				
Quality (Q)	The strength of credit reporting systems	–0.172 (–1.36)	–0.324*** (–2.75)	–0.200 (–0.11)	–0.684*** (–4.13)				
Interaction: U	(Percentage of adults who receive wages into an account) * Political risk rating		–0.182*** (–4.15)						
Interaction: A	(Percentage of adults with access to mobile banking at home) * Political risk ratings			–0.219*** (–4.27)					
Interaction: Q	(The strength of credit reporting systems) * Political risk ratings				–0.209*** (–4.20)				
Usage (U)	Percentage of adults using the Internet to payments					–0.016*** (–5.05)	–0.017*** (–5.20)	–0.016*** (–5.06)	–0.016*** (–5.12)
Access (A)	Number of debit cards per 1,000 adults					–0.013*** (–2.75)	–0.009 (–1.57)	–0.010 (–1.05)	–0.012*** (–2.60)

(*continued*)

Table 3.6 Cont.

Dimension	*Variables*	*Top indicators for each dimension (With interaction – specifications 2–4)*				*Second-ranked indicators for each dimension (With interaction – specifications 6–8)*			
		[1]	*[2]*	*[3]*	*[4]*	*[5]*	*[6]*	*[7]*	*[8]*
Quality (Q)	Financial knowledge					–0.483*** (–3.19)	–0.540*** (–3.46)	–0.462*** (–2.86)	–0.388** (–2.09)
Interaction: U	(Percentage of adults using the Internet to make payments) * Political risk ratings						–0.016 (–1.42)		
Interaction: A	(Number of debit cards per 1,000 adults) * Political risk ratings							–0.001 (–0.35)	
Interaction: Q	(Financial knowledge) * Political risk ratings								0.001 (0.86)
	Political risk ratings	–0.111** (–2.03)	–0.100 (–1.43)	–0.040** (–2.01)	–0.043** (–2.01)	–0.146*** (–3.38)	–0.127*** (–2.81)	–0.136*** (–2.64)	–0.106* (–1.68)
	Growth, per capita GDP	–0.033** (–2.13)	–0.024* (–1.77)	–0.038*** (–2.70)	–0.037*** (–2.68)	–0.027** (–2.22)	–0.040*** (–2.63)	–0.028** (–2.19)	–0.026** (–2.21)
	Literacy rate, adult female (% of females aged 15 and above)	–0.022 (–0.86)	–0.016 (–0.65)	–0.042* (–1.78)	–0.040* (–1.72)	–0.071*** (–4.27)	–0.062*** (–3.45)	–0.067*** (–3.30)	–0.075 (–4.41)
	Prevalence of undernourishment (% of population)	–0.001 (–0.05)	0.022 (1.08)	0.011 (0.56)	0.012 (0.58)	–0.011 (–0.82)	0.014 (0.63)	0.006 (0.29)	–0.001 (–0.07)
	Births attended by skilled health staff (% of total)	0.026 (0.96)	0.015 (0.63)	0.027 (1.15)	0.020 (0.84)	0.010 (0.72)	0.009 (0.67)	–0.009 (–0.68)	0.000 (0.02)

Government expenditure on health expenditure (% of GDP)	−0.065*** (−3.05)	0.016 (0.74)	−0.037* (−1.85)	−0.035* (−1.72)	−0.008 (−0.41)	0.001 (0.05)	−0.005 (−0.26)	−0.003 (−0.14)
Expected years of schooling	−0.206*** (−4.02)	−0.279*** (−5.73)	−0.267*** (−5.54)	−0.255*** (−5.43)	−0.273*** (−6.93)	−0.261*** (−6.54)	−0.265*** (−5.88)	−0.257*** (−6.04)

Source: Authors' own calculation.

Notes: The dependent variable is child mortality rate, under-5 (per 1,000 live births). The key independent variables are the top two indicators from each dimension of financial inclusion. All variables are expressed in logarithmic form. Unrestricted number of lags of endogenous variables is used. We, however, checked the consistency of the results by taking different lags of the endogenous variables and the qualitative nature of the results remains intact. ***, **, and * denote significance at the 1%, 5%, and 10% levels, respectively. Heteroscedasticity and autocorrelation robust t-statistics are in parentheses. Constant and country and time-fixed effects, which are not reported in the table, are included. The regressions include 133 observations and 20 Asian countries. Both Hansen test of overidentification restrictions and AR (2) test for serial correlation align with the conventional levels.

Table 3.7 Income inequality and financial inclusion: at index and dimension(s) levels

Variables	*[1] Index No interaction*	*[2] Index With interaction*	*[3] Dimension No interaction*	*[4] Dimension With interaction (U)*	*[5] Dimension With interaction (A)*	*[6] Dimension With interaction (Q)*
Financial inclusion	−0.033***	−0.016				
	(−2.72)	(−0.49)				
(Financial inclusion) x (Political risk ratings)		−0.018***				
		(3.38)				
Political risk ratings	−0.010	−0.002	0.118	0.237	0.097	0.492
	(−0.56)	(−0.05)	(0.95)	(1.33)	(0.41)	(0.40)
Financial inclusion dimension – Usage			−0.105***	−0.088***	−0.021***	−0.083***
			(−6.06)	(−3.52)	(−2.75)	(−4.74)
Financial inclusion dimension – Access			−0.076***	−0.022	0.016	−0.061***
			(−3.69)	(−0.67)	(0.77)	(−3.13)
Financial inclusion dimension – Quality			−0.003	0.012	−0.075***	0.052
			(−0.06)	(0.17)	(−3.71)	(0.97)
(Usage) × (Political risk ratings)				−0.001***		
				(−3.90)		
(Access) × (Political risk ratings)					−0.001*	
					(−1.83)	
(Quality) × (Political risk ratings)						−0.003***
						(−4.80)
Growth, per capita GDP	0.018***	0.060***	0.269***	0.301***	0.087***	0.229***
	(3.92)	(6.17)	(6.80)	(5.34)	(4.44)	(5.78)
Trade openness	0.000	−0.005***	−0.001***	−0.001**	−0.001	−0.001
	(−0.57)	(−2.94)	(−2.78)	(−2.01)	(−0.88)	(−0.89)
Inflation	−0.001	0.001*	−0.002	0.006**	0.001**	−0.001
	(−1.31)	(1.67)	(−1.04)	(2.43)	(2.51)	(−0.87)

Labour force, female (% of total labour force)	−0.047***	−0.076***	−0.688***	−0.564***	−0.147***	−0.352***
	(−4.07)	(−3.04)	(−7.04)	(−3.99)	(−4.35)	(−5.50)
Growth of population	0.151**	0.168	0.051**	0.050*	−0.001	−0.022
	(2.50)	(1.32)	(2.57)	(1.77)	(−0.04)	(−1.11)
Life expectancy at birth, total (years)	0.001	−0.004***	−0.021***	−0.022***	−0.001	−0.008*
	(0.48)	(−2.61)	(−3.69)	(−2.75)	(−0.60)	(−1.87)
Average years of schooling	−0.010***	−0.023***	−0.083***	−0.059***	−0.034***	−0.086***
	(−6.51)	(−6.95)	(−7.99)	(−3.64)	(−5.67)	(−7.24)

Source: Authors' own calculation.

Notes: The dependent variable is income inequality measured by Gini coefficient. The key independent variable is the financial inclusion index derived from the hybrid method and the dimensions of financial inclusion. To minimise the issue of multi-collinearity, all regressions consider rural population (% of total population) and population growth interchangeably, and the qualitative nature of the results remains intact. Moreover, ethnic fractionalisation, literacy rate, and adult female (% of females aged 15 and above) are included. However, they are not reported as their coefficients are insignificant. All variables are expressed in logarithmic form. Unrestricted number of lags of endogenous variables is used. We, however, checked the consistency of the results by taking different lags of the endogenous variables and the qualitative nature of the results remains intact. ***, **, and * denote significance at the 1%, 5%, and 10% levels, respectively. Heteroscedasticity and autocorrelation robust t-statistics are in parentheses. Constant and country and time-fixed effects, which are not reported in the table, are included. The regressions include 147 observations and 20 Asian countries. Both Hansen test of overidentification restrictions and AR (2) test for serial correlation align with the conventional levels.

When disaggregating financial inclusion into its dimension components, results in Table 3.7 show that usage represents the most dominant financial inclusion dimension that has a statistically significant influence on income inequality across all four model specifications (i.e., specifications 3–6). Its effectiveness is enhanced when interacted with political risk. Results show that the access dimension is significant under two specifications (i.e., specifications 3 and 6) whilst the quality dimension is statistically significant under one specification (i.e., specification 5). Again, we find that political risk is not statistically significant as a stand-alone variable. However, its effectiveness becomes statistically significant as an interaction effect for each of the three dimensions (i.e., specifications 4–6), thereby enhancing the influence of each dimension on inequality outcomes.

At the indicator level, results in Table 3.8 reveal that the first-ranked indicators are much more dominant than second-ranked indicators in terms of exerting a statistically significant relationship on reducing income inequality. The usage indicator yields a statistically significant influence on inequality outcome across all model specifications which included the second-ranked indicators (i.e., specifications 1–8). Interestingly, we find political risk has a statistically significant positive impact on income inequality as a stand-alone variable across all model specifications (but mostly at the 10% significance level) and is statistically significant as an interaction term across each of the three indicators. This implies that the influence of financial inclusion is enhanced in the presence of higher institutional risk ratings (specifications 2–4 and 6–7). Again, the sign of the coefficients for the statistically significant control variables was in accordance with expectations and consistent with results presented at the index and dimension levels (i.e. Table 3.7).

In sum, this study reveals that at an aggregate level, financial inclusion has a positive effect across all major development outcomes, namely, economic growth, education, health, and income inequality. Although the positive effect of an index measure is robust across different specifications, results reveal that at a dimension level, different financial inclusion dimensions matter more for particular development outcomes than others. More specifically, usage and, to a lesser extent, access are the dominant dimensions impacting across virtually all the development outcomes whilst the quality dimension yields very limited influence on any of the development outcomes.

At the indicator level, results reveal that the top-ranked indicators identified in this study exert a far greater positive influence on development outcomes than second-ranked indicators demonstrating the importance of select indicators. These indicators are the percentage of adults who receive wages into an account (usage), percentage of adults with access to mobile banking at home (access), and the strength of credit reporting systems (quality). Possible reasons as to why these indicators are more relevant than others are (i) increase of usage of the formal banking system as a medium to receive wages and salaries in most developing countries and (ii) advancement of digital technology in the banking industry. With the recent tightening of credit reporting laws and to curb corruption, many countries, such as India,[11] have introduced ownership and use of formal accounts

Table 3.8 Income inequality and indicators of financial inclusion

Dimension	*Variables*	*Top indicators from each dimension (With interaction – specifications 2–4)*				*Second-ranked indicators for each dimension (With interaction – specifications 6–8)*			
		[1]	*[2]*	*[3]*	*[4]*	*[5]*	*[6]*	*[7]*	*[8]*
Usage (U)	Percentage of adults who receive wages into an account	–0.284*** (–4.96)	–0.281*** (–3.53)	–0.206*** (–3.54)	–0.222*** (–4.48)				
Access (A)	Percentage of adults with access to mobile banking at home	–0.392*** (–5.18)	–0.003 (–0.03)	–0.118 (–0.35)	–0.496*** (–5.54)				
Quality (Q)	The strength of credit reporting systems	–0.142 (–1.30)	–0.061 (–0.78)	–0.086 (–0.85)	–0.568*** (–1.00)				
Interaction: U	(Percentage of adults who receive wages into an account) * Political risk ratings		–0.053*** (–2.86)						
Interaction: A	(Percentage of adults with access to mobile banking at home) * Political risk ratings			–0.006* (–1.69)					
Interaction: Q	(The strength of credit reporting systems) * Political risk ratings				–0.006*** (–2.79)				
Usage (U)	Percentage of adults using the Internet to payments					–0.028*** (–7.13)	–0.028*** (–7.56)	–0.028*** (–7.77)	–0.027*** (–6.55)

(*continued*)

Table 3.8 Cont.

Dimension	*Variables*	*Top indicators from each dimension (With interaction – specifications 2–4)*				*Second-ranked indicators for each dimension (With interaction – specifications 6–8)*			
		[1]	*[2]*	*[3]*	*[4]*	*[5]*	*[6]*	*[7]*	*[8]*
Access (A)	Number of debit cards per 1,000 adults					–0.001 (–0.22)	–0.001 (–0.01)	–0.010 (–1.46)	–0.002 (–0.32)
Quality (Q)	Financial knowledge					–0.001 (–0.15)	–0.001 (–0.55)	–0.002 (–0.58)	–0.001 (–0.55)
Interaction: U	(Percentage of adults using the Internet to make payments) * Political risk ratings						–0.023*** (–2.82)		
Interaction: A	(Number of debit cards per 1,000 adults) * Political risk ratings							–0.001*** (–2.94)	
Interaction: Q	(Financial knowledge) * Political risk ratings								–0.001 (–0.74)
	Political risk ratings	–0.103*** (–2.62)	–0.003* (–1.70)	–0.212* (–1.68)	–0.183* (–1.79)	–0.011* (–1.85)	–0.032* (–1.72)	–0.001* (–1.65)	–0.001** (–2.01)
	Growth, per capita GDP	0.102*** (6.01)	0.052*** (5.35)	0.065*** (6.99)	0.065*** (6.92)	0.058*** (4.65)	0.073*** (5.76)	0.067*** (5.51)	0.058*** (4.45)
	Trade openness	–0.001 (–1.12)	0.001 (0.56)	–0.001* (–1.84)	–0.001** (–2.30)	–0.001* (–1.82)	–0.001* (–1.66)	–0.001 (–1.12)	–0.001* (–1.97)
	Inflation	0.001 (1.01)	0.001 (1.06)	0.001 (0.45)	0.001 (0.62)	0.001* (1.80)	0.001 (1.49)	0.001* (1.85)	0.001* (1.77)
	Labour force, female (% of total labour force)	–0.168*** (–5.28)	–0.061** (–2.14)	–0.151*** (–5.43)	–0.197*** (–5.82)	–0.075*** (–3.22)	–0.065*** (–2.95)	–0.076*** (–3.52)	–0.082*** (–3.37)

Growth of population	0.023**	0.012*	0.015*	0.020***	0.016*	0.016**	0.013*	0.015*
	(2.47)	(1.65)	(1.99)	(2.60)	(1.89)	(2.02)	(1.65)	(1.73)
Life expectancy at birth, total (years)	–0.005**	–0.002	–0.005**	–0.006***	–0.002	–0.003	–0.004*	–0.003
	(–2.12)	(–1.12)	(–2.24)	(–2.68)	(–0.70)	(–1.46)	(–1.69)	(–1.06)
Average years of schooling	–0.031***	–0.027***	–0.029***	–0.028***	–0.017***	–0.018***	–0.018***	–0.017***
	(–6.05)	(–6.98)	(–6.26)	(–5.96)	(–5.91)	(–6.89)	(–6.82)	(–5.90)

Source: Authors' own calculation

Notes: The dependent variable is income inequality measured by Gini coefficient. The key independent variables are the top two indicators from each dimension of financial inclusion. To minimise the issue of multi-collinearity, all regressions consider rural population (% of total population) and population growth interchangeably, and the qualitative nature of the results remains intact. Moreover, ethnic fractionalisation, literacy rate, and adult female (% of females aged 15 and above) are included. However, they are not reported as their coefficients are insignificant. All variables are expressed in logarithmic form. Unrestricted number of lags of endogenous variables is used. We, however, checked the consistency of the results by taking different lags of the endogenous variables and the qualitative nature of the results remains intact. ***, **, and * denote significance at the 1%, 5%, and 10% levels, respectively. Heteroscedasticity and autocorrelation robust t-statistics are in parentheses. Constant and country and time-fixed effects, which are not reported in the table, are included. The regressions include 147 observations and 20 Asian countries. Both Hansen test of overidentification restrictions and AR (2) test for serial correlation align with the conventional levels.

as the main medium for receiving wages and salaries. Whilst a larger proportion of the population receives wages through formal accounts, the process of receiving money in this way makes it easier for the government to collect higher income tax and provides better insurance and credit availability. This, in turn, increases consumption, government expenditure, and investment in the economy, which has direct money multiplier effects on national income. The higher the marginal propensity to consume and the propensity to invest, the higher is the multiplier effect in the economy, which increases economic growth and lowers income inequality. Similarly, formal ownership of accounts in relation to wages and salaries also helps the government collect more taxes that influences better health and education outcomes. The effect on economic growth and development has been further enhanced by the advancement of banking technologies, particularly the use of mobile phones to transfer money and apply for credit. This provides easier access to money, credit, and insurance and increases financial inclusion in the economy.

Interestingly, whilst quality is not influential at the dimension level, at the indicator level, the quality indicator – that is, stronger credit reporting system – influences some development outcomes. This reveals that a stronger legal system and respect for creditors' and debtors' rights, which are all part of lower political risk factors, not only influence development outcomes but also enhance the impact of financial inclusion. Political risk thus represents an important parameter not just as a control variable but also as a policy-relevant parameter in the context of implementing financial inclusion in developing countries.

3.6 Conclusion and policy perspectives

This study contributes to the financial inclusion literature by broadening the array of development outcomes under analysis, and in utilising both aggregated and disaggregated measures of financial inclusion. Further, it has paid particular attention to the role of political risk rating and its interaction with financial inclusion in determining its effect on development outcomes. By drawing upon a comprehensive data set compiled from various sources in 20 Asian countries, this study finds that financial inclusion not only contributes to enhancing the domains of economic growth and reducing inequality, but also that its reach extends to improving other development outcomes, specifically education and health. In this context, financial inclusion represents a fundamental mechanism for enhancing human development and is, therefore, of key importance to policymakers.

The 'fibrous' nature of financial inclusion means it can be constructed at various levels of aggregation. Thus, whilst at the most aggregated level financial inclusion can be analysed using a composite index to establish possible linkages with development outcomes, a finer-grained conceptual lens is required for understanding which particular components of financial inclusion are more important for certain development outcomes. For instance, our results show that using an index measure, financial inclusion is positively associated with all development outcomes. Yet, when analysed at a dimensional level, we find that usage is the only dimension impacting economic growth, and access is the only dimension impacting health outcomes. However, both usage and, to a lesser extent, access influence the other two development outcomes, specifically education and income inequality. The corollary to this is that we do not find any circumstance where all three dimensions of financial inclusion are simultaneously relevant for any one particular development outcome. The implication here is that when policymakers select particular development outcomes, they need to be cognisant of supporting particular, and not necessarily all, elements of financial inclusion to enhance and support their development policy objective(s) most effectively.

Most telling regarding the fibrous nature of financial inclusion is when analysing at the indicator level. Notably, our results show a considerable difference amongst indicators where the first-order indicators, generated using the PCA method, exerted a far greater positive influence on development outcomes than the second-highest-ranked indicators. As a stand-alone measure, the percentage of adults who receive wages into an account (usage indicator) represents the most influential indicator as it exerted a statistically significant positive effect across all development outcomes and under most model specifications. In contrast, the percentage of adults with access to mobile banking at home (access indicator) is less influential, being important for particular development outcomes. Interestingly, we find that (first-ranked) quality indicator exerts a positive influence on particular outcomes for specifications which showed no influence at the dimensional level. Although outside the scope of this study, an in-depth analysis on why each indicator is more influential in each country is warranted in the future. Some possible explanations as to why the percentage of adults who receive wages into an account is highly significant is that greater ownership and use of formal bank accounts to receive salaries and wages have a direct implication on economic growth through the channels of higher consumption, government expenditure, and investment. The higher the propensity to consume and propensity to invest, the higher is the multiplier effect on national income. Higher use of bank accounts for wages and salaries also helps the government collect higher income tax, which can be better used for health and education outcomes. Similarly, recent developments in banking technologies, including greater access to mobile phone banking at home (access indicator), has made it easier for everyone to access financial knowledge, transfer money to others, and apply for credit and insurance. Together, all these factors influence economic development positively. Finally, a better credit reporting system (quality indicator) is a measure of lower political risk and higher institutional quality, which directly influences economic development. Thus, the influence of financial inclusion can hinge on very specific indicators, and policymakers need to understand and identify these critical indicators which impact most on the development outcome that is under policy focus.

The significance of political risk factors extends beyond that as a control variable, as it is typically used in the empirical literature, but as an interaction effect where it represents an important mechanism for enhancing the effects of financial inclusion on particular development outcomes. We find that its influence on financial inclusion occurs at all levels of aggregation – at the index, dimension, and indicator levels. Importantly also, institutional quality can extend the range of financial inclusion components that can exert a positive influence on outcomes. For instance, whilst the quality dimension appears to have no influence on any of the development outcomes, when interacted with political risk, it has a positive effect on income inequality. Similarly, at the indicator level, the access indicator now exerts a positive influence on health outcomes when interacted with political risk, where hitherto had no influence on the particular outcome. Again, for policymakers wishing to extend financial inclusion to the 'unbanked' population, the effectiveness of the policy approach will depend on the extent of the political risk factors that prevail in that country.

Ultimately policymakers need to refrain from adopting a broad blanket policy approach to maximise the full potential of expanding financial inclusion. Rather, there is the need to be cognisant of the particular development outcome under focus and the need to select the most effective channel of financial inclusion. Moreover, consideration needs to be given to the state of its political risk factors and how they can be strategically incorporated into the overall financial inclusion policy framework.

Finally, this study provides a basis for future research by recognising the importance of understanding financial inclusion both at the aggregate and disaggregate levels and the role of political risk factors in effecting financial inclusion across different development outcomes. To this end, countries are at different stages of human development and have varying levels of political risk factors. Therefore, the interaction of these two can lead to differences in the impact of financial inclusion. Thus, future research to inform policy development needs to be tailored to the specific circumstances of a country at a particular time to identify the critical components and channels by which the effectiveness of financial inclusion can be optimised across development outcomes. This includes finding the channels through which each indicator influences development outcomes and why some indicators are more influential than others. Another future research direction is to examine closely the relationship between access, usage, and quality in these countries. Since our findings suggest that usage is the most dominant dimension, there could exist a hierarchical relationship between the dimensions where usage becomes more important when the economy has reached a certain threshold level of access and, similarly, quality becomes more dominant when the economy has reached a certain threshold level of usage. However, given that every country is at a different transitional phase of development, a closer examination is required at the country level to establish this threshold relationship amongst dimensions.

Notes

1 Corresponding author. GPO Box 2471, Adelaide 5000, SA. Email: Rajabrata.Banerjee@unisa.edu.au

2 Lee and Kim (2009) also show that education plays important role in promoting long-run economic growth in developing countries. Barrientos and Hulme (2009) state

that education is increasingly important in ensuring employment and asset accumulation particularly in developing countries.

3 http://hdr.undp.org/en/content/expected-years-schooling-children-years
4 See www.prsgroup.com/
5 In unreported results, we have also run fixed-effect ordinary least squares (OLS model) regressions as a robustness check, and we find results are qualitatively similar.
6 We use one period lagged values of all explanatory variables to consider the timing issues that these variables may take a certain time to influence the development outcomes. The lagged independent variables also eliminate reverse causality concerns with the development outcome. In addition, we have checked that there is no endogeneity issue between the control variables and financial inclusion by regressing financial inclusion on all the other control variables.
7 As noted, we also use a fixed-effects OLS model as a robust check. Although we do not report the fixed-effects results here, we find a high degree of concordance between GMM and fixed-effects OLS model approaches suggesting that the results presented here are quite robust.
8 In specification 3, usage is statistically significant at 10%.
9 The financial inclusion index is significant at 10% when interacting with political risk rating (i.e., specification 2).
10 Note that as health outcomes are measured as childhood mortality, a negative coefficient implies a positive effect on health outcomes.
11 See www.bbc.com/news/world-asia-india-28962762

References

Acemoglu, D., S. Johnson, and J. Robinson (2005), 'Institutions as a Fundamental Cause of Long-Run Growth', *Handbook of Economic Growth*, 1A, pp. 386–472.

Agyemang-Badu, A., K. Agyei, and E. Kwaku Duah (2018), 'Financial Inclusion, Poverty and Income Inequality: Evidence from Africa', *Spiritan International Journal of Poverty Studies*, 2(2), pp.1–38.

Akresh, R., L. Lucchetti, and H. Thirumurthy (2012), 'Wars and Child Health: Evidence from the Eritrean–Ethiopian Conflict', *Journal of Development Economics*, 99(2), pp. 330–40.

Allen, F., A. Demirguc-Kunt, L. Klapper, and M. Peria (2012), 'The Foundations of Financial Inclusion: Understanding Ownership and Use of Formal Accounts', *The World Bank Policy Research Working Paper*, No. 6290. Washington, DC: World Bank.

Allen, F., E, Carletti, R. Cull, J. Qian, L. Senbet, and P. Valenzuela (2013), 'Resolving the African Financial Development Gap: Cross-Country Comparisons and a Within-Country Study of Kenya', *World Bank Policy Working Paper*, No. 6592. Washington, DC: World Bank.

Allen, F., A. Demirguc-Kunt, L. Klapper, and M. Peria (2016), 'The Foundations of Financial Inclusion: Understanding Ownership and Use of Formal Accounts', *Journal of Financial Intermediation*, 27, pp. 1–30.

Andrianaivo, M. and K. Kpodar (2011), 'ICT, Financial Inclusion, and Growth Evidence from African Countries', *IMF Working Paper* No. 11–73. Washington, DC: International Monetary Fund.

Ang, J. (2008) 'What Are the Mechanisms Linking Financial Development and Economic Growth in Malaysia?', *Economic Modelling*, 25(1), pp. 38–53.

Arellano, M. and S. Bond (1991), 'Some Tests of Specification for Panel Data: Monte Carlo Evidence and an Application to Employment Equations', *The Review of Economic Studies*, 58(2), pp. 277–97.

Arellano, M. and O. Bover (1995), 'Another Look at the Instrumental Variable Estimation of Error-Components Models', *Journal of Econometrics*, 68(1), pp. 29–51.

Banerjee, R. and S. Roy (2014), 'Human Capital, Technological Progress and Trade: What Explains India's Long-Run Growth?', *Journal of Asian Economics*, 30, pp. 15–31.

Barrientos, A. and D. Hulme (2009), 'Social Protection for the Poor and Poorest in Developing Countries: Reflections on a Quiet Revolution: Commentary', *Oxford Development Studies*, 37(4), pp. 439–56.

Beck, T., A. Demirgüç-Kunt, and R. Levine (2007), 'Finance, Inequality and the Poor', *Journal of Economic Growth*, 12(1), pp. 27–49.

Becker, G., E. Glaeser, and K. Murphy (1999), 'Population and Economic Growth', *American Economic Review*, 89(2), pp. 145–49.

Behrman, J. and A. Deolalikar (1991), 'School Repetition, Dropouts, and the Rates of Return to Schooling: The Case of Indonesia', *Oxford Bulletin of Economics and Statistics*, 53(4), pp. 467–80.

Bjørnskov, C. (2010), 'Do Elites Benefit from Democracy and Foreign Aid in Developing Countries?', *Journal of Development Economics*, 92(2), pp. 115–24.

Block, S. (2002), 'Political Business Cycles, Democratization, and Economic Reform: The Case of Africa', *Journal of Development Economics*, 67(1), pp. 205–28.

Blundell, R. and S. Bond (1998), 'Initial Conditions and Moment Restrictions in Dynamic Panel Data Models', *Journal of Econometrics*, 87(1), pp. 115–43.

Blundell, R. and S. Bond (2000), 'GMM Estimation with Persistent Panel Data: An Application to Production Functions', *Econometric Reviews*, 19(3), pp. 321–40.

Brune, L., X. Giné, J. Goldberg, and D. Yang (2011), 'Commitments to Save: A Field Experiment in Rural Malawi', *World Bank Policy Research Working Paper*, No. 5748. Washington, DC: World Bank.

Burgess, R. and R. Pande (2005), 'Do Rural Banks Matter? Evidence from the Indian Social Banking Experiment', *American Economic Review*, 95(3), pp. 780–95.

Camara, N. and D. Tuesta (2014), 'Measuring Financial Inclusion: A Multidimensional Index', *BBVA Research Paper* No. 14/26.

Cheston, S. and L. Kuhn (2002), 'Empowering Women through Microfinance', Draft, *Opportunity International,* 64. www.chs.ubc.ca/srilanka/PDFs/Empowering%20women%20through%20microfinance.pdf (accessed 10 September 2019).

Chong, A. and C. Calderon (2000), 'Institutional Quality and Income Inequality', *Economic Development and Cultural Change*, 48(4), pp. 761–86.

Claessens, S. and L. Leaven (2003), 'Financial Development, Property Rights, and Growth', *Journal of Finance*, 58(6), pp. 2401–36.

Dearden, L., J. Ferri, and C. Meghir (2002), 'The Effect of School Quality on Educational Attainment and Wages', *Review of Economics and Statistics*, 84(1), pp. 1–20.

De la Croix, D. and O. Licandro (1999), 'Life Expectancy and Endogenous Growth', *Economics Letters*, 65(2), pp. 255–63.

Demirgüç-Kunt, A. and L. Klapper (2012), *Measuring Financial Inclusion: The Global Findex Database*. Washington, DC: World Bank.

Demirgüç-Kunt, A., L. Klapper, D. Singer, S. Ansar, and J. Hess (2018), *The Global Findex Database 2017: Measuring Financial Inclusion and the Fintech Revolution*. Washington, DC: World Bank.

Dwyfor Evans, A., C. Green, and V. Murinde (2002), 'Human Capital and Financial Development in Economic Growth: New Evidence Using the Translog Production Function', *International Journal of Finance & Economics*, 7(2), pp. 123–40.

Feeny, S. and B. Ouattara (2013), 'The Effects of Health Aid on Child Health Promotion in Developing Countries: Cross-Country Evidence', *Applied Economics*, 45(7), pp. 911–19.

Fischer, S. (1993), 'The Role of Macroeconomic Factors in Growth', *Journal of Monetary Economics*, 32(3), pp. 485–512.

Gakidou, E., K. Cowling, R. Lozano, and C. Murray (2010), 'Increased Educational Attainment and Its Effect on Child Mortality in 175 Countries between 1970 and 2009: A Systematic Analysis', *The Lancet*, 376(9745), pp. 959–74.

Galiani, S., P. Gertler, and E. Schargrodsky (2005), 'Water for Life: The Impact of the Privatization of Water Services on Child Mortality', *Journal of Political Economy*, 113(1), pp. 83–120.

Glaeser, E.L., R. La Porta, F. Lopez-de-Silanes, and A. Shleifer (2004),. 'Do Institutions Cause Growth?', *Journal of Economic Growth*, 9(3), pp. 271–303.

Goldsmith, R. (1969), *Financial Structure and Development*. New Haven: Yale University Press.

Grohmann, A., T. Klühs, and L. Menkhoff (2018). 'Does Financial Literacy Improve Financial Inclusion? Cross-Country Evidence', *World Development*, 111, pp. 84–96.

Gupta, S., H. Davoodi, and E. Tiongson (2001), 'Corruption and the Provision of Health Care and Education Services', in A.K. Jain (ed.), *The Political Economy of Corruption*. London: Routledge. pp. 123–53.

Gylfason, T. (2001), 'Natural Resources, Education, and Economic Development', *European Economic Review*, 45(4–6), pp. 847–59.

Hakeem I. (2010), 'Banking Development, Human Capital and Economic Growth in Sub-Saharan Africa (SSA)', *Journal of Economic Studies*, 37(5), pp. 557–77.

Hasan, I., P. Wachtel, and M. Zhou (2009), 'Institutional Development, Financial Deepening and Economic Growth: Evidence from China', *Journal of Banking & Finance*, 33(1), pp. 157–70.

Honohan, P. (2008). 'Cross-Country Variation in Household Access to Financial Services', *Journal of Banking & Finance*, 32(11), pp. 2493–2500.

Huang, Y. and Y. Zhang (2020), 'Financial Inclusion and Urban–Rural Income Inequality: Long-Run and Short-Run Relationships', *Emerging Markets Finance and Trade*, 56(2), pp. 457–471.

IEG (2015), *Financial Inclusion: A Foothold on the Latter toward Prosperity? An Evaluation of the World Bank Group Support for Financial Inclusion for Low-Income Households and Microenterprises*. Washington, DC: IBRD and World Bank. http://ieg.worldbankgroup.org/sites/default/files/Data/Evaluation/files/financialinclusion.pdf (accessed 8 September 2019).

Inoue, T. and S. Hamori (2016), 'Financial Access and Economic Growth: Evidence from Sub-Saharan Africa', *Emerging Markets Finance and Trade*, 52(3), pp. 743–53.

Jahan, S., J. De, F. Jamaludin, P. Sodsriwiboon, and C. Sullivan (2019), 'The Financial Inclusion Landscape in the Asia–Pacific Region: A Dozen Key Findings', *IMF Working Paper*, www.imf.org/en/Publications/WP/Issues/2019/04/19/The-Financial-Inclusion-Landscape-in-the-Asia-Pacific-Region-A-Dozen-Key-Findings-46713 (accessed 30 September 2019).

Jung, H.S. and E. Thorbecke (2003), 'The Impact of Public Education Expenditure on Human Capital, Growth, and Poverty in Tanzania and Zambia: A General Equilibrium Approach', *Journal of Policy Modeling*, 25(8), pp. 701–25.

Justino, P., T. Brück, and P. Verwimp (eds.) (2013), *A Micro-Level Perspective on the Dynamics of Conflict, Violence, and Development.* New York: Oxford University Press.
Kim, D., J. Yu, and M. Hassan (2018), 'Financial Inclusion and Economic Growth in OIC Countries', *Research in International Business and Finance*, 43, pp. 1–14.
Krueger, A. and M. Lindahl (2001), 'Education for Growth: Why and For Whom?', *Journal of Economic Literature*, 39(4), pp. 1101–36.
LaPorta, R., F. Lopez-de-Silanes, A. Shleifer, and R. Vishny (1998), 'Law and Finance', *Journal of Political Economy*, 106(6), pp. 1113–55.
Lee, K. and B. Kim (2009), 'Both Institutions and Policies Matter But Differently for Different Income Groups of Countries: Determinants of Long-Run Economic Growth Revisited', *World Development*, 37(3), pp. 533–49.
Levin, M. and G. Satarov (2000), 'Corruption and Institutions in Russia', *European Journal of Political Economy*, 16(1), pp. 113–32.
Lin, F. and D. Fu (2016), 'Trade, Institution Quality and Income Inequality', *World Development*, 77, pp. 129–42.
McKinnon, R. (2010), *Money and Capital in Economic Development.* Washington, DC: Brookings Institution Press.
Mishkin, F. (2007), *The Economics of Money, Banking, and Financial Markets.* London: Pearson Education.
Mishra, P. and D. Newhouse (2009), 'Does Health Aid Matter?', *Journal of Health Economics*, 28(4), pp. 855–72.
Mor, N. and B. Ananth (2014), Financial Development and Health. https://papers.ssrn.com/sol3/papers.cfm?abstract_id=2418861 (accessed 15 September 2019).
Narayan, P., S. Narayan, and S. Mishra (2011), 'Do Remittances Induce Inflation? Fresh Evidence from Developing Countries', *Southern Economic Journal*, 77(4), pp. 914–33.
Neaime, S. and I. Gaysset (2018), 'Financial Inclusion and Stability in MENA: Evidence from Poverty and Inequality', *Finance Research Letters*, 24, pp. 230–37.
Park, C. and R. Mercado (2015), 'Financial Inclusion, Poverty, and Income Inequality in Developing Asia', *ADB Economics Working Paper Series* No. 426, Mandaluyong: ADB.
Park, C. and R. Mercado (2018), 'Financial Inclusion, Poverty, and Income Inequality', *The Singapore Economic Review*, 63(01), pp. 185–206.
Pena, X., C. Hoyo, and D. Tuesta (2014), 'Determinants of Financial Inclusion in Mexico based on the 2012 National Financial Inclusion Survey (ENIF)', *BBVA Research* No. 14/15.
Pritchett, L. and L. Summers (1996), 'Wealthier Is Healthier', *The Journal of Human Resources*, 31(4), pp. 841–68.
Ram, R. (1984), 'Population Increase, Economic Growth, Educational Inequality, and Income Distribution: Some Recent Evidence', *Journal of Development Economics*, 14(3), pp. 419–28.
Rasheed, B., S. Law, L. Chin, and M. Habibullah (2016), 'The Role of Financial Inclusion in Financial Development: International Evidence', *Abasyn University Journal of Social Sciences*, 9(2), pp. 330–48.
Rodrik, D., A. Subramanian, and F. Trebbi (2004), 'Institutions Rule: The Primacy of Institutions over Geography and Integration in Economic Development', *Journal of Economic Growth*, 9(2), pp. 131–65.
Rojas-Suarez, L. and M. Amado (2014), 'Understanding Latin America's Financial Inclusion Gap', *Working Paper* No. 367. Washington, DC: Center for Global Development.

Roodman, D. (2009), 'How to Do xtabond2: An Introduction to Difference and System GMM in Stata', *The Stata Journal*, 9(1), pp. 86–136.

Sarma, M. (2008), 'Index of Financial Inclusion', *ICRIER Working Paper* No. 215, http://icrier.org/pdf/Working_Paper_215.pdf (accessed 8 September 2019).

Sharma, D. (2016), 'Nexus between Financial Inclusion and Economic Growth: Evidence from the Emerging Indian Economy', *Journal of Financial Economic Policy*, 8(1), pp. 13–36.

Sarma, M. and J. Pais (2011), 'Financial Inclusion and Development', *Journal of International Development*, 23(5), pp. 613–28.

Shaw, E. (1973), *Financial Deepening in Economic Development*. New York: Oxford University Press.

Scully, G. (1982), 'The Institutional Framework and Economic Development', *Journal of Political Economy*, 96(3), pp. 652–62.

Shleifer, A. and R. Vishny (1993), 'Corruption', *The Quarterly Journal of Economics*, 108(3), pp. 599–617.

Simon, J. and A. Pilarski (1979), 'The Effect of Population Growth upon the Quantity of Education Children Receive', *The Review of Economics and Statistics*, 61(4), pp. 572–84.

Yanikkaya, H. (2003), 'Trade Openness and Economic Growth: A Cross-Country Empirical Investigation', *Journal of Development Economics*, 72(1), pp. 57–89.

World Bank (1994), 'Enhancing Women's Participation in Economic Development', *Report* No. 12972. Washington, DC: World Bank.

Appendix 3.1 Data, descriptions, and sources – dependent and independent variables

	Description	*Sources*
Dependent variables		
Economic growth	It indicates the annual percentage growth rate of GDP per capita based on constant $US 2010.	WDI
Education (expected years of schooling)	It denotes the number of years of schooling that a child of school entrance age can expect to receive if prevailing patterns of age-specific enrolment rates persist throughout the child's life.	UNDP
Health (under-5 mortality rate)	It shows the probability of dying between birth and age 5, expressed per 1,000 live births.	UNDP
Income inequality (Gini coefficient)	It measures the deviation of the distribution of income amongst individuals or households within a country from a perfectly equal distribution. A value of 0 represents absolute equality, a value of 100, absolute inequality.	UNDP
Independent variables		
Financial inclusion index	It shows a composite index of usage, access, and quality of financial services.	See Chapter 2
Political risk ratings	It covers 12 weighted variables including both social and political attributes of a country, such as government stability, internal conflict, corruption, religious tensions, law and order, and other attributes. It takes a value between 0 (highest risk) and 12 (lowest risk).	PRS group
Initial per capita income	It is per capita GDP measured based on the constant $US 2010 at the beginning of the relevant period.	WDI
Trade openness	It is calculated as the sum of merchandise exports and imports divided by the value of GDP, which is measured by constant $US 2010.	WDI
Life expectancy	It indicates the number of years a newborn infant would live if prevailing patterns of mortality at the time of his or her birth were to stay the same throughout his or her life.	WDI
Inflation	It is measured by the consumer price index which reflects the annual percentage change in the cost to the average consumer of acquiring a basket of goods and services that may be fixed or changed at specified intervals, such as yearly.	WDI
Domestic credit to the private sector (% of GDP)	It refers to financial resources provided to the private sector by financial corporations – such as through loans, purchases of non-equity securities, and trade credits and other accounts receivable – that establish a claim for repayment.	WDI

Appendix 3.1 Cont.

	Description	*Sources*
Population growth	It is the annual population growth rate for year t calculated as the exponential rate of growth of the mid-year population from year t-1 to t, expressed as a percentage. Population is based on the de facto definition of population, which counts all residents regardless of legal status or citizenship.	WDI
Labour force, female (% of total labour force)	It is the percentage of women who are in the total labour force. Labour force comprises people aged 15 years and older who supply labour for the production of goods and services during a specified period.	WDI
Population under 15 years	It is the total population between the ages of 15 and 64. Population is based on the de facto definition of population, which counts all residents regardless of legal status or citizenship.	WDI
Government expenditure on education expenditure (% of GDP)	It is the general government expenditure on education (current, capital, and transfers), expressed as a percentage of GDP. It includes expenditure funded by transfers from international sources to the government. General government usually refers to local, regional, and central governments.	WDI
Pupil–teacher ratio, primary	It is the average number of pupils per teacher in primary school.	WDI
Literacy rate, adult female (% of females aged 15 and above)	It is the percentage of people aged 15 years and above who can both read and write and understand a short simple statement about their everyday life.	WDI
Prevalence of undernourishment (% of population)	It is the percentage of the population whose food intake is insufficient to meet dietary energy requirements continuously.	WDI
Births attended by skilled health staff (% of total)	It shows the percentage of deliveries attended by personnel trained to give the necessary supervision, care, and advice to women during pregnancy, labour, and the postpartum period; to conduct deliveries on their own; and to care for newborn babies.	WDI
Government expenditure on health expenditure (% of GDP)	It is the public expenditure on health from domestic sources as a share of the economy as measured by GDP.	WDI

Source: Authors's own calculation

GDP = gross domestic product; PRS = political risk service; UNDP = United Nations Development Programme; WDI = World Development Index

4 Financial inclusion

New measurement and cross-country impact assessment[1]

Cyn-Young Park and Rogelio V. Mercado, Jr.

4.1 Introduction

Financial inclusion aids inclusive growth, economic development, and financial deepening. More practically, it can increase poor people's access to financial services, and so reduce poverty and narrow income inequality. Empirical evidence supports this view. Indeed, simply having a bank account increases savings, empowers women, boosts household consumption, and raises productive investment (Allen et al., 2012; Beck et al., 2009; Ramahan 2011; and Zhang and Posso, 2017). In recent years, G20 leaders have recognised financial inclusion as one of the pillars of the global development agenda, whilst policymakers around the world have pursued it as a major policy goal.

However, the empirical literature on the macro-level impact of financial inclusion remains limited given the limited data and consensus measures for financial inclusion. Whilst the World Bank recently made available the Global Financial Inclusion (Global Findex) database to measure and track the progress of financial access across member countries, comprehensiveness of any single indicator for financial inclusion has often been questioned.

Despite the challenges, some studies tried to construct a more comprehensive index for financial inclusion. Honohan (2008) introduced a composite measure for financial access and found a set of country-specific structural variables that matter for financial access. For example, more aid as a percentage of gross domestic product (GDP), a higher age-dependency ratio, and higher population density significantly reduced financial access, whilst increased mobile phone subscriptions and higher quality of institutions significantly boosted financial access. Looking at the cross-country link between poverty and financial access, his research indicated that financial access significantly lowers poverty. However, the result is valid only when financial access is the sole regressor. In an earlier version of his paper, Honohan (2007) tested the significance of financial access in reducing income equality. His results showed that higher financial access significantly reduces income inequality. However, the link between the two variables depends on the specification used.

Rojas-Suarez (2010) also used the same financial access indicator as Honohan (2008) to test the significance of various macroeconomic and country characteristics on financial access amongst a group of emerging economies. The results show that economic volatility, weak rule of law, higher income inequality, and social underdevelopment and regulatory constraints significantly lower financial inclusion. Park and Mercado (2016, 2018) confirmed these earlier findings, showing that per capita income, rule of law, and demographic characteristics are positively correlated with financial inclusion for both global and Asian samples. They also found that financial inclusion is significantly correlated with lower poverty for both global and developing Asia samples. Although their results point to a significant covariation between income inequality and financial inclusion in their full sample, no such covariance is found in the developing Asia sample.

This chapter aims to investigate the country-level impact of financial inclusion on overall poverty, income inequality, entrepreneurship, and female empowerment, which is in line with the literature on the role of financial access and its interaction with finance sector development in poverty reduction, such as shown in Burgess and Pande (2005), Gimet and Lagoarde-Segot (2012), Honohan (2004), Perez-Moreno (2011), and Rewilak (2017).

The question asked in this chapter is: does financial inclusion lower poverty and income inequality? In this context, we also test if financial inclusion also improves entrepreneurship and female borrowing. We employ female borrowing as a measure of female empowerment, which is the proportion of adult females amongst borrowers from a financial institution. Addressing these questions in a cross-country setting will provide evidence for policymakers on the importance of economy-wide conditions, including the pursuit of financial inclusion, on socio-economic and development outcomes.

Unlike many micro-development studies on similar topics of financial inclusion, this chapter introduces methodological innovations for creating a new composite index of financial inclusion (IFI) that is used to investigate cross-country evidence for the economic impacts of financial inclusion. Hence, this chapter offers macro-level evidence on cross-country differences in per capita income and poverty rates. On the methodological innovation, we use principal component analysis (PCA) in constructing a new IFI for 151 economies based on measures of ease of access, availability, and usage from the most recent published data from the World Bank Global Findex Database. Our new financial inclusion measure combines a multidimensional approach in identifying components of financial inclusion and the use of normalised weights from the PCA in determining the contribution of each component to the aggregate indicator. Our new index shows that the indicators and dimension weights from the PCA remain relatively stable across three survey years – 2011, 2014, and 2017.

Our key findings indicate that higher financial inclusion is important in reducing poverty in general. However, there are varying degrees of interaction effects between financial inclusion and country income groups, suggesting that for any given level of financial inclusion, an additional increase in financial inclusion has the largest impact on poverty reduction for low-income countries. This result implies nonlinearities in the relationship between financial inclusion and poverty, subject to the country-specific development stage and income factors that may influence the effects of financial inclusion.[2] This relates to Rewilak (2013), who found that financial development may alleviate poverty but the effect is not universal across different regions. For example, financial development is successful in raising the income of the lowest quintile in South Asia, but the converse is true for Latin America and the Caribbean. In contrast, our findings suggest that financial inclusion has heterogeneous effects on poverty depending on country incomes.

The chapter proceeds as follows. Section 4.2 discusses conceptual and measurement issues on financial inclusion. Section 4.3 explains the methodology in constructing a new financial inclusion index and provides stylised facts. Section 4.4 presents the empirical approach and discusses the results. Section 4.5 concludes.

4.2 Financial inclusion concepts and measurement

Conceptually, definitions of financial inclusion vary. Several studies defined the concept within the broader context of social inclusion. For example, Leyshon and Thrift (1995) highlighted the exclusion of some groups and individuals from access to formal financial systems, whilst Sinclair (2001) focused on the inability to access necessary financial services in an appropriate form. Amidžić et al. (2014) directly defined financial inclusion as an economic state in which individuals and firms are not denied access to basic financial services. Sarma (2008) provided a multidimensional approach in defining financial inclusion as a process that ensures ease of access, availability, and usage of formal financial systems for all members of an economy. In contrast, Camara and Tuesta (2014) defined an inclusive financial system as one that maximises usage and access whilst minimising involuntary exclusions. Hence, they focused more on usage, access, and barriers, which capture both the supply and demand sides of financial access.

And just as no single conceptual definition of financial inclusion exists, no standard measure of the concept is universally accepted. Consequently, measures of financial inclusion often varied across studies. For instance, Honohan (2007, 2008) constructed a financial access indicator that captures the fraction of the adult population in each economy with access to formal financial intermediaries – which captures only one dimension of financial inclusion. This composite financial access indicator was constructed using household survey data for economies with available data on financial access. For those without a household survey on financial access, the indicator was derived using information on bank account numbers and GDP per capita. The data set was constructed as a cross-section series using the most recent data as the reference year, which varies across economies.

Amidžić et al. (2014) constructed a financial inclusion indicator as a composite of variables concerning multiple dimensions: outreach (geographic and demographic penetration), usage (deposit and lending), and quality (disclosure requirement, dispute resolution, and cost of usage).[3] Each measure was normalised, statistically identified for each dimension, and then aggregated using statistical weights where the aggregation follows a weighted geometric mean. One drawback of this approach is that it used a factor analysis method to reduce a set of variables down to a smaller number of factors and, therefore, not fully utilising all available data for each country. Furthermore, it is very difficult to have a reliable and available cross-country data on quality measures.

Sarma (2008) followed a different approach to construct the indicator. She first computed a sub-index for each dimension of financial inclusion (access, availability, and usage) and then aggregated each index as the normalised inverse of Euclidean distance, where the distance was computed from a reference ideal point and then normalised by the number of dimensions included in the aggregate index. An advantage of this approach is that it is easy to compute and does not impose varying weights for each dimension. In Sarma (2015), dimensional weights were set at arbitrary values due to the lack of available data to fully characterise availability and usage dimensions. For example, the weights for access, availability, and usage were 1, 0.5, and 0.5, respectively.

Camara and Tuesta (2014) used two-stage PCA wherein, in the first stage, they estimated three sub-indexes – usage, access, and barriers – which define their financial inclusion measure. In the second stage, they estimated the dimension weights and the overall financial inclusion index with the dimension sub-indexes in the first stage as explanatory variables. In effect, their financial inclusion measure is a weighted average of three dimensions, where the weights are derived from the PCA. Whilst their methodology suffers from weaknesses of its own, the weights were drawn from available data, rather than relying on the researcher's discretion and potential biases.

This chapter adopts a multidimension approach in defining financial inclusion as a process that ensures ease of access, availability, and usage of financial services for all members of society, like Sarma (2008).[4] The advantage of this definition is that it builds the concept of financial inclusion based on several dimensions, each of which can be assessed separately. More importantly, it strictly delineates financial inclusion dimensions focusing on the financial access of a segment of the population included in the financial system. However, we compute the weights for aggregating indexes using the PCA, like Camara and Tuesta (2014).

4.3 Index of financial inclusion

Before assessing the impact of financial inclusion on reducing poverty, narrowing income inequality, and achieving other socioeconomic outcomes across different samples of countries, we first construct our financial inclusion indicator. The motivations for constructing a new index are to (i) develop a consistent and robust measure of financial inclusion using all available data for a large sample of economies, (ii) help standardise the measure and allow consistent economic analysis for all countries in our sample, and (iii) improve the quality of the measure by combining multiple dimensions of financial inclusion into a composite index using the PCA.

In computing our IFI, we follow a two-step approach. First, we combine various measures of access, availability, and usage into three-dimensional indexes that are related to financial inclusiveness, rather than financial exclusion.[5] Second, we combine three-dimension indexes into a composite IFI. The aggregate index is a weighted linear combination of dimensional indexes, which themselves are weighted linear combinations of various indicators. The weights for aggregating indexes are derived using the PCA. The PCA is a commonly used method combining a set of variables to extract maximum common information from individual indicators.[6] In effect, the PCA partitions the variance in a set of variables and uses it to determine weights that maximise the resulting principal component's variation. The derived principal component is a variable that captures variations in data to the maximum extent possible.

Using the PCA to derive the weights offers several advantages. First, in application to IFI, the weights of each dimension will now be data-driven, hence parametric, as opposed to exogenously determining the weights, which is a non-parametric method. Second, unlike common factor analysis, the PCA does not make any assumptions regarding the number of common factors, enhancing its feature as a data-driven parametric approach to indexing. Given the main advantages, we use the PCA to construct the weights in aggregating various indicators to dimension indexes and then into a composite financial inclusion index.

In the first step, we standardise each indictor in each dimension as:

$$X_{i,d} = \frac{x_i - m_i}{M_i - m_i} \tag{4.1}$$

where x_i is the actual value of indicator i, m_i is the minimum value of indicator i, and M_i is the maximum value of dimension i.[7] $X_{i,d}$ is the standardised value of indicator i of dimension d. In aggregating each indicator to a dimension index, we use the PCA. We denote λ_j (j = 1, ..., p) as the j-th eigenvalue, subscript j refers to the number of principal components that also coincides with the number of standardised indicators p. We assume that $\lambda_1 > \lambda_2 > \ldots > \lambda_p$ and denote P_k (k = 1, ..., p) as the k-th principal component. We derive each dimension index according to the weighted averages:

$$D_d = \frac{\Sigma_{j,k=1}^{p} \lambda_j P_k}{\Sigma_{j=1}^{p} \lambda_j} \tag{4.2}$$

where D_d is dimension d index and $P_k = X\lambda_j$. λ_j represents the variance of the k-th principal component (weights) and X is the indicators matrix. The weights given to each component are decreasing so that the larger proportion of the variation in each dimension is explained by the first principal component and so on. Following Camara and Tuesta (2014), we also account for 100% of the total variation in our dimension indexes to avoid discarding information that could accurately estimate the overall country financial inclusion index.

Once we have the dimension indexes, we run another PCA to derive the dimension weights for the overall financial inclusion.

$$IFI_i = \frac{\Sigma_{j=1}^{p} \lambda_j P_{ki}}{\Sigma_{j=1}^{p} \lambda_j} \tag{4.3}$$

where IFI_i is the aggregate financial inclusion index for country *i*. $P_k = X\lambda_j$. λ_j represents the variance of the k-th principal component (weights of each dimension) and X is the dimensions matrix. The weights given to each component are also decreasing, and we account for 100% of the total variation in our IFI. We can also represent Equation 4.3 as:

$$IFI_i = \omega_1 D_{1,i} + \omega_2 D_{2,i} + \omega_3 D_{3,i} \tag{4.4}$$

where ω are the weights derived from the PCA and D_i are the dimensions. Equation 4.4 states that our IFI for our sample of 151 advanced and emerging economies is a weighted average of individual dimensions.

For our indicators, we use the World Bank's Global Findex database. For access, the indicators include the ratio of the adult population with financial accounts to the total population (%). This indicator is a better measure of the segment of the adult population with bank accounts compared to the number of deposit accounts per adult population. We also include the proportion of the adult population with credit and debit cards as these measures complement those who have a bank account; that is, one must have a bank account before a debit and/or a credit card is issued. Our primary data source is the World Bank's Global Findex database, which is based on individual and household survey data for 2011, 2014, and 2017 aggregated to the country level. For our 2014 and 2017 data for access, we also include the percentage share of the adult population with a mobile money account for those with available data.[8]

For the availability dimension, we include the number of commercial bank branches and automatic teller machines (ATMs) per 100,000 adults, also taken from the Global Findex database. Both measures pertain to the geographic penetration of banking services. For the usage dimension, we include the share of the adult population who borrowed and saved from a financial institution. We also include the domestic credit-to-GDP ratio, sourced from the World Bank's World Development Indicators.[9]

Table 4.1 presents the computed normalised weights for each indicator. Several observations are notable. First, changing the number of indicators in a dimension index significantly alters the resulting weights. For the access dimension, the inclusion of a mobile money account altered the weights for 2014 and 2017 for countries with available mobile account data. For those without mobile account data, the weights remained mostly the same as in 2011. Second, the weight of commercial bank branches was significantly larger than the weight of ATMs per adult population for the availability dimension. This holds across country income groups. Third, the share of those who borrow from a financial institution is far greater than the share of those who saved and for the credit-to-GDP ratio for

Table 4.1 Principal component analysis of indicators for each index of financial inclusion dimension

	Full sample					*HIC*					*MHI*				
	2011	*2014*		*2017*		*2011*	*2014*		*2017*		*2011*	*2014*		*2017*	
Account (% age 15+)	0.314	0.321	0.263	0.321	0.273	0.312	0.289	0.290	0.310	0.294	0.284	0.292	0.336	0.295	0.274
Credit card (% age 15+)	0.367	0.363	0.250	0.365	0.239	0.488	0.432	0.181	0.436	0.146	0.412	0.408	0.065	0.403	0.180
Debit card (% age 15+)	0.318	0.316	0.273	0.314	0.254	0.200	0.279	0.297	0.255	0.284	0.304	0.300	0.324	0.302	0.255
Mobile money (% age 15+)			0.215		0.234			0.231		0.276			0.276		0.291
Branches per 100,000 pop.	0.626	0.649		0.640		0.767	0.794		0.746		0.647	0.710		0.749	
ATMs per 100,000 pop.	0.374	0.351		0.360		0.233	0.206		0.254		0.353	0.290		0.251	
Borrower (% age 15+)	0.437	0.447		0.441		0.305	0.174		0.148		0.444	0.443		0.508	
Saver (% age 15+)	0.247	0.268		0.276		0.209	0.294		0.314		0.323	0.291		0.277	
Credit (% GDP)	0.315	0.285		0.283		0.487	0.532		0.538		0.233	0.266		0.216	
Dimension 1 (Access)	0.300	0.291		0.284		0.302	0.250		0.260		0.237	0.231		0.173	
Dimension 2 (Availability)	0.402	0.395		0.399		0.434	0.426		0.436		0.229	0.481		0.475	
Dimension 3 (Usage)	0.298	0.314		0.317		0.264	0.324		0.304		0.534	0.288		0.353	

	MLI					*LIC*				
	2011	*2014*		*2017*		*2011*	*2014*		*2017*	
Account (% age 15+)	0.276	0.281	0.217	0.294	0.268	0.415	0.343	0.281	0.295	0.227
Credit card (% age 15+)	0.444	0.428	0.359	0.432	0.156	0.290	0.354	0.225	0.407	0.264
Debit card (% age 15+)	0.280	0.291	0.224	0.274	0.174	0.295	0.302	0.262	0.298	0.237
Mobile money (% age 15+)			0.200		0.401			0.232		0.272
Branches per 100,000 pop.	0.758	0.687		0.621		0.639	0.609		0.561	

ATMs per 100,000 pop.	0.242	0.313	0.379	0.361	0.391	0.439
Borrower (% age 15+)	0.135	0.246	0.355	0.280	0.257	0.281
Saver (% age 15+)	0.278	0.553	0.482	0.287	0.313	0.284
Credit (% GDP)	0.587	0.201	0.163	0.433	0.430	0.436
Dimension 1 (Access)	0.269	0.179	0.231	0.285	0.299	0.443
Dimension 2 (Availability)	0.261	0.461	0.543	0.430	0.489	0.246
Dimension 3 (Usage)	0.470	0.360	0.226	0.285	0.212	0.311

Source: Authors' calculations.

ATM = automatic teller machine; GDP = gross domestic product; HIC = high-income countries; MHI = middle-high-income countries; MLI = middle-low-income countries; LIC = low-income countries.

Notes: Weights are normalised. Dimension 1 (access) weights for 2014 and 2017 include weights for mobile money whenever data are available. Refer to Appendix 4.1 for data definition and sources.

middle-high-income countries. In contrast, the credit-to-GDP ratio has a higher weight for high- and low-income countries. Taken together, these imply that indicator weights in one dimension significantly vary across country income groups. Fourth, weights appear to be stable for all survey periods. This offers support for using the PCA to generate indicator and dimension weights in aggregating a financial inclusion index. Finally, amongst dimensions, availability appears to have greater importance than access and usage. This validates the findings of Demirgüç-Kunt and Klapper (2012), who found that distance or the lack of available bank branches in remote areas are primary reasons survey respondents are involuntarily excluded from financial services.[10]

Applying Equations 4.1–4.4 on the list of indicators, Table 4.2 presents our cross-country IFI, ordered from the highest to the lowest in 2017.[11] In principle, the IFI index could reach 100, suggesting very high financial inclusion. But our computed index reaches only up to 78.91 for Luxembourg in 2017. This could be attributed to the use of weighted averages for our indicators and dimensions, as weighted averages make it less likely for a country to score high points on each weight. Nonetheless, the ordering of economies based on IFI appears robust such that economies like Japan, Luxembourg, Spain, and the United States always scored highly on previous IFI rankings (see including Park and Mercado, 2016, 2018). Figure 4.1 illustrates IFI median values by country income groupings. As expected, high-income countries (as classified by the World Bank) score highly on our IFI measure, whilst low-income countries score the lowest. It also shows that financial inclusion has moderately increased across income groups between sample periods, but the increase is most notable for low-income countries.

4.4 Empirical methodology and results

To address the research question raised in this chapter, we test the significance of the aggregate level of financial inclusion in 2011–2014 on rates of poverty, income inequality, entrepreneurship, and female borrowing in 2014–2017. We expect economies with higher financial inclusion to have lower poverty rates and income inequality and higher entrepreneurship (Dupas and Robinson, 2009) and female empowerment (Ashraf et al., 2010). Figure 4.2 demonstrates this negative relationship between the average level of IFI in 2011–2014 and average poverty rates in 2014–2017. Figure 4.3 exhibits a similar pattern for income inequality. But to formally test the relationship, we estimate the equation:

$$\Upsilon_{2014-17,i} = \alpha + \beta_1 IFI_{2011-14,i} + \beta' X_{2011-2013,i} + \phi D_i + \varphi D_i * IFI_{2011-14,i} + \varepsilon_i \qquad (4.5)$$

where Υ pertains to the average values of poverty, income inequality, entrepreneurship, and female borrowing for 2014–2017. *IFI* is the average value for financial inclusion in 2011 and 2014. X is a row vector of regressors which includes the average values of secondary education completion and GDP growth rates for 2011–2013.[12] D is a dummy variable for country income groupings. $D*IFI$ is

Table 4.2 Index of financial inclusion ranking, 2017

Rank	*Economy*	*Code*	*Income group*	*Geographic group*	*IFI 2011*	*IFI 2014*	*IFI 2017*
1	Luxembourg	LUX	HIC	EUR	71.81	73.21	78.91
2	United States	USA	HIC	NAM	63.24	66.33	72.48
3	Canada	CAN	HIC	NAM	62.33	66.30	68.87
4	Spain	ESP	HIC	EUR	68.15	68.65	66.92
5	Australia	AUS	HIC	EAP	61.20	62.21	63.34
6	New Zealand	NZL	HIC	EAP	62.39	63.15	63.11
7	Switzerland	CHE	HIC	EUR	59.40	59.00	62.07
8	Korea	KOR	HIC	EAP	59.16	59.03	62.06
9	United Kingdom	GBR	HIC	EUR	54.06	59.06	59.73
10	Norway	NOR	HIC	EUR	58.95	56.08	59.34
11	Japan	JPN	HIC	EAP	49.83	59.20	59.24
12	Mongolia	MNG	MIL	EAP	48.31	56.99	59.16
13	Italy	ITA	HIC	EUR	43.30	51.57	57.58
14	Israel	ISR	HIC	MENA	45.99	56.80	56.37
15	Denmark	DNK	HIC	EUR	59.14	55.50	55.95
16	France	FRA	HIC	EUR	54.96	54.42	55.67
17	Portugal	PRT	HIC	EUR	58.70	54.82	54.75
18	Sweden	SWE	HIC	EUR	55.38	55.77	53.30
19	Germany	DEU	HIC	EUR	47.54	50.36	51.59
20	Hong Kong, China	HKG	HIC	EAP	48.33	50.53	51.35
21	Malta	M LT	HIC	EUR	51.08	48.33	49.87
22	Slovenia	SVN	HIC	CEE	51.25	47.45	49.61
23	Ireland	IRL	HIC	EUR	51.69	49.71	48.59
24	Austria	AUT	HIC	EUR	45.38	47.04	48.33
25	Croatia	HRV	MIH	CEE	46.48	49.99	47.70
26	Finland	FIN	HIC	EUR	52.02	49.60	46.80
27	Poland	POL	HIC	CEE	32.59	38.58	46.39
28	Belgium	BEL	HIC	EUR	43.45	44.58	45.75
29	Bulgaria	BGR	MIH	CEE	39.19	45.11	45.69
30	Cyprus	CYP	HIC	EUR	62.16	46.05	45.64
31	Slovakia	SVK	HIC	CEE	37.26	40.69	45.47
32	Iran	IRN	MIH	MENA	43.08	41.38	45.46
33	Netherlands	NLD	HIC	EUR	48.80	45.37	45.30
34	Singapore	SGP	HIC	EAP	37.17	39.06	44.07
35	Russia	RUS	MIH	FSU	32.07	41.53	42.55
36	Estonia	EST	HIC	CEE	40.85	40.70	41.71
37	Czech Republic	CZE	HIC	CEE	35.38	37.75	40.50
38	United Arab Emirates	ARE	HIC	MENA	30.38	35.69	40.23
39	Montenegro	MNE	MIH	EUR	35.54	38.39	39.52
40	Kuwait	KWT	HIC	MENA	46.50	34.48	38.71
41	Thailand	THA	MIH	EAP	36.84	35.45	38.45
42	Latvia	LVA	HIC	CEE	38.86	39.38	36.99
43	China	CHN	MIH	EAP	25.75	32.08	36.59
44	Georgia	GEO	MIL	FSU	21.58	29.39	36.27
45	Turkey	TUR	MIH	MENA	29.71	31.28	35.75
46	Colombia	COL	MIH	LAC	20.02	34.64	35.56
47	Malaysia	MYS	MIH	EAP	28.45	32.36	35.07
48	Chile	CHL	HIC	LAC	26.50	31.50	34.65
49	Serbia	SRB	MIH	CEE	34.50	32.88	34.56

(*continued*)

Table 4.2 Cont.

Rank	*Economy*	*Code*	*Income group*	*Geographic group*	*IFI 2011*	*IFI 2014*	*IFI 2017*
50	Mauritius	MUS	MIH	SSA	35.32	35.72	34.52
51	Trinidad and Tobago	TTO	HIC	LAC	29.84	30.38	34.47
52	Macedonia	MKD	M IH	CEE	29.33	33.11	34.46
53	Namibia	NAM	MIH	SSA	25.02	24.22	34.43
54	Costa Rica	CRI	MIH	LAC	27.97	33.04	33.74
55	Greece	GRC	HIC	EUR	38.07	35.95	33.46
56	Qatar	QAT	HIC	M ENA	31.14	31.25	32.57
57	Armenia	ARM	MIL	FSU	19.96	21.70	32.45
58	Brazil	BRA	MIH	LAC	30.73	33.38	32.42
59	Lithuania	LTU	HIC	CEE	29.09	30.56	32.38
60	Oman	OMN	HIC	M ENA	31.06	29.61	31.23
61	Romania	ROU	MIH	CEE	27.88	29.24	30.73
62	Lebanon	LBN	MIH	M ENA	27.16	28.32	30.60
63	Uruguay	URY	HIC	LAC	21.25	26.50	30.30
64	Saudi Arabia	SAU	HIC	M ENA	20.15	27.61	29.71
65	Hungary	HUN	HIC	CEE	30.63	28.43	29.65
66	Kenya	KEN	MIL	SSA	17.15	27.09	29.43
67	South Africa	ZAF	MIH	SSA	27.78	32.49	29.17
68	Bosnia and Herzegovina	BIH	MIH	CEE	29.63	30.24	29.14
69	Belize	BLZ	MIH	LAC	27.50	26.87	28.68
70	Belarus	BLR	MIH	FSU	23.20	22.73	28.60
71	Venezuela	VEN	MIH	LAC	18.69	22.36	27.95
72	Kazakhstan	KAZ	MIH	FSU	20.14	22.01	27.09
73	Dominican Republic	DOM	MIH	LAC	20.29	22.72	26.97
74	Sri Lanka	LKA	MIL	SAS	25.22	26.24	26.76
75	Panama	PAN	MIH	LAC	22.30	26.49	26.66
76	Indonesia	IDN	MIL	EAP	14.24	21.96	25.99
77	Ukraine	UKR	MIL	FSU	21.47	23.73	25.94
78	Bolivia	BOL	MIL	LAC	18.67	23.66	25.49
79	Guatemala	GTM	MIL	LAC	23.12	25.12	24.86
80	Kosovo	UVK	MIL	CEE	21.04	23.05	24.75
81	Jordan	JOR	MIL	M ENA	15.89	17.55	23.04
82	Peru	PER	MIH	LAC	15.60	16.74	22.96
83	Jamaica	JAM	MIH	LAC	22.00	22.20	22.91
84	Honduras	HND	MIL	LAC	16.03	19.40	22.29
85	Vietnam	VNM	MIL	EAP	17.20	18.65	22.29
86	Tunisia	TUN	MIL	M ENA	17.97	17.81	22.26
87	India	IND	MIL	SAS	14.18	17.12	21.59
88	Paraguay	PRY	MIH	LAC	16.00	17.71	20.91
89	Argentina	ARG	MIH	LAC	18.99	20.91	20.85
90	Uzbekistan	UZB	MIL	FSU	17.10	20.19	20.84
91	Ecuador	ECU	MIH	LAC	19.51	20.98	20.78
92	Albania	ALB	MIH	CEE	20.45	20.83	20.76
93	Cambodia	KHM	MIL	EAP	11.64	18.08	19.50
94	Moldova	MDA	MIL	CEE	12.76	14.03	19.30
95	Uganda	UGA	LIC	SSA	9.92	17.63	19.24
96	Ghana	GHA	MIL	SSA	10.48	13.23	19.16
97	Botswana	BWA	MIH	SSA	14.63	22.63	18.47
98	Nepal	NPL	LIC	SAS	12.85	14.42	18.38

Table 4.2 Cont.

Rank	*Economy*	*Code*	*Income group*	*Geographic group*	*IFI 2011*	*IFI 2014*	*IFI 2017*
99	Mexico	MEX	MIH	LAC	17.72	20.62	18.19
100	Gabon	GAB	MIH	SSA	7.19	12.82	18.01
101	Morocco	MAR	MIL	MENA	19.49	19.72	17.74
102	Azerbaijan	AZE	MIH	FSU	15.51	18.83	17.54
103	Bhutan	BTN	MIL	SAS	15.94	16.27	17.48
104	Swaziland	SWZ	MIL	SSA	16.95	16.49	17.19
105	Tajikistan	TJK	MIL	FSU	5.24	6.13	17.02
106	Philippines	PHL	MIL	EAP	14.38	15.79	16.13
107	Bangladesh	BGD	MIL	SAS	18.85	11.80	16.03
108	El Salvador	SLV	MIL	LAC	12.34	20.25	16.02
109	Nicaragua	NIC	MIL	LAC	9.91	13.12	15.78
110	Zambia	ZMB	MIL	SSA	9.80	11.80	15.62
111	Rwanda	RWA	LIC	SSA	11.56	14.10	15.47
112	Zimbabwe	ZWE	LIC	SSA	13.55	13.08	15.39
113	Burkina Faso	BFA	LIC	SSA	4.97	6.68	14.86
114	Togo	TGO	LIC	SSA	5.66	6.77	14.70
115	Kyrgyzstan	KGZ	MIL	FSU	8.64	12.42	14.42
116	Senegal	SEN	LIC	SSA	5.27	7.25	13.80
117	Nigeria	NGA	MIL	SSA	10.74	14.61	13.24
118	Lesotho	LSO	MIL	SSA	7.42	9.26	13.24
119	Angola	AGO	MIL	SSA	17.45	12.92	13.19
120	Myanmar	MMR	MIL	EAP	10.87	10.38	13.10
121	Benin	BEN	LIC	SSA	5.50	7.54	13.07
122	Lao PDR	LAO	MIL	EAP	15.54	15.37	13.05
123	Haiti	HTI	LIC	LAC	9.16	6.74	12.73
124	Mali	MLI	LIC	SSA	5.04	7.21	12.64
125	Tanzania	TZA	LIC	SSA	8.55	12.28	12.63
126	West Bank and Gaza	PSE	MIL	MENA	10.51	11.03	12.27
127	Ethiopia	ETH	LIC	SSA	7.63	7.18	11.69
128	Algeria	DZA	MIH	MENA	7.97	12.49	11.68
129	Egypt	EGY	MIL	MENA	6.19	7.72	11.55
130	Cote d'Ivoire	CIV	MIL	SSA	7.85	10.02	11.48
131	Malawi	MWI	LIC	SSA	8.38	7.38	11.46
132	Liberia	LBR	LIC	SSA	8.30	8.86	11.46
133	Syria	SYR	MIL	MENA	11.43	10.63	11.38
134	Mauritania	MRT	MIL	SSA	8.72	10.86	11.03
135	Cameroon	CMR	MIL	SSA	5.85	4.55	10.42
136	Pakistan	PAK	MIL	SAS	5.61	6.77	9.18
137	Comoros	COM	LIC	SSA	8.57	8.44	9.10
138	Republic of Congo	COG	MIL	SSA	5.02	7.03	8.65
139	Djibouti	DJI	MIL	MENA	7.42	7.49	8.14
140	Guinea	GIN	LIC	SSA	2.79	3.41	7.64
141	Sudan	SDN	MIL	SSA	3.59	6.23	6.60
142	Democratic Republic of Congo	COD	LIC	SSA	1.89	4.68	6.47
143	Sierra Leone	SLE	LIC	SSA	7.19	5.76	6.20
144	Madagascar	MDG	LIC	SSA	2.65	3.46	6.05
145	Iraq	IRQ	MIH	MENA	7.19	5.52	5.90
146	Chad	TCD	LIC	SSA	5.78	3.86	5.75

(*continued*)

Table 4.2 Cont.

Rank	*Economy*	*Code*	*Income group*	*Geographic group*	*IFI 2011*	*IFI 2014*	*IFI 2017*
147	Central African Republic	CAF	LIC	SSA	1.81	2.76	4.92
148	Niger	NER	LIC	SSA	1.78	2.79	4.91
149	Afghanistan	AFG	LIC	SAS	5.69	3.62	4.19
150	Burundi	BDI	LIC	SSA	3.40	3.39	3.58
151	Yemen	YEM	MIL	MENA	2.00	2.12	2.16

Source: Authors' calculations.

Notes
CEE = Central and Eastern Europe; EAP = East Asia and Pacific; EUR = Europe; FSU = Former Soviet Union; IFI = index of financial inclusion; HIC = high-income countries; LAC = Latin American countries; LIC = low-income countries; MENA = Middle East and North Africa; MHI = middle-high-income countries; MLI = middle-low-income countries; SAS = South Asia; SSA = Sub-Saharan Africa. Refer to Section 4.2 for the discussion of the construction of the IFI.

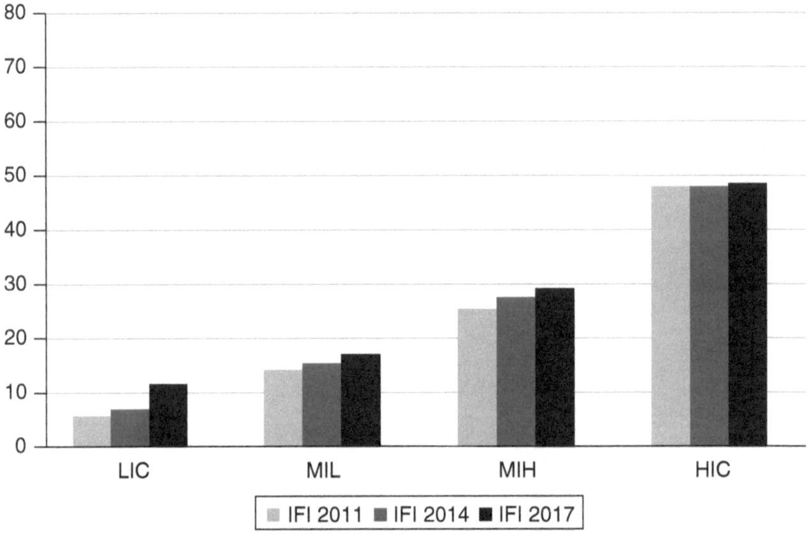

Figure 4.1 Index of financial inclusion by income group (median).

LIC = low-income countries; MLI = middle-low-income countries; MHI = middle-high-income countries; HIC = high-income countries. Median values based on the index of financial inclusion presented in Table 4.2.

Source: Authors' calculations.

the interaction term between the country income group and financial inclusion.[13] The interaction term in Equation 4.5 will indicate whether financial inclusion to a specific income group exerts a greater or lesser impact on poverty, income inequality, entrepreneurship, and female borrowing than in other income groups.

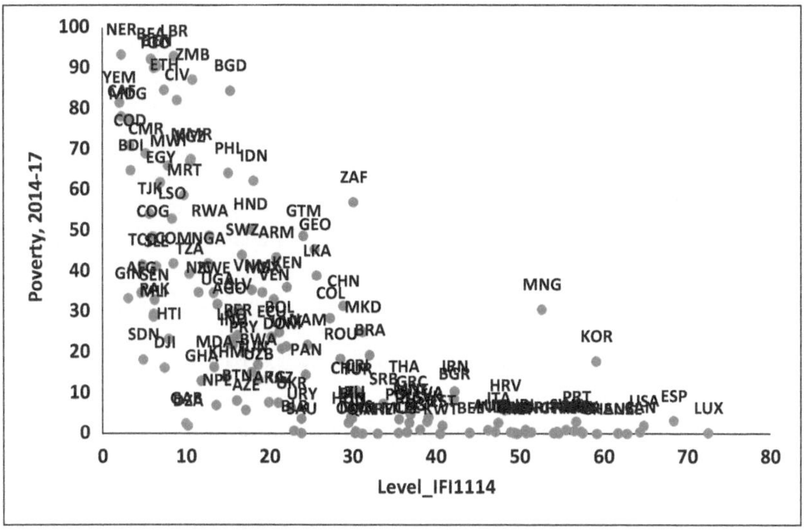

Figure 4.2 Poverty on index of financial inclusion.

Notes: Level_IFI1114 pertains to the average IFI for 2011 and 2014. Poverty refers to the average value of the poverty headcount ratio for 2014–2017.

Source: Authors' calculations.

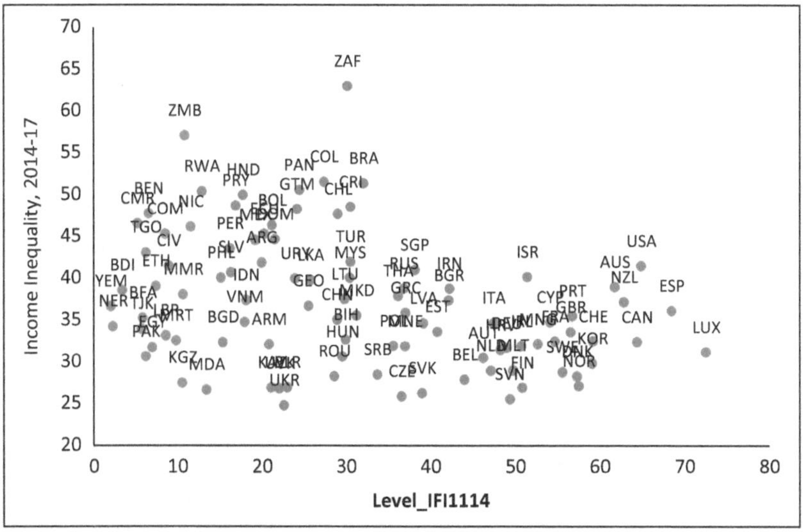

Figure 4.3 Income inequality on index of financial inclusion.

Notes: Level_IFI1114 pertains to the average IFI for 2011 and 2014. Income inequality refers to the average value of the Gini coefficient for 2014–2017.

Source: Authors' calculations.

We limit the number of regressors to avoid multicollinearity amongst regressors in Equation 4.5.[14] We also use robust standard errors to address potential heteroskedasticity. In addition, regressing the dependent and independent variables in two different periods reduces endogeneity; that is, the explanatory variables are lagged. This estimation approach is recommended in reducing endogeneity in a cross-section set-up without affecting the instrument variable approach. Finally, we analyse Equation 4.5 using ordinary least squares estimation. We do not use an instrument variable with two-stage least squares estimation due to the lack of a valid instrument. The use of a weak instrument will lead to inefficient estimation as the standard errors in the second-stage regression will be higher, yielding inconsistent results. However, in our sensitivity tests (discussed in the latter part of this chapter), we run Fuller's limited information maximum likelihood estimation (1977) with potential, though weak, instruments. The same results hold for the effects of financial inclusion, suggesting that our lagged regressor specification somehow minimises endogeneity issues, although we do acknowledge that endogeneity may persist due to omitted variables.

Tables 4.3–4.5 present the results on the impact of financial inclusion on poverty and income inequality. Besides poverty and inequality, we add entrepreneurship and female borrowing, which is used as a proxy for female empowerment, since financial inclusion is often discussed as a key driver for these two important economic variables in micro-level studies using individual and household survey data. Table 4.3 presents evidence that higher financial inclusion significantly lowers poverty and increases entrepreneurship and female bank borrowing.

Table 4.3 Estimates on poverty, income inequality, entrepreneurship, and female borrowing, full sample

Variables	$Poverty_{2014\text{–}17}$	$Income\ inequality_{2014\text{–}17}$	$Entrepre_{2014\text{–}17}$	$Female\ empower_{2014\text{–}17}$
Financial $inclusion_{2011\text{–}14}$	–0.891***	0.022	0.230***	0.457***
	[–5.422]	[0.413]	[8.538]	[4.488]
Education $completion_{2011\text{–}13}$	–0.120	–0.145***	–0.034**	–0.078
	[–1.197]	[–3.902]	[–2.057]	[–1.353]
$Growth_{2011\text{–}13}$	0.586	0.512**	0.190*	0.625
	[0.881]	[2.150]	[1.674]	[1.345]
Constant	55.075***	44.787***	4.933***	37.239***
	[7.915]	[18.439]	[4.540]	[7.843]
Observations	121	90	127	127
R-squared	0.501	0.300	0.426	0.200

Source: Authors' calculations.

Notes: Dependent variables are average values of poverty, income inequality, entrepreneurship and female borrowing for 2014–17. The regressors are average values of financial inclusion for 2011 and 2014; and education completion and GDP growth rates for 2011–13. *** p<0.01, ** p<0.05, * p<0.1. Robust standard errors are used for t-stats reported in brackets.

Table 4.4a Estimates on poverty, income inequality, entrepreneurship, and female borrowing, with high- and middle-high-income countries

Variables	$Poverty_{2014-17}$	*Income* $inequality_{2014-17}$	$Entrepre_{2014-17}$	*Female* $empower_{2014-17}$
Financial $inclusion_{2011-14}$	−0.253***	−0.001	0295***	0.706***
	[−2.800]	[−0.022]	[10.806]	[7.115]
Education $completion_{2011-13}$	−0.121**	−0.240***	0.014	0.097
	[−2.594]	[−5.394]	[0.562]	[1.262]
$Growth_{2011-13}$	0.163	0.787***	0.295*	1.788***
	[0.428]	[2.895]	[1.939]	[3.190]
Constant	25.944***	53.317***	−2.008	10.177
	[4.662]	[14.810]	[−0.967]	[1.575]
Observations	71	60	75	75
R-squared	0.257	0.474	0.567	0.484

Source: Authors' calculations.

Notes: Dependent variables are average values of poverty, income inequality, entrepreneurship, and female borrowing for 2014–17. The regressors are average values of financial inclusion for 2011 and 2014; and education completion and GDP growth rates for 2011–13. Refer to Table 4.2 for high (HIC) and middle-high-income MIH country list. *** p<0.01, ** p<0.05, * p<0.1. Robust standard errors are used for t-stats reported in brackets.

However, we do not find similar results for income inequality. These results hold whilst we control for educational attainment and higher output growth, which are significant for income inequality and entrepreneurship.

Tables 4.4a and 4.4b present the results when we split the sample into high-, middle-high-, middle-low-, and low-income country groups.[15] Table 4.4a illustrates that higher financial inclusion lowers poverty rates and increases entrepreneurship and female borrowing in high- and middle-high-income countries. This result is valid with other control variables, such as education completion and output growth. Economies with higher education completion have less poverty and income inequality, whilst those with stronger growth rates have higher income inequality, entrepreneurship, and female borrowing. For middle-low- and low-income country groups in Table 4.4b, higher financial inclusion lowers poverty rates and increases entrepreneurship. However, amongst other control variables, only higher education completion is significant for income inequality. These results indicate that whilst economies that have attained greater financial inclusion have significantly lower poverty rates for both income groups, the estimated reduction in poverty is larger for low-income countries.

Given the results presented in Tables 4.3, 4.4a, and 4.4b, we explore interaction effects between financial inclusion and country income groups. This helps in assessing whether financial inclusion is sufficient in lowering poverty and income inequality and how it interacts with other factors associated with country income levels. As suggested by Beck et al. (2009), financial access may

Table 4.4b Estimates on poverty, income inequality, entrepreneurship, and female borrowing, middle-low-, and low-income countries

Variables	*Poverty*$_{2014-17}$	*Income inequality*$_{2014-17}$	*Entrepre*$_{2014-17}$	*Female empower*$_{2014-17}$
Financial inclusion$_{2011-14}$	−1.403*** [−2.927]	0.168 [0.914]	0.112* [1.953]	−0.110 [−0.433]
Education completion$_{2011-13}$	0.100 [0.691]	−0.116* [−1.846]	−0.027 [−1.126]	−0.058 [−0.713]
Growth$_{2011-13}$	0.631 [0.478]	−0.339 [−0.758]	0.198 [1.580]	0.253 [0.426]
Constant	59.116*** [6.305]	44.530*** [14.177]	6.930*** [6.728]	47.575*** [9.648]
Observations	50	30	52	52
R-squared	0.169	0.167	0.103	0.030

Source: Authors' calculations

Notes: Dependent variables are average values of poverty, income inequality, entrepreneurship, and female borrowing for 2014–17. The regressors are average values of financial inclusion for 2011 and 2014; and education completion and GDP growth rates for 2011–13. Refer to Table 4.2 for middle-low (MLI) and low-income (LIC) country list. *** p<0.01, ** p<0.05, * p<0.1. Robust standard errors are used for t-stats reported in brackets.

reduce poverty and income inequality not only through the direct provision of financial services to low-income groups but also through higher wage savings and participation in the formal sector of an economy. For middle-low- and low-income countries, indirect effects may exceed the direct effects because of inefficient financial systems and the ineffective provision of financial services to the poor. More importantly, exploring the interaction effects between financial inclusion and country income groups allows us to assess whether the impact of financial inclusion on poverty for a specific income group is particularly greater or smaller than for other income groups. Such differences in the financial inclusion impact on poverty by country income groups would help understand the pattern of nonlinear financial inclusion effects across country groupings.

Tables 4.5a–4.5d present the results when we control for different income groups and their interaction effects with financial inclusion to assess whether belonging to a specific income group produces a significantly different impact on our parameters of interest compared to other groups. Table 4.5a validates that higher financial inclusion significantly lowers poverty rates and increases entrepreneurship for the high-income group, whilst we do not see the same effect for income inequality and female borrowing. Interestingly, however, the estimates for interactive terms indicate that, for high-income countries, a one-unit increase in financial inclusion raises poverty rates significantly by around 0.03% whilst for all other income groups it lowers poverty by about 1.40%. The finding that financial

Table 4.5a Estimates on poverty, income inequality, entrepreneurship, and female borrowing, with high-income interaction effects

Variables	$Poverty_{2014\text{–}17}$	*Income* $inequality_{2014\text{–}17}$	$Entrepre_{2014\text{–}17}$	*Female* $empower_{2014\text{–}17}$
Financial $inclusion_{2011\text{-}14}$	−1 397***	0.158	0.073*	0.022
	[−5.044]	[1.403]	[1.968]	[0.146]
Education $completion_{2011\text{-}13}$	−0.015	−0.155***	−0.017	−0.021
	[−0.146]	[−3.844]	[−0.967]	[−0.357]
$Growth_{2011\text{-}13}$	0.658	0.408	0.224**	0.674
	[0.906]	[1.388]	[2.305]	[1.605]
HIC	−59.342***	2.889	−7.506***	−28.228***
	[−8.329]	[0.591]	[−3.691]	[−4.116]
HIC*financial $inclusion_{2011\text{-}14}$	1 429* * *	−0.168	0.263***	0.851***
	[5.872]	[−1.320]	[4.979]	[4.394]
Constant	59.647***	43.546***	6.465***	41.581***
	[7.535]	[15.707]	[7.180]	[10.104]
Observations	121	90	127	127
R-squared	0.590	0.335	0.521	0.313

Source: Authors' calculations.

HIC = high-income countries

Notes: Dependent variables are average values of poverty, income inequality, entrepreneurship, and female borrowing for 2014–2017. The regressors are average values of financial inclusion for 2011 and 2014; and education completion and GDP growth rates for 2011–2013. Refer to Table 4.2 for the list of countries in each country income group. *** p<0.01, ** p<0.05, * p<0.1. Robust standard errors are used for t-stats reported in brackets.

inclusion increases poverty in high-income countries might reflect the impact of recent financial crises and economic downturn in advanced economies, which drove some households below the poverty line despite the increase in financial inclusiveness.[16] Table 4.5a also reveals that higher financial inclusion increases entrepreneurship for high-income countries more than for other income groups. This suggests that financial inclusion has a more potent impact on entrepreneurial activities for high-income countries.

Tables 4.5b–4.5d show that higher financial inclusion reduces poverty rates and increases entrepreneurship and female borrowing for all other income groups. However, the significance of interaction terms between financial inclusion and country income group varies across the income groups. In Table 5b, for middle-high-income countries, the interaction term is significant such that a one-unit increase in financial inclusion significantly reduces poverty rates by around 0.22%. But the decline for other income groups is even larger at around 1.00%. This finding may reflect that middle-high-income countries have significantly lower poverty rates than other income groups and that the marginal decline in poverty would be smaller for an additional increase in financial inclusion. For middle-low-income countries, in Table 4.5c, the interaction term is

Table 4.5b Estimates on poverty, income inequality, entrepreneurship, and female borrowing, with middle-high-income interaction effects

Variables	*Poverty*$_{2014-17}$	*Income inequality*$_{2014-17}$	*Entrepre*$_{2014-17}$	*Female empower*$_{2014-7}$
Financial inclusion$_{2011-14}$	–0.996***	0.037	0.221***	0.431***
	[–6.399]	[0.668]	[8.318]	[4.126]
Education completion$_{2011-13}$	–0.070	_0 149***	–0.027	–0.062
	[–0.730]	[–3.925]	[–1.590]	[–1.030]
Growth$_{2011-13}$	0.536	0.476**	0.137	0.546
	[0.832]	[2.097]	[1.136]	[1.172]
MHI	–34.489***	6.832*	–0.490	–4.294
	[–4.197]	[1.811]	[–0.322]	[–0.510]
MHI*Financial Inclusion$_{2011-14}$	0.773***	–0.092	–0.085	–0.036
	[3.303]	[–0.867]	[–1.407]	[–0.123]
Constant	58.194***	43.531***	5.669***	38.653***
	[8.530]	[18.763]	[5.004]	[8.110]
Observations	121	90	127	127
R-squared	0.553	0.359	0.490	0.228

Source: Authors' calculations.

Notes: Dependent variables are average values of poverty, income inequality, entrepreneurship, and female borrowing for 2014–2017. The regressors are average values of financial inclusion for 2011 and 2014; and education completion and GDP growth rates for 2011–2013. Refer to Table 4.2 for the list of countries in each country income group. *** p<0.01, ** p<0.05, * p<0.1. Robust standard errors are used for t-stats reported in brackets.

insignificant, suggesting that the impact of financial inclusion on middle-low-income countries is not statistically different from other income groups. For low-income countries in Table 4.5d, a one-unit increase in financial inclusion leads to a significant drop in poverty rates by around 3.33%, whereas the decline for other income groups is around 0.83%. Again, this result may be because low-income countries have significantly higher poverty rates than other income groups. So, the decline in poverty would be greater for any given increase in financial inclusion. On the contrary, the estimates show that a one-unit increase in financial inclusion leads to a slightly lower female borrowing (by around 0.19%) for the middle-low-income group. This contrasts with the finding that a unit increase in financial inclusion is positively correlated with female borrowing for all but high-income groups, consistent with Buvinić and Furst-Nichols (2016), Calderon et al. (2016), Ghosh and Vinod (2017), and Swamy (2014). This irregular income pattern suggests that the effect of financial inclusion on female borrowing may be subject to various socio-political and cultural backgrounds, irrespective of country income.

The estimates also show that educational attainment reduces poverty and income inequality, in line with previous studies. However, educational attainment has a negative relationship with entrepreneurship, which shows up consistently

Table 4.5c Estimates on poverty, income inequality, entrepreneurship, and female borrowing, with middle-low-income interaction effects

Variables	$Poverty_{2014\text{–}17}$	$Income\ inequality_{2014\text{–}17}$	$Entrepre_{2014\text{–}17}$	$Female\ empower_{2014\text{–}17}$
Financial inclusion$_{2011\text{–}14}$	−0.753***	0.034	0.251***	0.536***
	[−4.312]	[0.586]	[8.503]	[5.049]
Education completion$_{2011\text{–}13}$	−0.148	−0 145***	−0.036**	−0.080
	[−1.519]	[−3.988]	[−2.153]	[−1.381]
Growth$_{2011\text{–}13}$	0.492	0.605**	0.272**	1.140**
	[0.740]	[2.276]	[2.385]	[2.582]
MLI	12.921	1.190	2.470*	10.182*
	[1.206]	[0.305]	[1.880]	[1.870]
MLI*financial inclusion$_{2011\text{–}14}$	−0.087	−0.089	−0.131**	−0.727***
	[−0.193]	[−0.531]	[−2.089]	[−2.786]
Constant	50.342***	44.165***	4.058***	33.601***
	[6.255]	[14.176]	[3.276]	[7.165]
Observations	121	90	127	127
R-squared	0.528	0.303	0.437	0.244

Source: Authors' calculations.

Notes: Dependent variables are average values of poverty, income inequality, entrepreneurship, and female borrowing for 2014–2017. The regressors are average values of financial inclusion for 2011 and 2014; and education completion and GDP growth rates for 2011–2013. Refer to Table 4.2 for the list of countries in each country income group. *** p<0.01, ** p<0.05, * p<0.1. Robust standard errors are used for t-stats reported in brackets.

across our regression results. A possible explanation is that people without higher education are more likely to start their own business as they might have insufficient qualifications to be employed in the formal sector and, hence, they become more entrepreneurial.

Taken together, our key findings suggest that although higher financial inclusion lowers poverty rates for all income groups, the magnitude to which poverty drops given an increase in financial inclusion is higher for low-income groups. In other words, although financial inclusion in general lowers poverty across all income groups, the marginal reduction in poverty is the largest for low-income countries. This reflects the structural features associated with varying stages of economic development. This is new to the financial inclusion empirical literature, but in line with the model predictions of Bhattacharya and Patnaik (2015).

The baseline results hold in sensitivity tests. First, instead of using one indicator or dimension weight for all economies, we use varying weights across different income groups for alternative tests. The rationale for using varying income weights pertains more to the different degrees of financial development across the sample. Table 4.6 presents the results using varying dimension weights. The estimates show that the baseline findings hold. This is expected, as there is little

Table 4.5d Estimates on poverty, income inequality, entrepreneurship, and female borrowing, with low-income interaction effects

Variables	*Poverty*$_{2014-17}$	*Income inequality*$_{2014-17}$	*Entrepre*$_{2014-17}$	*Female empower*$_{2014-17}$
Financial inclusion$_{2011-14}$	−0.826***	0.012	0.237***	0.482***
	[−4.964]	[0.210]	[9.086]	[4.692]
Education completion$_{2011-13}$	−0.022	−0.193***	−0.013	−0.006
	[−0.209]	[−5.213]	[−0.719]	[−0.091]
Growth$_{2011-13}$	0.570	0.560**	0.135	0.425
	[0.803]	[2.291]	[1.157]	[0.877]
LIC	33.912**	−15.936***	2.578	8.381
	[2.566]	[−4.870]	[1.444]	[1.203]
LIC*financial inclusion$_{2011-14}$	−2.500**	1 149***	0.129	0.558
	[−2.042]	[5.317]	[0.524]	[0.854]
Constant	44.701***	48.966***	3.115**	30.871***
	[5.471]	[18.538]	[2.459]	[5.385]
Observations	121	90	127	127
R-squared	0.541	0.378	0.469	0.272

Source: Authors' calculations.

Notes: Dependent variables are average values of poverty, income inequality, entrepreneurship, and female borrowing for 2014–2017. The regressors are average values of financial inclusion for 2011 and 2014; and education completion and GDP growth rates for 2011–2013. Refer to Table 4.2 for the list of countries in each country income group. *** $p<0.01$, ** $p<0.05$, * $p<0.1$. Robust standard errors are used for t-stats reported in brackets.

difference between the financial inclusion index when country group weights are used (Table 4.1).

Second, Tables 4.3 and 4.6 present the baseline estimates in a cross-sectional lagged form. We run pooled ordinary least squares (OLS) estimation and panel-fixed effects regressions with country and time-fixed effects separately for robustness checks. Tables 4.7a–4.7c present the results for pooled panel with country-fixed effects and panel with time-fixed effects on the significance of financial inclusion on poverty, income inequality, entrepreneurship, and female borrowing. The estimation uses 2014 and 2017 values of dependent variables regressed on the 2011 and 2014 values of the regressors, such that the poverty rate for 2017 is regressed on financial inclusion for 2014. The estimates using pooled OLS (Table 4.7a) and panel with time-fixed effects (Table 4.7c) are consistent with the baseline estimates in Table 4.3, where we find that higher financial inclusion significantly reduces poverty rates and increases entrepreneurship and female borrowing. As expected, the results for panel estimation with country-fixed effects in Table 4.7b show no significant relationship. These suggest that the relationship between poverty, entrepreneurship, female borrowing, and financial inclusion lies within cross-country differences and not with the time variation, perhaps due to having a shorter sample period. These results not only

Table 4.6 Estimates on poverty, income inequality, entrepreneurship, and female borrowing using varying dimension weights

Variables	$Poverty_{2014\text{–}17}$	*Income* $Inequality_{2014\text{–}17}$	$Entrepre_{2014\text{–}17}$	*Female* $Empower_{2014\text{–}17}$
Financial inclusion$_{2011\text{–}14}$	−0.881***	0.036	0.212***	0.424***
	[−5.427]	[0.693]	[8.043]	[4.253]
Education completion$_{2011\text{–}13}$	−0.142	−0.149***	−0.023	−0.057
	[−1.486]	[−4.269]	[−1.389]	[−1.004]
Growth$_{2011\text{–}13}$	0.485	0.543**	0.184	0.617
	[0.729]	[2.191]	[1.632]	[1.329]
Constant	55.953***	44.562***	4.891***	37.132***
	[7.991]	[18.018]	[4.435]	[7.780]
Observations	121	90	127	127
R-squared	0.500	0.303	0.383	0.178

Source: Authors' calculations.

Notes: Dependent variables are average values of poverty, income inequality, entrepreneurship, and female borrowing for 2014–2017. The regressors are average values of financial inclusion for 2011 and 2014; and education completion and GDP growth rates for 2011–2013. *** p<0.01, ** p<0.05, * p<0.1. Robust standard errors are used for t-stats reported in brackets.

Table 4.7a Pooled OLS estimates on the index of financial inclusion

Variables	$Poverty_t$	*Income* $inequality_t$	$Entrepre_t$	*Female* $empower_t$
Financial inclusion$_{t-1}$	−0.811***	0.026	0.214***	0.423***
	[−7.441]	[0.746]	[4.198]	[6.030]
Education completion$_{t-1}$	−0.140*	−0.158***	−0.030	−0.080*
	[−1.913]	[−6.309]	[−1.348]	[−1.900]
Growth$_{t-1}$	0.250	0.357***	0.111	0.325
	[0.473]	[3.007]	[0.894]	[1.014]
Constant	53.413***	45.523***	5.428***	39.452***
	[10.379]	[26.570]	[4.263]	[12.582]
Observations	201	161	254	244
R-squared	0.482	0.310	0.124	0.180

Source: Authors' calculations.

Notes: Dependent variables are for 2014 and 2017. Regressors are lagged values for 2011 and 2014, respectively. *** p<0.01, ** p<0.05, * p<0.1. Robust standard errors are used.

validate the baseline estimates but also support the empirical specification shown in Equation 4.5.

Third, we perform a sensitivity test with the female labour force participation rate as a proxy for female empowerment instead of the female borrowing used in our baseline models. Female borrowing is defined as the percentage of the female population aged 15 years and above who borrowed from a financial

Table 4.7b Panel estimates with country fixed effects

Variables	*Poverty*$_t$	*Income inequality*$_t$	*Entrepre*$_t$	*Female empower*$_t$
Financial inclusion$_{t-1}$	–0.105	–0.098	–0.061	–0.134
	[–1.339]	[–1.531]	[–0.194]	[–0.585]
Education completion $_{t-1}$	–0.108	–0.039	2.757***	–0.860
	[–1.201]	[–0.230]	[2.685]	[–1.005]
Growth$_{t-1}$	–0.081	0.016	–0.123	0.115
	[–0.549]	[0.222]	[–0.512]	[0.443]
Constant	38.704***	34.329**	–59.158**	51.198**
	[13.082]	[2.460]	[–2.332]	[2.338]
Observations	201	161	254	244
R-squared	0.998	0.994	0.333	0.888

Source: Authors' calculations.

Notes: Dependent variables are for 2014 and 2017. Regressors are lagged values for 2011 and 2014, respectively. Country dummies are included. *** p<0.01, ** p<0.05, * p<0.1. Robust standard errors are used.

Table 4.7c Panel estimates with time-fixed effects

Variables	*Poverty*$_t$	*Income inequality*$_t$	*Entrepre*$_t$	*Female empower*$_t$
Financial inclusion$_{t-1}$	–0.802***	0.028	0.205***	0.429***
	[–7.388]	[0.818]	[4.782]	[6.137]
Education completion$_{t-1}$	–0.142*	–0.162***	–0.024	–0.083*
	[–1.940]	[–6.547]	[–1.106]	[–1.969]
Growth$_{t-1}$	0.208	0.380***	0.224*	0.262
	[0.397]	[3.131]	[1.802]	[0.839]
Constant	55.288***	45.142***	1.458	41.882***
	[10.215]	[25.863]	[0.847]	[12.444]
Observations	201	161	254	244
R-squared	0.487	0.317	0.257	0.201

Source: Author's calculation.

Notes: Dependent variables are for 2014 and 2017. Regressors are lagged values for 2011 and 2014, respectively. Time dummies are included. *** p<0.01, ** p<0.05, * p<0.1. Robust standard errors are used.

institution for any purpose, which might be correlated with our IFI. Instead, the female labour force participation rate is defined as the percentage of female population between ages 15 and 64 who are in the labour force. Table 4.8 presents the findings. They are consistent with the baseline results such that we find higher financial inclusion improves female borrowing, but mostly for

Table 4.8 Estimates on female borrowing, using female labour force participation rate

Variables	*Female* $empower_{2014\text{–}17}$	*Female* $empower_{2014\text{–}17}$	*Female* $empower_{2014\text{–}17}$
Financial inclusion$_{2011\text{–}14}$	0.391***	0.280***	–0.206
	[3.367]	[2.823]	[–0.739]
Education completion$_{2011\text{–}13}$	–0.041	0.330***	–0.195**
	[–0.619]	[3.610]	[–2.365]
Growth$_{2011\text{–}13}$	0.935	0.327	3.166***
	[1.508]	[0.512]	[2.969]
Constant	46.235***	23 419***	48.846***
	[7.814]	[2.677]	[7.705]
Sample	All	Advanced	Developing
Observations	130	77	53
R-squared	0.103	0.364	0.230

Source: Authors' calculations.

Notes: Dependent variable refers to female labour force participation rate for 2014–2017. The regressors are average values of financial inclusion for 2011 and 2014; and education completion and GDP growth rates for 2011–2013. Column 2 includes high- and middle-high-income countries, whilst column 3 includes middle-low- and low-income countries. *** p<0.01, ** p<0.05, * p<0.1.

developed economies. The results may reflect the well-known phenomenon of the U-shaped relationship between women's labour force participation and economic development (Goldin, 1995).

Finally, we run sensitivity tests using instrument variables to mitigate the endogeneity concerns. Whilst we used lagged regressors in our baseline models, which could address endogeneity concerns, the persistence of our regressors might bias our estimates. But the efficiency of two-stage least squares estimation depends on the validity or strength of the instrument candidate. Unfortunately, finding a suitable or valid instrument in a cross-country regression set-up is extremely difficult. Nonetheless, we use alternative instruments given our small sample size with Fuller's (1977) modified limited information maximum likelihood estimation (LIML), where we set Fuller's α parameter to 4. In effect, the FLIML modifies the LIML estimator by subtracting from LIML root, λ_0, a number which is asymptotically negligible as the sample size increases (Davidson and MacKinnon, 1993; Kadiyala and Oberhelman, 1992). We employ the savings rate and a measure of rule of law as instrument variables. The savings rate is a potential candidate as it reflects differentials across income groups, whilst the rule of law may represent lesser market imperfections. Both candidates are weak instruments based on Cragg-Donald Wald F statistics. Nevertheless, our results hold under these weak instruments, which justifies the use of lagged regressors in our baseline specification. Tables 4.9a and 4.9b present the results using the savings rate and rule of law as instruments. The estimates are in line with the baseline results in Table 4.3.

Table 4.9a Estimates on poverty, income inequality, entrepreneurship, and female borrowing, using savings rate as instrument

Variables	*Poverty*$_{2014-17}$	*Income inequality*$_{2014-17}$	*Entrepre*$_{2014-17}$	*Female empower*$_{2014-17}$
Financial inclusion$_{2011-14}$	-0891*** [-5.422]	0.022 [0.413]	0230*** [8.538]	0.457*** [4.488]
Education completion$_{2011-13}$	-0.120 [-1.197]	-0.145*** [-3.902]	-0.034** [-2.057]	-0.078 [-1.353]
Growth$_{2011-13}$	0.586 [0.881]	0.512** [2.150]	0.190* [1.674]	0.625 [1.345]
Constant	55.075*** [7.915]	44.787*** [18.439]	4.933*** [4.540]	37.239*** [7.843]
Observations	121	90	127	127
R-squared	0.501	0.300	0.426	0.200

Source: Authors' calculations.

Notes: Dependent variables are average values of poverty, income inequality, entrepreneurship, and female borrowing for 2014–2017. The regressors are average values of financial inclusion for 2011 and 2014; and education completion and GDP growth rates for 2011–2013. Financial inclusion measure instrumented with savings rate for 2011–2014. Estimates based on Fuller limited information maximum likelihood with alpha set to 4. *** p<0.01, ** p<0.05, * p<0.1.

Table 4.9b Estimates on poverty, income inequality, entrepreneurship, and female borrowing, using rule of law as instrument

Variables	*Poverty*$_{2014-17}$	*Income Inequality*$_{2014-17}$	*Entrepre*$_{2014-17}$	*Female Empower*$_{2014-17}$
Financial inclusion$_{2011-14}$	−1.080*** [−5.165]	0.013 [0.169]	0265*** [6.556]	0.458*** [3.532]
Education completion$_{2011-13}$	−0.049 [−0.472]	−0.142*** [−3.526]	−0.046** [−2.329]	−0.078 [−1.223]
Growth$_{2011-13}$	0.246 [0.349]	0.494* [1.809]	0.252* [1.857]	0.627 [1.438]
Constant	57.323*** [9.061]	44.898*** [17.601]	4.530*** [3.706]	37.222*** [9.474]
Observations	121	90	127	127
R-squared	0.494	0.300	0.419	0.200

Source: Authors' calculations.

Notes: Dependent variables are average values of poverty, income inequality, entrepreneurship, and female borrowing for 2014–2017. The regressors are average values of financial inclusion for 2011 and 2014; and education completion and GDP growth rates for 2011–2013. Financial inclusion measure instrumented with rule of law for 2011–2014. Estimates based on Fuller limited information maximum likelihood with alpha set to 4. *** p<0.01, ** p<0.05, * p<0.1.

4.5 Conclusions

Financial inclusion has emerged as a major policy goal for governments across the world, but empirical evidence of its effects on poverty reduction and other social benefits has been elusive at the macro level. In this chapter, we assess the heterogeneous effects of financial inclusion on poverty and other social goals across different country income levels.

To overcome data limitations for a comprehensive financial inclusion measure at the macro level, we constructed a new IFI for 151 economies using weights derived from the PCA in aggregating indicators for access, availability, and usage to examine the cross-country variations in the relationship between financial inclusion and other economic variables. Using the World Bank Global Findex database, we combined a multidimensional approach with the normalised weights from the PCA in deriving our index. The IFI shows that the weights using the PCA are relatively stable for three survey periods, suggesting its suitability in measuring cross-country variations in financial inclusion.

Using our new index, this chapter assessed the cross-country impact of financial inclusion on poverty, income inequality, entrepreneurship, and female empowerment. Using a cross-sectional approach, our estimates provided robust evidence that higher financial inclusion significantly lowers poverty rates, raises entrepreneurship, and boosts female borrowing. Also, splitting the sample by country income groups, we found that higher financial inclusion significantly lowers poverty rates and increases entrepreneurship for all income groups. However, the impacts of financial inclusion on poverty and other social goals are heterogeneous across country income groups, with the unit increase in financial inclusion associated with the largest reduction in poverty for low-income countries.

Notes

1 An earlier version of this draft was presented at the Financial Development and Inclusion Workshop hosted by the Centre for Applied Finance and Economics of the University of South Australia, Adelaide, Australia, on 1–2 December 2017; and at the University of South Australia–ERIA–Lee Kuan Yew School of Public Policy Financial Inclusion Workshop, 30–31 May 2019, in Singapore. The authors thank the discussant and participants for comments and suggestions which have been incorporated in this chapter. The views expressed in this chapter are those of the authors and do not necessarily reflect the views and policies of the Asian Development Bank, its Board of Governors, or the governments they represent.

2 We define nonlinearities as a case when the impact varies across country income groups such that it is relevant for certain income groups, and not for others. We do not mean nonlinearities in functional form.

3 Although Amidžić et al. (2014) defined proxies for a quality measure, they did not include it in their composite indicator due to a lack of reliable and available data.

4 Camara and Tuesta (2014) argued that barriers to financial access must be included as a dimension of financial inclusion as they reflect demand-side measures of financial services. However, demand-side indicators could also be included in a multidimensional approach. In other words, the lack of demand-side measures in existing financial

inclusion measures does not fully justify the inclusion of a barriers dimension in the aggregate financial inclusion measure.

5 We classify the percentage of the adult population with bank accounts as access and not as usage, in line with the existing studies on financial access (Beck et al., 2009; Honohan, 2007, 2008; Park and Mercado, 2016, 2018; Sarma, 2008, 2015).

6 Some institutional measures using PCA include the KOF Index of Globalization (KOF Swiss Economic Institute), the Economic Freedom of the World Index (Economic Freedom Network), the Chicago Fed National Activity Index (Federal Reserve Bank of Chicago), the Kansas City Financial Stress Index (Federal Reserve Bank of Kansas City), and the General Indicator of Science and Technology (National Institute of Science and Technology Policy, Japan).

7 We set the minimum value for each indicator at zero.

8 Appendix 4.1 lists data definitions and sources.

9 We explored the option of including point-of-sales data from the Global Findex database. Unfortunately, data are available for only 78 economies and the survey period is unspecified.

10 Table 4.1 also presents the weights of each indicator and dimension using country income group samples. Note that similar patterns hold as in the full sample weights.

11 We tested for the significance of each indicator on each dimension and the significance of each dimension on individual country overall financial inclusion index. The regression results show that all indicators and dimensions indices are significant.

12 We considered including productivity as one of our explanatory variables. However, any changes in productivity are captured by the average GDP growth rate. Moreover, we include overall GDP growth rate, rather than the determinants of growth rates, to avoid multicollinearities. We included education completion as control for human capital and average income.

13 Refer to Table 4.2 for the country income groups, and Appendix 4.1 for the full list of data notes and sources.

14 We ran similar estimation including rule of law. However, we found that it is highly correlated with financial inclusion, such that the unconditional correlation between rule of law and financial inclusion is significant at 0.83. This leads to multicollinearity when both rule of law and financial inclusion are included in the empirical specification. Hence, we opted to drop rule of law in our current specification.

15 We combined high- and middle-high-income and middle-low- and low-income countries in both regressions to have enough sample size to assume normality of both samples.

16 This result is in line with the actual poverty trends for most advanced economies in recent years, 2014–2017. In most cases, high-income countries have not reduced their poverty. However, poverty rates have been rising in a significant number of high-income countries, including the likes of Austria, Germany, Spain, the United Kingdom, and even Sweden.

References

Allen, F., A. Demirgüç-Kunt, L. Klapper, and M.S. Martinez Peria (2012), 'The Foundations of Financial Inclusion: Understanding Ownership and Use of Formal Accounts', *World Bank Policy Research Working Paper*, No. 6290. Washington, DC: World Bank.

Amidžić, G., A. Massara, and A. Mialou (2014), 'Assessing Countries' Financial Inclusion Standing – A New Composite Index', *IMF Working Paper*, No. 14/36. Washington, DC: IMF.

Ashraf, N., D. Karlan, and W. Yin (2010), 'Female Empowerment; Further Evidence from a Commitment Savings Product in the Philippines', *World Development,* 28(3), pp.333–44.

Barro, R.J. and J-W Lee (2013), 'A New Data Set of Educational Attainment in the World, 1950–2010', *Journal of Development Economics,* 104(C), pp.184–98.

Beck, T., A. Demirgüç-Kunt, and P. Honohan (2009), 'Access to Financial Services: Measurement, Impact, and Policies', *The World Bank Research Observer,* 24(1), pp.119–45.

Bhattacharya, R. and I. Patnaik (2015), 'Financial Inclusion, Productivity Shocks, and Consumption Volatility in Emerging Economies', *The World Bank Economic Review,* 30(1), pp.171–201.

Burgess, R. and R. Pande (2005), 'Do Rural Banks Matter? Evidence from the Indian Social Banking Experiment', *American Economic Review* 95(3), pp.780–95.

Buvinić, M. and R. Furst-Nichols (2016), 'Promoting Women's Economic Empowerment: What Works?', *The World Bank Research Observer,* 31(1), pp.59–101.

Calderon, G., L. Iacovone, and L. Juarez (2016), 'Opportunity versus Necessity: Understanding the Heterogeneity of Female Micro-Entrepreneurs', *The World Bank Economic Review,* 30(1), pp.86–96.

Camara, N. and D. Tuesta (2014), 'Measuring Financial Inclusion: A Multidimensional Index', *BBVA Research Working Paper,* No. 14/26. Madrid: BBVA.

Davidson, R. and J.G. MacKinnon (1993), *Estimation and Inference in Econometrics.* New York: Oxford University Press.

Demirgüç-Kunt, A. and L. Klapper (2012), 'Measuring Financial Inclusion: The Global Findex Database', *World Bank Policy Research Working Paper,* No. 6025. Washington, DC: World Bank.

Dupas, P. and J. Robinson (2009), 'Savings Constraints and Microenterprise Development: Evidence from a Field Experiment in Kenya', *NBER Working Paper,* No. 14693. Cambridge, MA: National Bureau of Economic Research.

Fuller, W.A. (1977), 'Some Properties of a Modification of the Limited Information Estimator', *Econometrica,* 45(4), pp.939–53.

Ghosh, S. and D. Vinod (2017), 'What Constrains Financial Inclusion for Women? Evidence from Indian Micro Data', *World Development,* 92 (C), pp.60–81.

Gimet, C. and T. Lagoarde-Segot (2012), 'Financial Sector Development and Access to Finance. Does Size Say It All?', *Emerging Markets Review,* 13 (3), pp.316–37.

Goldin, C. (1995), 'The U-Shaped Female Labor Force Function in Economic Development and Economic History', in T. Paul Schultz (ed.), *Investment in Women's Human Capital and Economic Development.* Chicago: University of Chicago Press, pp.61–90.

Honohan, P. (2004), 'Financial Development, Growth, and Poverty: How Close Are the Links?', *World Bank Policy Research Working Paper,* No. 3203. Washington, DC: World Bank.

Honohan, P. (2007), 'Cross-Country Variation in Household Access to Financial Services', World Bank paper prepared for the conference 'Access to Finance', 15–16 March, Washington, DC.

Honohan, P. (2008), 'Cross-Country Variation in Household Access to Financial Services', *Journal of Banking and Finance,* 32 (11), pp.2493–2500.

Kadiyala, K.R. and D. Oberhelman (1992), 'Optimizing in the Class of Fuller Modified Limited Information Maximum Likelihood Estimators', *Journal of Multivariate Analysis,* 43 (2), pp.218–36.

Leyshon, A. and N. Thrift (1995), 'Geographies of Financial Exclusion: Financial Abandonment in Britain and the United States', *Transactions of the Institute of British Geographers,* 20(3), pp.312–41.

Organisation for Economic Co-operation and Development (n.d.), OECD Statistics, https://stats.oecd.org/ (accessed 15 November 2017).

Park, C-Y. and R.V. Mercado Jr. (2016), 'Does Financial Inclusion Reduce Poverty and Income Inequality in Developing Asia?', in S. Gopalan and T. Kikuchi (eds.), *Financial Inclusion in Asia: Issues and Policy Concerns.* London: Palgrave Macmillan, pp.61–92.

Park, C-Y. and R.V. Mercado Jr. (2018). 'Financial Inclusion, Poverty, and Income Inequality', *Singapore Economic Review,* 63(1), pp.1–22.

Perez-Moreno, S. (2011), 'Financial Development and Poverty in Developing Countries: A Causal Analysis', *Empirical Economics,* 41(1), pp.57–80.

Ramahan, M. (2011), 'Access to Financing and Firm Growth', *Journal of Banking and Finance,* 35(3), pp.709–23.

Rewilak, J. (2013), 'Finance Is Good for the Poor but It Depends Where You Live', *Journal of Banking and Finance,* 37 (5), pp.1451–59.

Rewilak, J. (2017), 'The Role of Financial Development in Poverty Reduction', *Review of Development Finance,* 7 (2), pp.169–76.

Rojas-Suarez, L. (2010), 'Access to Financial Services in Emerging Powers: Facts, Obstacles, and Policy Implications', *OECD Global Development Background Papers.* Paris: Organisation for Economic Co-operation and Development.

Sarma, M. (2008), 'Index of Financial Inclusion', *Working Paper,* No. 215. New Delhi: Indian Council for Research on International Economic Relations.

Sarma, M. (2015), 'Measuring Financial Inclusion', *Economics Bulletin,* 35(1), pp.604–11.

Sinclair, S. (2001), 'Financial Exclusion: An Introductory Survey', Report from the Centre for Research in Socially Inclusive Services. Edinburgh: Heriot-Watt University.

Swamy, V. (2014), 'Financial Inclusion, Gender Dimension, and Economic Impact on Poor Households', *World Development,* 56(C), pp.1–15.

UNESCO Institute for Statistics, http://uis.unesco.org/ (accessed 15 November 2017).

United Nations University World Institute for Development Economics Research (UNU-WIDER) (n.d.), World Income Inequality Database (accessed 15 November 2017).

World Bank (2014), *Global Financial Development Report 2014: Financial Inclusion.* Washington, DC: World Bank.

World Bank (2017), PovcalNet, http://iresearch.worldbank.org/PovcalNet/povOnDemand.aspx (accessed 15 November 2017).

World Bank, Global Financial Inclusion Database, https://datacatalog.worldbank.org/dataset/global-financial-inclusion-global-findex-database (accessed 15 November 2017).

World Bank, World Development Indicators, http://datatopics.worldbank.org/world-development-indicators/ (accessed 15 November 2017).

Zhang, Q. and A. Posso (2017), 'Thinking Inside the Box: A Closer Look at Financial Inclusion and Household Income', *The Journal of Development Studies,* 55(7), https://doi.org/10.1080/00220388.2017.1380798.

Appendix 4.1 Data, definitions, and sources

Variable	*Definitions*	*Sources*
Account (% ages 15+)	Population 15 years old and above to total population with an account in a financial institution	World Bank, Global Financial Inclusion database
Credit card (% ages 15+)	Population 15 years old and above to total population with a credit card	World Bank, Global Financial Inclusion database
Debit card (% ages 15+)	Population 15 years old and above to total population with a debit card	World Bank, Global Financial Inclusion database
Mobile money account (% age 15+)	Population 15 years old and above to total population with mobile money account	World Bank, Global Financial Inclusion database
Branches	Number of commercial bank branches per 100,000 adult population	World Bank, World Development Indicators
ATMs	Number of ATMs per 100,000 adult population	World Bank, World Development Indicators
Borrower (% ages 15+)	Borrowed from a financial institution, percentage of population 15 years old and above	World Bank, Global Financial Inclusion database
Saver (% ages 15+)	Saved in a financial institution, percentage of population 15 years old and above	World Bank, Global Financial Inclusion database
Credit (% GDP)	Domestic credit to the private sector as percentage of nominal GDP	World Bank, World Development Indicators
$\text{Poverty}_{2014\text{–}17}$	Average of poverty headcount ratio at national poverty lines for 2014–2017 (percentage of population)	Asian Development Bank, World Bank (World Development Indicators) and World Poverty Clock at www.worldpoverty.io
$\text{Income inequality}_{2014\text{–}17}$	Average of Gini index for 2014–2017	Asian Development Bank, Chart Book Economic Inequality, OECD Statistics, UNU-WIDER, and World Bank (World Development Indicators and PovcalNet)
$\text{Entrepreneurship}_{2014\text{–}17}$	Average values for 2014 and 2017 of population aged 15 and above who borrowed to start, operate, or expand a farm or business (%)	World Bank, Global Financial Inclusion database

(*continued*)

Appendix 4.1 Cont.

Variable	*Definitions*	*Sources*
Female $\text{empower}_{2014\text{–}17}$	Average values for 2014 and 2017 of the percentage of female population aged 15 and above who borrowed in a financial institution for any purpose (%) Alternative measure: female labour force participation rate (% of female population aged 15–64 years)	World Bank, Global Financial Inclusion database
Financial $\text{inclusion}_{2011\text{-}14}$	Average financial inclusion index for 2011 and 2014	Financial $\text{inclusion}_{2011\text{-}14}$
Education $\text{completion}_{2011\text{-}13}$	Average value of the percentage of population aged 25 and above who attained or completed lower secondary education; values can be for an earlier period of 2011–2013 for which data are unavailable	Barro and Lee Database, UNESCO Institute of Statistics, World Bank (World Development Indicators)
Savings $\text{rate}_{2011\text{-}14}$	Savings rate in percent of GDP is calculated as GDP less final consumption expenditure	World Bank, World Governance Indicators
Rule of $\text{law}_{2011\text{-}14}$	Values refer to the average of the percentile ranking of countries	World Bank, World Governance Indicators

Source: Authors' enumeration.

5 Financial inclusion and macroeconomic volatility in Asia[1]

Sasidaran Gopalan, Ramkishen S. Rajan, and Aizhan Sharipova*

5.1 Introduction

Greater financial inclusion remains a key policy priority for several emerging market and developing economies (EMDEs), especially those in Asia, and is likely to enable several of the UN's sustainable development goals (SDGs) (Klapper, El-Zoghbi, and Hess, 2016). While the related literature has recognised that expanding financial services can promote equitable economic growth, scant attention seems to have been paid to the nexus between financial inclusion and output volatility.

Why should output volatility matter? Over the past three decades, several papers have documented the importance of moderating output volatility and insulating economies from exogenous shocks by smoothing aggregate fluctuations. One of the central reasons why output volatility matters is because of its impact on economic growth.

Since the channels through which financial inclusion can influence output volatility have generally not been explored in the literature, an intuitive starting point would be to consider the various components of aggregate demand. Starting with household consumption, greater financial inclusion could possibly enhance consumption smoothing by allowing agents to adjust their consumption patterns over time (Mehrotra and Yetman, 2015) in a way that potentially dampens macroeconomic volatility. When it comes to firms' investments, based on the 'creative destruction' thesis, as long as greater financial inclusion results in firms and entrepreneurs gaining more access to bank credit, it tends to lead to more innovation (Ayyagari, Demirgüç-Kunt, and Maksimovic, 2011), which could amplify output volatility. On the flip side, the economy may become less concentrated amongst a handful of firms (Chauvet and Jacolin, 2017), which could in turn reduce output volatility.

Yet another important channel comes from the effectiveness of monetary policy transmission. Greater financial inclusion reduces the unbanked population, which makes monetary policy via interest rate transmission more effective, thus dampening macroeconomic volatility. However, as Mehrotra and Yetman (2014) point out, if central banks focus more on stabilising inflation as part of their optimal monetary policy, it may make output more volatile.

The final component of aggregate demand is exports. If greater financial inclusion increases credit availability for trade financing, more firms could export and also engage in diversification, thus moderating output volatility (Calderon and Schmidt-Hebbel, 2008).

Given this background, we are interested in empirically probing the nexus between financial inclusion and macroeconomic volatility, specifically focusing on 16 Asian EMDEs between 1995 and 2017. The main contributions of this chapter to the literature are four-fold. First, we focus exclusively on the Asian EMDEs using all available data. Second, we test for the relationship between reckless financial inclusion in the form of excessive credit growth and output volatility.[2] Third, we investigate the importance of macroprudential policies in moderating output volatility induced by such reckless financial inclusion. Finally, we go beyond conventional measures to understand the relationship between digital financial inclusion ('fintech') and output volatility for a broader sample of EMDEs.

To preview the main findings, we observe a strong and robust negative relationship between financial inclusion and output volatility, that is, greater financial inclusion stabilises output. However, our results also highlight a cautionary note: the joint association of financial inclusion and excessive credit growth tends to amplify output volatility. Our empirical analysis further shows that macroprudential policies (MaPs) limit the impact of reckless financial inclusion on output fluctuations, highlighting their promise and potential. Finally, our analysis also reveals that the output stabilising effects of traditional financial inclusion measures do not extend to advancements in digital financial inclusion; in other words, we find that greater digital financial inclusion amplifies output volatility in EMDEs.

The remainder of the chapter is structured as follows: We offer a succinct overview of the key literature on determinants of output volatility in Section 5.2. We start Section 5.3 by discussing some stylised facts on financial inclusion in Asia. We then provide an overview of the data used, the empirical model, and the associated priors. In Section 5.4, we present our empirical results on the nexus between financial inclusion and output volatility along with robustness checks. Section 5.5 focuses on the empirical relationship between digital financial inclusion and output volatility using a larger sample of EMDEs. Section 5.6 concludes the chapter.

5.2 Key literature[3]

There are two distinct strands of relevant literature. The first deals with the importance of output volatility and its determinants. Although the literature establishes that output volatility significantly affects economic growth, there is no consensus about the direction of this relationship. An early set of papers, including that of Kormendi and Meguire (1985), Grier and Tullock (1989), and Caballero and Hammour (1991), fall under the Schumpeterian tradition of 'creative destruction' and argue that output volatility increases economic growth due to the 'cleansing effect' of recessions.

However, there has also been a notable strand of empirical literature starting with the influential contribution of Ramey and Ramey (1995) that shows a strong negative relationship between output volatility and growth due to 'uncertainty-induced planning errors by firms'. Following Ramey and Ramey (1995), several papers, such as those by Martin and Rogers (2000), Kneller and Young (2001), have empirically established a negative relationship between output volatility and growth. More recent works by Aghion and Howitt (2006) and Badinger (2010) find similar results, though they argue that the negative relationship could be the result of diminishing returns to investments.[4]

Regardless of whether output volatility increases or reduces growth, many related studies have attempted to understand the determinants of output volatility.[5] This brings us to the second related, small and yet growing strand of literature that has attempted to empirically understand the relationship between different dimensions of financial sector development and output volatility. Some notable relevant papers include the following: Easterly, Islam, and Stiglitz (2000); Bekaert, Harvey, and Lundblad (2006); Dabla-Norris and Srivisal (2013); Meller (2013); and Wang, Wen, and Xu (2017).

In one of the earliest papers discussing the role of the financial sector in understanding growth volatility, Easterly, Islam, and Stiglitz (2000), using a panel of 60 countries, found that a deeper financial system, as signified by greater credit to gross domestic product (GDP) ratio, is significantly associated with lower output volatility, although the relationship is non-linear in that a large financial sector amplifies output volatility.

Against the backdrop of several EMDEs liberalising their financial sectors since the 1990s, one of the empirical questions of interest at that time was whether this was aggravating volatility in the real economy. In an important contribution, Bekaert et al. (2006) specifically probed this relationship between greater equity market liberalisation and capital account openness on the volatility of real consumption growth using a panel of 95 emerging market economies between 1980 and 2000. They found that financial liberalisation is mostly associated with lower consumption growth volatility, and a resulting decline in the latter's ratio with GDP, which they interpret as evidence for improved risk sharing.

In a related paper, Meller (2013) focused on a sample of 26 developed and 36 developing countries from 1980 to 2007 and found that the impact of financial openness on output volatility is conditioned on a country's financial risk rating, where low-risk countries see international financial openness mitigating output volatility and vice versa for high-risk countries.

Focusing particularly on financial deepening for a panel of 110 advanced and developing economies covering the period 1974–2008, Dabla-Norris and Srivisal (2013) found that the volatility of output, consumption, and investment growth are notably dampened by greater financial depth. They also observed significant non-linear effects in this relationship for advanced economies wherein, beyond a certain threshold, higher financial depth amplifies output volatility.

Finally, using aggregate data for more than 100 countries covering the period 1989–2006, Wang et al. (2017) empirically explored the relationship between financial development and volatility of aggregate output and investment. In line with other papers, the authors also found a significantly robust negative relationship between the two variables of interest, implying that countries characterised by high financial development experience lower aggregate output volatility. They also presented evidence of non-linearity governing this relationship in that the mitigating effect on output volatility is substantially higher at lower levels of financial development compared to very high degrees of financial deepening.

While a majority of papers in this literature focuses on financial deepening and output volatility, no paper to our knowledge examines the specific nexus between financial inclusion and output volatility, with the notable exception of that of Mehrotra and Yetman (2014). In their paper, in addition to a theoretical model that attempts to explain how different levels of financial inclusion affect welfare-maximising monetary policy, Mehrotra and Yetman (2014), using a cross-section of 130 countries, empirically test for the impact of greater degrees of financial inclusion on the ratio of output to inflation volatilities. Further, they also empirically check whether consumption volatility declines relative to output volatility for higher degrees of financial inclusion. Their results suggest that while higher financial inclusion increases the ratio of output to inflation volatility, it reduces the ratio of consumption to output volatility, confirming the predictions of their theoretical model.

As this review illustrates, the bulk of the literature has focused on financial deepening and output volatility rather than the impact of financial inclusion per se, which will be the focus of our analysis.

5.3 Data and empirical model

We construct a panel dataset for about 16 EMDEs in Asia over the period 1995–2017. The choice of the time period and the sample of countries were purely based on consistent availability of data. Before we proceed with the empirics, we present some stylised facts about the trends and patterns in financial inclusion indicators across our sample economies.

5.3.1 Stylised facts

Asian EMDEs have seen a sharp increase in financial inclusion since the late 1990s. As Figure 5.1 points out, the degree of financial inclusion in Asia compares very favourably with the rest of the world. We can note that the average score of the (composite) index of financial inclusion for all EMDEs in Asia closely trailed the rest of the world through the 2000s. However, since 2012, we can see that the average penetration of financial inclusion in the Asian region overtook that of all the other regions significantly, underlining the speed with which policymakers in EMDEs have embraced efforts to achieve financial inclusivity in their economies.

While the region on the whole has been dynamic and vibrant, a disaggregated picture shown in Figure 5.2 reveals that a few countries have consistently contributed to this significant rise in financial inclusion over the years. Interestingly,

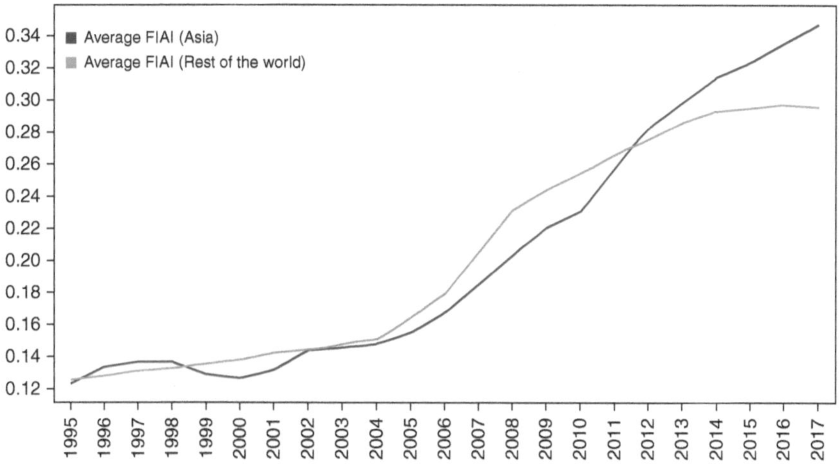

Figure 5.1 Financial inclusion access index in Asian EMDEs (1995–2017).
EMDE = emerging market and developing economy; FIAI = financial inclusion access index
Source: Authors based on IMF financial access statistics.

we can see that, until 2004, on average the high index scores were largely driven by a handful of Central Asian countries like Mongolia and Uzbekistan, while other fast-growing Southeast Asian EMDEs like Malaysia and Thailand also had notable contributions. While these economies continued to consistently improve their financial inclusion, since 2005, many more EMDEs such as China, India, Indonesia, the Philippines, and Vietnam have experienced increases in financial inclusion.

We also present the trends in specific financial access indicators (e.g., ATMs and bank branches) for the 17 EMDEs in Asia over the years (Figures 5.3 and 5.4). The dominance of Mongolia and Uzbekistan is more visible when it comes to the presence of bank branches relative to ATMs, while the opposite appears to be true for other EMDEs noted earlier.

5.3.2 Empirical model

The basic estimating equation will be as follows:

$$y_{it} = \delta_i + \beta fi_{it} + {}^{3}\boldsymbol{D}_{it} + \cdot\, \boldsymbol{E}_{it} + \text{»}\boldsymbol{B}_{it} + \rho_t + u_{it} \quad (5.1)$$

y_{it} is the measure of output volatility of country i at time t;
fi_{it} is the level of financial inclusion in country i at time t;
$\boldsymbol{D}_{it}$ is the vector of variables representing domestic conditions that affect output volatility;

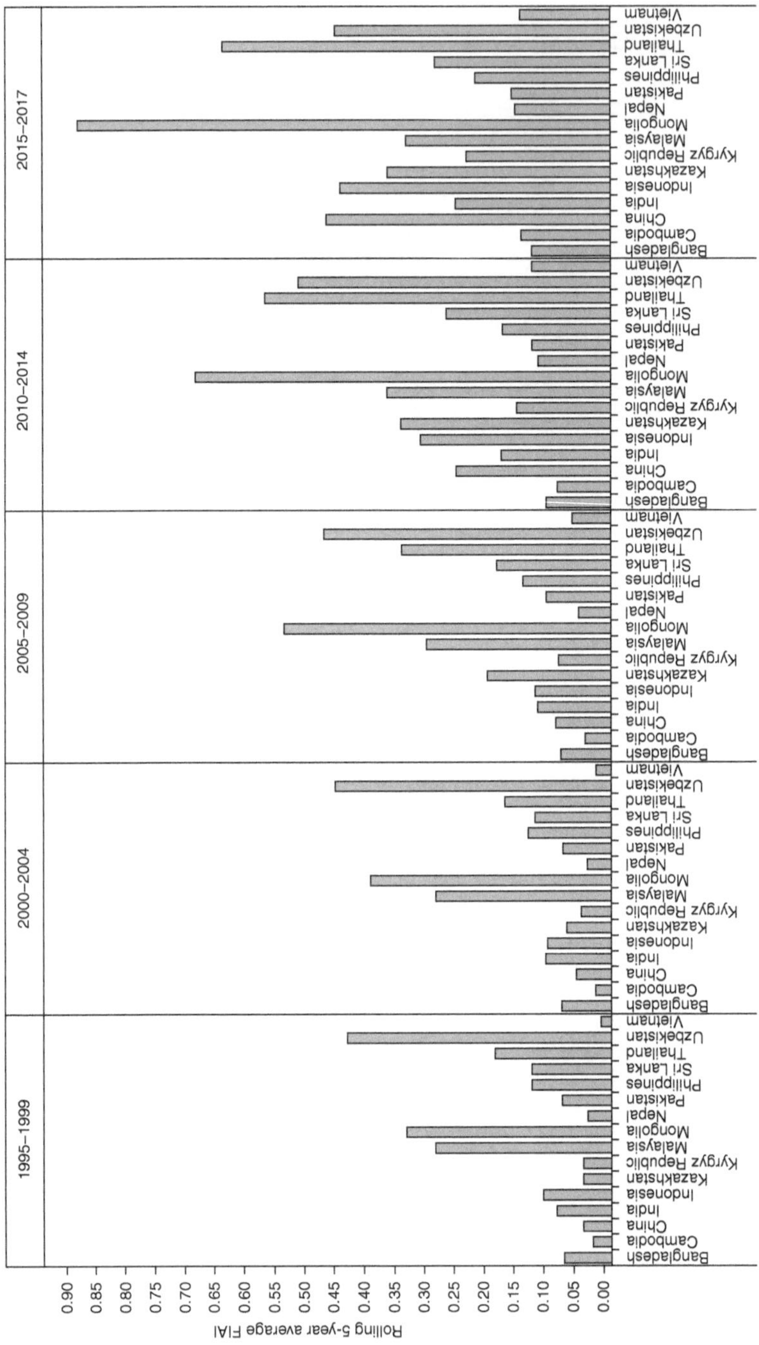

Figure 5.2 Financial inclusion access index in Asia: country breakdown.

FIAI = financial inclusion access index

Source: Authors based on IMF financial access statistics.

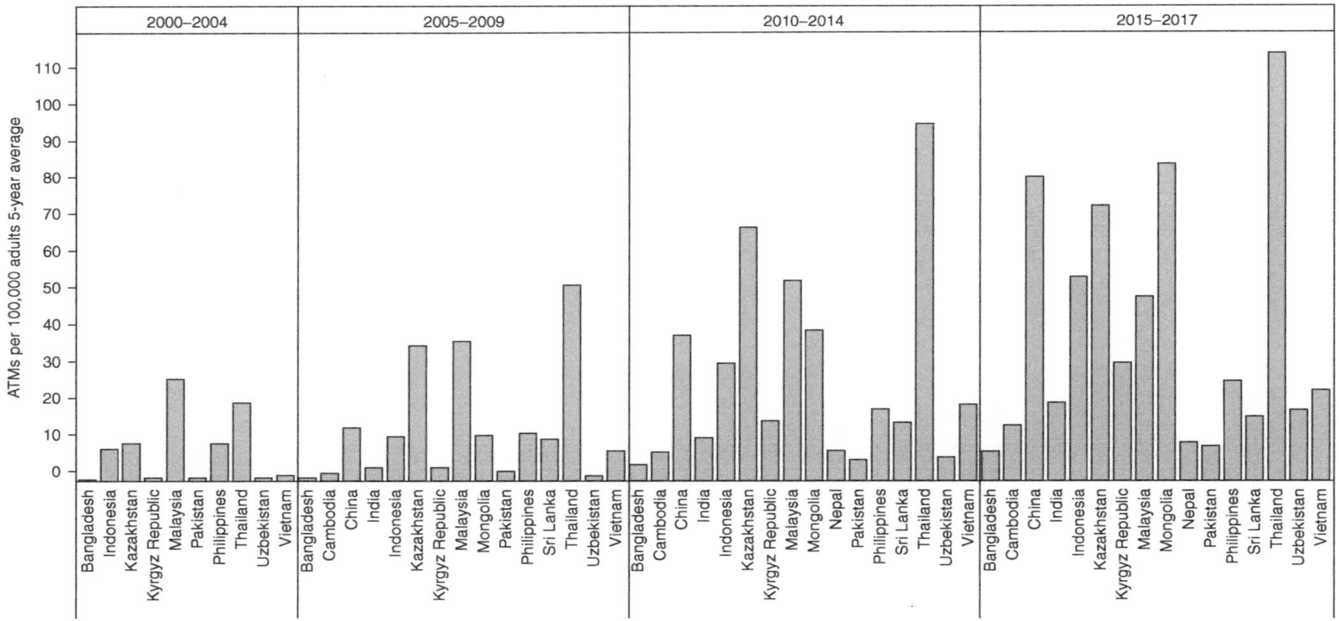

Figure 5.3 Trends in ATMs per capita in Asian EMDEs (1995–2017).

ATM = automated teller machine; EMDE = emerging market and developing economy

Source: Authors based on IMF financial access statistics.

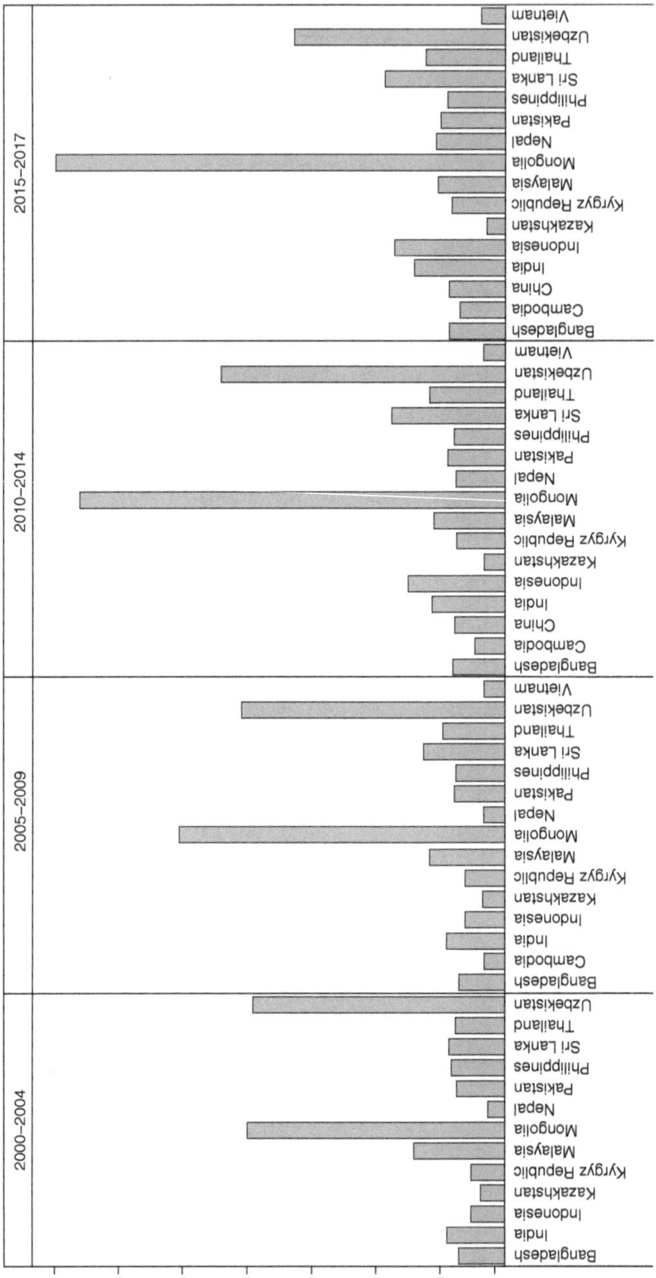

Figure 5.4 Trends in bank branches per capita in Asian EMDEs (1995–2017).

EMDE = emerging market and developing economy

Source: Authors based on IMF financial access statistics.

E_{it} is the vector of variables capturing external conditions that affect output volatility;
B_{it} is the vector of banking sector variables that affect output volatility;
δ_i is country-fixed effects;
ρ_t *is* time-fixed effects; and
u_{it} is the idiosyncratic error term.

The dependent variable in our empirics is output volatility measured as a three-year rolling standard deviation of GDP per capita growth rate, which is consistent with the literature on volatility. While we use this in our baseline estimation for consistency, we also use other definitions of output volatility as robustness checks. Our focal independent variable is the financial inclusion access index compiled by the International Monetary Fund. We re-run our empirics using alternative indicators of financial inclusion under robustness checks.

Most estimating models, such as the one given in Equation (5.1), tend to violate conditional mean independence, which is a prerequisite to obtain unbiased and consistent estimates. The specific source of violation of conditional mean independence typically arises from omitted variable bias. As has been well-established in the literature, the unobserved effects model, as given in Equation (5.1), allows us to undertake a within transformation which in turn enables us to handle the unobserved heterogeneity bias resulting from estimating it, as long as the unobserved variables that could be potentially correlated with our regressors are time-invariant in nature. In such circumstances, we can reasonably argue that our fixed effects model produces unbiased and robust estimates.

However, an important point is that the fixed effects setup outlined above is generally the norm in literature for 'short panels', wherein the number of entities (N) is significantly larger than the number of time periods (T). In our case, the panel we construct is of a 'long form' wherein our number of entities N (16 countries in total) is relatively less than the number of time periods T, which is 22 (1995–2017). Given that our N is less than T, it is generally recommended that our fixed effects model can be modelled with first-order auto-regressive (AR [1]) disturbances. So, a generic version of this model can then be written as follows:

$$Y_{it} = \alpha_i + X_{it}\beta + u_{it} \tag{5.2}$$

where error term $u_{it} = \rho u_{it-1} + \varepsilon_{it}$ follows an AR (1) error structure and α_i is modelled as a fixed effect. In other words, we allow the error term u_{it} in our model to be correlated over i instead of the independently and identically distributed error model assumed in a conventional fixed effects estimation. This permits potentially more efficient parameter estimates. So, we estimate a variant of Equation (5.2) applied to Equation (5.1) as our main estimating equation. However, we also present the results of a conventional fixed effects estimation as a robustness check to facilitate comparisons.

5.3.3 Control variables and priors

The literature on determinants of output volatility lists a wide-ranging set of control variables that can be grouped under at least three different categories. As noted in Equation (5.1), the first set of determining factors is a vector of domestic macroeconomic and financial variables. The second set pertains to variables reflecting external conditions that could possibly influence output volatility. Finally, the last group of variables are related to the domestic banking sector. In what follows, we will briefly discuss the control variables we include in our empirics and their priors based on the literature.[6]

5.3.3.1 Domestic conditions

- *Inflation*: With regard to the priors, higher inflation could amplify output volatility if it results in overall macroeconomic price instability. However, this nexus is ambiguous because if there is a Phillips curve-type trade-off between inflation and output, higher inflation could dampen output volatility.
- *Fiscal policy volatility*: We control for volatility of fiscal policy as it is a component of aggregate demand. Studies such as Herrera and Vincent (1994) point out that fiscal policy volatility could also result in higher consumption volatility, in turn amplifying output volatility. Fatas and Mihov (2013) show that fiscal policy volatility influences growth negatively. However, (lagged) fiscal policy volatility can also be counter-cyclical, moderating output volatility. Thus, the expected direction of the relationship can go either way.
- *Credit growth*: An important source of domestic macroeconomic and financial instability is excessive and volatile credit growth. Aggregate credit growth that is excessive on its own can lead to greater instability in aggregate demand. However, if greater financial inclusion is associated with excessive credit growth, we can expect it to contribute to higher rather than lower output volatility.

5.3.3.2 External conditions

- *Trade openness*: Amongst the external conditions that influence output volatility, the empirical literature identifies a country's trade openness as a determining factor. Many studies argue that higher trade openness could leave EMDEs more vulnerable to external shocks, hence amplifying output volatility (Kose, Otrok, and Whiteman, 2003; di Giovanni and Levchenko, 2008). In addition, Cavallo (2008), for instance, argues that countries with higher trade openness signal higher creditworthiness, making them less prone to sudden stops in capital inflows, which in turn stabilises output volatility.
- *Financial openness*: While wider access to global capital markets could make countries more vulnerable to global transmission of shocks and crises (Furman and Stiglitz, 1998), any financial openness that leads to greater

international risk sharing could reduce consumption and output volatility (Bekaert et al., 2006).

- *Exchange rate volatility*: In addition to controlling for trade and financial openness (in levels), we control for real effective exchange rate (REER) volatility that would be expected to amplify domestic output volatility.

5.3.3.3 Banking sector variables

As specified in Equation (5.1), we also add a vector of banking sector variables that could influence output volatility. They include:

- *Bank z-score:* Generally, an unstable banking system could amplify output volatility, with vulnerability to a crisis represented by the bank z-score. When economies undertake higher financial inclusion, it could result in more firms having access to credit, weakening bank balance sheets and worsening output volatility. If, on the contrary, greater financial inclusion results in a more diversified bank asset base, it consequently reduces the riskiness of bank portfolios, thus lowering output volatility (Khan, 2011).
- *Banking concentration*: A concentrated banking sector becomes important only in the context of financial inclusion and output volatility. If greater financial inclusion is associated with a more concentrated banking system, the pressure for imprudent lending could be significantly lower, which might decrease output volatility. This is broadly in line with the 'competition-fragility' literature that finds that a concentrated banking system tends to be more stable (Cetorelli and Peretto, 2000; Doll, 2010).

5.4 Empirical results

5.4.1 Financial inclusion and output volatility in Asia

First, we present a simple scatterplot that captures the basic relationship between financial inclusion and output volatility for our sample of Asian EMDEs. As Figure 5.5 shows, the fit is not quite strong despite the seemingly upward-sloping positive relationship between the two variables of interest. This is at best a weak positive relationship, although nothing conclusive can be drawn from simple cross-country averages over the entire sample period.

To ascertain the true underlying relationship when controlling for other observable and unobservable factors more systematically, we estimate Equation (5.1) using fixed effects with AR(1) disturbances. Table 5.1 shows the results. Column (1) displays the results of economic determinants of output volatility controlling for domestic factors, while columns (2) and (3) show the results of the augmented model with controls on external and banking conditions, respectively.

Focusing on column (1), we can clearly see that there is a strong negative relationship between financial inclusion and output volatility. The coefficient is not

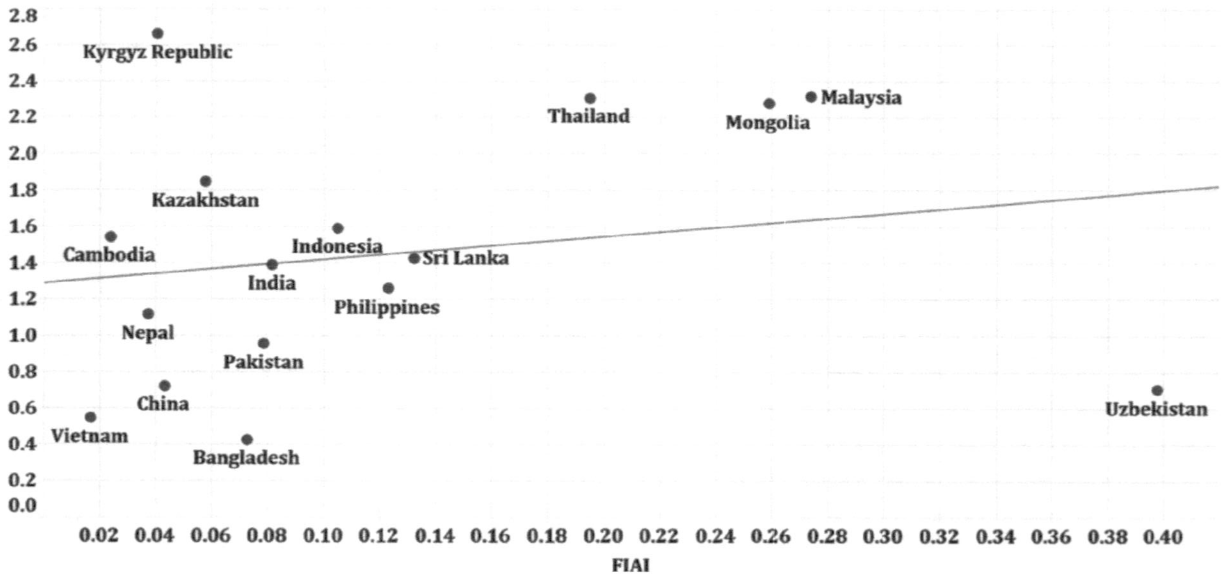

Figure 5.5 Scatterplot of financial inclusion and output volatility in Asia.

FIAI = Financial inclusion access index

Source: Authors.

only negative but also statistically significant at the 5% level, implying that greater financial inclusion moderates output volatility in our sample of Asian EMDEs after controlling for domestic conditions. In terms of magnitude, we can interpret this result as a standard deviation change in the financial inclusion index being associated with a 2.2 standard deviation change in output volatility. In terms of the control variables, although all the variables carry the right sign in accordance with our priors, only government consumption expenditure appears to be statistically significant.

We next augment the model with a matrix of controls capturing the external conditions that could affect output volatility. The results in column (2) show that the fundamental relationship between financial inclusion and output volatility remains persistently negative and statistically significant. The magnitude of the coefficient is also comparable to that of the baseline results reported in column (1), reflecting the consistency of this result. In terms of controls, both trade improvement and REER volatility appear to amplify output volatility, while the remaining variables carry the right sign but are statistically insignificant. In the final column of Table 5.1, we can see the robustness of the basic result of interest established so far: higher financial inclusion appears to dampen output volatility in Asia.

Overall, our baseline results have established a strong robust negative relationship between higher levels of financial inclusion and higher output volatility, implying that the beneficial impacts of financial inclusion extend to dampening the fluctuations in per capita GDP growth. With several EMDEs in Asia characterised by such volatility, this bears crucial policy significance.

5.4.2 Reckless financial inclusion and output volatility

Having established the fundamental relationship between financial inclusion and output volatility, we next turn to empirically examining how the joint interaction between financial inclusion and credit growth affects output volatility. Our working hypothesis is that when the greater policy push for financial access and usage coincides with excessive credit growth, output volatility could worsen. If a statistically and economically meaningful result is unearthed from this interaction, then this is a clear sign for policymakers to proceed with caution.

In Table 5.2, we show the results of this exercise. We re-run the baseline model, but with an interaction term between financial inclusion and credit growth. The results are quite striking, with two important points worth underlining. First, the coefficient of financial inclusion continues to be persistently negative and highly statistically significant, with larger magnitudes across all specifications as shown in columns (1)–(3). This implies that the fundamental results have not been altered. Second, while credit growth on its own turns out to be statistically insignificant in most cases, the interaction term of interest shows a strong positive and statistically significant relationship. This suggests that when higher financial inclusion coincides with excessive credit growth, it amplifies output volatility. In other

Table 5.1 Financial inclusion and output volatility in Asian EMDEs

Dep. var.: output volatility	*(1)*	*(2)*	*(3)*
	Domestic conditions	*External conditions*	*Banking conditions*
FIAI	**–2.218****	**–2.544****	**–2.359****
	(1.118)	(1.115)	(1.173)
Inflation	0.00945	0.00974	0.00939
	(0.00701)	(0.00785)	(0.00799)
Govt. cons. exp.	0.0695**	0.0742**	0.0771**
	(0.0339)	(0.0360)	(0.0377)
Credit growth	0.00208	0.000788	0.000425
	(0.00212)	(0.00267)	(0.00272)
Trade % of GDP		0.00585	0.00530
		(0.00510)	(0.00529)
Total		0.0148***	0.0141***
		(0.00410)	(0.00424)
Fin openness		0.501	0.617
		(0.391)	(0.404)
REER volatility		0.0332**	0.0335**
		(0.0160)	(0.0163)
Bk concentration			0.00238
			(0.00480)
Z-score			–0.0115
			(0.0208)
Observations	285	253	245
Number of countries	15	15	15

Source: Authors.

Note: Fixed effects estimates with AR(1) disturbances.
*** p<0.01, ** p<0.05, * p<0.1
EMDE = emerging market and developing economy; FIAI = financial inclusion access index; GDP = gross domestic product; REER = real effective exchange rate; ToT = terms of trade

words, reckless financial inclusion in the form of high credit growth appears to jeopardise output stability.

5.4.3 Macroprudential policies and output volatility

Our empirical results have shown that although financial inclusion in general tends to contribute to output stability, when it coincides with higher credit growth, it tends to produce undesirable effects. How best to tackle that? We empirically verify whether there is a role for MaPs to moderate output volatility, especially when induced by reckless financial inclusion.

MaPs have become an important component of a broader tool kit for EMDEs to limit systemic vulnerabilities, reducing the extent of financial interconnectedness,

Table 5.2 Reckless financial inclusion and output volatility

Dep. var.: output volatility	*(1)*	*(2)*	*(3)*
	Domestic	*External*	*Banking*
FIAI	**-8.128*** **	**-7.445** **	**-7.107** **
	(2.862)	(3.000)	(3.082)
Inflation	0.0207**	0.0174*	0.0165
	(0.00969)	(0.0102)	(0.0104)
Govt. cons. exp.	0.0632	0.0707	0.0695
	(0.0446)	(0.0441)	(0.0466)
Credit growth	-0.00312	0.00614	0.00630
	(0.00919)	(0.00965)	(0.00984)
FI*credit growth	**0.0735*** **	**0.0555** **	**0.0541** **
	(0.0251)	(0.0249)	(0.0252)
Trade% of GDP		0.00605	0.00499
		(0.00679)	(0.00701)
ToT		0.0227***	0.0213***
		(0.00574)	(0.00591)
Fin openness		1.843***	2.007***
		(0.571)	(0.589)
REER volatility		0.0468**	0.0483**
		(0.0208)	(0.0211)
Bk concentration			0.00109
			(0.00640)
Z-score			-0.0203
			(0.0268)
Observations	285	253	245
Number of countries	15	15	15

Source: Authors.

Note: Fixed effects estimates with AR(1) disturbances
*** $p<0.01$, ** $p<0.05$, * $p<0.1$
FI = financial inclusion; FIAI = financial inclusion access index; GDP = gross domestic product; REER = real effective exchange rate; ToT = terms of trade

and managing excessive credit growth. We begin by exploiting the comprehensive dataset on MaPs compiled by Cerutti, Claessens, and Laeven (2017) for a large panel of EMDEs for 2000–2017. By extracting the relevant data on MaPs for this period for our sample of Asian EMDEs, we empirically verify whether they moderate output volatility, especially in light of the joint effects induced by reckless financial inclusion.

Our empirical approach involves first including MaPs as an additional determinant of output volatility and then augmenting the specification with a triple interaction term between MaPs, credit growth, and financial inclusion. Our priors state that if MaPs play the desired role of contributing to financial stability, we would observe a strong negative relationship in that it dampens output volatility.

Table 5.3 What role for macroprudential policies?

Dep. var.: output volatility	*(1)*	*(2)*	*(3)*	*(4)*
	Dom-MaP	*Dom-FI*Cr*MaP*	*Ext-MaP*	*Ext-FI*Cr*MaP*
FIAI	**-3.906**	**-5.169***	**-3.967***	**-5.616***
	(2.823)	(2.856)	(2.186)	(3.013)
Inflation	0.000495	0.000306	0.000665	0.00464
	(0.0143)	(0.0141)	(0.0116)	(0.0150)
Govt. cons. exp.	0.131***	0.128***	0.0743*	0.123**
	(0.0482)	(0.0476)	(0.0389)	(0.0485)
Credit growth	-0.00800	-0.00504	-0.000208	-0.000890
	(0.0111)	(0.0111)	(0.00864)	(0.0113)
Trade % of GDP			0.00150	-0.0104
			(0.00583)	(0.00835)
ToT			0.0188***	0.00302
			(0.00455)	(0.00599)
Fin openness			0.555	0.885
			(0.436)	(0.605)
REER volatility			0.0117	0.00368
			(0.0241)	(0.0290)
FI*credit growth	0.0273	0.0702**	0.0127	0.0641**
	(0.0236)	(0.0299)	(0.0174)	(0.0309)
MaP	-0.0316	0.148	-0.0618	0.137
	(0.122)	(0.144)	(0.0863)	(0.147)
FI*Cr*MaP		**-0.0107****		**-0.00913***
		(0.00468)		(0.00495)
Observations	210	210	218	210
Number of countries	15	15	15	15

Source: Authors.

Note: Fixed effects estimates with AR(1) disturbances
*** p<0.01, ** p<0.05, * p<0.1
FI = financial inclusion; FIAI = financial inclusion access index; GDP = gross domestic product; MaP = macroprudential policy; REER = real effective exchange rate; ToT = terms of trade

Table 5.3 summarises the results of this empirical exercise. While column (1) shows the baseline regression results for determinants of output volatility with MaPs as an additional regressor controlling for domestic conditions, column (2) captures the impact of the triple interaction term of interest. The same exercise is repeated in columns (3) and (4), with the matrix of control variables expanded to include external conditions affecting output volatility.

Our results support our priors in that the triple interaction term is statistically significant and enters the regression with the appropriate negative sign (columns 2 and 4). These results imply the moderating impact of MaPs on output volatility induced by excessive credit growth. However, we do not find any MaPs on their own to have any significant relationship with output volatility.

5.4.4 Robustness checks

We undertake two types of robustness checks. First, we use alternative indicators of financial inclusion. So far, the empirical results we have obtained use an access index as the main proxy for financial inclusion. To verify the robustness of our findings using other indicators, we re-run all the fundamental results established so far using alternative indicators such as the use of ATMs, bank branches, and deposit accounts, representing both the access and usage dimensions of financial inclusion.

Table 5.4 presents the results of the estimation using all the alternative indicators of financial inclusion. As we can observe, regardless of the proxy used, we consistently find that greater financial inclusion contributes to output stability in Asian EMDEs, which is a strong policy result. Further, we observe that the interaction between the different financial inclusion indicators and credit growth always yields a strong positive and statistically significant coefficient, implying that higher financial inclusion coinciding with higher credit growth amplifies output volatility consistently across all specifications. This result is robust to using both access and usage indicators of financial inclusion. Most of the results pertaining to the sign and significance of the control variables remain consistent with those established so far.

The second type of sensitivity check is to revert to a more traditional two-way fixed effects estimation of the key regressions. Table 5.5 shows the results of the fixed effects estimates for all four types of financial inclusion indicators used so far. We start with the composite index of financial inclusion used in the baseline results, followed by ATMs, branches, and deposit accounts. For all four specifications, we re-run the same set of basic regressions, while controlling for country and year fixed effects. As the results in Table 5.5 show, all the key results continue to be robust.[7]

5.5 Digital financial inclusion and output volatility in EMDEs

Our final section of the chapter focuses on probing the empirical relationship between the digital component of financial inclusion and output volatility. Financial innovations enabled by digital technology have seen phenomenal growth across EMDEs all over the world. As Figure 5.6 shows, since 2010, EMDEs across the board have witnessed a meteoric rise in indicators such as mobile money transactions, underlining the prevalence of digital financial inclusion in these countries.

Despite its prevalence and significance, there has not been much work empirically focusing on the macroeconomic impacts of digital financial inclusion, largely due to inconsistent data availability. Although the so-called 'fintech revolution' can promote financial inclusion, enhance entrepreneurship, lower the cost of credit, and spur overall investment and growth, concerns have been raised about its possible impact on traditional banking, monetary policy, and growth volatility.

Table 5.4 Alternative indicators of financial inclusion

Dep. var.: output volatility	*(1)*	*(2)*	*(3)*	*(4)*	*(5)*	*(6)*
	ATMs	*ATMs*cr*	*Branches*	*Branches*cr*	*Deposit accounts*	*Deposit acc*cr*
ATMs	**–0.633****	**–0.577***				**–0.569****
	(0.250)	(0.308)				(0.246)
Inflation	–0.00308	0.0180	–0.00728	0.00480	–0.0147	–0.0202
	(0.0167)	(0.0160)	(0.0162)	(0.0157)	(0.0177)	(0.0196)
Gov. cons. exp.	0.135**	0.185***	0.0874	0.104*	0.0550	0.0451
	(0.0632)	(0.0600)	(0.0648)	(0.0613)	(0.0886)	(0.0949)
Credit growth	0.00398	–0.0121	0.00685	–0.0378***	0.000663	–0.117*
	(0.0112)	(0.0142)	(0.00441)	(0.0129)	(0.00710)	(0.0668)
ATMs*credit		**0.00855****				
		(0.00399)				
Trade % of GDP	0.0177*	0.0128	0.0227**	0.0250**	0.00428	0.00804
	(0.00906)	(0.00936)	(0.0108)	(0.0104)	(0.00830)	(0.00852)
ToT	0.00923	0.00449	0.0124	0.00920	0.0222**	0.0142
	(0.00870)	(0.00916)	(0.00970)	(0.00933)	(0.0104)	(0.0123)
Fin openness	1.397*	–0.574	1.620**	1.826**	0.0516	0.145
	(0.800)	(0.874)	(0.719)	(0.714)	(0.520)	(0.700)
REER volatility	0.00753	0.0174	0.0198	0.00162	0.00807	–0.00443
	(0.0358)	(0.0332)	(0.0389)	(0.0372)	(0.0331)	(0.0339)
Bk concentration	0.00654	0.0101	0.00437	0.00549	0.00297	0.00319
	(0.00920)	(0.00878)	(0.00948)	(0.00918)	(0.00830)	(0.00861)
Z-score	–0.00685	–0.0300	–0.0662	–0.0520	–0.0620	–0.0666
	(0.0576)	(0.0533)	(0.0615)	(0.0583)	(0.0460)	(0.0566)
Branches			**–0.108***	**–0.219*****		
			(0.0582)	(0.0628)		

Branches*credit				**0.0213***** (0.00582)		
Deposit acc					**−1.120**** (0.447)	
Deposit acc*credit						**0.00748*** (0.00421)
Constant	0.694 (0.907)	1.547* (0.884)	−0.435 (0.778)	−0.429 (0.682)	17.39*** (4.217)	0.104 (0.836)
Observations	146	131	135	135	112	107
Number of countries	15	15	15	15	12	12

Source: Authors.

Note: Fixed effects estimates with AR (1) disturbances
*** $p<0.01$, ** $p<0.05$, * $p<0.1$
ATM = automated teller machine; GDP = gross domestic product; REER = real effective exchange rate; ToT = terms of trade

Table 5.5 Two-way fixed effects estimation using all indicators of financial inclusion

	(1)	*(2)*	*(3)*	*(4)*
	FIAI	*ATMs*	*Branches*	*Deposit accounts*
FIAI	**–2.071****			
	(0.961)			
Inflation	0.0485***	0.0115	0.0241	–0.0147
	(0.0167)	(0.0218)	(0.0205)	(0.0177)
Gov. cons. exp.	0.0475	0.210**	0.216***	0.0550
	(0.0800)	(0.0747)	(0.0791)	(0.0886)
Credit growth	0.00918	0.00454	0.00561	0.000663
	(0.00560)	(0.00336)	(0.00568)	(0.00710)
Trade % of GDP	–0.00184	0.0116*	0.00161	0.00428
	(0.00600)	(0.00615)	(0.00797)	(0.00830)
ToT	0.0129***	0.00792*	0.00746	0.0222**
	(0.00400)	(0.00409)	(0.00626)	(0.0104)
Fin openness	–0.0162	1.579***	1.736***	0.0516
	(0.397)	(0.404)	(0.477)	(0.520)
REER volatility	0.191***	0.0415	0.0626	0.00807
	(0.0287)	(0.0323)	(0.0385)	(0.0331)
Bk concentration	0.00326	0.0214**	0.0241***	0.00297
	(0.00545)	(0.00796)	(0.00727)	(0.00830)
Z-score	–0.0578**	–0.00384	–0.0692	–0.0620
	(0.0270)	(0.0491)	(0.0585)	(0.0460)
ATMs		**–0.152***		
		(0.0776)		
Branches			**–0.171****	
			(0.0711)	
Deposit acc.				**–1.120****
				(0.447)
Constant	0.162	–0.943	0.267	17.39***
	(0.800)	(1.060)	(1.546)	(4.217)
Observations	260	161	150	112
R-squared	0.303	0.289	0.299	
Number of countries	15	15	15	12

Source: Authors.

Note: Robust standard errors in parentheses; all regressions include year and country FE
*** p<0.01, ** p<0.05, * p<0.1
ATM = automated teller machine; FIAI = financial inclusion access index; GDP = gross domestic product; REER = real effective exchange rate; ToT = terms of trade

All the empirical results established thus far have essentially focused on traditional modes of financial inclusion, covering both access and usage dimensions. In this section, we focus on available digital financial inclusion measures for a broader sample of EMDEs. Consistent data are available only for two measures: the first is the number of mobile money transactions per 1,000 adults, which captures the access dimension of digital financial inclusion, while the second is the number of active mobile money accounts, which represents the

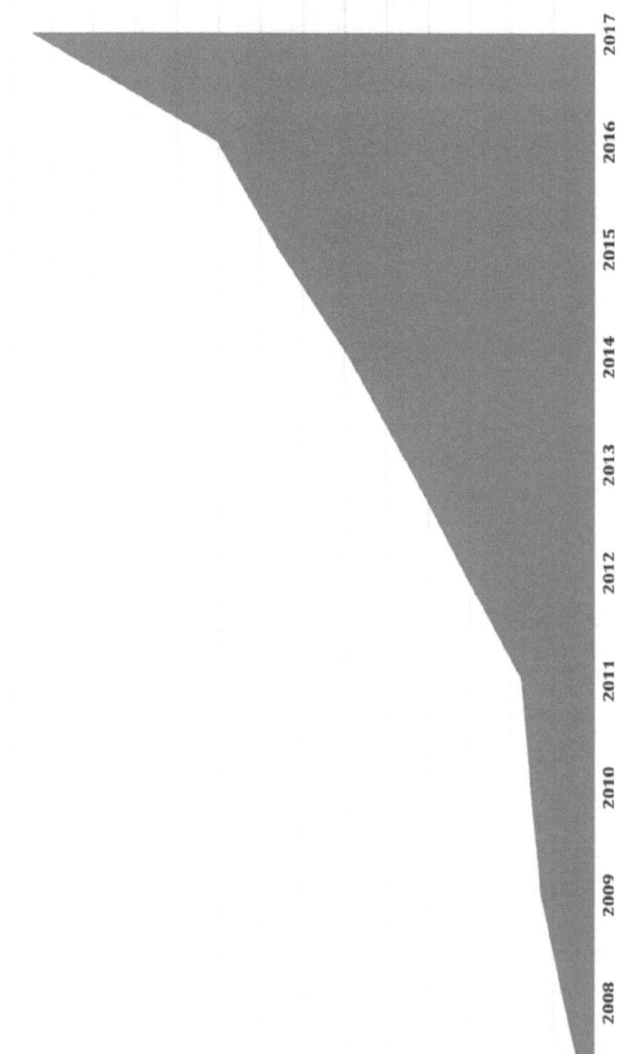

Figure 5.6 Trends in digital financial inclusion in EMDEs (2007–2017).

EMDE = emerging market and developing economy

Source: Authors based on IMF financial access statistics.

Table 5.6 Digital financial inclusion and output volatility

	(1)	(2)
	Mobile money transactions (MM1)	*Mobile money accounts (MM2)*
Inflation	−0.171	2.086
	(1.707)	(1.927)
Change in gov. exp.	0.0889	0.113
	(0.0576)	(0.126)
Trade % of GDP	−0.00335	−0.00385
	(0.0211)	(0.0131)
ToT	0.0178**	0.0418***
	(0.00746)	(0.0143)
Financial openness	−0.0210	0.842
	(0.800)	(0.923)
REER volatility	0.0808*	0.0453
	(0.0458)	(0.0629)
Credit growth	0.174	0.353
	(0.164)	(0.263)
MM1	**0.131****	
	(0.0508)	
MM2		**0.490*****
		(0.141)
Observations	158	100
R-squared	0.424	0.450
Number of countries	38	26

Source: Authors.

Note: Robust standard errors in parentheses.
All regressions include country and year FE.
*** p<0.01, ** p<0.05, * p<0.1
FI = financial inclusion; GDP = gross domestic product; REER = real effective exchange rate; ToT = terms of trade

usage dimension. Meaningful data are available for about 40 EMDEs in the period 2009–2017, including in the Asian countries from the sample used so far. However, restricting the analysis for just the Asian countries leaves inadequate observations for a panel analysis.

We make use of a standard two-way fixed effects model to estimate this relationship. The control variables are the same as what we have used so far to ensure consistency in comparisons. Our results are shown in Table 5.6 for both proxies of digital financial inclusion. Interestingly, in strict contrast to the conventional measures of financial inclusion, we find a strong positive statistical and economic relationship between digital financial inclusion and output volatility. The coefficients of both the access and usage measures of digital financial inclusion are not only positive but also statistically significant at the 5% level, implying that advances in digital financial inclusion persistently amplify output volatility in EMDEs after controlling for other plausible determinants.

5.6 Conclusions

In this chapter, we have empirically explored the nexus between financial inclusion and macroeconomic volatility, focusing on a sample of Asian EMDEs covering 1995–2017. Our results show that financial inclusion and output volatility are negatively related, in that greater levels of financial inclusion tend to promote output stability in Asian EMDEs. That said, we also find that the interactive effects of financial inclusion and excessive credit growth tend to compromise this stability and instead amplify output volatility. Our empirical findings also show that policymakers in Asia can use macroprudential policies to moderate the impact of such reckless financial inclusion on output volatility. Finally, we also show that, in contrast to traditional financial inclusion measures tending to moderate output volatility, advancements in digital financial inclusion appear to produce the opposite effect; that is, greater digital financial inclusion amplifies output volatility in EMDEs, underlining the importance of focusing on such trade-offs for policymakers in Asia going forward.

Notes

1 This chapter draws upon and significantly builds on Cavoli, Gopalan, and Rajan (2020).
2 Any policy attempt to expand financial access and usage in a significant way could have unintended consequences that are not well understood. A build-up of excessive credit growth could be a potentially reliable early warning indicator of future financial crises, while an interaction between financial access and usage coinciding with excessive credit expansion could produce undesirable output volatility. This is a trade-off that policymakers must consider (see Cavoli et al., 2020, for more discussion).
3 This section is an abbreviated discussion based on Cavoli et al. (2020).
4 See Norrbin and Yigit (2005) and Bakas, Chortareas, and Magkonis (2017) for a comprehensive discussion on the relationship between growth and output volatility.
5 Some selected papers from this strand of literature include Kose et al. (2003); di Giovanni and Levchenko (2008); Hakura (2009); Malik and Temple (2009); and Iseringhausen and Vierke (2018).
6 See Appendix 5.1 for details of data sources.
7 The results also hold when testing for the impact of macroprudential policies on output volatility induced by reckless financial inclusion by using the alternative indicators. Results are available upon request.

References

Aghion, P. and P. Howitt (2006), 'Appropriate Growth Policy: A Unifying Framework', *Journal of the European Economic Association*, Papers and Proceedings of the Twentieth Annual Congress of the European Economic Association, 4(2–3), pp.269–314.

Ayyagari, M., A. Demirgüç-Kunt, and V. Maksimovic (2011), 'Firm Innovation in Emerging Markets: The Role of Finance, Governance, and Competition', *Journal of Financial and Quantitative Analysis*, 46(6), pp.1545–80.

Badinger, H. (2010), 'Output Volatility and Economic Growth', *Economic Letters*, 106(2010), pp.15–18.

Bakas, D., G. Chortareas, and G. Magkonis (2017), 'Volatility and Growth: A Not So Straightforward Relationship', Mimeo. February.

Bekaert, G., C.R. Harvey, and C. Lundblad (2006), 'Growth Volatility and Financial Liberalization', *Journal of International Money and Finance*, 25(3), pp.370–403.

Caballero, R. and M. Hammour (1991), 'The Cleansing Effect of Recessions', *American Economic Review*, 84(5), pp.1350–68.

Calderon, C. and K. Schmidt-Hebbel (2008), 'Openness and Growth Volatility', *Central Bank of Chile Working Paper*, No. 483. Santiago, Chile: Central Bank of Chile.

Cavallo, E.A. (2008), 'Output Volatility and Openness to Trade: A Reassessment', *Economía*, 9(1), pp.105–38.

Cavoli, T., S. Gopalan, and R.S. Rajan (2020), 'Does Financial Inclusion Amplify Output Volatility in Emerging and Developing Economies?', *Open Economies Review.* **31**, pp.901–930.

Cerutti, E., Claessens, S., and L. Laeven, (2017), 'The Use and Effectiveness of Macroprudential Policies: New Evidence,' *Journal of Financial Stability*, 28, February, pp. 203–24.

Cetorelli, N. and P.F. Peretto, 'Oligopoly Banking and Capital Accumulation', Federal Reserve Bank of Chicago Working Paper, No. 2000–12. Duke Department of Economics Research Paper No. 19. Available at SSRN, https://ssrn.com/abstract=254343 or http://dx.doi.org/10.2139/ssrn.254343. (accessed October 31, 2020).

Chauvet, L. and L. Jacolin (2017), 'Financial Inclusion, Bank Concentration and Firm Performance', *World Development*, 97, pp.1–13.

Dabla-Norris, E. and N. Srivisal (2013), 'Revisiting the Link between Finance and Macroeconomic Volatility', *IMF Working Paper*, No. WP/13/29. Washington, DC: IMF.

di Giovanni, J. and A.A. Levchenko (2008), 'Trade Openness and Volatility', *IMF Working Paper*, No. WP/08/146. Washington, DC: IMF.

Doll, M. (2010), 'Bank Concentration, Competition and Financial Stability', Universteit Van Tilburg. July.

Easterly, W., R. Islam, and J.S. Stiglitz (2000), 'Explaining Growth Volatility', *World Bank Working Paper*, No. 28159. Washington, DC: World Bank.

Fatas, A. and I. Mihov (2013), 'Policy Volatility, Institutions, and Economic Growth', *Review of Economics and Statistics*, 95(2), pp.362–76.

Furman, J. and J. Stiglitz (1998), 'Economic Crises: Evidence and Insights from East Asia', *Brookings Papers on Economic Activity*, 2, 1–114. www.brookings.edu/wp-content/uploads/1998/06/1998b_bpea_furman_stiglitz_bosworth_radelet.pdf

Grier, K. B. and G. Tullock (1989), 'An Empirical Analysis of Cross-National Economic Growth, 1951–1980', *Journal of Monetary Economics*, 24 (2), pp.259–76.

Hakura, D.S. (2009), 'Output Volatility in Emerging Market and Developing Countries: What Explains the "Great Moderation" of 1970–2003?', *Czech Journal of Economics and Finance*, 59(3), pp.229–54.

Herrera, S. and B. Vincent (1994), 'Public Expenditure and Consumption Volatility', *World Bank Policy Research Working Paper*, No. 4633. Washington, DC; World Bank.

Iseringhausen, M. and H. Vierke (2018), 'What Drives Output Volatility? The Role of Demographics and Government Size Revisited', *European Commission Directorate-General for Economic and Financial Affairs Discussion Paper* 075. Luxembourg: European Commission.

Khan, S.H.R. (2011), 'Financial Inclusion and Financial Stability: Are They Two Sides of the Same Coin?', Address by Shri HR Khan, Deputy Governor of the Reserve Bank of India, 04 November. www.bis.org/review/r111229f.pdf?ql=1#:~:text=The%20twin%20objectives%20of%20financial,not%20work%20at%20cross%20purposes

Klapper, L., M. El-Zoghbi, and J. Hess (2016), 'Achieving the Sustainable Development Goals: The Role of Financial Inclusion', Consultative Group to Assist the Poor (CGAP), April.

Kneller, R. and Young, G. (2001), 'Business Cycle Volatility, Uncertainty and Long-Run Growth', *The Manchester School*, 69 (5), pp.534–52.

Kormendi, R.C. and P.G. Meguire (1985), 'Macroeconomic Determinants of Growth: Cross-Country Evidence', *Journal of Monetary Economics*, 16 (2), pp.141–63.

Kose, M.A., Otrok, C and C.H. Whiteman (2003), 'International Business Cycles: World, Region, and Country-Specific Factors', *American Economic Review*, 93(4), pp.1216–39.

Malik, A. and J.R.W. Temple (2009), 'The Geography of Output Volatility', *Journal of Development Economics*, 90 (2), pp.163–78.

Martine, P. and C.A Rogers (2000), 'Long-term Growth and Short-Term Economic Stability', *European Economic Review*, 44(2), pp. 359–81.

Mehrotra, A. and J. Yetman (2014), 'Financial Inclusion and Optimal Monetary Policy', *BIS Working Papers*, No. 476. Basel, Switzerland: BIS.

Mehrotra, A. and J. Yetman (2015), 'Financial Inclusion – Issues for Central Banks', *BIS Quarterly Review*, March, 83–96. www.bis.org/publ/qtrpdf/r_qt1503h.pdf

Meller, B. (2013), 'The Two-Sided Effect of Financial Globalization on Output Volatility', *Review of World Economics*, 149, pp.477–504.

Norrbin, S.C. and F.P. Yigit (2005), 'The Robustness of the Link between Volatility and Growth of Output', *Review of World Economics*, 141(2), pp.343–56.

Organisation for Economic Cooperation and Development (OECD) (2018), 'Enhancing SME Access to Diversified Financing Instruments', Discussion Paper, 2018 SME Ministerial Conference, Plenary Session 2. Paris: OECD.

Ramey, G., and V.A. Ramey (1995), 'Cross-Country Evidence on the Link between Volatility and Growth', *American Economic Review*, 85(5), pp.1138–51.

Wang, P., Y. Wen, and Z. Xu (2017), 'Financial Development and Long-Run Volatility Trends', *Federal Reserve Bank of St. Louis Working Paper Series* 2013-003C. St. Louis: Federal Reserve Bank.

Appendix 5.1 Data, definitions, and sources

Variable	*Definitions*	*Sources*
Volatility of GDP per capita (constant 2005 US$)	Three-year rolling standard deviation of GDP per capita growth rate. GDP per capita is GDP divided by mid-year population. GDP is the sum of gross value added by all resident producers in the economy plus any product taxes and minus any subsidies not included in the value of the products. It is calculated without making deductions for depreciation of fabricated assets or for depletion and degradation of natural resources. Data are in constant 2005 US dollars.	World Bank national accounts data, and OECD National Accounts data files
Financial Institutions Access Index	A composite index based on branches and ATMs per capita from the IMF Financial Market Development Database.	International Monetary Fund (IMF)
Inflation	Inflation calculated as year-on-year percentage change in consumer price index (CPI). CPI reflects changes in the cost to the average consumer of acquiring a basket of goods and services that may be fixed or changed at specified intervals, such as yearly. The Laspeyres formula is generally used. Data are period averages.	IMF
Fiscal policy volatility	Year-on-year percentage change in government final consumption used as a measure of volatility. General government final consumption expenditure (formerly general government consumption) includes all government current expenditures for purchases of goods and services (including compensation of employees). It also includes most expenditures on national defence and security but excludes government military expenditures that are part of government capital formation.	World Bank
Credit growth	Year-on-year growth rate of domestic credit to the private sector. Domestic credit to the private sector refers to financial resources provided to the private sector by financial corporations, such as through loans, purchases of non-equity securities, and trade credits and other accounts receivable, which establish a claim for repayment.	World Bank

(*continued*)

Appendix 5.1 Cont.

Variable	*Definitions*	*Sources*
Trade openness	Merchandise trade as a share of GDP is the sum of merchandise exports and imports divided by the value of GDP, all in current US dollars.	World Trade Organization and World Bank GDP estimates
Financial openness	Stock of external liabilities to GDP	Philip R. Lane and Gian Maria Milesi-Ferretti (2017), 'International Financial Integration in the Aftermath of the Global Financial Crisis', IMF Working Paper, No. 17/115
REER volatility	Three-year rolling standard deviation of annual real effective exchange rate (REER). REER, which measures the development of the real value of a country's currency against the basket of the trading partners of the country, is a frequently used variable in both theoretical and applied economic research and policy analysis.	Bruegel
Bank z-score	It captures the probability of default of a country's banking system. Z-score compares the buffer of a country's banking system (capitalisation and returns) with the volatility of those returns. It is estimated as (ROA+[equity/assets])/sd(ROA); sd(ROA) is the standard deviation of ROA. ROA, equity, and assets are country-level aggregate figures calculated from underlying bank-by-bank unconsolidated data from Bankscope.	Bankscope, Bureau van Dijk (BvD)
Non-performing loans	Bank non-performing loans to gross loans (%). Reported by IMF staff. Note that due to differences in national accounting, taxation, and supervisory regimes, these data are not strictly comparable across countries.	Financial Soundness Indicators Database (fsi.imf.org), IMF
Bank concentration	Raw data are from Bankscope. (Sum [data 2025] for three largest banks in Bankscope) / (Sum [data 2025] for all banks in Bankscope). This is reported only when the number of banks in Bankscope is three or more. Calculated from underlying bank-by-bank unconsolidated data from Bankscope.	Bankscope, Bureau van Dijk (BvD)

6 Empowering the powerless

Financial inclusion in developing Africa and Asia

Firmin Doko Tchatoka and Ha Trang Vo

6.1 Introduction

Financial inclusion is usually defined as individuals and businesses having access to affordable financial products and services that meet their needs (i.e., transactions, payments, savings, credit, and insurance) delivered in a responsible and sustainable way. Financial inclusion has emerged as a building block for both poverty reduction and economic growth, as it offers incremental and complementary solutions to tackle poverty, promote inclusive development, and address the millennium development goals.

Since 2011, the World Bank Group has launched Global Findex, a database that tracks global financial inclusion efforts. Many media outlets and organisations have written about or used the database, including Bloomberg, CNN, *The Financial Times*, *Forbes*, *The New York Times*, *The Wall Street Journal*, and the World Economic Forum. In 2015, the World Bank Group developed a framework for enabling 1 billion people around the world to gain access to a transaction account through targeted interventions by 2020. This was referred to as Universal Financial Access 2020 (UFA2020). To date, over 30 partners, including the United Nations, have committed to achieving the UFA2020 goals,[1] and the benefits of financial inclusion are increasingly undeniable. Gallup's most recent survey in 2017 showed that 1.2 billion adults worldwide have opened a bank account since 2011, including 515 million in the preceding 3 years. Globally, 69% of adults—3.8 billion people—now have an account at a bank or with a mobile money provider. Bank accounts combat poverty by helping individuals invest in education and business opportunities, as well as manage unexpected expenses like a hospital bill or the loss of a breadwinner that can push families into hardship.

Despite this progress, 1.7 billion adults remain unbanked (Demirguc-Kunt et al., 2015) around the world. Several studies that examine the financially excluded have looked at the demand side; see, for example, Allen et al. (2012), Fungacova and Weill (2015), and Demirguc-Kunt and Klapper (2012). This narrow focus is usually justified by the lack of supply side data. The current study is one of the first to exploit a rich dataset from the supply side, using *Financial Inclusion Insights*, an InterMedia programme funded by the Bill and Melinda

Gates Foundation that spans eight countries, four in Africa (Kenya, Nigeria, Uganda, Tanzania), and four in Asia (India, Indonesia, Bangladesh, Pakistan).

The literature on global financial inclusion falls into three main categories. The first looks at the benefits of financial inclusion, with most studies examining its impact on either poverty and inequality,[2] or economic growth and unemployment.[3] Specifically, financial inclusion educates children and reduces child labour through easy access to credit that enables households to smooth consumption expenditures over time (Becker, 1975). Moreover, greater access to credit services can promote self-employment, thus reducing unemployment (Menon and van der Meulen Rodgers, 2011). Financial inclusion can also impact macroeconomic policies. For example, Mbutor and Uba (2013) found an inverse relationship between the inflation rate and the size of commercial banks' loans and advances, meaning that financial inclusion is likely to improve monetary policy. The second category explores financial inclusion access. While some of these studies were conducted at the individual country level (see, e.g., Fungacova and Weill, 2015; and Efobi et al., 2014 for China and Nigeria, respectively), others focused on African countries (see, e.g., Allen et al., 2012; Demirguc-Kunt and Klapper, 2012). In general, these studies conclude that education, income, and age are key determinants of financial services access (Allen et al., 2012; Fungacova and Weill, 2015), but gender and religion also matter (Demirguc-Kunt and Klapper, 2012). The third category focuses on building an index to measure the degree of financial inclusion or the performance of financial systems (see, e.g., Sharma, 2008; Gupte et al., 2012; Camara and Tuesta, 2014).

Despite this widespread literature, whether financial inclusion can empower the poorest around the globe remains unclear. Further, none of these studies has established a typology of financial inclusion service users over time. Providing such a typology is paramount, not only to gauge financial services access, but also to design policies that boost access for vulnerable groups, for example, women and rural producers.

Taking advantage of the rich *Financial Inclusion Insights* survey data, our study contributes to the financial inclusion literature in two main ways. First, by employing multiple correspondence analysis (MCA) – a statistical analysis technique for nominal categorical data, used to detect and represent underlying structures in a data set – we establish the association over time between user characteristics and the financial inclusion services provided (banking, mobile money, and both banking and mobile money). Although major regional differences in financial inclusion service usage exist between Africa and Asia, MCA results clearly outlined that gender, poverty, education, age, and location are key determinants of financial inclusion services access in both regions. The results also show that while the dynamic of financial services usage in the African sample seems to shift from banking to mobile money, the Asian countries have seen a steady increase in all financial services usage since 2013. The shift from banking to mobile money in Africa could be explained by increasing mobilisation to lift people out of poverty, especially women and rural producers, through financial inclusion (see, e.g., Atkinson and Messy, 2013; Triki and Faye, 2013). Since banking is rarely available to rural and female Africans, the expansion of mobile phones and Internet access in rural areas has enabled mobile money as the only alternative to financial inclusion (see, e.g., the M-PESA mobile money service in Kenya; Van Hove and Dubus, 2019; Johnson and Nino-Zarazua, 2011; and the surveys for Kenya and Uganda).

Interestingly, our results also show that the overall share of financially excluded individuals, as well as that of most subgroups in the sample (classified by age, gender, poverty, location, education), has decreased significantly over time for Asia. In this region, for example, the overall share of financially excluded individuals has dropped from about 60% in 2013 to about 34% in 2017. Similarly, the share of financially excluded poor (respectively, female) has decreased from around 50% (respectively, 38%) in 2013 to roughly 21% (respectively, 20%) in 2017. Only the proportions of financially excluded non-poor individuals, individuals living in urban areas, and those with tertiary education have remained constant in the Asian sample. As such, financial exclusion has been a relative success in the Asian countries studied.

More importantly, many disadvantaged groups (e.g., poor, females, and rural Asians) have seen a drop in their shares of financially excluded individuals, although their use of financial services has steadily increased since 2013. This also suggests that financial inclusion has empowered the poorest in Asia. By contrast, the African countries in the sample show mixed results. With the exception of poor individuals, the proportion of financially excluded individuals in most of the other subgroups has not changed much during the period. The share of financially excluded poor individuals, however, has dropped slightly from around 45% in 2013 to about 38% in 2017. These results suggest that financial inclusion has yet to be effective in Africa compared with Asia. But the fact that the share of financially excluded poor individuals has been dropping since 2016 indicates that Africa is moving toward financial inclusion.

The second way our study contributes to the financial inclusion literature is by providing a typology of financial inclusion service users in both regions, as well as its dynamic over time by employing clustering. We found that while young, rural, and female financial inclusion service users in Africa seem to shift toward mobile money, the same group in Asia prefers either banking or mobile money. In both Africa and Asia, financial inclusion service users in urban areas who are not poor and have basic education combine both banking and mobile money. Poor males and young females under 45 years old who live mostly in rural areas in Asia prefer banking, while the same group in Africa tends toward mobile money.

The rest of the chapter is organised as follows. Section 6.2 studies the determinants of financial inclusion access. Section 6.3 establishes the typology of financial inclusion services users over time. Conclusions are drawn in Section 6.4.

6.2 Determinants of financial inclusion service usage

In this study, we use MCA to describe the associations between individuals' socio-economic characteristics and the financial inclusion services offered. From the geometric point of view, MCA represents data as points in a low-dimensional

Euclidean space. With the exception of Dungey et al. (2018), MCA technique is not well known in the financial literature, so we shall introduce the method briefly in Section 6.2.1. Section 6.2.2 presents the data used for the analysis, and Section 6.2.3 contains the main results.

6.2.1 MCA method

MCA applies the correspondence analysis algorithm to an indicator matrix[4] known as a Burt table (see, e.g., Greenacre, 2017). Analysing the indicator matrix allows the direct representation of individuals as points in geometric space. The Burt table is the symmetric matrix of all two-way cross-tabulations between the categorical variables and has an analogy with the covariance matrix of continuous variables. Analysing the Burt table is a more natural generalisation of simple correspondence analysis, and individuals or the means of groups of individuals can be added as supplementary points to the graphical display.

Specifically, let I be a set of n individuals with p characteristics $X=\left[X_1,\dots,X_p\right]$. Each characteristic $X_j, j=1,\dots,p$, has k_j categories. The total number of categories is $k=\sum_{j=1}^{q}k_j$. Define x_{i,k_j} such that

$$x_{i,k_j}=\begin{cases}1 & \textit{if } i\in I \textit{ is in category } k_j,\\ 0 & \textit{otherwise}\end{cases} \tag{6.1}$$

and let $X_k=\left[X_{k_1},\dots,X_{k_p}\right]\in\mathbb{R}^{n\times k}$. MCA analyses the data matrix X_k consisting of entries 1 or 0 depending on whether or not individual $i\in I$ chooses category k_j. Let $\phi_{k_j}=\left(\phi_{jl}\right)_{l=1,\dots,k_j}$ denote the scale value vector of category $l=1,\dots,k_j$ and $\tilde{X}_k=\sum_{j=1}^{p}X_{k_j}\phi_{k_j}$ be the scaled variable induced by scaling X_k. Let $\phi_k=\left(\phi_{k_1}',\dots,\phi_{k_p}'\right)'$ be the k dimension vector of scale values, and $\tilde{X}=\left[\tilde{X}_1,\dots,\tilde{X}_p\right]$ be the matrix of scaled variables.

The MCA principle solves:

$$\max_{\phi_k} Var\left[\frac{1}{p}\sum_{j=1}^{p}\sum_{l=1}^{k}\phi_{jl}x_{jl}\right] \quad s.t. \quad e_k'D\phi_k=0,\ \phi_k'D\phi_k=np \tag{6.2}$$

$$\Leftrightarrow \max_{a_{jl}} Var\left[\frac{1}{p}\sum_{j=1}^{p}\sum_{l=1}^{k}\sqrt{\frac{a_{jl}^2 n}{pn_{jl}}}\,y_{jl}\right] \quad s.t. \quad \sum_{j=1}^{p}\sum_{l=1}^{k}n_{jl}^{\frac{1}{2}}a_{jl}=0,\ \sum_{j=1}^{p}\sum_{l=1}^{k}a_{jl}^{\frac{1}{2}}=1, \tag{6.3}$$

where D is a k-dimensional diagonal matrix constructed with non-null frequencies n_{jl}, e_k a k-dimensional vector of ones, and $a_k=\sqrt{\frac{n_{jl}}{np}}$ \ π*_{ji} • . The solution ϕ^* in (2) and a^* in (3) are related as

$$\phi^* = (np)^{\frac{1}{2}} D^{\frac{-1}{2}} a^*. \tag{6.4}$$

Equation (6.4) shows that the optimal scaling parameters ϕ^* and a^* depend on the number of characteristics p, the number of individuals n, and the frequency of occurrence D.

The k components of $\phi^*$are the category factors, $\hat{\psi}^* = \left(\frac{1}{Q}\right) X\phi^*$, and the subject factors (normalised variables) are $\psi^* = \frac{\hat{\psi}^*}{(\lambda_h)^{\frac{1}{2}}}$, where λ_h is the hth eigenvalue of the *Burt* matrix and it represents the variance explained by the hth principal component. As such, $p\lambda_h / (k - p)$ is the proportion of the variance explained by the hth component. The contribution of category l, $l = 1,\ldots,k$, to the hth principal component, c_l^h, and the correlation between $\tilde{X}_j^h$ and ψ^* are then given by

$$c_{jl}^h = \frac{n_{jl}\left(\phi_{jl}^*\right)^2}{np}, \; corr\left(\tilde{X}_j^h, \psi^*\right) = \left(\lambda_{hp} \sum_{l=1}^{k} c_{jl}^h\right)^2. \tag{6.5}$$

Contributions c_{jl}^h help locate the observations or variables important for a given factor, while correlations $corr\left(\tilde{X}_j^h, \psi^*\right)$ help locate the factors important for a given observation or variable. It is important to note that MCA codes data by creating several binary columns for each variable with the constraint that only one of the columns takes the value 1. This creates artificial additional dimensions because one categorical variable is coded with several columns. As such, the inertia, that is, the variance of the solution space, is artificially inflated, leading to the percentage explained by the first dimension being severely underestimated. This problem can be alleviated by using, for example, the correction of the data matrix eigenvalues in Greenacre (1993).

6.2.2 Data description

We use survey data from *Financial Inclusion Insights*. The surveys started in 2013 in partnership with the Bill and Melinda Gates Foundation, with the goal of building meaningful knowledge about the financial landscape in four countries in Africa (Kenya, Nigeria, Tanzania, and Uganda) and four in Asia (Bangladesh, India, Indonesia, and Pakistan). These eight countries have a combined population of over 2 billion. While the survey is conducted each year with updates in the questionnaire and tabulated data, the number of respondents in each country is fixed over time and depends on the country population size. Table 6.1 shows the sample size for each country, with India representing over seven times the samples of Bangladesh, Indonesia, Nigeria, and Pakistan, and over 14 times those of Kenya, Tanzania, and Uganda.

Financial Inclusion Insights describes financial inclusion as a journey in which customers move from being financially excluded to financially included. Figure 6.1 depicts this journey.

Table 6.1 Survey samples per country

Bangladesh	6,000
India	45,000
Indonesia	6,000
Kenya	3,000
Nigeria	6,000
Pakistan	6,000
Uganda	3,000
Tanzania	3,000

Source: *Financial Inclusion Insights.*

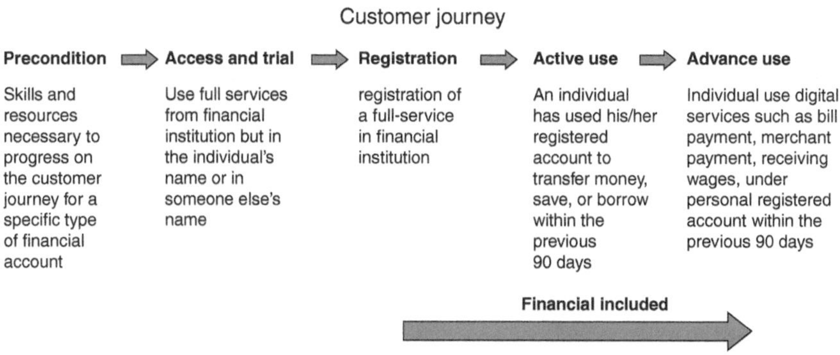

Figure 6.1 Financial inclusion process.
Source: *Financial Inclusion Insights.*

At each level, customers are further classified into different types based on their engagement with various ranges of financial services. To enable this classification, the surveys were designed to collect an extended level of information from the respondents. First, data on age, gender, family status, education, and wealth status were collected. Second, the surveys also queried the preconditions to access to financial services, such as whether respondents own a mobile phone, national ID, or a subscriber identification module card; the distance from respondents' location to the nearest financial service; and the availability of local networks. Third, respondents were asked how they use the financial services, including whether they own a financial account under their own name, how often they use financial services, the type of services they use, and whether they encounter difficulties in using them.

Financial Inclusion Insights considers respondents to be financially included if they have an account under their own name at a financial institution. As such, individuals owning mobile money accounts under their name are classified as financially included.

The data obtained from the surveys cover 5 years (2013–2017). The pooled sample of all eight countries includes 381,542 observations. Although this is a

Table 6.2 Individual characteristics and financial services provided

Variables	*Description*
Age	Age from 15 to 24 years (15–24); age from 25 to 34 years (25–34); age from 35 to 44 years (35–44); age from 45 to 54 years (45–54); age above 55 years (>55)
Poverty	Poor (P); not poor (NP)
Gender	Male (M); female (F)
Location	Urban (UR); rural (RU)
Specialty	Female living in rural (RuF) area; female living in urban (NRuF) area; poor living in rural (RP) area; living in urban area and not poor (NRP)
Literacy skill	Respondents have basic literacy skill (L1); respondents without basic literacy skill (L0)
Numeration skill	Respondents with basic financial numeration skill (N1); respondents without basic financial numeration skill (N0)
Financial services	Respondents do not use any services (*financially excluded*); respondents only use bank services (BK); respondents only use mobile money services (MM); respondents use both bank and mobile money services (BM)

Source: *Financial Inclusion Insights.*

pooled sample, the respondents' country can be identified. Table 6.2 reports the data variables (characteristics), along with the type of financial services provided. Note that the continuous variables, such as respondent age, are categorised in ranges.

Table 6.3 presents summary statistics of the respondents' characteristics as well as their use of the financial services provided. The first part of the table contains the results of the pooled four African countries, while the second part reports those of the pooled four Asian countries. In each region (Africa or Asia), respondents are classified into four distinct groups based on their financial inclusion status. The first group consists of respondents who do not use any service provided, that is, *financially excluded* individuals. The second group consists of individuals who have only a registered bank account under their own name, that is, *bank* users. The third group consists of respondents who have a registered mobile money account under their own name, that is, *mobile money* users. Finally, the fourth group consists of individuals with both registered bank and mobile money accounts under their name, that is, *bank and mobile money* users.

As seen in Table 6.3, the average individual in the Africa region is about 34 years old, while that in the Asian region is nearly 38 years old. The three groups of financial service users in Africa are not much different in age, with the average bank user being the youngest (about 34 years old) while the average user of both banks and mobile money being the oldest (about 37 years old). The average financially excluded individual is relatively young in the Africa region (slightly below 33 years old). In the Asia region, the average mobile money

Table 6.3 Characteristics of financial services users

Characteristics ↓ Services →	*Financially excluded*	*BK*	*MM*	*BM*	*All*
Africa					
Age	33.705	34.28	35.142	37.407	34.459
Urban	24.61%	51.28%	37.77%	52.58%	34.29%
Rural	75.39%	48.72%	62.23%	47.42%	65.71%
Male	42.40%	63.86%	41.26%	56.22%	46.81%
Female	57.60%	36.14%	58.74%	43.78%	53.19%
Poor	79.90%	65.13%	57.06%	29.08%	67.80%
Not poor	20.10%	34.87%	42.94%	70.92%	32.20%
Literacy	58.58%	92.30%	81.00%	91.22%	71.85%
Numeracy	88.18%	95.32%	94.17%	96.20%	91.39%
Total Obs.	**39,299**	**11,977**	**16,874**	**6,853**	**75,003**
ASIA					
Age	36.421	39.595	30.383	33.366	37.9
Urban	30.88%	34.23%	38.51%	60.43%	32.87%
Rural	69.12%	65.77%	61.49%	39.57%	67.13%
Male	39.93%	48.84%	68.89%	74.41%	44.75%
Female	60.07%	51.16%	31.11%	25.59%	55.25%
Poor	73.42%	66.95%	63.51%	51.93%	70.01%
Not poor	26.58%	33.05%	36.49%	48.07%	29.99%
Literacy	61.55%	70.68%	80.82%	90.20%	66.40%
Numeracy	82.54%	88.80%	98.65%	98.70%	85.83%
Total Obs.	**152,506**	**148,753**	**1,857**	**2,775**	**305,891**

Source: *Financial Inclusion Insights.*

BK = banking; BM = both banking and mobile money; MM = mobile money

user is the youngest (about 30 years old), followed by the banking and mobile money user (about 33 years old) and the bank user (slightly below 40 years old). The average financially excluded individual in Asian countries is 36 years old. The percentage of people living in rural areas is quite similar in both regions (65.71% in Africa compared with 67.13% in Asia). However, there appears to be a substantial difference between the two regions regarding financial services usage. First, most financially excluded people in the African countries live in rural areas (75.39%), while this proportion is 69.12% for the Asian countries. Second, 48.72% of banking users, 62.23% of mobile money users, and 47.42% of both banking and mobile money users live in rural Africa, while these shares stand at 65.77%, 61.49%, and 39.57%, respectively, in Asia. As such, in the African countries surveyed, an individual living in an urban area is more likely to use banking (51.28%) or both banking and mobile money (52.58%), while an individual who lives in urban area is more likely to use banking and mobile money (60.43%) in Asia.

Males appear to be different from females in their choices of financial services. While mobile money seems to be preferred by females in Africa (58.74%), banking is predominant for females (51.16%) in Asia. The share of male banking and both banking and mobile money users is very high in Africa, while that of male mobile money and both banking and mobile money users is the highest in Asia. There is a clear gender gap in Asia in terms of financial service usage compared with Africa. For example, 74.41% of males in the Asian countries use both banking and mobile money against 25.59% of females, while this share is 46.81% of males (vs 53.19% of females) in the African countries. For the African countries, with the exception of users of both banking and mobile money, users of the other financial services and the financially excluded individuals are mostly poor. This contrasts slightly with the Asian countries, where poverty distribution is quite uniform across all financial services users and the financially excluded individuals; all are mostly poor. Note that in both regions, the financially excluded individuals are the poorest.

The overall share of individuals with basic literacy and numeracy skills is high in both regions (71.85% and 91.39%, respectively, in Africa, versus 66.40% and 85.83%, respectively, in Asia). However, the sample of each region still contains non-negligible shares of people with no basic literacy and numeracy skills (28.15% and 8.61%, respectively, in Africa, versus 33.60% and 14.17%, respectively, in Asia). Interestingly, even the majority of financially excluded people in both regions have basic literacy and numeracy skills. Despite this similarity, there appears to be a slight difference between the two regions. Indeed, while the mobile money users' group for Africa shows the lowest share of basic literacy and numeracy skills, it is the banking users' group that has the lowest share of basic literacy and numeracy skills in the Asian sample.

6.2.3 MCA results

The section has two main goals. First, it aims to establish the link between the type of financial services provided and the characteristics of their users. This can help map users to the financial services provided, thus enabling policymakers and stakeholders to design targeted policies toward, for example, achieving the UFA2020 goals. Second, the section evaluates the progress of financial inclusion in Africa and Asia toward the UFA2020 goals. Of particular interest is to understand how financial inclusion has evolved since 2013, and whether the inclusion process has empowered those in need (rural producers, poor, women, etc.).

To achieve these goals, we employ the MCA technique described in Section 6.2.1. To enable regional comparison of the financial inclusion process between Africa and Asia, we run the MCA separately for each region. As the data cover the period 2013–2017, we show only the graphical representations of the MCA results for 2013 (start period) and 2017 (end period) to ease readability. Presenting the results in detail for all years and both countries would lengthen the study without adding any qualitative value. Nevertheless, we analyse the dynamic over time of financial inclusion in both continents.

6.2.3.1 Financial inclusion in 2013

Figures 6.2 and 6.3 present the MCA results for both the African and Asian samples in the variable space (user characteristics). In both regions, the first three principal dimensions summarise most of the data variability. More specifically, their contribution to the total data inertia is 68.3% for Africa and 80.1% for Asia. Each of the remaining dimensions contributes less than 2% to the total variability; correspondingly, they are left out, as is often the case in most MCA applications.

The results for dimensions 1 and 2 are presented in Figure 6.2, while those of dimensions 1 and 3 are shown in Figure 6.3. Showing the figures side by side makes it easier to see the differences between both regions. In these figures, the variables that are significant (thus can be interpreted) are located farther away from the origin, and categories (or variables) that are highly associated are located close to each other and usually contribute to the same dimensions. Each dimension is a principal factor formed by a linear combination of the variables, and the contribution of each variable to this dimension can be quantified. For both regions, we see that *Dimension 1* on the right contrasts financial services users who are poor, over 35 years old, have low education (thus no basic literacy and numeracy skills) with younger users (less than 35 years old), not poor, and highly educated on the left. While *education* contributes mostly to *Dimension 1* in Africa, *poverty* and *location* are also important determinants of this dimension for Asia. As such, *Dimension 1* is labelled *Education* for Africa, and *Education, poverty, location* for Asia. This is the first difference between the two regions. *Dimension 2* (i.e., the vertical axes in Figure 6.2) fundamentally differs between the two regions. For the African sample, it is mainly described by *gender* and *poverty*, while for the Asian sample, *age* and *location* mostly form the dimension. A look at *Dimension 3* reveals that both regions also differ slightly in the sense that *gender* mostly contributes to it in the Asian sample, although, in addition to *gender, age* also plays an important role in the African sample. Table 6.4 describes the three dimensions for each region in 2013.

Because MCA allows plotting the financial inclusion indicators in the variable space to find out their association with user characteristics, each financial service

Table 6.4 Multiple correspondence analysis main dimensions in 2013

Dimensions Variables	*Description*	*Description*
	Africa	*Asia*
1	Education	Education, poverty, location
2	Gender, poverty	Age, location
3	Age, gender	Gender

Source: *Financial Inclusion Insights.*

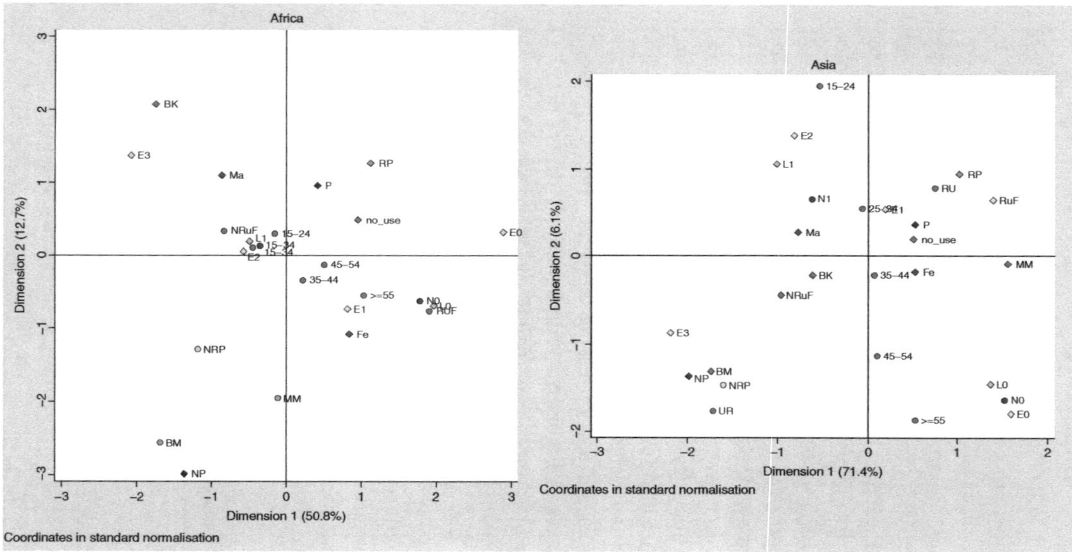

Figure 6.2 2013 MCA results in dimensions 1 and 2 – Africa versus Asia.
MCA = multiple correspondence analysis.
Four main types of financial users are: excluded people (no_use); bank users (BK), mobile money users (MM); bank and mobile money users (BM). Other characteristics of financial users are the following:
Age categories: (15–24), (25–34), (35–44), (45–54), > 55.
Poverty status: poor (P), not poor (NP).
Literacy ability: basic (L1), not basic (L0).
Numeration ability: basic (N1), not basic (N0). Location: rural (RU), urban (UR).
Gender: Male (Ma), female (Fe).
Education status: no-formal education (E0), primary education (E1), secondary education (E2), higher education (E3).
Special status: female in rural area (RuF), female in urban area (NRuF), poor in rural area (RP), not poor (NP).
Source: *Financial Inclusion Insights.*

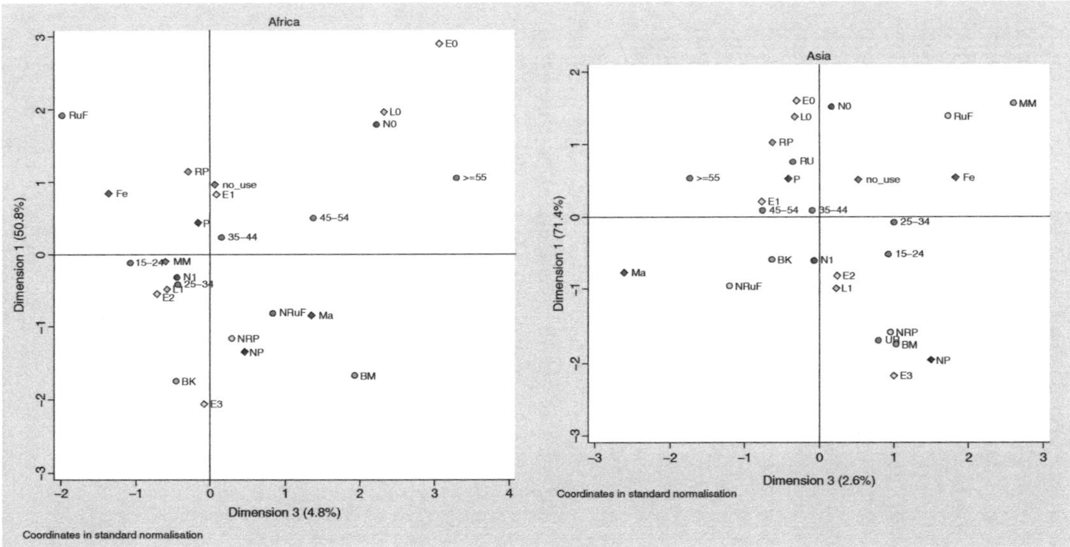

Figure 6.3 2013 MCA results in dimensions 1 and 3 – Africa versus Asia.
MCA = multiple correspondence analysis.
Four main types of financial users are: excluded people (no_use); bank users (BK), mobile money users (MM); bank and mobile money users (BM). Other characteristics of financial users are the following:
Age categories: (15–24), (25–34), (35–44), (45–54), > 55.
Poverty status: poor (P), not poor (NP).
Literacy ability: basic (L1), not basic (L0).
Numeration ability: basic (N1), not basic (N0). Location: rural (RU), urban (UR).
Gender: Male (Ma), female (Fe).
Education status: no-formal education (E0), primary education (E1), secondary education (E2), higher education (E3).
Special status: female in rural area (RuF), female in urban area (NRuF), poor in rural area (RP), not poor (NP).

Source: *Financial Inclusion Insights*.

is mainly associated with the characteristics of a group of its users (those users can be exhaustively described through their characteristics). As such, Figure 6.2 shows bank users at the top upper left corner close to highly educated male individuals in the African sample, with both mobile money and bank and mobile money users at the bottom left corner. These individuals are not poor and live in urban areas. On the right-hand side of the figure are individuals who are not associated with any of the financial services provided and thus are *financially excluded*. This group consists of females over 35 years old, who are less educated (no formal education or having only a primary education), poor, and living in a rural area. For the Asian sample (Figure 6.2), bank and mobile money users are located at the bottom left corner of the figure. The group consists of highly educated individuals, not poor, and living in an urban area. Bank users are males with secondary education and basic literacy and numeracy skills (see the top left corner of Figure 6.2 for Asia). On the top right-hand side of the figure is *financially excluded* individuals and mobile money users. Mobile money users for Asia are young, living mostly in a rural area, or poor females with a primary education. At the bottom right corner (Figure 6.2 for Asia) is the group of individuals over 55 years old with no formal education and lacking literacy and numeracy skills. This group of individuals is close to mobile money or no financial service; thus, those amongst them who use financial services mostly choose mobile money. The space of dimensions 1 and 3 (Figure 6.3) can be described in the same way, thereby complementing our analysis.

Figures 6.4 and 6.5 formally highlight dimensions 1–3 and suggest three to four possible groupings of individuals as per their usage and non-usage of financial services provided, and also locate the available services in the space. For example, in Figure 6.4, the group at the top left corner for the African sample captures highly educated male individuals who are mostly bank users. The group in the right-hand side (Figure 6.4 for Africa) captures females over 35 years old, with no formal education or only a primary education, poor, and living in a rural area. It is also apparent in the African sample that, in these two dimensions, there is no financial service that is contained in the grouping of these individuals, that is, they were financially excluded in 2013. In contrast, the bottom left grouping in the African sample is individuals who are not poor and live in an urban area. Mobile money and bank and mobile money services are in this dimension space.

Table 6.5 describes each group, with the two regions side by side to enable easy comparison. As shown, both regions share some similarities in terms of their financial services usage, as well as some dissimilarities. First, bank users in both regions are educated males, but the African users are more educated, having typically reached tertiary levels, as compared with the Asian users who only have secondary education. Second, mobile money users are young (under 35 years old) and not poor, with a secondary education in the African sample, while in Asia, mobile money users are either rural females under 54 years old with primary education, or older people (more than 55 years old) with no basic literacy and numeracy skills. Third, users of both bank and mobile money in Africa are young (under 35 years old), not poor, and have secondary education, whereas

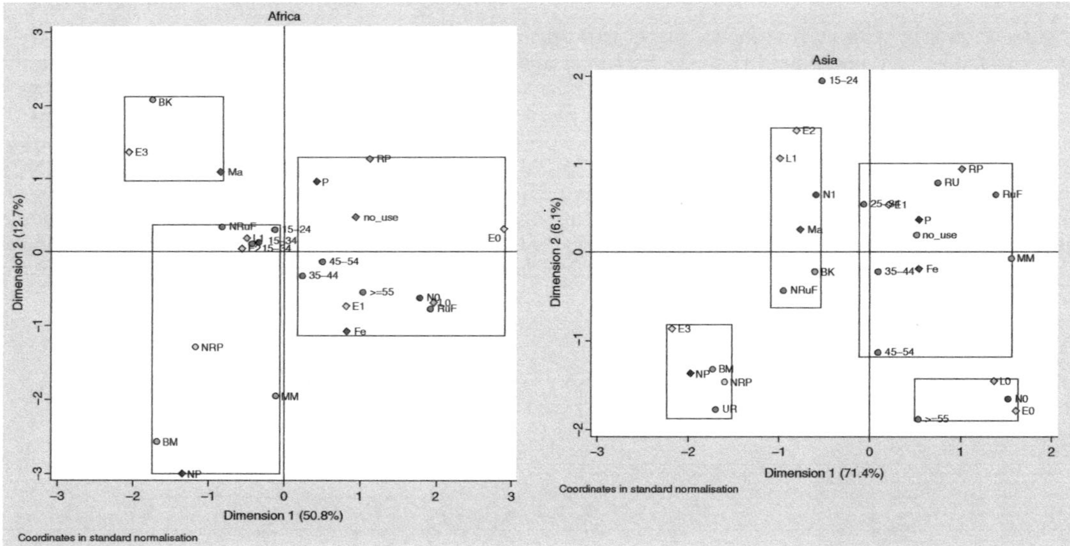

Figure 6.4 Use of financial services in 2013: dimensions 1 and 2 – Africa versus Asia.
Four main types of financial users are: excluded people (no_use); bank users (BK), mobile money users (MM); bank and mobile money users (BM). Other characteristics of financial users are the following:
Age categories: (15–24), (25–34), (35–44), (45–54), > 55.
Poverty status: poor (P), not poor (NP).
Literacy ability: basic (L1), not basic (L0).
Numeration ability: basic (N1), not basic (N0). Location: rural (RU), urban (UR).
Gender: Male (Ma), female (Fe).
Education status: no-formal education (E0), primary education (E1), secondary education (E2), higher education (E3).
Special status: female in rural area (RuF), female in urban area (NRuF), poor in rural area (RP), not poor (NP).
Source: *Financial Inclusion Insights.*

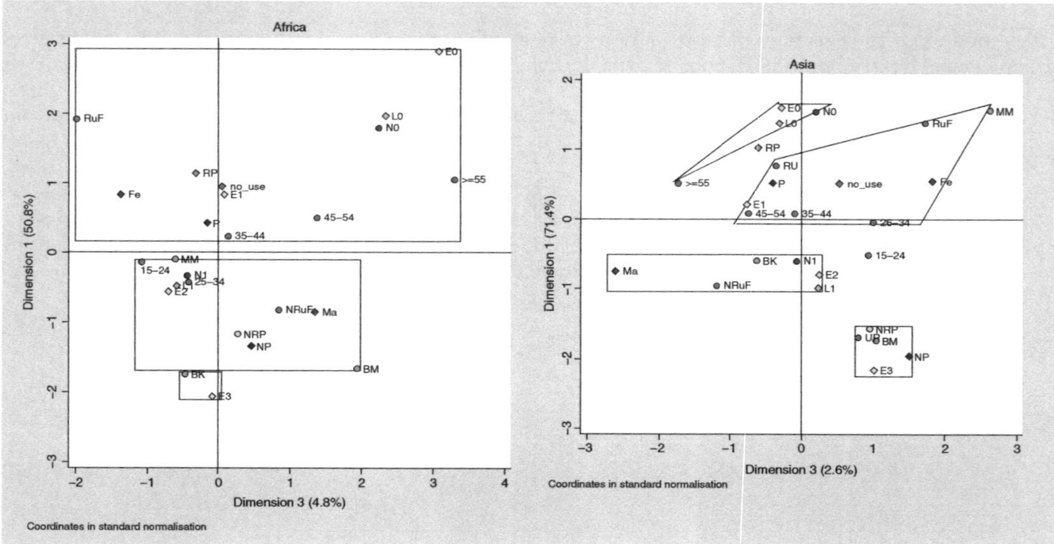

Figure 6.5 Use of financial services in 2013: dimensions 1 and 3 – Africa versus Asia.
Four main types of financial users are: excluded people (no_use); bank users (BK), mobile money users (MM); bank and mobile money users (BM). Other characteristics of financial users are the following:
Age categories: (15–24), (25–34), (35–44), (45–54), > 55.
Poverty status: poor (P), not poor (NP).
Literacy ability: basic (L1), not basic (L0).
Numeration ability: basic (N1), not basic (N0). Location: rural (RU), urban (UR).
Gender: Male (Ma), female (Fe).
Education status: no-formal education (E0), primary education (E1), secondary education (E2), higher education (E3).
Special status: female in rural area (RuF), female in urban area (NRuF), poor in rural area (RP), not poor (NP).

Source: Financial Inclusion Insights.

Table 6.5 Characteristics of financial users in 2013: Africa versus Asia

	Africa	*Asian*
BK	Tertiary education, males	Males, secondary education (have basic literacy and numeration skills)
MM	Not poor, under 35 years old, secondary education	Females, rural, poor, under 54 years old, primary education; or older than 55 years, no formal education (thus have no literacy and numeration skills)
BM	Not poor, under 35 years old, secondary education	Not poor, urban, high education
Financially excluded	Females, poor, rural, over 35 years old, low education	Females, rural, poor, under 54 years old, primary education; or older than 55 years, no formal education (thus have no literacy and numeration skills)

Source: *Financial Inclusion Insights.*

BK = banking; BM = both banking and mobile money; MM = mobile money

in Asia, users of both bank and mobile money are highly educated, live in urban areas, and are not poor. Finally, financially excluded people in the African sample are poor, older, and less educated rural females, while in the Asian sample, those are either poor rural females under 54 years old with primary education, or older individuals (over 55 years old) with no basic literacy and numeracy skills.

6.2.3.2 State of financial inclusion in 2017

We now focus on financial inclusion in 2017. As in Section 6.2.3.1, three principal dimensions explained most of the data variability (80.1% for the African sample and 68.2% for the Asian sample). Note that these numbers have flipped compared with those in Section 6.2.3.1, with the African sample now capturing more variability in the data than the Asian sample. Figures 6.6 and 6.7 illustrate how financial service user characteristics are located in the spaces of these three dimensions. It is important to note that the factors that form these dimensions have changed in many instances compared with the 2013 results. While education remains a key factor in Dimension 1 in both regions (similar to 2013), poverty now is no longer a significant determinant of Dimension 1 in the Asian sample; instead, it plays an important role in the African data. This suggests that the inclusion process may have evolved in both regions. Also, education appears important in Dimension 2 for Africa, whereas poverty is a key factor of that dimension in the Asian data. Age, which was not an important determinant of Dimension 2 in 2013 in the African sample, is now contributing to it in 2017, while the contribution of poverty and location has flipped sides compared with 2013. Similarly, Dimension 3 in 2017 is the reverse of that of 2013, with now

Table 6.6 MCA main dimensions in 2017

Dimensions	*Africa*	*Asia*
	Description	*Description*
1	Education, poverty, location	Education, location
2	Age, education	Age, poverty
3	Gender	Age, gender

Source: *Financial Inclusion Insights.*

MCA = multiple correspondence analysis

only gender mostly explaining it in the African data, whereas age and gender are its key determinants in the Asian data. Table 6.6 summarises these dimensions.

As before, we can plot the financial inclusion service indicators in the variable spaces to find out their association with user characteristics. Considering first the sample of African countries, we see from Figure 6.6 that bank users and those who combine both bank and mobile money are located on the left-hand side of the figure. Those individuals are highly educated, not poor, and live in urban areas. Mobile money users are at the bottom of Figure 6.6 (see subfigure *Africa*) and are young females with secondary education, mostly living in rural areas. This represents a change compared with 2013, where the age group 15–24 years was not significant (close to the origin). Financially excluded individuals are poor who live in rural areas and have at most a primary education. Those individuals are located on the right-hand side of Figure 6.6 (see subfigure *Africa*), and they also appear at the top right-hand side of Figure 6.7 (see subfigure *Africa*). These individuals lack basic literacy and numeracy skills and are over 55 years old.

Looking at the sample of Asian countries (Figures 6.6 and 6.7, subfigure *Asia*), we see that both mobile money and bank and mobile money users are located on the top left part of Figure 6.6 *(Asia)* and bottom left part of Figure 6.7 *(Asia)*. They are highly educated males, not poor, and living in urban areas. As the banking service variable and the 'no financial service' variable are close to the origin in both the Dimensions (1, 2) and (1, 3) spaces, they are difficult to interpret. However, it is likely that they are together with impoverished individuals between 25 and 44 years old with primary educations, and living in rural areas. Individuals without formal education and basic numeracy and literacy skills are located at the bottom right part of Figure 6.7 *(Asia)* and the first upper two quadrants of Figure 6.7 *(Asia)*. As in 2013, this group of individuals are mostly older people.

Table 6.7 contains a summary of each financial service user characteristic. The table enables both regional (Africa vs Asia) and dynamic (2013 vs 2017) comparisons. Considering regional differences first, with the exception of *financially excluded* individuals, while bank users in the African sample are not poor, highly educated, and live in urban areas, the Asian countries' bank users are poor, with only a primary education, living in rural areas, and under 45 years old.

Table 6.7 Characteristics of financial services users in 2017

	Africa	*Asia*
BK	Not poor, urban, high education	Rural, poor, under 45 years old, primary education
MM	Females, under 35 years old, secondary education	High education, males, under 25 years old, not poor, urban
BM	Not poor, urban, high education	High education, urban, males, under 25 years old, not poor
Financially excluded	Males, 35–55 years old, primary education; or rural poor females, over 55 years old with no formal education (thus lacking basic literacy and numeracy skills)	Rural, poor, under 45 years old, primary education; or rural poor females, over 55 years old with no formal education (thus lacking basic literacy and numeracy skills)

Source: *Financial Inclusion Insights.*

BK = banking; BM = both banking and mobile money; MM = mobile money

Mobile money users in the African sample are young females (under 35 years old) with secondary education, whereas in the Asian sample, mobile money users are young, highly educated males (under 25 years old), not poor, and living in urban areas. African users of both bank and mobile money services are highly educated, not poor individuals living in urban areas, while in the Asian sample, users of both bank and mobile money services, although they are highly educated, not poor, and live in urban areas, are mostly young males (under 25 years old).

Temporal differences show that financial service usage has evolved over time. Indeed, comparing the description of each financial service user group in 2013 with that in 2017 (Table 6.5 vs Table 6.7) shows noticeable differences in both regions. For example, in 2017, bank users are no longer associated with gender in both regions (so the service is now available to females), and less educated individuals have access to bank accounts in Asia. Similarly, mobile money users are now associated with gender, with educated young females dominating the market in Africa, while educated young males who are not poor and live in urban areas prevail in Asia. These results substantially contrast with those found in 2013.

Clearly, these results show that financial inclusion has evolved between 2013 and 2017. However, whether the inclusion process has empowered the poorest (rural producers, poor, women, etc.) is still unclear. Since each financial service is associated with specific users, and the fact that the decomposition of the survey sample has remained the same over time, we can trace how the share of the main subpopulation groups of financial services users has changed over time. This analysis allows, for example, tracking the switch of individuals from a service to another. To enable this, we must run MCA not only for 2013 and 2017, but also the other survey years (2014, 2015, and 2016). Since the survey sampling was drawn independently each year, we believe that running separate MCAs will capture the dynamic of financial inclusion over time. Section 6.2.3.3 presents the details.

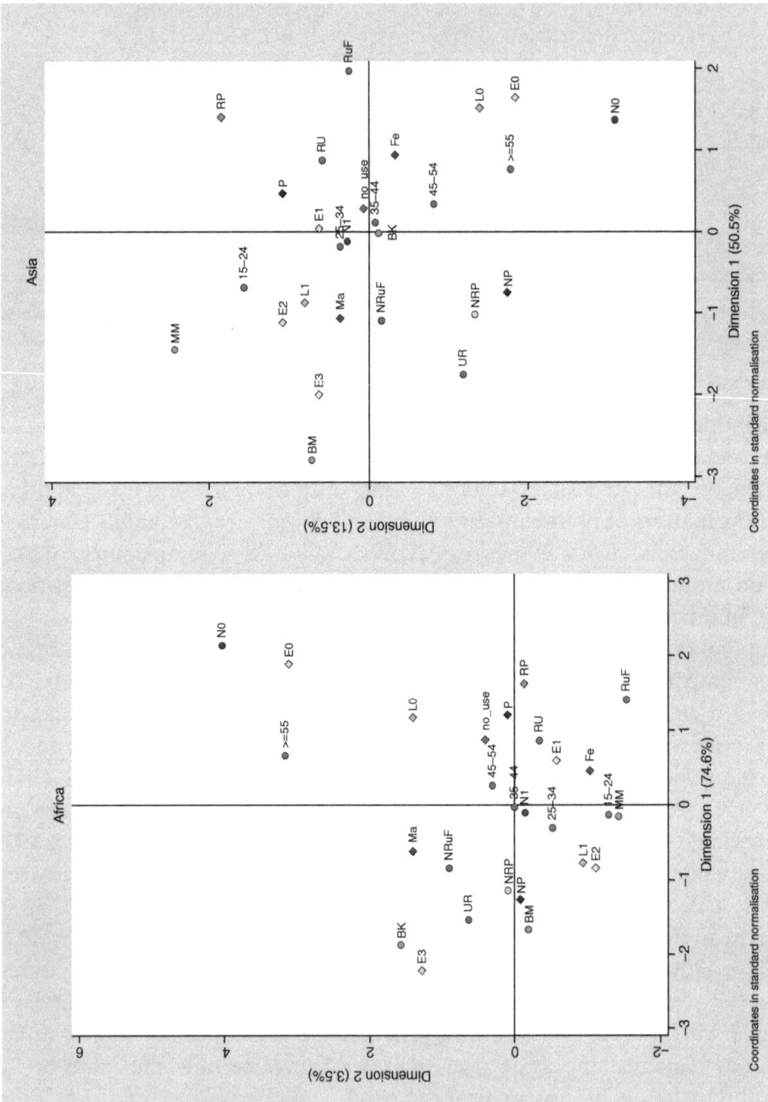

Figure 6.6 2017 MCA results in dimensions 1 and 2 – Africa versus Asia.

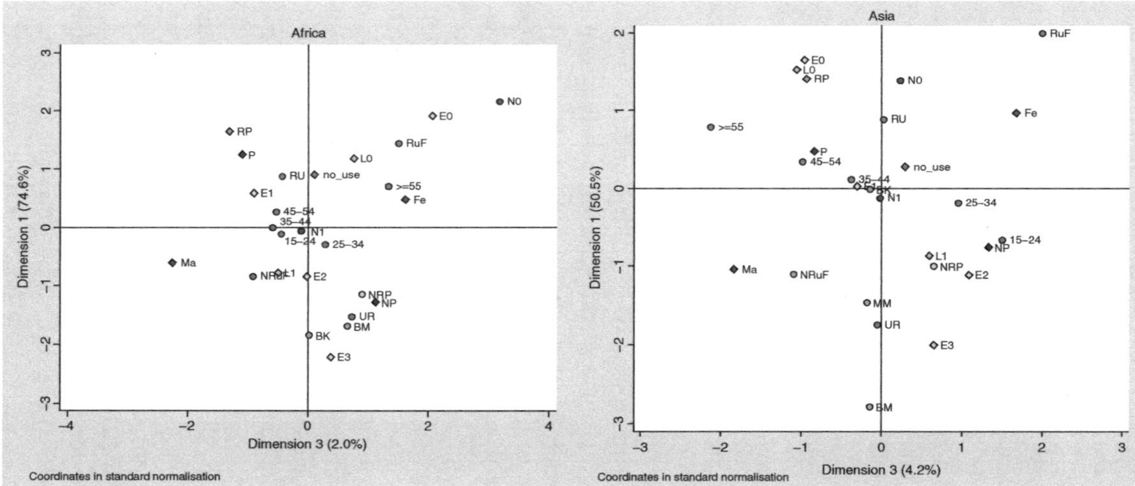

Figure 6.7 2017 MCA results in dimensions 1 and 3 – Africa versus Asia.
MCA = multiple correspondence analysis.
Four main types of financial users are: excluded people (no_use); bank users (BK), mobile money users (MM); bank and mobile money users (BM). Other characteristics of financial users are the following:
Age categories: (15–24), (25–34), (35–44), (45–54), > 55.
Poverty status: poor (P), not poor (NP).
Literacy ability: basic (L1), not basic (L0).
Numeration ability: basic (N1), not basic (N0). Location: rural (RU), urban (UR).
Gender: Male (Ma), female (Fe).
Education status: no-formal education (E0), primary education (E1), secondary education (E2), higher education (E3).
Special status: female in rural area (RuF), female in urban area (NRuF), poor in rural area (RP), not poor (NP).

Source: *Financial Inclusion Insights*.

6.2.3.3 Dynamic of financial inclusion between 2013 and 2017

Our previous analysis in Tables 6.5 and 6.7 showed that poverty, location, education, age, and gender explain most of the differences in the choice of the financial services provided in both continents. Each of these variables separates financial service users and non-users into several distinct subgroups. For example, *age* separates all bank, mobile money, and bank and mobile money users, as well as financially excluded individuals into five groups (15–24; 25–34; 35–44; 45–54; and ≥ 55). Similarly, *poverty* separates them into two groups, poor (P) and not poor (NP), and so does *gender* (females and males). As such, the dynamic of financial inclusion can be assessed by examining, for example, how the share of each subgroup of service users and non-users has changed over time. For clarity, we separate financial services users and non-users in this analysis. Section 6.2.3.4 deals with the dynamic of users, while Section 6.2.3.5 is concerned with that of non-users.

6.2.3.4 Financial inclusion services usage over time

Considering first the usage of banking services, Figure 6.8 shows the plots over time of the share of the overall bank users, as well as that of the main subgroups using this service (age, education, gender, location, and poverty). As in the MCA section, the plots are shown for both regions side by side (Africa in the first row and Asia in the second). For a given year, the share of each subgroup is computed as the number of bank users in that group divided by the total number of observations in the sample, that is, the entire surveyed population that year. As the question related to location was not included in the survey questionnaire of the African countries in 2013, the plots related to the subgroups resulting from this variable start from 2014 (see the bottom left subfigure in Figure 6.8). Looking first at the sample of African countries (first row), with the exception of the groups of individuals with no formal education and individuals over 55 years old that remained constant over time (top left subfigure), and the group of individuals who are not poor (bottom left subfigure) which trended upward, there is a downward trend in bank usage for the other subgroups, including the overall bank usage. For example, overall bank usage has fallen from roughly 18% in 2013 to around 12% in 2017. Similarly, the share of young bank users (under 24 years old) has decreased from around 14% in 2013 to about 7.5% in 2017 (top left subfigure). Remarkably, the share of bank users who were poor has decreased drastically, from slightly over 15% in 2013 to around 2.5% in 2017 (bottom left subfigure). Meanwhile, all subgroups of bank users in the Asian sample, including poor bank users, have steadily increased over the period (top right and bottom right subfigures). As such, most bank users in the African sample seem to have shifted from banking services to alternate financial inclusion services. In the Asian sample, however, the size of most bank user subgroups has steadily increased over time. Nevertheless, some similarities between the two regions exist. In particular, the share of individuals over 55 years old has remained constant over the period in both regions, while that of individuals who are not poor has trended upward.

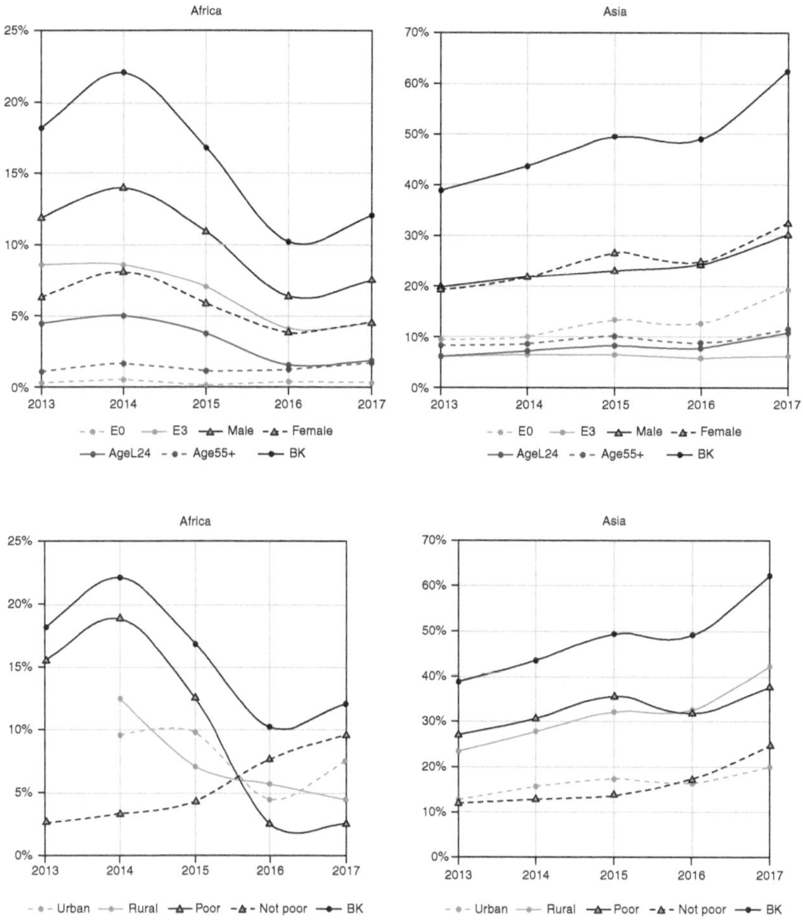

Figure 6.8 Bank usage over time – Africa versus Asia.
Bank account (BK) financial service. The main characteristics of this service users from the multiple correspondence analysis results are the following:
Age categories: (15–24), (25–34), (35–44), (45–54), > 55.
Poverty: poor (P), not poor (NP).
Location: rural (RU), urban (UR).
Gender: Male (Ma), female (Fe).
Education: no formal education (E0), primary education (E1), secondary education (E2), higher education (E3).

Source: *Financial Inclusion Insights.*

Now, looking at mobile money (Figure 6.9), we see that, in the African sample, the proportion of users in most subgroups has either slightly increased, or remained constant over time, with overall usage increasing from 20% in 2013 to roughly 25% in 2017. In particular, the proportion of female mobile money

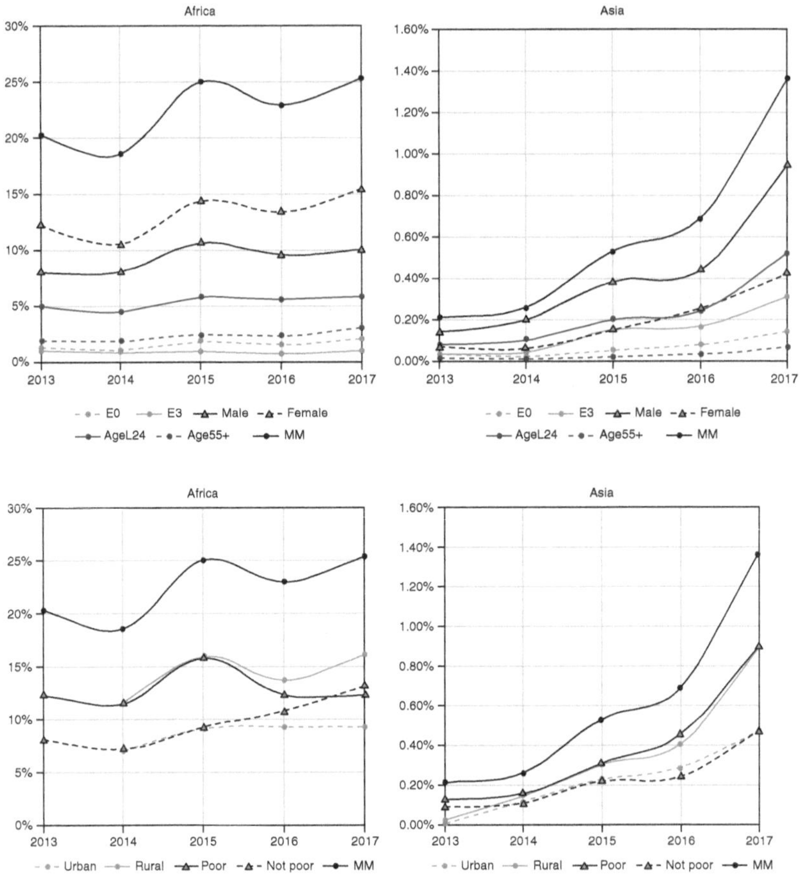

Figure 6.9 Mobile money usage over time – Africa versus Asia.
Mobile Money (MM) financial service.
The main characteristics of this service users from the multiple correspondence analysis results are the following:
Age categories: (15–24), (25–34), (35–44), (45–54), > 55.
Poverty: poor (P), not poor (NP).
Location: rural (RU), urban (UR).
Gender: Male (Ma), female (Fe).
Education: no formal education (E0), primary education (E1), secondary education (E2), higher education (E3).

Source: *Financial Inclusion Insights.*

users has increased steadily from around 12.5% in 2013 to slightly above 15% in 2017. Similarly, the proportions of mobile money users who are not poor and those living in rural areas have also increased steadily over the period. This suggests that the drop in bank usages observed in these subgroups may have benefitted mobile money usage, that is, there may have been a shift from banking to mobile money amongst these subgroups. Another explanation could be that the increasing effort in the Africa region to lift people out of poverty through financial inclusion has seen strong mobilisation in educating females and rural Africans to use these services (see, e.g., Atkinson and Messy, 2013; Triki and Faye, 2013). As previously noted, since banking is rarely available to rural and female Africans, the expansion of mobile phones and Internet even in rural areas has made mobile money the only viable solution (see, e.g., the M-PESA in Kenya; Van Hove and Dubus 2019; Kenya and Uganda; Johnson and Nino-Zarazua 2011). This could explain the steady increase in female and rural mobile money usage for the African region.

Similar to banking service, the share of mobile money users in most subgroups has increased in the Asian sample (top and bottom right subfigures of Figure 6.9). Note that the numbers shown in the vertical axis in these subfigures are small compared with the African sample due to the large sample size in this region, with India alone tripling all individuals surveyed in the Africa region. Unlike the African sample, males dominate females in mobile money usage in the Asian sample, while the shares of poor and rural Asians are identical after 2014. The latter pattern is also observed between the non-poor and rural Asian mobile money users.

Figure 6.10 presents the change in usage of both banking and mobile money within each subgroup. Considering the African sample (top and bottom left subfigures), with the exception of the share of poor individuals, all other subgroups have seen either an increasing trend or a constant evolution in their shares over time. The drop in usage of both banking and mobile money amongst the poorest Asians may be associated with that of banking usage in the same group. Meanwhile, the proportion of non-poor users of both banking and mobile money has increased from around 5.7% in 2013 to about 8.2% in 2017. Clearly, males dominate females in usage of both banking and mobile money, while urban Asians use this service more often than rural Asians. This is no surprise seeing the discrepancy in bank usage between males and females on one hand, and urban and rural on the other hand (Figure 6.8). Again, the proportion of usage of both banking and mobile money has steadily increased in most subgroups, including the poor, in the Asian sample (top and bottom right subfigures). While male users of both banking and mobile money dominate females (similar to Africa), the increase in the fraction of poor users of both banking and mobile money is more pronounced than that of non-poor users in Asia. Poor users of both banking and mobile money dominate non-poor users at the end of the period, which is contrary to the African case.

6.2.3.5 Financially excluded individuals over time

Figure 6.11 plots the proportion of financially excluded over time in the African sample (top and bottom left subfigures) and the Asian sample (top and bottom right subfigures). Looking first at the Asian sample (top and bottom right subfigures), we see that the overall proportion of financially excluded individuals,

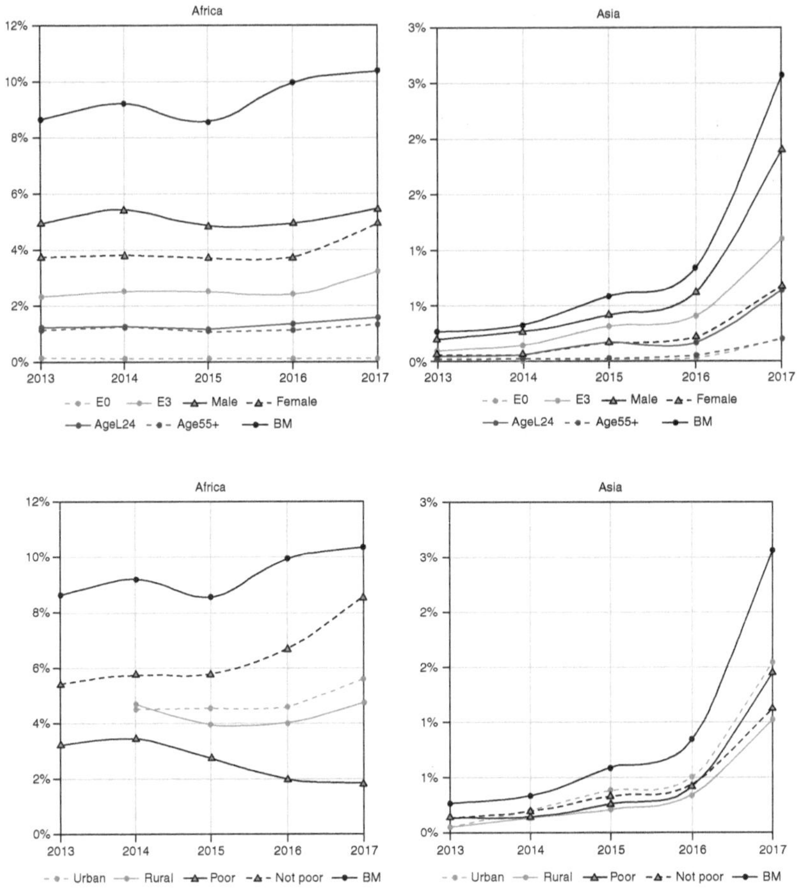

Figure 6.10 BM usage over time – Africa versus Asia.
Bank and Mobile money (BM) financial service.
The main characteristics of this service users from the multiple correspondence analysis results are the following:
Age categories: (15–24), (25–34), (35–44), (45–54), > 55.
Poverty: poor (P), not poor (NP).
Location: rural (RU), urban (UR).
Gender: Male (Ma), female (Fe).
Education: no formal education (E0), primary education (E1), secondary education (E2), higher education (E3).

Source: *Financial Inclusion Insights.*

as well as that of most subgroups, has decreased significantly over time. For example, this fraction has dropped drastically from slightly above 60% in 2013 to about 34% in 2017. Similarly, the fraction of financially excluded poor (respectively, females) has substantially decreased from around 50% (respectively, 38%) in

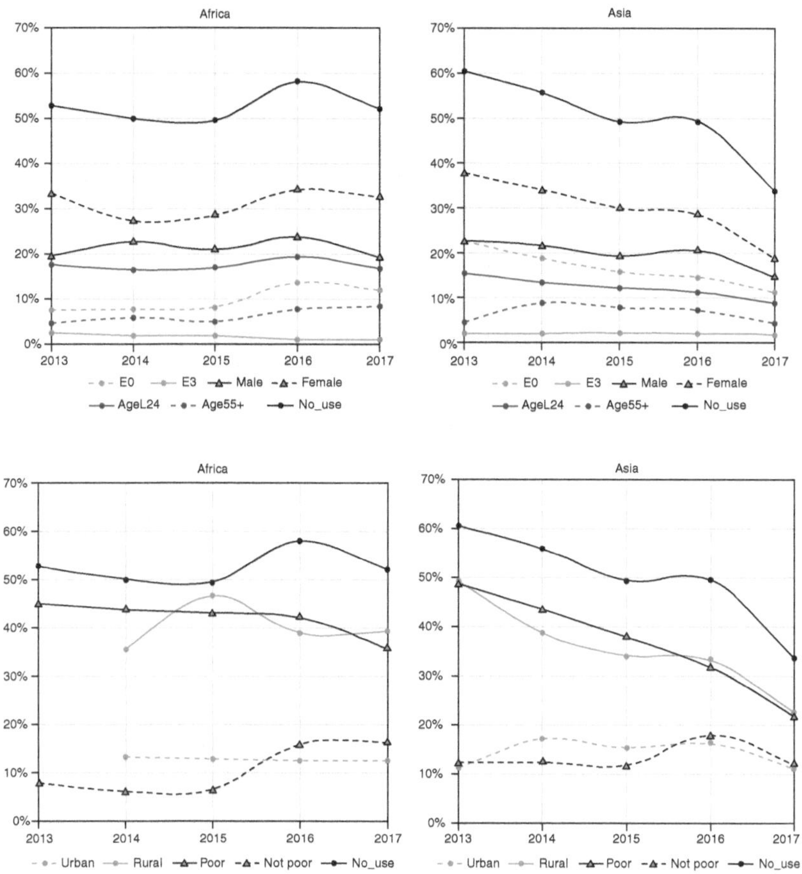

Figure 6.11 Financially excluded individuals over time – Africa versus Asia.
Non-users (no_use).
Age categories: (15–24), (25–34), (35–44), (45–54), > 55.
Poverty: poor (P), not poor (NP).
Location: rural (RU), urban (UR).
Gender: Male (Ma), female (Fe).
Education: no formal education (E0), primary education (E1), secondary education (E2), higher education (E3).

Source: *Financial Inclusion Insights.*

2013 to roughly 21% (respectively, 20%) in 2017. Only the proportions of financially excluded non-poor, urban, and higher educated individuals have remained steadily constant in the Asian sample during the period. Coupling these with the significant increase in financial services usage evidenced in Section 6.2.3.4, it is apparent that financial exclusion has been a relative success in the Asian countries studied. More importantly, many disadvantaged groups (e.g., poor, women, and rural Asians) have seen a drop in their fraction of financially excluded individuals, while their usage of financial services has increased steadily since 2013. As such, financial inclusion also seems to have empowered the poorest in the Asian countries studied.

In the results of the Africa sample (top and bottom left subfigures), there is a slight difference compared with Asia. With the exception of financially excluded poor individuals, the proportion of financially excluded individuals in most of the other subgroups has not changed much during the period. The proportion of financially excluded poor individuals, however, has dropped slightly from around 45% in 2013 to about 38% in 2017. Therefore, financial inclusion has yet to materialise in the African countries compared with Asia. However, the fact that the proportion of financially excluded poor individuals has dropped since 2016 indicates that these African countries are moving toward financial inclusion.

Although Section 6.2.1 provides an extensive characterisation of each group of financial inclusion service users (see, e.g., Tables 6.5 and 6.7), there is evidence of clusters amongst users based on their characteristics. This makes it difficult at this stage of the analysis to know exactly the profile of each service user or that of the financially excluded individuals. In the next section, we use cluster analysis to build the typology (i.e., distinct subgroups) of financial services users.

6.3 Typology of financial inclusion service users

Because the MCA results describe the association between the financial services provided and the characteristics of their users, it is possible to build a typology of financial services users based on these characteristics. To do it, we use cluster analysis to map the financial services users according to the services provided. As cluster analysis is not well known in finance literature, we first describe the technique briefly in Section 6.3.1.

6.3.1 Cluster analysis

Cluster analysis (or clustering) is a technique of grouping a set of data objects into clusters. It can, for example, help policymakers or stakeholders discover distinct groups amongst financial services users, and then use this knowledge to develop targeted policy programmes to increase accessibility to financial services. The clustering methodology in this study builds on the factors (dimensions) obtained from the MCA. The results of the MCA suggest that three main (principal) dimensions summarise most of the data variability in both the African and Asian samples. As the need to know both the number of factors which span the data and the initial number of clusters to be formed is paramount to any cluster analysis, especially when working with large datasets, conducting the MCA analysis as the first step was crucial.

We perform k-means clustering due to the size of the dataset. This method maximises the between-cluster variance and minimises the within-cluster variance relative to the mean of the cluster. The within-cluster variation forms homogeneous clusters. The algorithm initially assigns objects to a pre-assigned number of clusters, and these observations are successively reassigned between clusters by minimising the within-cluster variation. Observations are reassigned to new clusters only when the within-cluster variation is reduced by that reallocation. In our application, the initial distribution of observations into the clusters is random, although robustness tests to alternative initial conditions (first observation, last observation, and observation by predefined category) yielded qualitatively the same results.

Specifically, let $\mathbb{F} = (\mathbf{F}_1, \mathbf{F}_2, \mathbf{F}_3)$ be the space spanned by the three factors obtained from MCA. Each individual $i\,(i = 1,\ldots,n)$ in the sample is associated with its coordinate $f_i = \left(f_{ji}\right)_{1\le j\le 3}$. Let $\mathbb{S} = \{S_k; k = 1,\ldots,4\}$ be a partition of the n individuals into four subgroups, $n_k = |S_k|$, and $\mu_k = \left(\overline{f}_{jk}\right)_{1\le j\le 3}$, $\overline{f}_{jk} = \frac{1}{n_k}\sum_{i\in S_k} f^i_{jk}$. The algorithm for each individual i, solves:

$$min_{S_k \in S} \left\| f_i - \mu_k \right\|^2, \tag{6.6}$$

where $\|\cdot\|$ is the Euclidean norm. The algorithm has three steps:

1. Specify the initial clusters, $\mathbb{S}^0 = \{S_k^0;\ k = 1,\ldots,k\}$, and define the centroids $\mu_k^0 = \left(\overline{f}_{jk}^{\,0}\right)_{1\le j\le 3}$;
2. For each observation i, compute $\left\| f_i - \mu_k \right\|^2$ and set $i \in S_{\overline{k}}^{(t)}$ if $\left\| f_i - \mu_{\overline{k}} \right\|^2 \le \left\| f_i - \mu_k \right\|^2$ for all $k \ne \overline{k}$. Recalculate the centroids $\mu_k^{(t)} = \left(\overline{f}_{jk}^{(t)}\right)_{1\le j\le 3}$;
3. Iterate step 2 until $\left\| f_i - \mu_{\overline{k}} \right\|^2 < \varepsilon$, for some $\varepsilon > 0$.

The number of clusters to be pre-assigned in step 1, as well as the initial distribution of observations into these clusters, is obtained from the MCA, which again underscores the importance of conducting MCA first.

6.3.2 Classification of financial services users

We apply the above algorithm to our samples (Africa and Asia). As the goal is to describe whether individuals cluster based on their financial service usage, we only consider the users of the three financial services available. From the previous sections, we know that our data span a 5-year interval, so we conduct a year-by-year cluster analysis in each region. This allows us to study the dynamic of the clusters formed over time, as well as regional differences.

Considering the African sample of financial services users, the MCA results suggest two clusters for the first 3 years (2013–2015) and three clusters the past 2 years (2016 and 2017). Meanwhile, these numbers reversed in the Asian sample, with three clusters the first 3 years (2013–2015) and two clusters in the past 2 years (2016 and 2017). This is the first discrepancy between both regions.

Tables 6.8 and 6.9 describe the clusters over time in the African and Asian samples, respectively. Figures 6.12 (a and b) and 6.13 (a and b) show the plots of the clusters in each region in 2013 and 2017, as well as the financial services available to each group (cluster). We only present these 2 years for brevity. Similar graphs for the other years are available upon request.

Focusing first on 2013, we see from Figure 6.12a (African sample) that cluster 1 consists of young users (under 36 years old) who are mostly female with at least a primary education. This group usually uses mobile money. Cluster 2 is formed by poor educated young who are mostly males. This group likely uses banking. Clearly, most financial services users in the African countries were young in 2013 and predominantly used either banking or mobile money. We know from the MCA results that in 2013, users of both banking and mobile money were associated with individuals with secondary education, under 35 years old, and not poor. This group does not appear in 2013 as a cluster, probably because its size is small. Also, we see that individuals over 35 years (poor or low educated) were financially excluded in 2013 in the African sample. The clustering confirms these results. Regarding the Asian sample, the description of the three 2013 clusters, as well as their financial service usage, differs slightly from that observed in the African sample. Specifically, cluster 1 is mostly urban educated users who are not poor. This group mostly chooses either the banking service or both bank and mobile money services. Cluster 2 is formed by poor males living mostly in rural areas. This group mostly chooses banking. Finally, cluster 3 consists of rural female users who are on average in their late thirties and mostly poor. This group mainly chooses either banking or mobile money. The main similarity between the two regions is that financially excluded individuals are older with no formal education.

Considering the 2017 results Figure 6.13 shows three clusters in the African sample, while the Asian sample contains two clusters, thus reversing the 2013 cluster numbers between the two regions. In the African sample, individuals in cluster 1 are still mostly mobile money users. They are still young (on average in their late thirties) but all males (a contrast with 2013), mostly poor with basic education (primary and secondary), and mostly living in rural areas. Cluster 2 consists of young females with primary or secondary education also living mostly in rural areas. They are also mostly mobile money users, and their characteristics are much closer to those of the 2013 cluster 1. Cluster 3 is formed by educated non-poor individuals. This group mostly consists of either bank users or users of both banking and mobile money. If we analyse the Asian sample, we can find that there are now two clusters. Cluster 1 is formed by rural poor individuals with mostly no tertiary education. They mainly use banking, but sometimes mobile money. Cluster 2 consists of non-poor rural individuals or educated individuals mostly over 25 years old. This group likely prefers either banking or both banking and mobile money.

Table 6.8 Typology of financial users over time – Africa

Cluster	*Profile*	*2013*		*Cluster*	*Profile*	*2014*	
		User characteristics	*Product*			*User characteristics*	*Product*
1	Young, mostly females	Mostly females, under 45 years old, primary or secondary education education	MM	1	Poor, ed-ucated, young, mostly males	Mostly males, under 35 years old, mostly in the rural, poor, high education (secondary or higher level)	BK
2	Poor, ed-ucated, young males	Males, under 35 years old, poor, high educated (secondary or higher level)	BK	2	Young, mostly not poor females	Mostly females, under 35 years old, mostly urban and not poor primary or secondary	MM
Cluster	*Profile*	*2015*		*Cluster*	*Profile*	*2016*	
		User characteristics	*Product*			*User characteristics*	*Product*
1	Young, not poor, mostly females	Mostly females, under 35 years old, mostly not poor, mixed be-tween rural and urban, primary and secondary	MM	1	Young, not poor, educated males	Males, from 25 to 44 years old, not poor, mixed between rural and urban, high educated (secondary or higher level)	BK, BM
2	Young, poor, educated mostly males	Mostly males, under 45 years old, poor, mixed between rural and urban, high educated (secondary or higher	BK	2	Young, not poor, educated females	Females, under 35 years old, not poor, mixed between rural and urban, primary and secondary education	MM

(*continued*)

Table 6.8 Cont.

Cluster	*Profile*	*2015*		*Cluster*	*Profile*	*2016*	
		User characteristics	*Product*			*User characteristics*	*Product*
		level)		3	Rural, mostly poor	Under 45 years old, mostly Under 45 years old, poor and in the rural, primary education level	MM

Cluster	*Profile*	*2017*	
		User characteristics	*Product*
1	Young, rural, educated males	Males, under 45 years old, mostly poor, in the rural, primary or secondary education	MM
2	Young females, mostly in rural	Females, under 45 years old, mostly in the rural, primary or secondary education	MM
3	Educated, non-poor	Under 45 years old, mostly in the urban, not poor, high education level (secondary or higher)	BK, BM

Source: *Financial Inclusion Insights.*

BK = banking; BM = both banking and mobile money; MM = mobile money

Table 6.9 Typology of financial users over time – Asia

Cluster	*Profile*	*2013*		*Cluster*	*Profile*	*2014*	
		User characteristics	*Product*			*User characteristics*	*Product*
1	Educated, non-poor, mostly urban	From 25 to 44 years old, mostly from urban and not poor, high educated (secondary or higher level)	BK, BM	1	Poor males, mostly rural	Males, older than 44 years old, poor, mostly in the rural, secondary education	BK
2	Poor males, mostly rural	Males, over 35 years old, poor, in the rural, secondary education	BK	2	Rural, poor females	Females, from 25 to 44 years old, poor, in the rural, low education and numeration skill	BK
3	Rural females, mostly poor	Females, from 25 to 44 years old, poor, in the rural, low education and literacy skill	BK, MM	3	Educated, mostly urban non-poor	Mostly not poor and in the urban, high education (secondary or higher level)	BK, MM
Cluster	*Profile*	*2015*		*Cluster*	*Profile*	*2016*	
		User characteristics	*Product*			*User characteristics*	*Product*
1	Rural, poor females	Females, under 45 years old, poor, in the rural, low education and literacy skill	BK	1	Rural poor	Under 45 years old, poor, in the rural, secondary or no education	BK, MM
2	Educated, mostly	Mostly not poor and in the urban, high education	BK, MM	2	Educated, mostly	From 25 to 44 years old, mostly not poor,	BK

(*continued*)

Table 6.9 Cont.

Cluster	*Profile*	*2015*		*Cluster*	*Profile*	*2016*	
		User characteristics	*Product*			*User characteristics*	*Product*
	urban non-poor	(secondary and higher level)			non-poor	mixed between rural and urban, secondary education	
3	Poor males, mostly rural	Males, poor, mostly in the rural, secondary education	BK				

Cluster	*Profile*	*2017*	
		User characteristics	*Product*
1	Rural poor	Under 45 years old, poor, in the rural, low education (no education or primary education)	BK
2	Educated, not rural poorest	From 25 to 44 years old, mostly not poor, mostly educated	BK

Source: Financial Inclusion Insights.

BK = banking; BM = both banking and mobile mone;, MM = mobile money

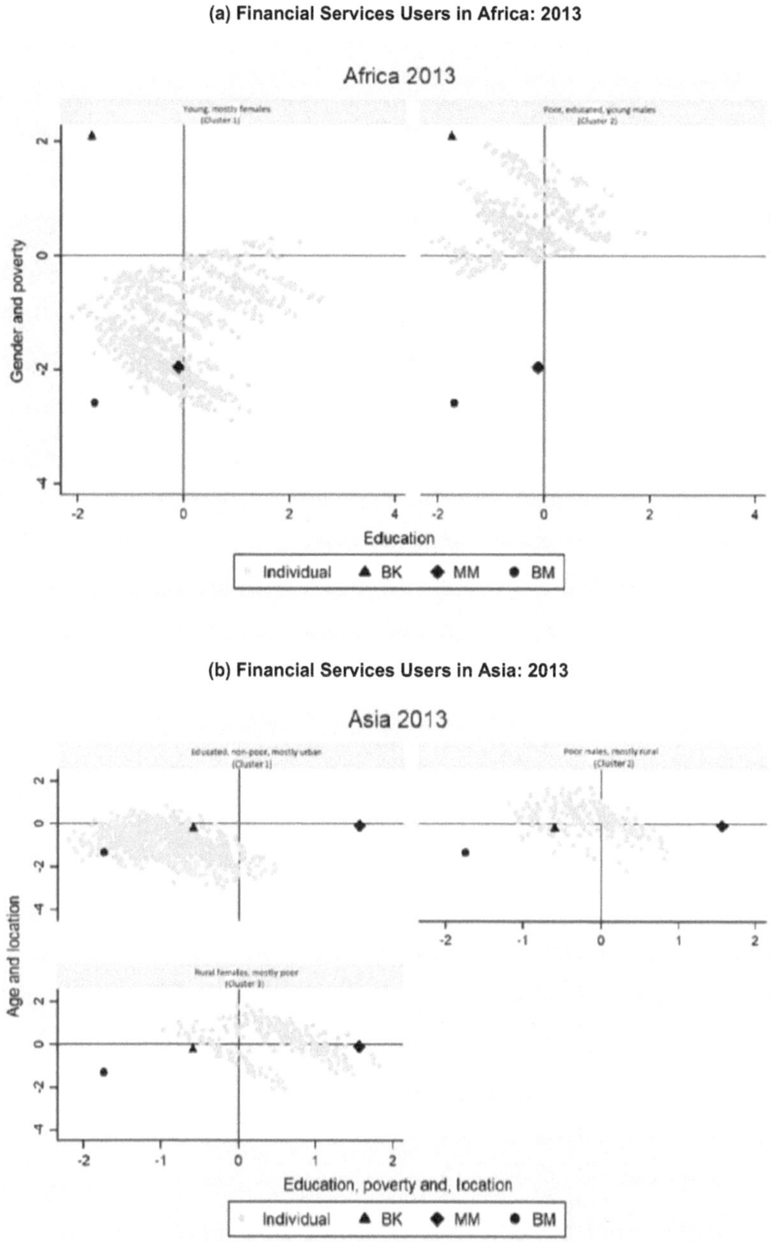

Figure 6.12 Clusters of financial services users in Africa and Asia – 2013
(a) Financial services users in Africa: 2013
(b) Financial services users in Asia: 2013
BK = banking, BM = both banking and mobile money, MM = mobile money
Source: Authors' calculations.

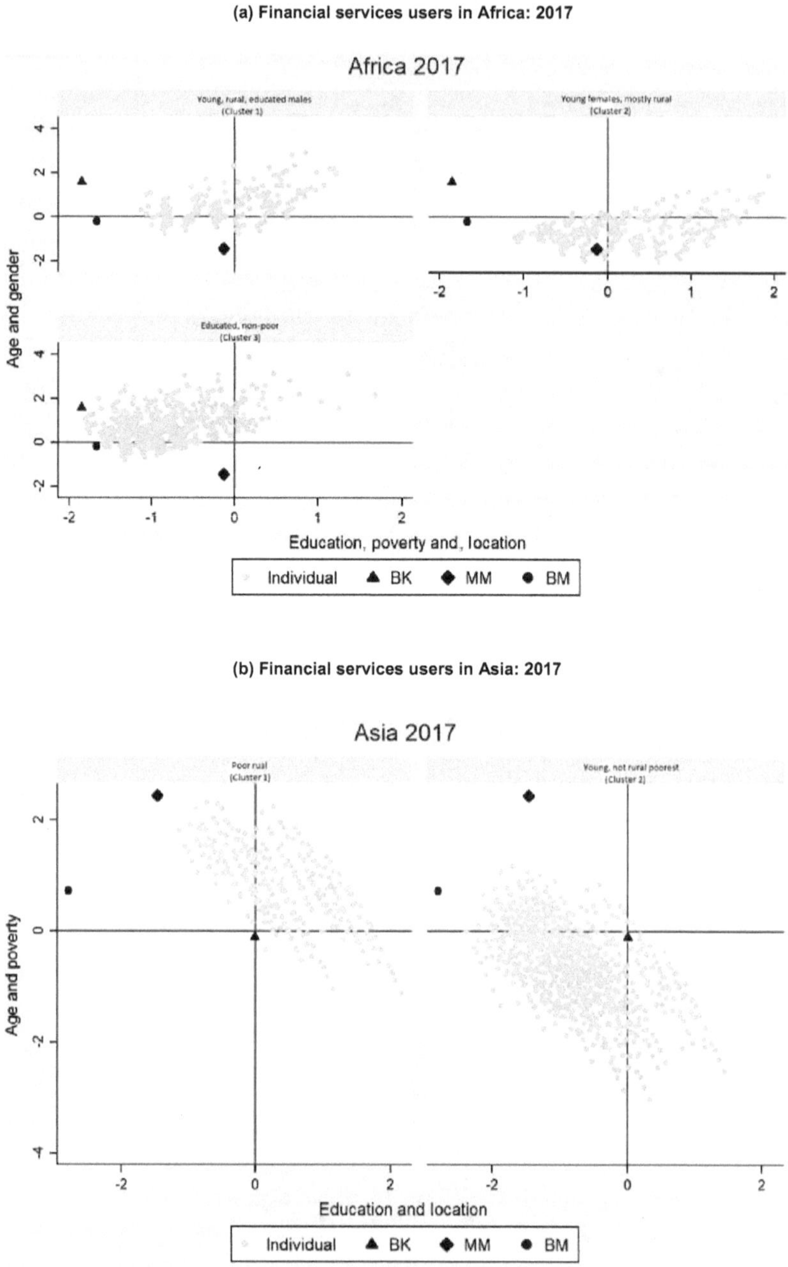

Figure 6.13 Clusters of financial services users in Africa and Asia – 2017
(a) Financial services users in Africa: 2017
(b) Financial services users in Asia: 2017
BK = banking, BM = both banking and mobile money, MM = mobile money
Source: Authors' calculations.

Detailed descriptive statistics of each cluster in 2013 and 2017 are included in Tables 6.A1–6.A4 in the Appendix. More importantly, a complete characterisation of each cluster for all years (2013–2017) is provided in Tables 6.8 and 6.9. This represents the typology of financial services users, as well as its dynamic in Africa (Table 6.8) and Asia (Table 6.9).

6.4 Conclusion

Financial inclusion has become one of the most powerful tools for poverty reduction and economic growth in developing nations. In this study, we examined the association between financial inclusion services and the characteristics of their users in eight developing countries in Africa and Asia. Using survey data from *Financial Inclusion Insights* over 5 years (2013–2017), we employ MCA to find that poverty, education, age, gender, and location are the main determinants of financial service usage in these countries. While the dynamic of financial service usage in the African countries seems to have shifted from banking toward mobile money, the Asian countries have seen a steady increase in all financial services usage since 2013.

The shift from banking to mobile money in Africa could be explained by the increasing mobilisation to lift people out of poverty, especially women and rural Africans, through financial inclusion. Since banking services are rarely available to rural and female Africans, the expansion of mobile phones and access to Internet in rural areas has made mobile money service usage a viable path to financial inclusion.

Interestingly, our results show that the overall proportion of financially excluded individuals, as well as that of most subgroups of the population (classified by age, gender, poverty, location, education), has decreased significantly over time in the Asian sample. Only the proportions of financially excluded non-poor individuals, individuals living in urban areas, and those with tertiary education have remained constant in the Asian sample. These groups are likely not engaged in any financial activity. These results, along with the significant increase in all financial service usage in the Asian sample, suggest that financial inclusion has been a relative success in Asia. More importantly, many disadvantaged groups (e.g., poor, women, and rural Asians) have seen a drop in their proportion of financially excluded individuals, while their use of financial services has steadily increased since 2013. Therefore, financial inclusion also seems to have empowered the poorest in Asia. By contrast, the African countries have seen mixed results. With the exception of poor individuals, the proportion of financially excluded individuals in most of the other subgroups has not changed much during the period. The proportion of financially excluded poor individuals, however, has dropped slightly from around 45% in 2013 to about 38% in 2017, thus suggesting that financial inclusion has yet to be effective in Africa compared with Asia. Nevertheless, the fact that the proportion of financially excluded poor individuals has dropped since 2016 indicates that the African countries are moving toward financial inclusion.

Moreover, we provide a typology of service users in both regions, as well as financial inclusion's dynamic over time. While young, rural, and female financial service users in Africa seem to move toward mobile money, the same groups prefer either banking or mobile money in the Asian sample. In both regions, financial service users who are not poor, live in urban areas, and have basic education combine both banking service and mobile money. Poor males and young females under 45 years old who live mostly in rural areas prefer banking, while the same groups tend toward mobile money in the African sample.

Notes

1 The UFA2020 initiative focuses on 25 priority countries representing almost 70% of all financially excluded in the world. The goals are to provide advanced financial access and inclusion, create a regulatory environment to enable access to transaction accounts, expand access points and financial capability, drive high-volume government programmes into those transaction accounts, and reach disadvantaged populations, that is, women and rural producers.

2 See, for example, Jeanneney and Kpodar (2011); Sarma and Pais (2011); Beck et al. (2005, 2007); Clarke et al. (2006); Burgess and Pande (2005); Honohan (2004); and Galor and Zeira (1993).

3 See, for example, Abu-Bader and Abu-Qarn (2008); Menon and van der Meulen Rodgers (2011); Bittencourt (2012); Pal (2011); and Yang and Yi (2008).

4 An indicator matrix is an individuals-by-variables matrix, where the rows represent individuals and the columns are dummy variables representing categories of the variables.

References

Abu-Bader, S. and A.S. Abu-Qarn (2008), 'Financial Development and Economic Growth: The Egyptian Experience', *Journal of Policy Modeling* 30(5), pp.887–98.

Allen, F., A. Demirguc-Kunt, L. Klapper, and M.S.M. Peria (2012), *The Foundations of Financial Inclusion: Understanding Ownership and Use of Formal Accounts*. Washington, DC: World Bank.

Atkinson, A. and F.-A. Messy (2013), 'Promoting Financial Inclusion through Financial Education: OECD/INFE Evidence, Policies and Practice', *OECD Working Papers on Finance, Insurance and Private Pensions*, No. 34. Paris: OECD.

Beck, T., A. Demirguc-Kunt, and R. Levine (2007), 'Finance, Inequality and the Poor', *Journal of Economic Growth* 12(1), pp.27–49.

Beck, T., A. Demirguc-Kunt, and M.S. Martinez Peria (2005), *Reaching Out: Access to and Use of Banking Services across Countries*. Washington, DC: World Bank.

Becker, G. (1975), *Human Capital: A Theoretical and Empirical Analysis with Special Reference to Education*. New York: Columbia University Press.

Bittencourt, M. (2012), 'Financial Development and Economic Growth in Latin America: Is Schumpeter Right?', *Journal of Policy Modeling* 34(3), pp.341–55.

Burgess, R. and R. Pande (2005), 'Do Rural Banks Matter? Evidence from the Indian Social Banking Experiment', *American Economic Review* 95(3), pp.780–95.

Cámara, N. and D. Tuesta (2014), 'Measuring Financial Inclusion: A Multidimensional Index', *BBVA Research Paper*, No. 14/26, Madrid: BBVA.

Clarke, G.R., L.C. Xu, and H.-F. Zou (2006), 'Finance and Income Inequality: What Do the Data Tell Us?', *Southern Economic Journal* 72(3), pp.578–96.

Demirguc-Kunt, A. and L. Klapper (2012), *Financial Inclusion in Africa: An Overview*. Washington, DC: World Bank.

Demirguc-Kunt, A., L. Klapper, D. Singer, S. Ansar, and J. Hess (2018), *The Global Findex Database 2017: Measuring Financial Inclusion and the Fintech Revolution*. Washington, DC: World Bank.

Demirguc-Kunt, A., L. Klapper, D. Singer, and P. Van Oudheusden (2015), *The Global Findex Database 2014: Measuring Financial Inclusion around the World*. Washington, DC: World Bank.

Dungey, M., F.D. Tchatoka, and M.B. Yanotti (2018), 'Using Multiple Correspondence Analysis for Finance: A Tool for Assessing Financial Inclusion', *International Review of Financial Analysis* 59, pp.212–22.

Efobi, U., I. Beecroft, and E. Osabuohien (2014), 'Access to and Use of Bank Services in Nigeria: Micro-econometric Evidence', *Review of Development Finance* 4(2), pp.104–14.

Fungacova, Z. and L. Weill, (2015), 'Understanding Financial Inclusion in China', *China Economic Review* 34, pp.196–206.

Galor, O. and J. Zeira (1993), 'Income Distribution and Macroeconomics', *The Review of Economic Studies* 60(1), pp.35–52.

Greenacre, M. (2017), *Correspondence Analysis in Practice*. Abingdon: Chapman and Hall/CRC.

Greenacre, M.J. (1993), 'Biplots in Correspondence Analysis', *Journal of Applied Statistics* 20(2), pp.251–69.

Gupte, R., B. Venkataramani, and D. Gupta (2012), 'Computation of Financial Inclusion Index for India', *Procedia-Social and Behavioral Sciences* 37, pp.133–49.

Honohan, P. (2004), 'Financial Development, Growth and Poverty: How Close Are the Links?', in C.A.E. Goodhart (ed.), *Financial Development and Economic Growth*. London: Palgrave Macmillan, pp.1–37.

Jeanneney, S.G. and K. Kpodar (2011), 'Financial Development and Poverty Reduction: Can There Be a Benefit without a Cost?', *The Journal of Development Studies* 47(1), pp.143–63.

Johnson, S. and M. Nino-Zarazua (2011), 'Financial Access and Exclusion in Kenya and Uganda', *The Journal of Development Studies* 47(3), pp.475–96.

Mbutor, M.O. and I.A. Uba (2013), 'The Impact of Financial Inclusion on Monetary Policy in Nigeria', *Journal of Economics and International Finance* 5(8), pp.318–26.

Menon, N. and Y. van der Meulen Rodgers (2011), 'How Access to Credit Affects Self-employment: Differences by Gender during India's Rural Banking Reform', *The Journal of Development Studies* 47(1), pp.48–69.

Pal, R. (2011), 'The Relative Impacts of Banking, Infrastructure and Labour on Industrial Growth: Evidence from Indian States', *Macroeconomics and Finance in Emerging Market Economies* 4(1), pp.101–24.

Sarma, M. and J. Pais, (2011), 'Financial Inclusion and Development', *Journal of International Development* 23(5), pp.613–28.

Sharma, M. (2008), 'Index of Financial Inclusion', Working Paper, No. 215, Indian Council for Research on International Economic Relations (ICRIER). New Delhi: ICRIER.

Triki, T. and I. Faye (2013), *Financial Inclusion in Africa*. Tunis: African Development Bank.
Van Hove, L. and A. Dubus (2019), 'M-pesa and Financial Inclusion in Kenya: Of Paying Comes Saving?', *Sustainability* 11(3), p.568.
Yang, Y.Y. and M.H. Yi (2008), 'Does Financial Development Cause Economic Growth? Implication for Policy in Korea', *Journal of Policy Modeling* 30(5), pp.827–40.

Appendices

Appendix 6.1 Clusters' descriptive statistics: 2013 financial users – Africa

Variables	*Cluster 1*		*Cluster 2*	
	Mean	*Std. dev.*	*Mean*	*Std. dev.*
Age	35.55	13.589	33.13	11.799
Age 24 less	21%	0.411	24%	0.426
Age 25–34	33%	0.470	41%	0.491
Age 35–44	23%	0.419	18%	0.388
Age 45–54	11%	0.313	10%	0.298
Age 55 plus	11%	0.308	7%	0.248
Male	32%	0.465	76%	0.430
Literacy	81%	0.396	96%	0.200
Numeration	85%	0.359	94%	0.242
Poverty	41%	0.493	92%	0.271
Rural poor	22%	0.411	53%	0.499
Rural female	34%	0.473	10%	0.298
No education	5%	0.216	2%	0.155
Primary	44%	0.497	15%	0.359
Secondary	38%	0.487	41%	0.493
High education	12%	0.322	40%	0.489
Observations	3,655		3,412	

Source: Authors' calculations.

Appendix 6.2 Clusters' descriptive statistics: 2013 financial users – Asia

Variables	*Cluster 1*		*Cluster 2*		*Cluster 3*	
	Mean	*Std. dev.*	*Mean*	*Std. dev.*	*Mean*	*Std. dev.*
Age	40.25	15.281	42.58	15.937	38.60	15.087
Age 24 or less	16%	0.370	13%	0.341	17%	0.378
Age 25–34	24%	0.428	19%	0.396	26%	0.438
Age 35–44	22%	0.413	24%	0.428	25%	0.434
Age 45–54	18%	0.380	17%	0.376	13%	0.341
Age 55 plus	20%	0.401	26%	0.438	18%	0.386
Urban	81%	0.396	1%	0.105	0%	0.000
Male	55%	0.497	100%	0.000	0%	0.045
Literacy	85%	0.359	67%	0.470	47%	0.499
Numeration	90%	0.294	84%	0.368	63%	0.483
Poverty	38%	0.485	100%	0.000	90%	0.302
Rural poor	0%	0.020	97%	0.179	90%	0.305
Rural female	5%	0.211	0%	0.000	100%	0.060
No education	10%	0.305	24%	0.425	45%	0.498
Primary	11%	0.308	20%	0.401	14%	0.350
Secondary	51%	0.500	48%	0.500	37%	0.482
High education	28%	0.450	8%	0.274	4%	0.195
Observations	9,983		5,931		6,542	

Source: Authors' calculations.

Appendix 6.3 Clusters' descriptive statistics: 2017 financial users – Africa

Variables	*Cluster 1*		*Cluster 2*		*Cluster 3*	
	Mean	*Std. dev.*	*Mean*	*Std. dev.*	*Mean*	*Std. dev.*
Age	37.41	13.89048	34.96	12.47355	37.64	14.89873
Age 24 or less	20%	0.396746	22%	0.411345	18%	0.38161
Age 25–34	26%	0.439785	36%	0.479731	35%	0.477025
Age 35–44	26%	0.438308	21%	0.408961	19%	0.393929
Age 45–54	17%	0.375009	12%	0.330674	11%	0.315702
Age 55 plus	11%	0.318336	9%	0.284015	17%	0.374792
Urban	13%	0.341456	27%	0.444205	79%	0.406896
Male	100%	0	0%	0	64%	0.481348
Literacy	77%	0.421434	73%	0.443019	82%	0.381343
Numeration	99%	0.112688	98%	0.150436	98%	0.131713
Poverty	73%	0.445135	46%	0.498084	8%	0.27194
Rural poor	62%	0.485443	36%	0.479842	0%	0.050165
Rural female	0%	0	73%	0.444205	2%	0.124577
No education	4%	0.190993	7%	0.251721	5%	0.21026
Primary	58%	0.493752	50%	0.500086	16%	0.362664
Secondary	32%	0.465591	38%	0.485203	43%	0.495463
High education	5%	0.227674	5%	0.220555	36%	0.479434
Observations	1,478		2,634		3,172	

Source: Authors' calculations.

Appendix 6.4 Clusters' descriptive statistics: 2017 financial users – Asia

Variables	*Cluster 1*		*Cluster 2*	
	Mean	*Std. dev.*	*Mean*	*Std. dev.*
Age	38.39	15.015	38.59	14.607
Age 24 and less	19%	0.395	17%	0.378
Age 25–34	25%	0.431	27%	0.444
Age 35–44	23%	0.420	23%	0.420
age 45–54	15%	0.359	15%	0.361
Age 55 plus	18%	0.383	17%	0.379
Urban	0%	0.000	56%	0.496
Male	48%	0.500	51%	0.500
Literacy	61%	0.488	70%	0.459
Numeration	93%	0.251	92%	0.274
Poverty	100%	0.000	33%	0.472
Rural poor	100%	0.000	0%	0.000
Rural female	52%	0.500	22%	0.416
No education	33%	0.469	27%	0.446
Primary	33%	0.471	26%	0.441
Secondary	26%	0.439	32%	0.466
High education	8%	0.270	14%	0.347
Observations	15,872		23,304	

Source: Authors' calculations.

7 The poverty-reducing effects of financial inclusion

Evidence from Cambodia

Kimty Seng

7.1 Introduction

Financial inclusion, defined as access to and use of services offered by financial institutions, is one of the main goals of economic development via financial development, and accordingly has been argued to serve as a key policy tool for achieving the sustainable development goals (SDGs) (Klapper, El-Zoghbi, and Hess, 2016). The intended effects of financial deepening on economic growth, income inequality, and poverty alleviation have been evidenced in many studies (Levine, Loayza, and Beck, 2000; Beck, Demirguc-Kunt, and Peria, 2007). Nonetheless, less evidence has been provided on the effects of financial inclusion on inclusive growth and poverty, even though previous studies have made marginal efforts to address this (Demirguc-Kunt, Klapper, and Singer, 2017). Although financial inclusion is likely beneficial to economic development, poverty alleviation in particular, three strands of literature have come to different and controversial conclusions.

On the positive side, financial inclusion, through microcredit for needy households, is likely to fight poverty (e.g., Karlan and Zinman, 2010; Imai, Arun, and Annim, 2010; Imai and Azam, 2012; Asad, Issam, and Imai, 2014; Rahman, Luo, and Minjuan, 2014; Kulb, Hennink, Kiiti, and Mutinda, 2015; Akotey and Adjasi, 2016). It has been found to increase household income (Burgess and Pande, 2005; Swamy, 2014), create jobs (Bruhn and Love, 2014), and increase expenditures (Dupas and Robinson, 2013) and savings (Brune, Giné, Goldberg, and Yang, 2016). Access to such financial services as microcredit can minimise households' socio-economic risk through empowering women, relaxing credit constraints, acquiring needed inputs and necessary assets, and helping them in a timely manner to meet certain unexpected expenditures (Kulb et al., 2015; Akotey and Adjasi, 2016). Furthermore, it allows the poor to take control of their lives and avoid less desirable factory jobs and insecure wage labour (Bornstein, 1996) by bankrolling microbusinesses, raising household income, and smoothing household consumption (Seng, 2018b). Such a pro-poor mission is underpinned by the success of Yunus's Grameen Bank in Bangladesh. These findings confirm that financial inclusion can produce welfare-enhancing effects, extending beyond its benefits in the financial realm to the economy (Grohmann, Klühs, and Menkhoff, 2018).

On the negative side, microcredit offered by microfinance institutions (MFIs) is likely to trap needy borrowers into a vicious cycle of poverty and has even weakened rather than empowered women (e.g., Maldonado and González-Vega, 2008; Bateman, 2010; Schicks, 2013; Ganle, Afriyie, and Segbefia, 2015; Seng, 2018a and 2018b). In between, some studies have questioned the pro-poor effects of financial inclusion and have argued that financial services, especially credit, should be used with caution (e.g., Bello, 2006; Banerjee, Dufio, Glennerster, and Kinnan, 2009; Duvendack and Palmer, 2012).

The empirical evidence on the intended effects of financial development on needy households has drawn recent studies' attention to the determinants of financial inclusion (e.g., Zins and Weill, 2016; Ouma, Odongo, and Were, 2017; Ghosh and Vinod, 2017; Masino and Niño-Zarazúa, 2020; Grohmann et al., 2018). Ghosh and Vinod (2017) and Grohmann et al. (2018) provided evidence that financial literacy has roles to play in promoting financial inclusion. Nonetheless, the most recent evidence on the unwanted effects of financial services still questions the pro-poor effects of financial development, in Cambodia in particular (e.g., Bylander, 2015; Bateman, 2017; Seng, 2018a and 2018b). However, these studies do not account for financial literacy in their empirical model analysis, even while attributing the undesirable effects to borrowers' limited financial literacy. In particular, Seng (2018a and 2018b) argued that the borrowers' limited financial knowledge is very likely to constrain the pro-poor development of microfinance in Cambodia. These studies make room for others on the poverty-reducing effects of financial development, a priori revealing that financial literacy is very likely to promote pro-poor financial inclusion in developing countries such as Cambodia.

To bridge this study gap, the current study analyses the effects of financial inclusion on poverty in terms of household income per capita, taking financial literacy into account. To accomplish this, the analysis uses an endogenous switching model by households' financial literacy status, with data from the 2015 global FinScope survey on Cambodia. The endogenous switching model addresses the endogeneity of the use of financial services, accounting not only for selection bias arising from unobserved factors determining both the decisions to use financial services and household income per capita, but also for the inherent differences between the users and non-users in terms of income functions.

A complementary analysis also investigates the effects on household budget deficits with an endogenous switching probit (ESP) model. The study concludes that the use of financial services is very likely to reduce household budget deficits and poverty if the users have at least basic financial knowledge. Although over the past two decades Cambodia's financial sector has developed remarkably,[1] with arguments that it has made a tremendous contribution to economic growth and household welfare, the empirical evidence is still limited.

The remainder of the study is structured as follows. Section 7.2 presents an overview of financial inclusion in Cambodia. Section 7.3 reviews relevant literature. Section 7.4 describes the analytical framework. Section 7.5 reports data and descriptive analysis. Section 7.6 presents the estimated results, and the final section concludes the study.

7.2 Overview of financial inclusion in Cambodia

Over the past two decades, Cambodia has achieved remarkably rapid growth in banking, particularly microfinance. From 1997 to 2011, the sector had a leading role in Cambodia's economy, especially in the rural communities (Bylander, 2015). The government has made efforts to promote the sector's growth, aiming at contributing to socio-economic development and poverty reduction (Seng, 2018a and 2018b). Cambodia's banking sector started with microfinance in the early 1990s, emerging from not-for-profit microcredit projects supported by international donors and nongovernmental organisations (NGOs). Microfinance was developed to create jobs for demobilised soldiers and fill the non-existent banking sector. In 2017, in the banking sector, there were 39 commercial banks, 15 specialised banks, 7 microfinance deposit institutions (MDIs), 69 MFIs, 313 rural credit institutions, 11 leasing companies, 15 third-party processors, 1 credit bureau, 6 representatives offices, and 2,476 money changers (National Bank of Cambodia [NBC], 2017).

Cambodia's financial inclusion has been promoted with a focus on access to credit and savings accounts, payment instruments, and payment services. According to the Financial Stability Review published by the NBC in 2019, the credit to businesses as a percentage of gross domestic product (GDP) increased from approximately 29% in 2012 to 58.3% in 2018, while the credit to individuals increased from approximately 15.5% in 2012 to 56.5% in 2018. However, the credit to businesses as a percentage of the total had a declining trend from approximately 62% in 2012 to 45% in 2018, while the credit to individuals had an increasing trend from approximately 38% in 2012 to 55% in 2018.

Furthermore, Figure 7.1 suggests that the total amount of deposits at banks and MDIs increased remarkably from approximately KR17.64 trillion in 2010 to KR76.78 trillion in 2017, while the total amount of loans offered by banks, MDIs, and MFIs also increased from approximately KR14.86 trillion in 2010 to KR81.40 trillion in 2017. Of note, from 2013 to 2017, the amount of deposits each year was smaller than that of loans. This trend suggests that deposit and loan growth is likely inclusive. This is illustrated by Figure 7.2, with the number of borrowers increasing from 1,264,423 in 2010 to 2,698,216 in 2017 and the number of depositors increasing from 1,211,915 in 2010 to 4,529,288 in 2017.

With this inclusiveness, people living in rural areas have easier access to financial services, epitomised by increased credit for income-generating activities (Cambodia Socio-Economic Survey, 2017). The rural credit offered by MFIs contributes to the expansion of cultivated land, enhancing agricultural production and living standards (Eliste and Zorya, 2015). Furthermore, the extension of MFI services benefited 3,878,618 Cambodians, or nearly five people per household (CMA, 2014). Arguably, this is attributable to Cambodian needy

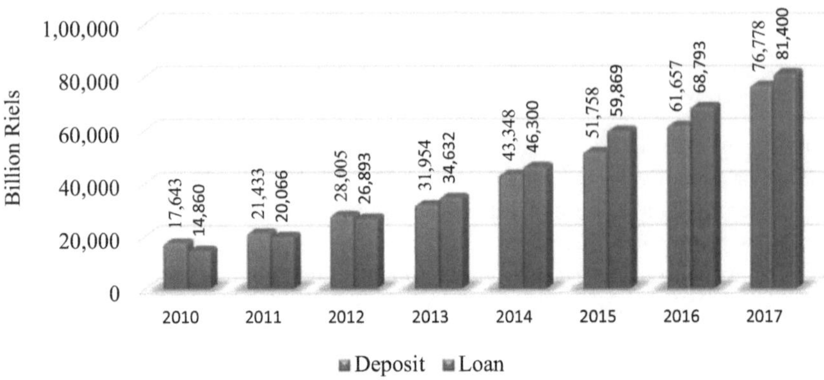

Figure 7.1 Total deposit and loan (2010–2017) (in KR billions).
Source: National Bank of Cambodia (2017).

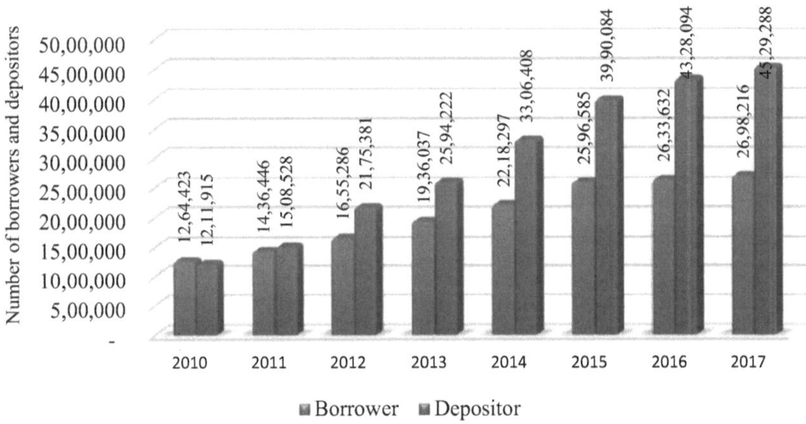

Figure 7.2 Number of borrowers and depositors (2010–2017).
Source: National Bank of Cambodia (2017).

households being able to access credit. Although there has been an increasing number of households included in financial development, high credit costs and financial illiteracy are still challenging many borrowers and other household users of financial services, in particular those living in rural locales. The recent development of financial technology (fintech), such as mobile money for payments, has improved household access to financial services at low transaction costs. In this context, an empirical study by Seng (2017) suggested that mobile money is likely to promote household access to MFI credit for non-agricultural investment but is likely to reduce the credit for non-productive purposes.

To promote financial inclusion, the NBC prioritises the following: access to credit for small and medium-sized enterprises; savings; access to small insurance services; payment systems; increasing the number of financial regulators; client protection; and financial literacy (NBC, 2018a). As far as financial literacy is concerned, basic financial courses such as some calculations are included in the education curriculum for high schools, and the NBC generates other advertisements oriented to the general public. In addition, the NBC enhances financial technology by developing relevant regulations and human resources. With the development of financial technology, the NBC introduced e-payment, so-called 'Bakong' using blockchain technology, allowing for the use of digital currency in both Khmer riels and US dollars (NBC, 2018b).

7.3 Literature review

The positive effect of finance on poverty reduction has been documented at both the macro and micro levels. Several studies (e.g., Deininger and Squire, 1998; White and Anderson, 2001; Ravallion, 2001; Dollar and Kraay, 2002; Bourguignon, 2003) found that economies with higher levels of financial development achieve faster poverty alleviation. Financial services that allow individuals access to formal savings instruments can augment a country's net savings (Aportela, 1999; Ashraf, Gons, Karlan, and Yin, 2003. Limited access to financial services can plunge many people into the poverty trap (Galor and Zeira, 1993; Banerjee and Newman, 1994; Aghion and Bolton, 1997; Beck et al., 2007). Although there are data limitations at the micro level and methodological challenges, for instance, in addressing sample selection bias related to the use of financial services or controlling for unobservable confounders regarding users' characteristics, there are various studies on quantifying the effects of access to microcredit on poverty alleviation.

However, micro-level empirical studies produced inconclusive results with very controversial conclusions; while some confirm poverty-reducing effects (e.g., Karlan and Zinman, 2010; Imai et al., 2010; Imai and Azam, 2012; Asad, Issam, and Imai, 2014; Rahman et al., 2014; Kulb et al., 2015; Akotey and Adjasi, 2016), others debunk them (e.g., Maldonado and González-Vega, 2008; Bateman, 2010; Schicks, 2013; Ganle et al., 2015; Seng, 2018a and 2018b). In between, some studies showed mixed effects on poverty reduction; for example, in northeast Thailand, affluent borrowers, in particular the members of the village committee, are very likely to gain welfare benefits from microcredit outreach, while rank-and-file members are unlikely to do so (Coleman, 1999 and 2006). Other mixed effects are also found in the Philippines (Kondo, Orbeta, Dingcong, and Infantado, 2008) and in Ghana (Ganle et al., 2015).

Alam (2012) analysed the impacts of gender-based returns to credit on intrahousehold resource allocation in rural Bangladesh by dealing with endogeneity of microcredit use with an instrumental variable method. The findings illustrate that female borrowers allocate household earnings more efficiently, indicating that microcredit empowers women. Imai and Azam (2012) and Asad et al. (2015) used a propensity score matching (PSM) approach to quantify the poverty-reducing effects of MFI credit at the household level in Bangladesh and in Pakistan, respectively, with the results confirming the pro-poor effects. Rahman et al. (2014) analysed the welfare-enhancing effects of microloans on households by adopting a difference-in-difference (DID) approach, with the data collected from the Shaanxi province of China. Their findings illustrated the intended effects. Swamy (2014) examined the economic effects of financial inclusion on poor households by gender in India by using the DID method with panel ordinary least squares (OLS) and generalised methods of moments with standard errors for a robust analysis. The findings suggest that financial inclusion reduces poverty in terms of household income per capita, with the income-increasing effects on women being significantly higher than those on men. However, the PSM approach cannot control for such unobservable characteristics as borrowers' wealth, entrepreneurial skills, motivation, and so forth that potentially determine both the use of credit and the outcome variables (Seng, 2015), while the DID procedure may still be subject to such biases as reverse causality and omitted variable bias.

Other empirical studies tried to address endogeneity regarding the household uptake of microloans by using a treatment effects method (e.g., Imai et al., 2010) to evaluate the pro-poor effects of MFI credit for productive purposes in India and Heckman sample selection approach (e.g., Akotey and Adjasi, 2016) to access the effects of microcredit in Ghana. These studies confirm the favourable effects. Still, these econometric approaches fail to account for structural differences between borrowers and non-borrowers in terms of outcome functions because of the assumptions that the functions differ only by constant terms (Seng, 2018a), yielding bias and inconsistent results.

Other strands of studies confirmed unfavourable effects of poverty alleviation. For instance, Coleman's 2006 studies illustrate that northeast Thailand's microcredit, used in non-productive ways, traps women in a vicious cycle of high-interest debts. The failure of financial inclusion in terms of access to credit to break women's poverty cycle results from women generally making low return on investment and repaying loans by borrowing from other micro-lenders, bearing a heavy debt burden (Seng, 2018a). Schicks's 2013 analysis of Ghana's credit market shows that 30% of Accra borrowers from the major microlenders experience over-indebtedness, while over-indebtedness puts a large burden on many borrowers in Kosovo (Pytkowska and Spannuth, 2012). Furthermore, the most influential studies by Seng (2018a and 2018b) suggest that microcredit is very likely to worsen borrowers' household welfare and even trap the needy borrowers in a vicious cycle of poverty in Cambodia. These findings indicate that MFIs are seemingly drifting away from their social mission, raising concerns over the poverty-reducing effects of financial inclusion in terms of access to credit. Although Seng's 2018 studies did not account for the effects of financial literacy in their empirical model, they nonetheless argued that the borrowers' limited financial knowledge is very likely to constrain the pro-poor development of microfinance in Cambodia.

These studies make room for further studies on the poverty-reducing effects of financial development, a priori revealing that financial literacy is very likely to promote pro-poor financial inclusion in developing countries such as Cambodia. In addition, Cole, Sampson, and Zia (2011), and Grohmann et al. (2018) found that higher financial literacy substitutes for financial infrastructure and promotes more financial inclusion, possibly reinforcing the desirable effects of financial services on household welfare and poverty reduction. Nevertheless, some studies (e.g., Bello, 2006; Banerjee et al., 2009; Karlan and Zinman, 2009; Duvendack and Palmer Jones, 2012) cautioned against considering financial inclusion in terms of microloans as a tool to fight poverty, although still advocating it, arguing that it should be used with 'cautious optimism'.

7.4 Analytical framework

This study analyses the effects of financial inclusion in terms of uptake of financial services on household poverty in terms of household income per capita, accounting for financial literacy, with the endogenous switching model to control for endogeneity of household use of financial services. The endogenous switching model controls for selection bias arising from unobservable factors affecting both the use of financial services and household income and for inherent differences between the users and non-users in terms of income functions. The ESP model is complementarily adopted to quantify the effects of financial inclusion on household budget deficits.

7.4.1 Household decision to use financial services and its implications

Following Seng (2018a and 2018b), household decisions to use financial services and their implications in terms of income per capita can be modelled within a two-stage framework, with the first corresponding to the decision and the second corresponding to its implications. A model for household *i*'s decision regarding the use of financial services is built on the empirical models proposed by Imai and Azam (2012), and Akotey and Adjasi (2016), and examined with a probit model estimation (Seng, 2018a and 2018b). Thus, the probit model can be specified in the following latent variable:

$$T_i^* = \alpha Z_i + u_i \ \ with \ \ T_i = \begin{cases} 1 \ if \ T_i^* > 0 \\ 0 \ otherwise \end{cases} \tag{7.1}$$

where T_i is a binary variable that is equal to 1, if household i takes up financial services, and zero otherwise. Z_i is covariates correlated with the decision to use or not to use financial services. α is parameter to be estimated. u_i is error term that is assumed to be normally distributed, that is, $u_i \sim N(0,1)$.

The simplest approach to quantify the effects of financial inclusion would be to use the dummy variable T_i in a household income function as a regressor and then to apply an OLS estimation. In this case, a commonly used model in the literature on impact evaluation is expressed as follows:

$$Y_i = \beta_1 X_i + \beta_2 T_i + \varepsilon_i \tag{7.2}$$

where Y_i is household *i*'s per capita income; X_i is controlling factors expected to determine the income; T_i is a dummy for the use of financial services; and β_2 is the coefficient capturing the effects of financial inclusion on the income. However, this procedure is very likely to yield biased and inconsistent estimates because the decisions to use financial services are potentially endogenous. That is, the decisions can be voluntarily made and may be based on individual households' self-selection (Seng, 2018b). Standard treatment effects models can be used to account for this self-selection bias and other unobservable confounders. Nevertheless, these models cannot control for the inherent differences between the household users and non-users in terms of income functions due to the assumption that the functions differ by only constant terms. The failure to address this structural issue may still yield biased and inconsistent estimates of the effects. Addressing the inherent differences, the PSM approach can be adopted. However, this approach fails to account for unobservable confounders, more possibly still producing biased and inconsistent estimates. Thus, to provide reliable empirical evidence, a proper empirical approach should be adopted.

7.4.2 Endogenous switching model

Following Seng (2018a and 2018b), to deal with the earlier mentioned econometric challenges, the endogenous switching model that treats the household's financial choices (use vs. do not use the services) as regimes is employed and specified as follows:[2]

$$T_i^* = \alpha Z_i + u_i \tag{7.3}$$

$$\text{Regime 1}: y_{1i} = \beta_1 X_{1i} + \varepsilon_{1i} \; if \; T_i = 1 \tag{7.4a}$$

$$\text{Regime 2}: y_{2i} = \beta_2 X_{2i} + \varepsilon_{2i} \; if \; T_i = 0 \tag{7.4b}$$

where T_i^* is the latent variable for household *i*'s use of financial services, with T_i being its observable counterpart. α, β_{1i}, and β_{2i} are vectors of parameters to be estimated. y_i represents household income per capita in regimes 1 (users) and 2 (non-users). X_i represents a vector of exogenous factors expected to determine the household income. The set of variables Z_i can overlap X_i; nonetheless, to properly identify the selection equation, at least one variable that directly affects the decisions to use financial services, but would indirectly influence the income through the use of financial services, is used as an instrument restriction. Imai et al. (2010) used the availability of formal banks in the village as a possible instrument to evaluate the effects of microcredit on household poverty with the treatment-effects model. Owing to the unavailability of such information in the current study's dataset, a dummy for income proof documents (the variable is 1 if the household has income proof documents and zero otherwise) and a dummy for family books are used as an identification restriction.

In addition to other documents such as land title, when borrowers apply for loans, the income proof documents and family books are also required by banks and MFIs in Cambodia. Moreover, the family book is also required for opening a bank account to identify savers. Thus, the study hypothesises that their availability influences the decisions regarding the use of financial services, but does not determine the income. Following Di Falco, Veronesi, and Yesuf (2011), a simple rejection falsification test is also conducted to justify admissibility, that is, instruments are valid if they affect the financial decision but not the non-users' household income per capita. Appendix 7.1 confirms that the availability of income proof documents and family books jointly influence the decisions to use financial services, but do not affect household income per capita; thus, they can be used as valid instruments. Finally, the error terms u_i, ε_{1i} and ε_{2i} are assumed to be correlated and jointly normally distributed with a zero mean vector and covariance matrix; that is, $(v_i, \varepsilon_{1i}, \varepsilon_{2i}) \sim N(0, cov(.))$:

$$cov(v_i, \varepsilon_{1i}, \varepsilon_{2i}) = \begin{pmatrix} \sigma^2_{v_i} & \sigma_{\varepsilon_{1i}v_i} & \sigma_{\varepsilon_{2i}v_i} \\ \sigma_{\varepsilon_{1i}v_i} & \sigma^2_{\varepsilon_{1i}} & . \\ \sigma_{\varepsilon_{2i}v_i} & . & \sigma^2_{\varepsilon_{2i}} \end{pmatrix} \tag{7.5}$$

where $var(v_i) = \sigma^2_{v_i}, var(\varepsilon_{1i}) = \sigma^2_{\varepsilon_{1i}}, var(\varepsilon_{2i}) = \sigma^2_{\varepsilon_{2i}}, cov(\varepsilon_{1i}, \varepsilon_{2i}) = \sigma_{\varepsilon_{1i}\varepsilon_{2i}}, cov(\varepsilon_{1i}, v_i) = \sigma_{\varepsilon_{1i}v_i}$, and $cov(\varepsilon_{2i}, v_i) = \sigma_{\varepsilon_{2i}v_i}$. The variance $\sigma^2_{v_i}$ equals 1, as α is estimated only up to a scale factor, and the covariance $\sigma_{\varepsilon_{1i}\varepsilon_{2i}}$ is not defined as y_{1i} and y_{2i} are not observed together (Maddala, 1986).

The correlation between the error term v_i of Equation (7.3) and the error terms ε_{1i} and ε_{2i} of Equations (7.4a) and (7.4b) suggests potential unobservable effects. Thus, the expected values of ε_{1i} and ε_{2i} conditional on regime selection would be nonzero and can be derived as follows:

$$E(\varepsilon_{1i} \mid T_i = 1, X_{1i}) = E(\varepsilon_{1i} \mid v_i \rangle - \alpha Z_i) = \sigma_{\varepsilon_{1i}v_i} \frac{\phi(Z_i\alpha)}{\Phi(Z_i\alpha)} = \sigma_{\varepsilon_{1i}v_i} \lambda_{1i} \tag{7.6a}$$

$$E(\varepsilon_{2i} \mid T_i = 0, X_{2i}) = E(\varepsilon_{2i} \mid v_i \leq -\alpha Z_i) = \sigma_{\varepsilon_{2i}v_i} \frac{-\phi(Z_i\alpha)}{1 - \Phi(Z_i\alpha)} = \sigma_{\varepsilon_{2i}v_i} \lambda_{2i} \tag{7.6b}$$

where ϕ is the standard normal probability density function and Φ is the cumulative distribution function of the standard normal distribution. λ_{1i} and λ_{2i} are the inverse Mills ratios (IMRs) predicted at $Z_i\alpha$ for household users and non-users, respectively (Greene, 2008). Then, one can conduct an endogeneity test with the estimated covariances $\sigma_{\varepsilon_{1i}v_i}$ and $\sigma_{\varepsilon_{2i}v_i}$. Either significantly nonzero $\sigma_{\varepsilon_{1i}v_i}$ or $\sigma_{\varepsilon_{2i}v_i}$ rejects the null hypothesis that there is no sample selection bias, confirming the endogenous switching (Maddala, 1986). Thus, a test for significant coefficients of the correlation between ε_{1i} and v_i ($\rho_{\varepsilon_{1i}v_i} = \sigma_{\varepsilon_{1i}v_i} / \sigma_{\varepsilon_{1i}}\sigma_{v_i}$) and between ε_{2i} and v_i ($\rho_{\varepsilon_{2i}v_i} = \sigma_{\varepsilon_{2i}v_i} / \sigma_{\varepsilon_{2i}}\sigma_{v_i}$) is necessarily carried out (Lokshin and Sajaia, 2004).

A full information maximum likelihood (FIML) approach is the most efficient at estimating the endogenous switching model (Lokshin and Sajaia, 2004). The FIML approach simultaneously estimates the selection and outcome equations with the availability of income proof documents restricting the model identification, and then provides consistent standard errors. Given the assumption that the error terms follow trivariate normal distribution, the logarithmic likelihood function for the system of Equations (7.3) and (7.4a and 7.4b) can be:

$$\ln \mathrm{L_i} = \Sigma \mathrm{T_i}\left[\ln \phi\left(\frac{\mu_{1i}}{\tilde{\mathrm{A}}_{\mu_{1i}}}\right) - \ln \tilde{\mathrm{A}}_{\mu_{1i}} + \ln \Phi(\theta_{1i})\right]$$

$$+(1-T_i)\left[\ln \phi\left(\frac{\varepsilon_{2i}}{\sigma_{\varepsilon_{2i}}}\right) - \ln \sigma_{\varepsilon_{2i}} + \ln\left(1-\Phi(\theta_{2i})\right)\right]$$

where $\theta_{ji} = \dfrac{Z_i\alpha + \rho_j\varepsilon_{ji} / \sigma_j}{\sqrt{1-\rho_j^2}}$, j = 1, 2, with ρ_j being the correlation between the error term v_i of Equation (7.3) and the error terms ε_{1i} and ε_{2i} of Equations (7.4a) and (7.4b), respectively. That is, ρ_1 and ρ_2 are equal to $\rho_{\varepsilon_{1i}v_i} = \sigma_{\varepsilon_{1i}v_i} / \sigma_{\varepsilon_{1i}}\sigma_{v_i}$ and $\rho_{\varepsilon_{2i}v_i} = \sigma_{\varepsilon_{2i}v_i} / \sigma_{\varepsilon_{2i}}\sigma_{v_i}$, respectively.

Furthermore, the pro-poor effects of financial inclusion can be estimated by comparing the users' conditional expected income derived from the endogenous switching regression with the counterfactual case that the same households have not used financial services. The conditional expected income a user enjoys with characteristics X and Z, and the conditional expected income that the same user would enjoy without using financial services are derived as follows (Lokshin and Sajaia, 2004):

$$E(y_{1i}|T_i = 1, X_{1i}) = \beta_1 X_{1i} + \sigma_{\varepsilon_{1i}v_i}\lambda_{1i} \quad (7.7a)$$

$$E(y_{2i}|T_i = 1, X_{1i}) = \beta_2 X_{1i} + \sigma_{\varepsilon_{2i}v_i}\lambda_{1i} \quad (7.7b)$$

where $\sigma_{\varepsilon_{1i}v_i}\lambda_{1i}$ control for a sample selection arising from the fact that a user is different from others with characteristics X and Z due to unobserved confounders. Following Heckman, Tobias, and Vytlacil (2001) and Di Falco et al. (2011), the effects of the treatment on the treated (TT) that accounts for all factors potentially determining the differences in income can be derived as follows:

$$TT = E(y_{1i}|T_i = 1) - E(y_{2i}|T_i = 1) = (\beta_1 - \beta_2)X_{1i} + (\sigma_{\varepsilon_1 v_i} - \sigma_{\varepsilon_2 v_i})\lambda_{1i} \quad (7.8)$$

The TT results from the differences in the coefficients in Equations (7.7a) and (7.7b) ($\beta_1 - \beta_2$ and $\sigma_{\varepsilon_1 v_i} - \sigma_{\varepsilon_2 v_i}$). Thus, simply comparing average household income in the user group $E(y_{1i}|T_i = 1)$ to that in the non-user group $E(y_{2i}|T_i = 0)$ would confirm a bias of the treatment effects. If a household self-selects to use or not use financial services based on comparative advantage, $\sigma_{\varepsilon_1 v_i} - \sigma_{\varepsilon_2 v_i}$ would be positive, suggesting that the use of financial services would increase household income under self-selection rather than under random assignment (Maddala, 1983).

7.4.3 Endogenous switching probit model

To give more insights into the potential effects of financial inclusion on poverty alleviation, an analysis on the effects of financial inclusion on household budget deficits is also conducted with the ESP model developed by Aakvik, Heckman, and Vytlacil (2005), and Lokshin and Sajaia (2011). In the model, the treatment T_i is earlier defined by Equation (7.3) and the outcome is a binary variable for the households' behaviours towards household budget deficits (the variable is 1 if the household runs a budget deficit and zero if otherwise) being used as the outcome variable. The outcome equations are specified as follows:

$$\text{Regime 1}: y_{1i}^* = \beta_1 X_{1i} + v_{1i}, y_{1i} = 1\,(y_{1i}^* > 0) \quad (7.9a)$$

$$\text{Regime 2}: y_{2i}^* = \beta_2 X_{2i} + v_{2i},\ y_{2i} = 1\,(y_{2i}^* > 0) \quad (7.9b)$$

$$\text{Observed } y_i \text{ is defined as } y_i = \begin{cases} y_{1i}\, if \;\; T_i = 1 \\ y_{2i}\, if \;\; T_i = 0 \end{cases}$$

where y_{1i}^* and y_{2i}^* are the latent variables determining the observed binary outcomes y_{1i} and y_{2i}. X_i represents a vector of exogenous factors expected to determine the household budget deficit. β_{1i} and β_{2i} are vectors of parameters to be estimated. The error terms u_i of Equation(7.3), and v_{1i} and v_{2i} of Equations (7.9a) and (7.9b), respectively, are assumed to be correlated and jointly normally distributed with a zero mean vector and covariance matrix; that is, $(u_i,\ v_{1i}, v_{2i}) \sim N(0, cov(.))$. The ESP model is also estimated with the FIML (Lokshin and Sajaia, 2011). To properly identify the selection equation, at least one variable that directly affects the decisions to use financial services, but would indirectly influence the household budget deficit through their use, is used as an instrument restriction. To justify the admissibility of the availability of income proof documents and family books being used as the instruments, the same simple rejection falsification test as in the endogenous switching model is performed. The results reported in Appendix 7.1 confirm that the availability of income proof documents and family books can be used as the valid instruments. Similar to the TT derived from Equation (7.8) for the effects on household income per capita, accounting for all factors potentially affecting the differences in probability of household budget deficits, the treatment effects on the treated (TT) can be derived as follows:

$$TT = \Pr\left(y_{1i} = 1 \mid T_i = 1\right) - \Pr\left(y_{2i} = 1 \mid T_i = 1\right) \tag{7.10}$$

The average treatment effects on the treated (ATT), for the corresponding subgroups of the sample, is commonly computed by averaging TT from Equation (7.10) which is the mean effects of the treatment on those who use financial services. In this case, the ATT can be computed as follows (Lokshin and Sajaia, 2011):

$$ATT = \frac{1}{N_T} \Sigma TT_i \tag{7.11}$$

where N_T is the number of observations with $T_i = 1$ (i.e., the number of financial users). The ATT also provides the robustness check on the effects of financial inclusion on poverty in terms of household income per capita.

7.5 Data and variables

This section describes the source of data and main variables used in the analysis. A descriptive statistical analysis is also presented at the end of the section. The analysis is also conducted with simple statistical tests of differences in means.

7.5.1 Data used in the analysis

The current study uses the data from the FinScope Consumer Survey conducted in 2015. The FinScope survey was carried out by South Africa's FinMark Trust in partnership with the United Nations Capital Development Fund, Cape Town–based think tank Cenfri, as well as local partners including the NBC and the National Institute of Statistics (NIS). The survey contains household information based on a nationwide representative sample of the adult population over 18 years of age. The sampling frame and data weighting were carried out by the NIS and weighted to the NIS estimates and validated against census data and the 2013 Cambodia Inter-Censal Population Survey. In the survey, the total of 3,150 household representatives over 18 years of age in both rural and urban areas were selected as the sample. Nevertheless, because some representatives did not provide full information on the variables of interest, there are some missing observations in the analysis. Adjusting for the missing observations, the final sample count is 2,693 individuals in the regression analysis.

7.5.2 Variables

The dependent variable in the selection equation is binary for the use of financial services, while the dependent variables in the outcome equation are the household income per capita for the endogenous switching model and the household budget deficit for the ESP model. Following Lusardi and Mitchell (2007) and Drexler, Greg, and Antoinette (2014), financial literacy in the current study is defined as an ability to understand basic financial concepts. A dummy for financial literacy (i.e., the variable is 1 if the household understands how banks work and benefits from a saving account at banks, and zero otherwise) is built on the availability of data in the FinScope survey.

Owing to the limitations on data, following previous studies (e.g., Imai et al., 2010; Akotey and Adjasi, 2016; Seng, 2018a and 2018b), the study uses the available information such as household head characteristics, household characteristics, and means of access to information, and income proof documents as the explanatory variables in the model. The head's characteristics consist of age, gender, ethnicity, and marriage status. Following Seng (2018a and 2018b), the heads are also grouped into four categories according to educational level: training, primary education, secondary education, and tertiary education. The numbers of household income generators are included to capture the effects of household characteristics. Households are also characterised by their geographical locations: Coastal area, Plain area, Plateau area, and Tonlé Sap area. The analysis also controls for rural areas, as a geographical characteristic, to capture rural household behaviour towards the decisions concerning financial services, as well as its effect on household income (e.g., Akotey and Adjasi, 2016).

The means of communication and access to information, proxied by cell phone and email, is used to capture the effects of access to financial information on households' financial decisions. This facilitates the diffusion of information on financial services amongst households because it can serve as a tool to build social networks, and then, more likely, to induce households to use the services, and more probably in an efficient way. Of note, social networks are very likely to promote access to microfinance services (Wydick, Hayes, and Kempf, 2011). Cell phones can also be used as mobile money, which is found to promote household welfare and financial inclusion (Munyegera and Matsumoto, 2015; Ouma et al., 2017). Finally, as noted, the availability of household income proof documents and a family book are also critical when applying for any financial services. Thus, they are expected to determine household income per capita indirectly through access to financial services. All these variables are summarised in Table A7.2.

7.5.3 Descriptive analysis

The survey suggests that approximately 61.14% of the sampled households use formal financial services, suggesting that approximately 38.86% are excluded from access to financial services. Approximately 30% of the financial users take out credit, while approximately 10% save money at formal financial institutions. Moreover, approximately 89.37% of the sampled households have at least basic financial knowledge (i.e., understanding how banks work and benefit from a savings account).[3]

The descriptive statistics summarised in Table 7.1 illustrate some non-significant and significant differences between household users and non-users in terms of each variable, which are supported by simple statistical tests of differences in means. For example, there are non-significant differences in per capita household income between the users, who enjoy an average household income per capita of KR291,889 (US$73), and non-users, who enjoy an average household income per capita of KR302,222 (US$76).[4] Moreover, on average, approximately 51% of the users run household budget deficits, while approximately 52% of the non-users run household budget deficits. The figures illustrate the non-significant difference between the users and the non-users in terms of household budget deficits. Nevertheless, the users and the non-users are significantly different in terms of household head's ethnicity, gender, education achievement, number of income generators, access to information and social communication, and geographical locations. Particularly, approximately 16.2% of the users are headed by a person having access to secondary school and approximately 2% by a person having access to higher education, while approximately 13% of the non-users are headed by a person having access to secondary school and approximately 1% headed by a person having access to tertiary education. These results indicate that the households headed by a secondary school person are likely to have more access to financial services.

Furthermore, on average, approximately 7.4% of the users possess income proof documents, while approximately 4.2% of the non-users have them, suggesting a significant difference between users and non-users. This simple statistical test reveals that income documents are likely to facilitate the use of financial services, in particular when households apply for credit.

Table 7.2 demonstrates the simple statistical test results regarding the differences between households headed by a person with financial literacy and those headed by a person without financial literacy in terms of each variable. The results suggest a non-significant difference between the groups in terms of household income per capita. However, households headed by a financially literate person enjoy an average per capita income of KR303,992 (US$76), while those headed by a financially non-literate person enjoy an average income of KR227,813 (US$57). Concerning the use of financial services, albeit non-significant, the percentage of households headed by a financially literate person is approximately 62%, while those headed by a financially non-literate person is

Table 7.1 Household characteristics by users and non-users of financial services

Variables	*Users*		*Non-users*		*Difference in mean*
	Mean	*SD*	*Mean*	*SD*	
Household income per capita	291,888.60	1,030,364.00	302,222.10	3,284,952.00	–10,333.52
Household budget deficit	0.507	0.500	0.518	0.500	–0.011
Financial literacy	0.898	0.302	0.886	0.317	0.012
Household head's age	44.045	13.961	43.081	16.569	0.964
Household head's ethnicity	0.944	0.230	0.957	0.204	–0.013*
Household head's gender	0.074	0.261	0.094	0.292	–0.020**
Single	0.004	0.060	0.007	0.002	–0.003
Marriage	0.459	0.498	0.455	0.498	0.004
Divorced	0.009	0.096	0.010	0.099	0.000
Widowed	0.052	0.222	0.067	0.250	–0.015**
Training	0.003	0.051	0.004	0.064	–0.001
Primary	0.241	0.428	0.292	0.455	–0.051***
Secondary	0.162	0.369	0.127	0.333	0.035***
Tertiary	0.019	0.135	0.010	0.099	0.009**
Income generators	2.469	1.287	2.368	1.233	0.101**
Cellphone	0.800	0.400	0.646	0.478	0.154***
Email	0.062	0.241	0.019	0.136	0.043***
Rural	0.676	0.467	0.741	0.438	–0.064***
Coastal	0.076	0.266	0.068	0.252	0.009
Plain	0.502	0.500	0.476	0.500	0.026*
Plateau	0.094	0.293	0.154	0.361	–0.059***
Tonlé Sap	0.327	0.469	0.302	0.459	0.025*
Income proof	0.074	0.261	0.042	0.200	0.032***
Family book	0.909	0.287	0.883	0.320	0.025***

Source: Author's calculation.

Notes: Income per capita is the monthly income in riel.
SD = standard deviation.
* denotes test statistic significance at 10% level.
** denotes test statistic significance at 5% level.
*** denotes test statistic significance at 1% level.

approximately 59%. Related to household budget deficits (spending more than earning), on average, the percentage of households headed by a financially literate person is approximately 52%, which is significantly higher than that of those headed by a financially non-literate person, with approximately 44%.

Nonetheless, the results of this simple descriptive statistical analysis do not necessarily suggest that households headed by a financially literate person are more likely to enjoy higher household income per capita and more likely to run a household budget deficit than do those headed by a financially non-literate person. This is because this simple statistical approach cannot address such issues as endogeneity of financial literacy and household decisions to use financial

Table 7.2 Main household characteristics by financial literacy status

	With financial literacy		*Without financial literacy*		*Difference in mean*
	Mean	*SD*	*Mean*	*SD*	
Household income per capita	303,991.5	2,302,071	227,813.1	689,760.6	76,178.36
Use of financial services	0.615	0.487	0.585	0.493	0.029
Household budget deficit	0.520	0.500	0.439	0.497	0.081**
Household head's age	43.794	15.009	42.636	15.217	1.158
Household head's ethnicity	0.947	0.224	0.964	0.186	−0.017
Household head's gender	0.081	0.272	0.090	0.286	−0.009
Single	0.005	0.001	0.0001	0.001	0.005
Marriage	0.457	0.498	0.463	0.499	−0.006
Divorced	0.010	0.097	0.009	0.094	0.001
Widowed	0.056	0.230	0.072	0.258	−0.016
Training	0.004	0.060	0.0001	0.001	0.004
Primary	0.259	0.438	0.278	0.448	−0.018
Secondary	0.151	0.358	0.125	0.332	0.026
Tertiary	0.015	0.121	0.018	0.133	−0.003
Income generators	2.426	1.262	2.457	1.317	−0.030
Cellphone	0.742	0.438	0.725	0.447	0.017
Email	0.045	0.208	0.045	0.207	0.000
Rural	0.701	0.458	0.710	0.454	−0.010
Coastal	0.069	0.253	0.107	0.310	−0.039**
Plain	0.503	0.500	0.403	0.491	0.100***
Plateau	0.115	0.319	0.137	0.345	−0.022
Tonlé Sap	0.313	0.464	0.352	0.478	−0.039*

Source: Author's calculation.

Notes: Income per capita is the monthly income in riels.
SD = standard deviation.
* denotes test statistic significance at 10% level.
** denotes test statistic significance at 5% level.
*** denotes test statistic significance at 1% level.

services. Further analyses addressing such a challenge control for financial literacy in the evaluation of the effects of financial inclusion on household income.

7.6 Results and discussion

The descriptive statistical analysis suggests the non-significant differences in household income per capita and in household budget deficit between users and non-users. The econometric analysis further quantifies the poverty-reducing effects of financial inclusion on households, controlling for endogeneity issues regarding the decision to use financial services.

7.6.1 Use of financial services

Table 7.3 reports the results of the probit model, describing the decision to use financial services, jointly estimated with the income equations by using the FIML method. The life-cycle effects of the household head on the probability of using financial services are quadratic, confirmed by the significantly positive coefficient of age and the significantly negative coefficient of the age-squared term. Similar to the previous studies by Seng (2018a and 2018b), the likelihood of using financial

Table 7.3 Determinants of households' financial uses (simultaneously estimated probit[a])

Variables	*Use of financial services*		
	Coef.	*SE*	*P-value*
Household head's age	7.547***	1.394	0.000
Household head's age squared	–0.977***	0.190	0.000
Household head's gender	0.041	0.152	0.785
Household head's ethnicity	–0.246**	0.114	0.030
Single	–0.354	0.393	0.368
Marriage	0.054	0.096	0.575
Divorced	0.007	0.321	0.983
Widowed	–0.086	0.178	0.630
Training	–0.610	0.426	0.152
Primary	–0.026	0.096	0.783
Secondary	0.100	0.109	0.359
Tertiary	0.157	0.284	0.579
Income generators	0.031	0.021	0.136
Cellphone	0.459***	0.061	0.000
Email	0.784***	0.158	0.000
Rural	–0.013	0.061	0.834
Coastal	0.321***	0.117	0.006
Plain	0.199**	0.081	0.015
Plateau	Dropped		
Tonlé Sap	0.245***	0.083	0.003
Income proof	0.431***	0.107	0.000
Family book	0.021	0.086	0.809
Constant	–14.600***	2.552	0.000
Observations	2,693		
Prob. > χ^2	0.000		

Source: Author's calculation.

Notes: Standard errors (SE) is robust SE.
* denotes test statistic significance at 10% level.
** denotes test statistic significance at 5% level.
*** denotes test statistic significance at 1% level.
a Probit model is simultaneously estimated with the income regime equations by using the FIML method.

services increases, but starts to decrease by degrees after attaining 48 years of age. With age, the head gains more experience and has increasing economic opportunities, becoming eager for financial services, but starts to lose by degrees the opportunities after reaching this age (Seng, 2018a and 2018b).

Nevertheless, the significantly negative coefficient of the household head's ethnicity suggests that households headed by Khmer are less likely to use financial services. As expected, cellphone and email have significantly positive correlations with the decision to use financial services. These findings are consistent with the arguments by previous studies (e.g., Wydick et al., 2011; Munyegera and Matsumoto, 2015; Ouma et al., 2017) that access to information and social networks facilitate microfinance services. Furthermore, households in Coastal, Plain, and Tonlé Sap are likely to use more financial services offered by formal financial institutions. As expected, although the coefficient of family books is non-significant, it is positive and the coefficient of income proof documents is significantly positive, confirming that their availability is important for the use of financial services, in particular credit applications.

7.6.2 Household income per capita

Table 7.4 presents the estimates for the income equations of the endogenous switching model. The likelihood ratio test for joint independence of Equations (7.3)–(7.4b) is reported at the bottom of the table. The testing result suggests that the three equations are jointly dependent, confirmed by the significant likelihood ratio, indicating the problem of endogeneity that needs to be controlled for in the model specification of household income equations. That is, the endogeneity is caused by the presence of both observed and unobserved confounders determining the decision to use financial services and the income outcome given the decision to use the services. In this case, the endogenous switching model is appropriate to account for self-selection and inherent differences between users and non-users (Seng, 2018a and 2018b).

The differences in the income equations' coefficients between users and non-users, corresponding to the structural differences across the two regimes in terms of each explanatory variable, show the presence of heterogeneity in the samples. These bring about the differences between the users and non-users in terms of income functions. For example, the household heads' tertiary educations are significantly and positively associated with the income for both users and non-users; the coefficients' magnitudes are, however, lower for the users than those for the non-users. These results suggest that the effects of tertiary educations are greater amongst the non-users. Furthermore, the detailed results corresponding to other explanatory variables can be found in Table 7.4 and interpreted in a similar fashion.

7.6.3 Poverty-reducing effects of financial inclusion

Table 7.5 presents the effects of financial inclusion on poverty, with the second column corresponding to the income effects. The treatment effects (TT) are

Table 7.4 Determinants of household income per capita

Variables	*Users*			*Non-users*		
	Coef.	*SE*	*P-value*	*Coef.*	*SE*	*P-value*
Household head's age	6.410***	1.856	0.001	8.819**	3.856	0.022
Household head's age squared	–0.922***	0.253	0.000	–1.250**	0.533	0.019
Household head's gender	–0.166	0.124	0.181	–0.172	0.204	0.401
Household head's ethnicity	–0.065	0.108	0.545	0.216	0.169	0.202
Single	–0.216	0.405	0.594	–0.550**	0.253	0.030
Marriage	–0.297**	0.122	0.015	–0.722***	0.194	0.000
Divorced	0.142	0.297	0.633	–0.162	0.331	0.624
Widowed	–0.214	0.169	0.205	–0.377	0.275	0.170
Training	0.814	0.806	0.313	0.462*	0.260	0.076
Primary	0.051	0.115	0.655	0.438**	0.177	0.013
Secondary	0.160	0.147	0.275	0.523**	0.226	0.021
Tertiary	0.587*	0.310	0.058	1.240**	0.513	0.016
Income generators	–0.166***	0.025	0.000	–0.151***	0.034	0.000
Cellphone	0.492***	0.078	0.000	0.406***	0.101	0.000
Email	0.522***	0.131	0.000	–0.797	0.848	0.347
Rural	–0.616***	0.068	0.000	–0.713***	0.109	0.000
Coastal	0.441***	0.128	0.001	0.185	0.149	0.214
Plain	0.022	0.092	0.813	–0.246**	0.106	0.020
Plateau	Dropped			Dropped		
Tonlé Sap	0.155*	0.090	0.084	–0.077	0.105	0.461
Constant	1.020	3.405	0.765	–3.514	6.837	0.607
$\ln \sigma_{\varepsilon_1 v}$	0.219***	0.051	0.000			
$\rho_{\varepsilon_1 v}$	0.055	0.095	0.564			
$\ln \sigma_{\varepsilon_2 v}$				0.305***	0.052	0.000
$\rho_{\varepsilon_2 v}$				–0.151	0.111	0.174
LR test of indep. Eqns.	Prob. > χ^2 = 0.000					
Log pseudo-likelihood	–6,184.469					

Source: Author's calculation.

Notes: Standard errors (SE) is robust SE. The dependent variable is the natural log of monthly household income per capita. These outcome equations are jointly estimated with the selection equation reported in Table 7.2 by using the FIML method with robust SE. LR = Likelihood ratio.
* denotes test statistic significance at 10% level.
** denotes test statistic significance at 5% level.
*** denotes test statistic significance at 1% level.

described via household head's financial literacy and gender interacted with financial literacy. The estimated results demonstrate that, for households headed by a person without financial literacy, the conditional expected income by the financial users $E(y_1|I=1)$ is KR123,399 (US\$31) per month. The conditional expected

Table 7.5 Effects of financial inclusion on household income per capita

	Income effects	
	Mean	*SE*
Without financial literacy		
$E(y_{1i} \| T = 1)$	123,398.600	5,487.527
$E(y_{2i} \| T = 1)$	93,560.460	5,419.053
TT	29,838.140***	77,12.269
With financial literacy		
$E(y_{1i} \| T = 1)$	123,949.200	1,885.205
$E(y_{2i} \| T = 1)$	93,349.010	1,867.451
TT	30,600.140***	2,653.558
Male head without financial literacy		
$E(y_{1i} \| T = 1)$	125,012.800	5,820.670
$E(y_{2i} \| T = 1)$	96,095.590	5,915.732
TT	28,917.170***	8,299.161
Male head with financial literacy		
$E(y_{1i} \| T = 1)$	124,281.900	1,972.431
$E(y_{2i} \| T = 1)$	95,054.390	1,994.227
TT	29,227.480***	2,804.893
Female head without financial literacy		
$E(y_{1i} \| T = 1)$	105,239.300	14,937.650
$E(y_{2i} \| T = 1)$	70,925.410	8,415.328
TT	34,313.910***	17,145.000
Female head with financial literacy		
$E(y_{1i} \| T = 1)$	119,713.600	6,298.973
$E(y_{2i} \| T = 1)$	76,734.270	4,710.588
TT	42,979.310***	7,865.539

Source: Author's calculation.

Notes: The expected values of monthly household income per capita in riels by individual households are transformed from log terms.
SE = standard error; TT = treatment effects
*** denotes test statistical significance at 1% level.

income users would have enjoyed if they did not use financial services $E(y_2 | I = 1)$ is KR93,560 (US$23) per month. Thus, when using financial services, on average, households are likely to increase the per capita income by KR29,838 (US$7) per month. In a similar fashion, when using financial services, on average, households headed by a person with financial literacy are likely to increase the per capita income by KR30,600 (US$8) per month. These results suggest that financial users with financial literacy are much better off in terms of household income per capita than those without financial literacy. Overall, the results reveal that financial literacy is very likely to reinforce the favourable effects of financial inclusion on poverty reduction. These results support the findings by previous studies (e.g., Cole et al., 2011; Grohmann et al., 2018). They also confirm the argument by Seng (2018a and 2018b) that the lack of financial knowledge is very likely to be an obstacle to the pro-poor growth of microfinance, and, even worse, bring about the unwanted effects of financial inclusion in Cambodia.

Taking gender into consideration, when using financial services, on average, households headed by a man without financial literacy are likely to increase the household income per capita by KR28,917 (US$7) per month, while those headed by a man with financial literacy are likely to increase the income by KR29,227 (US$7) per month. Furthermore, households headed by a woman without financial literacy are likely, when using financial services, to increase the income by KR34,314 (US$9) per month, while those with financial literacy are likely to increase the income by approximately KR42,979 (US$11). The results show that, regardless of financial literacy, female-headed users of financial services are very likely to gain more than male-headed users in terms of household income per capita. These results are consistent with arguments that female users of financial services allocate household incomes more efficiently (e.g., Alam, 2012; Akotey and Adjasi, 2016). Of note, financial users headed by a woman with financial literacy are more likely to make the greatest gains from using financial services, suggesting that promoting financial inclusion and financial literacy for women is one of the best ways to lift needy households out of poverty. These findings complement both of Seng's 2018 studies that focused only on credit and did not account for gender and financial literacy in the estimation of the treatment effects of microcredit on household welfare and poverty.

Table 7.6 presents the household budget deficit effects of financial inclusion, with the second column being described via household head's financial literacy and gender interacted with financial literacy. The estimated results demonstrate that, when using financial services, on average, households headed by a person without financial literacy are likely to reduce the probability of running household budget deficits by approximately 26%. Similarly, when using financial services, on average, households headed by a person with financial literacy are likely to reduce the probability of running a household budget deficit by approximately 27%. These results suggest that financial users with financial literacy are likely to reduce the likelihood of household budget deficits at a greater level than do those without financial literacy. Overall, these results reveal that financial literacy is very likely to help financial users mitigate the risk of household budget deficits, reinforcing the income effects of financial inclusion. The estimated results of the probit model describing the household decision to use financial services are consistent with those reported in Table 7.2 and are available on request. Moreover, the detailed results related to outcome equations describing the budget deficit for the users and non-users are also available on request.

Table 7.6 reports the average treatment effects of financial inclusion on household budget deficits. Taking gender into account, when using financial services, on average, households headed by a man without financial literacy are likely to reduce the probability of household budget deficit by approximately 12%, while those headed by a woman without financial literacy are likely to reduce the probability by approximately 17%. Furthermore, households headed by a man with financial literacy are likely, when using financial services, to reduce the probability by approximately 12%, while those headed by a woman with financial literacy are

Table 7.6 Effects of financial inclusion on household budget deficits

	ATT		*Difference in ATT*
	Male	*Female*	
Without financial literacy	−0.116 (0.005)	−0.170 (0.024)	0.054*** (0.017)
With financial literacy	−0.118 (0.001)	−0.200 (0.009)	0.082*** (0.006)

Source: Author's calculation.

ATT = average treatment effects on the treated
*** denotes test statistical significance at 1% level. Standard errors are in parentheses.

likely to reduce the probability by approximately 20%. The results demonstrate that, regardless of financial literacy, female-headed users of financial services are very likely to perform much better than male-headed users in terms of reducing household budget deficits. These results confirm the arguments by Alam (2012), and Akotey and Adjasi (2016) that women manage cash more efficiently. Of note, financial users headed by a woman with financial literacy are more likely to reduce the probability of a household budget deficit by the greatest level, indicating that promoting both financial inclusion and financial literacy for women is beneficial. These complementary findings provide evidence that financial literacy is likely to reinforce the poverty-alleviating effects of financial inclusion, more possibly through reducing household budget deficits.

7.7 Conclusion

The empirical evidence on the beneficial effects of financial development on needy households has drawn recent studies' attention to the determinants of financial inclusion and suggests that financial literacy has roles to play in enhancing financial inclusion. While the most recent studies do not control for financial literacy in their empirical model analysis, the evidence on the unwanted socio-economic effects of financial services is still ambivalent about the poverty-alleviating effects of financial development.

This study analyses the effects of financial inclusion on poverty in terms of household income per capita via financial literacy and household gender interacted with financial literacy in Cambodia by applying the endogenous switching model to data from the FinScope Survey conducted in 2015. The endogenous switching results suggest that the use of financial services is very likely to make a great contribution to increasing household income per capita, in particular for household users headed by a woman with financial literacy. A complementary analysis was also performed to further quantify the household budget deficit effects of financial inclusion with the ESP model. The ESP results demonstrate that the use of financial services is more likely to reduce the probability of a household budget deficit, for the users headed by a woman with financial literacy in particular. These results suggest that financial inclusion is very likely to make a great contribution to poverty reduction if the users have at least basic financial knowledge. Women with financial literacy are more likely to gain from financial inclusion. These findings are robust and consistent with the NBC's prioritised policies towards enhancing financial inclusion, giving insight into how financial inclusion can promote poverty alleviation and in particular underscoring the need for effective financial education for the current and next generations, and gender access to financial services as a strategy for sustained poverty reduction in Cambodia.

Finally, the study has its limitations as the panel data are unavailable and those used in the analysis, in particular the variable capturing financial literacy, are not ideal for estimating treatment effects. With such accurate data, this study can be improved with more appropriate instruments and financial literacy measurement to address the issues of endogeneity regarding financial services and the issues of financial literacy when estimating treatment effects. This is an opportunity for future studies when better data are available.

Acknowledgements

I am very grateful to Prof. Shujiro Urata from Waseda University, Japan, for his encouragement. Also, I would like to sincerely thank Dr. Rashesh Shresstha from Economic Research Institute for ASEAN and East Asia (ERIA) for his useful comments. Furthermore, I wish to express my gratitude to the National Bank of Cambodia for giving me the data and opportunities to conduct this study. All remaining errors are my sole responsibility.

Disclosure statement

No potential conflict of interest was reported by the author.

Notes

1 Bangladesh is the highest MFI-penetrated economy, with a rate of 25% followed by Bosnia Herzegovina (15%), Mongolia (15%), Cambodia (13%), and Nicaragua (11%) (Gonzalez, 2010; Seng, 2018a and 2018b).

2 Following the previous studies (e.g., Chang and Mishra, 2008; Akotey and Adjasi, 2016; Seng, 2018a and 2018b), the selection model is estimated with a probit model describing the household decision to use financial services.

3 Owing to the unavailability of appropriate data on financial literacy from the FinScope survey, the study constructs a proxy for financial literacy based on a question: do you understand how banks work and benefit from having a savings account at a bank?

4 The amount is converted into US dollars at the exchange rate of US$1 = KR4,000.

References

Aakvik, A., J.J. Heckman, and E.J. Vytlacil (2005), 'Estimating Treatment Effects for Discrete Outcomes When Responses to Treatment Vary: An Application to Norwegian Vocational Rehabilitation Programs', *Journal of Econometrics*, 125(1-2), pp.15–51. doi:10.1016/j.jeconom.2004.04.002.

Aghion, P., and P. Bolton (1997), 'A Theory of Trickle-Down Growth and Development', *Review of Economic Studies*, 64(2), pp.151–72. https://www.jstor.org/stable/2971707 (accessed 25 June 2020).

Akotey, J.O., and C.K.D. Adjasi (2016), 'Does Microcredit Increase Household Welfare in the Absence of Microinsurance?', *World Development*, 77(2016), pp.380–94. doi:10.1016/j.worlddev.2015.09.005.

Alam, A. (2012), 'The Effects of Gender-Based Returns to Borrowing on Intra-Household Resource Allocation in Rural Bangladesh', *World Development*, 40(6), pp.1164–80. doi:10.1016/j.worlddev.2011.12.009

Aportela, F. (1999), 'Effects of Financial Access on Savings by Low-Income People', Banco De México, Research Department. http://users.nber.org/~rdehejia/!@$devo/Lecture%2006%20Microcredit/supplemental/Aportela.pdf (accessed 25 June 2020).

Asad K.G., M. Issam, and K.S. Imai (2015), 'Microfinance and Household Poverty Reduction: Empirical Evidence from Rural Pakistan', *Oxford Development Studies*, 43(1), pp.84–104. https://doi.org/10.1080/13600818.2014.980228

Ashraf, N., N. Gons, D. Karlan, and W. Yin (2003), *A Review of Commitment Savings Products in Developing Countries* (ERD Working Paper Series No. 45), Tokyo: Asian Development Bank Institute. http://hdl.handle.net/11540/1969 (accessed 25 June 2020).

Banerjee, A., and A. Newman (1994), 'Poverty, Incentives and Development', *American Economic Review Papers and Proceedings,* 84(2), pp.211–15.

Banerjee, A.V., E. Dufio, R. Glennerster, and C. Kinnan (2009), 'The Miracle of Microfinance? Evidence from a Randomized Evaluation', *MIT Poverty Action Lab.* Cambridge, MA: Massachusetts Institute of Technology.

Bateman, M. (2010), *Why Doesn't Microfinance Work? The Destructive Rise of Local Neoliberalism.* Zed Books: London.

Bateman, M. (2017), *Post-War Reconstruction and Development in Cambodia and The Destructive Role of Microcredit. Paper Presented at the 8th International Scientific Conference 'Future World By* 2050. Pula, Croatia, 1–3 June 2017. www.researchgate.net/publication/315788551_post-war_reconstruction_and_development_in_cambodia_and_the_destructive_role_of_microcredit (accessed 25 June 2020).

Beck, T., A. Demirguc-Kunt, and M.S.M. Peria (2007), 'Reaching Out: Access to and Use of Banking Services across Countries', *Journal of Monetary Economics*, 85(1), pp.234–66. http://refhub.elsevier.com/s0305-750x(18)30212-2/h0040 (accessed 25 June 2020).

Bello, W. (2006), 'Microcredit, Macro Issues', *The Nation.* 30 October. www.thenation.com/article/archive/microcredit-macro-issues/ (accessed 25 June 2020).Bornstein, D. (1996), *The Price of a Dream. The Story of the Grameen Bank and the Idea That It Is Helping the Poor to Change Their Lives.* New York: Simon and Schuster.

Bourguignon, F. (2003), 'The Growth Elasticity of Poverty Reduction: Explaining Heterogeneity across Countries and Time Periods', in T. Eicher, and S. Turnovsky (eds.), *Inequality and Growth: Theory and Policy Implications.* Cambridge, MA: MIT Press.

Bruhn, M., and I. Love (2014), 'The Real Impact of Improved Access to Finance: Evidence from Mexico', *The Journal of Finance,* 69(3), pp.1347–69. http://refhub.elsevier.com/s0305-750x(18)30212-2/h0055 (accessed 25 June 2020).

Brune, L., X. Giné, J. Goldberg, and D. Yang (2016), 'Facilitating Savings for Agriculture: Field Experimental Evidence from Malawi', *Economic Development and Cultural Change*, 64(2), pp.187–220. http://refhub.elsevier.com/s0305-750x(18)30212-2/h0060 (accessed 25 June 2020).

Burgess, R., and P. Rohini (2005), 'Do Rural Banks Matter? Evidence from the Indian Social Banking Experiment', *American Economic Review,* 95(3), pp.780–95. http://refhub.elsevier.com/s0305-750x(18)30212-2/h0065 (accessed 25 June 2020).

Bylander, M. (2015), 'Credit as Coping: Rethinking Microcredit in the Cambodian Context', *Oxford Development Studies,* 43(4), pp.533–53. https://doi.org/10.1080/13600818.2015.1064880

Cambodia Microfinance Association (2014), *Annual Report 2014.* Phnom Penh: Cambodia Microfinance Association. www.cma-network.org/en/microfinance-in-cambodia (accessed 25 June 2020).

Cambodia Socio-Economic Survey (2017), *Cambodia Socio-Economic Survey* 2017. Phnom Penh: National Institute of Statistics.

Cole, S., T. Sampson, and B. Zia (2011), 'Prices or Knowledge? What Drives Demand for Financial Services in Emerging Markets?', *Journal of Finance,* 66(6), pp.1933–67. https://doi.org/10.1111/j.1540-6261.2011.01696.x

Coleman, B.E. (1999), 'The Impact of Group Lending in Northeast Thailand', *Journal of Development Economics,* 60(1), pp.105–42. doi:10.1016/s0304-3878(99)00038-3

Coleman, B.E. (2006), 'Microfinance in Northeast Thailand: Who Benefits and How Much?', *World Development,* 34(9), pp.1612–38. doi:10.1016/J.Worlddev.2006.01.006

Deininger, K., and L. Squire (1998), 'New Perspectives on Old Issues: Inequality and Growth', *Journal of Development Economics,* 57(2), pp.259–87.

Demirguc-Kunt, A., L. Klapper, and D. Singer (2017), 'Financial Inclusion and Inclusive Growth – A Review of Recent Empirical Evidence', *World Bank Policy Research Paper,* No. 8040, Washington, DC: World Bank. https://ideas.repec.org/p/wbk/wbrwps/8040.html (accessed 25 June 2020).

Di Falco, S., M. Veronesi, and M. Yesuf (2011), 'Does Adaptation to Climate Change Provide Food Security? A Micro-Perspective from Ethiopia', *American Journal of Agricultural Economics,* 93(3), pp.829–46. doi:10.1093/ajae/aar006.

Dollar, D., and A. Kraay (2002), 'Growth Is Good for the Poor', *Journal of Economic Growth,* 7(3), pp.195–225.

Drexler, A., F. Greg, and S. Antoinette (2014), 'Keeping It Simple: Financial Literacy and Rules of Thumb', *American Economic Journal: Applied Economics,* 6(2), pp.1–31.

Dupas, P., and J. Robinson (2013), 'Savings Constraints and Microenterprise Development: Evidence from a Field Experiment in Kenya', *American Economic Journal: Applied Economics,* 5(1), pp.163–92. http://refhub.elsevier.com/s0305-750x(18)30212-2/h0115 (accessed 25 June 2020).

Duvendack, M., and J.R. Palmer (2012), 'High Noon for Microfinance Impact Evaluations: Re-Investigating the Evidence from Bangladesh', *The Journal of Development Studies,* 48(12), pp.1864–80. https://doi.org/10.1080/00220388.2011.646989

Eliste, P., and S. Zorya (2015), Cambodian Agriculture in Transition: Opportunities and Risks. Washington, DC: World Bank. http://documents.worldbank.org/curated/en/2015/08/24919384/cambodian-agriculture-transition-opportunities-risks (accessed 25 June 2020).

Galor, O., and J. Zeira (1993), 'Income Distribution and Macroeconomics', *The Review of Economic Studies,* 60(1), pp.35–52.

Ganle, J.K., K. Afriyie, and A.Y. Segbefia (2015), 'Microcredit: Empowerment and Disempowerment of Rural Women in Ghana', *World Development,* 66, pp.335–45. doi:10.1016/j.worlddev.2014.08.027

Ghosh, S., and D. Vinod (2017), 'What Constrains Financial Inclusion for Women? Evidence from Indian Micro Data', *World Development,* 92, pp.60–81. http://dx.doi.org/10.1016/j.worlddev.2016.11.011

Gonzalez, A. (2010), 'Is Microfinance Growing too Fast?', *MIX Data Brief*, No. 5, Microfinance Information Exchange. https://papers.ssrn.com/sol3/papers.cfm?abstract_id=1644948 (accessed 25 June 2020).

Greene, W.H. (2008), *Econometric Analysis*. Upper Saddle River, NJ: Prentice Hall.

Grohmann, A., T. Klühs, and L. Menkhoff (2018), 'Does Financial Literacy Improve Financial Inclusion? Cross-Country Evidence', *World Development*, 111, pp.84–96. https://doi.org/10.1016/j.worlddev.2018.06.020

Heckman, J.J, J.L. Tobias, and E.J. Vytlacil (2001), 'Four Parameters of Interest in the Evaluation of Social Programs', *Southern Economic Journal*, 68(2), pp.210–33. https://doi.org/10.2307/1061591

Imai, K.S., and M.D.S. Azam (2012), 'Does Microfinance Reduce Poverty in Bangladesh? New Evidence from Household Panel Data', *The Journal of Development Studies*, 48(5), pp.633–53. doi:10.1080/00220388.2012.661853

Imai, K.S., T. Arun, and S.K. Annim (2010), 'Microfinance and Household Poverty Reduction: New Evidence from India', *World Development*, 38(12), pp.1760–74. doi:10.1016/j.worlddev.2010.04.006

Karlan, D., and J. Zinman (2010), 'Expanding Credit Access: Using Randomized Supply Decisions to Estimate the Impacts', *Review of Financial Studies*, 23(1), pp.433–64. https://doi.org/10.1093/rfs/hhp092

Klapper, L., M. El-Zoghbi, and J. Hess (2016), 'Achieving the Sustainable Development Goals – The Role of Financial Inclusion', *CGAP Working Paper*. www.unsgsa.org/files/3114/6489/8605/sdgs_paper_final_003.pdf (accessed 25 June 2020).

Kondo, T., A.J. Orbeta, C. Dingcong, and C. Infantado (2008), 'Impact of Microfinance on Rural Households in The Philippines', *IDS Discussion Paper Series*, No. 2008-05. Manila: Philippine Institute for Development Studies. www.eaber.org/node/22639 (accessed 25 June 2020).

Kulb C., M. Hennink, N. Kiiti, and J. Mutinda (2015), 'How Does Microcredit Lead to Empowerment? A Case Study of the Vinya Wa Aka Group in Kenya', *Journal of International Development*, 28(5), 715–32. doi: 10.1002/jid.3130

Levine, R., N. Loayza, and T. Beck (2000), 'Financial Intermediation and Growth: Causality and Causes', *Journal of Monetary Economics*, 46(1), pp.31–77. https://doi.org/10.1016/S0304-3932(00)00017-9

Lokshin, M., and Z. Sajaia (2004), 'Maximum Likelihood Estimation of Endogenous Switching Regression Models', *Stata Journal*, 4(3), pp.282–89.

Lokshin, M., and Z. Sajaia (2011), 'Impact of Interventions on Discrete Outcomes: Maximum Likelihood Estimation of the Binary Choice Models with Binary Endogenous Regressors', *The Stata Journal*, 11(3), pp.368–85.

Lusardi, A., and S.M. Olivia (2007), 'Financial Literacy and Retirement Preparedness: Evidence and Implications for Financial Education', *Business Economics*, 42(1), pp.35–44.

Maldonado, J.H., and C. González-Vega (2008), 'Impact of Microfinance on Schooling: Evidence from Poor Rural Households in Bolivia', *World Development*, 36(11), pp.2440–55. doi:10.1016/j.worlddev.2008.04.004

Maddala, G.S. (1983), *Limited-Dependent and Qualitative Variables in Econometrics*. Cambridge: Cambridge University Press.

Maddala, G.S. (1986), 'Disequilibrium, Self-Selection, and Switching Models', in Z. Griliches, and D. I. Michael (Eds.), *Handbook of Econometrics*, pp. 1633–82. North-Holland: Elsevier.

Masino, S., and M. Niño-Zarazúa (2020), 'Improving Financial Inclusion through the Delivery of Cash Transfer Programmes: The Case of Mexico's Progresa-Oportunidades-Prospera Programme', *The Journal of Development Studies,* 56(1), pp.151–68. https://doi.org/10.1080/00220388.2018.1546845

Munyegera, C.K., and T. Matsumoto (2015), 'Mobile Money, Remittances, and Household Welfare: Panel Evidence from Rural Uganda', *World Development,* 79, pp.127–37. http://dx.doi.org/10.1016/j.worlddev.2015.11.006

NBC (2017), *Annual Report* 2017. Phnom Penh: National Bank of Cambodia.

NBC (2018a), *Annual Report* 2018. Phnom Penh: National Bank of Cambodia.

NBC (2018b), *Semi-Annual Report* 2018. Phnom Penh: National Bank of Cambodia.

NBC (2019), *Financial Stability Review* 2019. Phnom Penh: National Bank of Cambodia.

Ouma, S.A., T.M. Odongo, and M. Were (2017), 'Mobile Financial Services and Financial Inclusion: Is It a Boon for Savings Mobilization?', *Review of Development Finance,* 7(1), pp.29–35 https://doi.org/10.1016/j.rdf.2017.01.001

Pytkowska, J., and S. Spannuth (2012), *Indebtedness of Microcredit Clients in Kosovo: Results from a Comprehensive Field Study.* Frankfurt Am Main: Microfinance Centre, Finance in Motion, EFSE.

Rahman, M.W., J. Luo, and Z. Minjuan (2014), 'Welfare Impacts of Microcredit Programmes: An Empirical Investigation in the State-Designated Poor Counties of Shaanxi, China', *Journal of International Development,* 27(7), pp.1012–26. doi: 10.1002/jid.3020

Ravallion, M. (2001), 'Growth, Inequality and Poverty: Looking Beyond Averages', *World Development,* 29(11), pp.1803–15.

Schicks, J. (2013), 'The Sacrifices of Micro-Borrowers in Ghana–A Customer-Protection Perspective on Measuring Over-Indebtedness', *The Journal of Development Studies,* pp.49(9), 1238–55. https://doi.org/10.1080/00220388.2013.775421

Seng, K. (2015), 'The Effects of Nonfarm Activities on Farm Households' Food Consumption in Rural Cambodia', *Development Studies Research,* 2(1), pp.77–89. doi: 10.1080/21665095.2015.1098554

Seng, K. (2017), 'Considering the Effects of Mobile Phones on Financial Inclusion in Cambodia', *MPRA Paper,* No. 82225. Germany: University Library of Munich.

Seng, K. (2018a), 'Rethinking the Effects of Microcredit on Household Welfare in Cambodia', *The Journal of Development Studies,* 54(9), pp.1496–1512. https://doi.org/10.1080/00220388.2017.1299139

Seng, K. (2018b), 'Revisiting the Microcredit's Poverty-Reducing Promise: Evidence from Cambodia', *Journal of International Development,* 30(4), pp.615–42. https://doi.org/10.1002/jid.3336

Swamy, V. (2014), 'Financial Inclusion, Gender Dimension, and Economic Impact on Poor Households', *World Development,* 56, pp.1–15. http://dx.doi.org/10.1016/j.worlddev.2013.10.019

White, H., and E. Anderson (2001), 'Growth Vs. Redistribution: Does the Pattern of Growth Matter?', *Development Policy Review,* 19(3), pp.167–289.

Wydick, B., H.K. Hayes, and S.H. Kempf (2011), 'Social Networks, Neighborhood Effects, and Credit Access: Evidence from Rural Guatemala', *World Development,* 39(6), pp.974–82. https://doi.org/10.1016/j.worlddev.2009.10.015

Zins, A., and L. Weill (2016), 'The Determinants of Financial Inclusion in Africa', *Review of Development Finance,* 6, pp.46–57. http://dx.doi.org/10.1016/j.rdf.2016.05.001

Appendix 7.1 Parameter estimates – test for validity of the selected instruments

Variables	*Per capita income by non-users (OLS)*			*Use of financial services (probit)*			*Budget deficit by non-users (probit)*		
	Coef.	*SE*	*P-value*	*Coef.*	*SE*	*P-value*	*Coef.*	*SE*	*P-value*
HH's age	9.71***	2.10	0.00	9.26***	1.20	0.00	3.26*	1.65	0.05
HH's age squared	–1.37***	0.29	0.00	–1.22***	0.16	0.00	–0.43*	0.23	0.06
HH's ethnicity	0.17	0.21	0.43	–0.19*	0.11	0.08	–0.14	0.18	0.44
HH's gender	–0.17	0.27	0.52	–0.02	0.14	0.87	0.10	0.22	0.66
Single	–0.57	0.61	0.35	–0.33	0.36	0.37	–0.13	0.50	0.80
Marriage	–0.70***	0.16	0.00	0.07	0.09	0.44	0.04	0.14	0.76
Divorced	–0.13	0.48	0.79	0.25	0.27	0.37	–0.20	0.43	0.64
Widowed	–0.37	0.31	0.23	–0.01	0.17	0.94	0.05	0.26	0.85
Training	0.30	0.70	0.67	–0.54	0.43	0.21	0.91	0.67	0.18
Primary	0.41**	0.16	0.01	–0.07	0.09	0.44	–0.04	0.13	0.76
Secondary	0.52**	0.19	0.01	0.11	0.10	0.26	0.18	0.16	0.26
Tertiary	1.25**	0.54	0.02	0.12	0.22	0.59	0.15	0.39	0.71
Income generators	–0.15***	0.04	0.00	0.04*	0.02	0.05	–0.03	0.03	0.30
Cellphone	0.47***	0.10	0.00	0.43***	0.06	0.00	–0.02	0.08	0.82
Email	–0.68*	0.37	0.06	0.66***	0.14	0.00	0.14	0.28	0.62
Rural	–0.71***	0.11	0.00	–0.02	0.05	0.68	0.05	0.09	0.55
Coastal	0.22	0.20	0.26	0.09	0.10	0.38	–0.12	0.15	0.44
Plain	–0.24*	0.13	0.06	–0.03	0.05	0.54	0.03	0.09	0.77
Plateau	Dropped			–0.27***	0.08	0.00	–0.05	0.11	0.69
Tonlé sap	–0.04	0.13	0.75	Dropped					
Income proof[a]	0.29	0.21	0.17	0.43***	0.11	0.00	–0.03	0.19	0.85
Family book[a]	0.08	0.14	0.54	0.01	0.08	0.91	0.25**	0.12	0.03

Constant	–5.12	3.83	0.18	–17.39***	2.19	0.00	–6.15**	3.00	0.04
Observations	1031			2693			1221		
Adj. R^2	0.14								
Prob. > Chi^2						0.00			0.48
Pseudo R^2				0.06			0.01		
Log likelihood				–1979.36			–835.20		

Source: Author's calculation.

Notes

OLS = ordinary least squares.

a the test for the joint effects income proof and family book under the null hypothesis: (1) for per capita income by non-users (OLS), $H_0 : \lambda_1 = \lambda_2 = 0$, the critical value F = 1.10 and Prob. > F = 0.33; (2) for the use of financial services (probit), $H_0 : \lambda_1 = \lambda_2 = 0$, the critical value Chi^2 = 16.33 and Prob. > Chi^2 = 0.00; and (3) for the budget deficit by non-users (probit), $H_0 : \lambda_1 = \lambda_2 = 0$, the critical value Chi^2 = 4.65 and Prob. > Chi^2 = 0.10.

* denotes test statistic significance at 10% level.

** denotes test statistic significance at 5% level.

*** denotes test statistic significance at 1% level.

Appendix 7.2 Summary of variables

Variables	*Definition*
Dependent	
Household income per capita	Natural log of monthly income per household member
Household budget deficit	= 1 if the household runs budget deficit (i.e., spending > income)
Financial inclusion	= 1 if the household uses financial services (i.e., saving and borrowing etc.)
Independent	
Household head's age	Natural log of household head age
Household head's gender	= 1 if the household head is female
Household head's ethnicity	= 1 if the household head is Khmer
Single	= 1 if the household head is single
Marriage	= 1 if the household head is married
Divorced	= 1 if the household head is devoiced
Widowed	= 1 if the household head is widowed
Training	= 1 if the household head had access to any training
Primary	= 1 if the household head had access to primary school
Secondary	= 1 if the household head had access to secondary school
Tertiary	= 1 if the household had access to higher education
Income generators	The number of household members who contribute to income generation
Cellphone	= 1 if the household communicates and access to information by cellphone
Email	= 1 if the household communicates and access to information by email
Rural	= 1 if the household lives in rural area
Coastal	= 1 if the household settles in Coastal area
Plain	= 1 if the household settles in Plain area
Plateau	= 1 if the household settles in Plateau area
Tonlé Sap	= 1 if the household settles in Tonlé Sap area
Income proof	= 1 if the household possesses income proof documents

8 Financial inclusion and savings in Indonesia

Rashesh Shrestha and Samuel Nursamsu

8.1 Introduction

Financial inclusion can contribute towards poverty alleviation by enabling poor households to use products and services of formal financial institutions to optimally save, invest, and manage risks, and to benefit from the financial deepening of the broader economy. The benefits of financial products are well known (Beck and Demirguc-Kunt, 2006; Karlan and Morduch, 2010): with savings, households can accumulate assets, which in turn can enable them to invest in capital and access credit. If they can obtain credit at a reasonable interest rate, they can make profitable investments and grow their enterprise. With insurance, poor households can prepare for unanticipated income and health shocks due to environmental conditions (e.g., inclement weather, pollution, natural disasters), macroeconomic upheaval (recession, financial crisis), or other reasons. Currently, many poor households rely on informal sources to meet their financial needs – borrowing from family and friends or village moneylenders who charge exorbitant fees, and saving in informal groups. These sources are usually costly, inadequate, risky, and insufficiently regulated, which may lead to exploitation. Recognising the importance of access to formal finance in improving household welfare, many developing countries have been emphasising on financial inclusion over the past decade.

Focused financial inclusion policies have met with some success in encouraging bank account openings, which remain the most basic financial service. However, existing studies find that while opening a bank account is an important first step towards financial inclusion, it does not reliably translate into usage. When poor households were offered the opportunity to open a savings account at low cost, Prina (2015) found, there was high frequency of usage amongst new account holders in Nepal. However, a similar intervention in three African countries did not prove to be a success – studies by Dupas et al. (2018) found that new bank account holders did not actively use them. Lack of income was an important barrier in the latter setting. This suggests income growth and financial inclusion interact positively to improve welfare. The question then is whether financial inclusion in a high growth economic environment enables households to make investments that puts them in a stable trajectory of welfare gains.

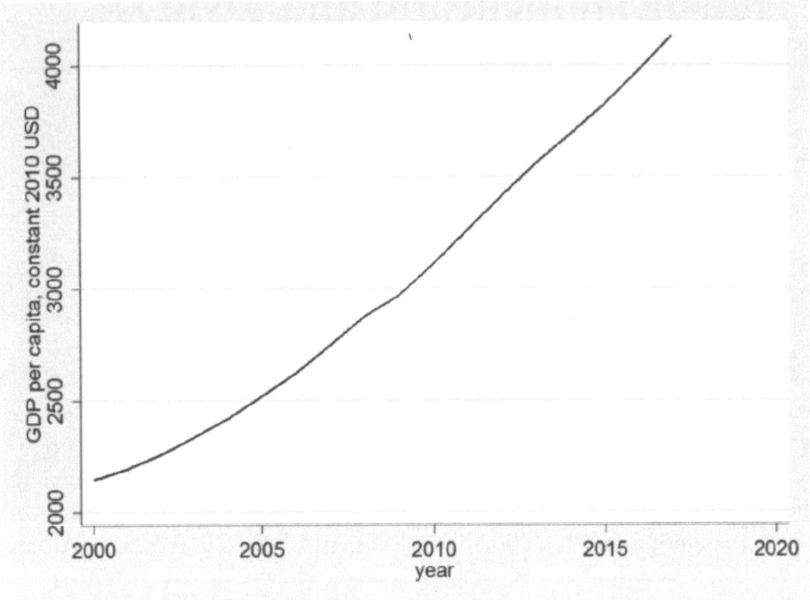

Figure 8.1 Indonesia's real GDP per capita in 2010 US$.
GDP = gross domestic product.
Source: Authors' calculation from World Development Indicators.

This chapter studies the relationship between financial inclusion and household savings in Indonesia, a setting with rapid economic growth *and* concerted government effort to expand financial inclusion over the past decade. The setting allows us to explore how financial inclusion translates income growth into accumulation of financial assets. Indonesia has consistently grown at over 5.5% per year over the past decade, with nominal income per capita rising by US$1,300 between 2006 and 2016, an increase of 50% (see Figure 8.1). The additional income would have enabled households to expand their consumption and move out of poverty. Indeed, the World Bank estimated that during this period poverty headcount fell from 22.5% to 6.5%.[1] Nonetheless, many households in Indonesia remain vulnerable to falling back into poverty, and rising inequality is a concern, making inclusivity an important policy concern (Tim Nasional Percepatan Penanggulangan Kemiskinan, 2018). Thus, understanding the relationship between financial inclusion and savings behaviour can contribute to the discussion about sustained poverty alleviation.

We use the Indonesian Family Life Survey (IFLS) data on household income, assets, consumption, and economic characteristics. The same households can be observed at two points in time, that is, 2007 and 2014, which allows investigating how households with different characteristics benefit from financial inclusion. We focus on households whose baseline characteristics (in 2007) made them likely to experience income growth during the 2007–2014 period, and study variation in savings in 2014 by the level of financial inclusion. To measure the level of financial inclusion of the households, we construct a sub-district (***kecamatan***)[2] index derived from the density of bank branches. The calculation follows the methodology of Sarma and Pais (2014) and uses the 2014 Village Potential Survey (PODES) data.

We find that poor households have higher probability of owning a savings account if they live in areas with a higher density of bank branches. According to our baseline results, a 0.1 increase in the index of financial inclusion (whose average value in the sample is 0.23) increases the probability of savings ownership by 2.9 percentage points amongst the poorest consumption quintile households in 2014 (the sample savings rate amongst the poorest quintile is 14%). The marginal effect on each of the four higher quintiles is approximately equal to 1.3%. Using different proxies for household welfare level (e.g., education level of the household head) does not alter the main inference. Thus, access to formal financial institutions can be most beneficial to increase savings amongst the poorest households.

The chapter contributes to our understanding of the role of financial inclusion in moving households securely out of poverty by enabling them to accumulate savings and other assets. The importance of savings on household welfare has been well-argued in the literature (Karlan et al., 2010). This is especially important in Indonesia given the vulnerability of many non-poor households to many types of shocks and lack of access to financial services for a sizable population. With rising income, Indonesia is also facing increasing inequality. It has been argued that as the country becomes more advanced, financial development can exacerbate inequality (Greenwood and Jovanovic, 1990). Hence, universal financial inclusion becomes a key factor for financial expansion to generate positive impact for economic development (Sarma and Pais, 2011).

8.2 Background: financial inclusion in Indonesia

Although financial development can increase economic growth (Levine, 2005; Beck et al., 2007), one concern is that it may leave behind individuals who lack access to the formal financial system and thus exacerbate inequality. Owing to low profitability and information problems, the private market tends to underserve the poor. At the same time, high monetary costs vis-à-vis informal financial services or low financial literacy (or both) may prevent use of formal financial services in developing countries like Indonesia (Cole et al., 2011). Thus, expanding financial inclusion requires additional incentives, innovative financial products, and financial education. Policymakers are now actively pursuing strategies to expand financial services amongst the poorer and underserved segments of the population. Indonesia, too, has been focused on giving a larger share of the population access to formal financial services, and, by recent statistics, has had some success in this regard.

In the first decade of 2000s, Indonesia was seriously underbanked despite steady economic recovery in the aftermath of the Asian Financial Crisis (Rosengard and Prasetyantoko, 2011). Indonesia remained well below its peers on available metrics of financial depth relative to its economic position.

The World Bank's 2010 nationwide household survey of access to financial services found that 50% of Indonesia's population had access to formal financial services (World Bank, 2010). Kikkawa and Xing (2014) report that, at the time, the government pursued various strategies to improve financial access of SMEs and poor households, including financial deregulation, education, no-frills bank accounts, financial identity programmes, and government-backed small business loan programmes, while also encouraging commercial banks to establish bank branches and install more automated teller machines. This was also when Indonesia reformed financial regulations to allow operation of mobile money and enable telecommunication companies to provide financial services.

Since 2011, available data provide evidence of the progress in financial inclusion. In this discussion, we mainly use the information from the World Bank's Financial Inclusion Database (FINDEX) (see Demirguc-Kunt et al. 2015, 2018 for detailed data description). Summary statistics of selected information from the Findex data are provided in Table 8.1. In terms of access, the percentage of individuals with a bank account was just 20% in 2011,[3] but it increased to almost 50% in 2017; this was the fastest progress amongst developing countries in East Asia and the Pacific, although the level is still lower than the global average of 69% (Demirguc-Kunt et al., 2018). The International Monetary Fund Financial Access Survey shows that, during this period, the number of deposit accounts with commercial banks increased from 109 million to 300 million, which is remarkable for a country with a population of 264 million. The same data show that 100 million accounts were added in 2017 alone.[4]

There is also a trend of the poorer segments of the population being included in the formal financial system in greater numbers. While the gain between 2011 and 2014 was greater for individuals in the upper 60th percentile of income, the gains between 2014 and 2017 were more pro-poor. Still, the gap by income level remains high. In 2017, 57% of those in the upper 60% income distribution had bank accounts, compared to only 37% of those in the bottom 40%.

Progress is slower on the actual usage of financial accounts. Only 21% of the respondents reported saving at a financial institution account, which is an increase of 6 percentage points from 2011. Nonetheless, about 30% of respondents saved in an informal way using savings clubs or with a person outside the family. Debit card ownership has increased, but credit card usage remains low. Likewise, regular use of financial institutional accounts has not increased as rapidly. While 80% of the respondents with a financial institution account made a deposit in 2014, this reduced to 52% in 2017. This is partly due to the large share of newly opened accounts not being utilised. Moreover, the fraction of respondents who reported not being able to come up with emergency funds remained almost the same in 2014 and 2017.

The progress in account ownership has been possible due to a concerted government effort to expand financial inclusion. Indonesia has adopted a comprehensive financial inclusion strategy touching upon all three of its dimensions: access, usage, and quality. Commitment to a National Strategy for Financial Inclusion was specified in the Chairman Statement in the ASEAN Summit in 2011. In June 2012, Bank Indonesia cooperated with the Vice President's Secretariat – National

Table 8.1 Summary of selected Findex variables

FINDEX variable	*2011*	*2014*	*2017*
Account (% age 15+)	19.6	36.1	48.9
Financial institution account (% age 15+)	19.6	35.9	48.4
Account, rural (% age 15+)	16.2	28.6	47
Account, female (% age 15+)	19.2	37.5	51.4
Account, male (% age 15+)	20	34.6	46.2
Account, income, poorest 40% (% ages 15+)	11	22.1	36.6
Account, income, richest 60% (% ages 15+)	25.3	45.3	57
Account, primary education or less (% ages 15+)	10.2	15.8	33.6
Account, secondary education or more (% ages 15+)	29.4	53.7	62.7
Account, young adults (% ages 15–24)	12.8	35.2	46.8
Saved at a financial institution (% age 15+)	15.3	26.6	21.5
Saved using a savings club or a person outside the family (% age 15+)	13.9	25.2	29.9
Borrowed from a financial institution (% age 15+)	8.5	13.1	17.2
Borrowed from family or friends (% age 15+)	42.3	41.5	35.7
Credit card ownership (% age 15+)	0.5	1.6	2.4
Debit card ownership (% age 15+)	10.5	25.9	30.8
Received government payments: into a financial institution account (% payment recipients, age 15+)		22.7	41
Received government payments: into an account (% payment recipients, age 15+)		22.7	41
Received government payments: through a mobile phone (% payment recipients, age 15+)		0.3	0.8
Received government transfers: first account opened to receive government transfers (% receiving transfers into an account, age 15+)		52.8	50.5
Received wages: into a financial institution account (% wage recipients, age 15+)		22.5	24.5
Borrowed any money in the past year (% age 15+)		56.8	54.8
Borrowed from a financial institution or used a credit card (% age 15+)		13.7	18.4
Debit card used to make a purchase in the past year (% age 15+)		8.5	11.3
Deposit in the past year (% with a financial institution account, age 15+)		80.4	51.7
No deposit and no withdrawal from a financial institution account in the past year (% age 15+)		4.6	14.7
Coming up with emergency funds: not possible (% age 15+)		50.2	49.6
Coming up with emergency funds: possible (% age 15+)		43	46.3

Source: World Bank FINDEX database. Not all variables were covered each year.

Team of Poverty Alleviation Acceleration (TNP2K) and Fiscal Policy Agency of Ministry of Finance to issue a National Strategy for Financial Inclusion. The National Strategy, promulgated as Presidential Regulation 82/2016,[5] set an ambitious target of covering 75% of the adult population by formal financial institutions by 2019. The progress towards this goal is tracked by a specially designed National Financial Literacy and Inclusion Survey, which shows a higher rate of financial inclusion at 68% in 2016, with bank account ownership at 63.6%. To coordinate various government agencies, Indonesia has established a National Secretariat for Financial Inclusion, an inter-governmental body comprising Indonesia's Financial Authority (OJK), Bank Indonesia, TNP2K, and the Ministry of Finance.

The national strategy pays special attention to the underserved groups: poor households, Small and Micro Enterprises (SMEs), and students. One effective strategy has been to convert government assistance from in-kind to cash and transfer them through the bank. Furthermore, Indonesia instituted a policy of directly transferring welfare payments into a recipient's bank account rather than providing cash, thus requiring them to open bank accounts. The conditional cash transfer (Family Hope Program or PKH) is now channelled through the banks in areas where the infrastructure is present. Other agencies are also encouraged to convert their programmes, but the complexity of some makes this approach not feasible for all programmes. The strategy to combine poverty programmes and financial inclusion seems to be working. Between 2014 and 2017, the share of adults receiving government transfers into a financial institution account almost doubled to 41%. Half of the respondents reported that they first opened an account to receive government transfers.

The Indonesia policy initiative is well-rounded as it targets multiple aspects of financial inclusion: access, availability, usage, and quality. According to the National Financial Literacy and Inclusion Survey conducted by the OJK, the financial inclusion index in 2016 was 67.82%, increasing from 59.74% in 2013. On the contrary, the financial literacy index in 2016 was 29.66%, increasing from 21.84% in 2013.

The OJK also monitors the financial landscape in such areas as knowledge/literacy, usage, and access. According to the OJK survey, conventional methods and physical access are still prominent in Indonesia, with physical offices becoming the main access channel of financial products. In addition, ATMs have also become the second-largest channel for people accessing financial products. On the contrary, the utilisation of the digital technology is still small, with only 5.8% respondents using phone banking and only 25% of respondents using online transactions to access the stock market.

The number of bank branches – the most basic conduit for access to financial service for a large majority of Indonesians – is expanding. The number of commercial bank offices increased from 26,894 in 2012 to 31,618 in 2018, while the number of rural bank offices increased from 4,425 to 6,273 over the same period (Otoritas Jasa Keuangan, 2015, 2019). However, the expansion of commercial bank branches has plateaued since 2015, although the number of rural banks (Bank Perkreditan Rakyat)[6] continues to rise. Moreover, there is substantial variation across locations. Using PODES, we create two indicators of bank branches: the share of families living in villages with a commercial bank branch, and the number of commercial bank branches per 1,000 families. These are reported in Table 8.2. Given the uneven distribution of Indonesia's population, the density and share of families living close to bank branches is different. While

Table 8.2 Bank branches density by province

Province	*Share of families*	*Density*
Aceh	10.86	0.33
Sumatera Utara	23.53	0.29
Sumatera Barat	35.63	0.35
Riau	35.53	0.36
Jambi	21.18	0.35
Sumatera Selatan	22.67	0.27
Bengkulu	16.67	0.38
Lampung	16.58	0.20
Kepulauan Bangka Belitung	26.64	0.39
Kepulauan Riau	51.19	0.37
Dki Jakarta	96.02	0.62
Jawa Barat	32.36	0.23
Jawa Tengah	22.92	0.24
D I Yogyakarta	51.89	0.39
Jawa Timur	25.32	0.23
Banten	30.36	0.22
Bali	42.88	0.43
Nusa Tenggara Barat	18.21	0.18
Nusa Tenggara Timur	14.31	0.27
Kalimantan Barat	30.47	0.29
Kalimantan Tengah	31.07	0.25
Kalimantan Selatan	28.90	0.31
Kalimantan Timur	53.07	0.40
Sulawesi Utara	16.52	0.33
Sulawesi Tengah	16.54	0.28
Sulawesi Selatan	24.37	0.31
Sulawesi Tenggara	14.09	0.34
Gorontalo	12.23	0.31
Sulawesi Barat	16.50	0.25
Maluku	21.03	0.29
Maluku Utara	10.93	0.30
Papua Barat	35.10	0.52
Papua	24.13	0.28
Total	**28.17**	**0.32**
N	**33**	

Source: Authors' calculation from PODES 2014. Kalimantan Utara, which was a newly formed province in 2014, is included into its parent Kalimantan Timur.

96% of the population in DKI Jakarta lives in 'villages' with a bank branch, the rate is less than 11% in Aceh. Bank branches tend to be highly concentrated in urban and peri-urban locations.

The traditional model of bank branches is not commercially viable everywhere across the archipelago, which means branchless banking will play a central strategic role in expanding access to financial services. Indonesia's attempt to make progress in this respect started with regulatory changes that enabled the launch of Digital Financial Services in 2009. The take-up of digital banking had been

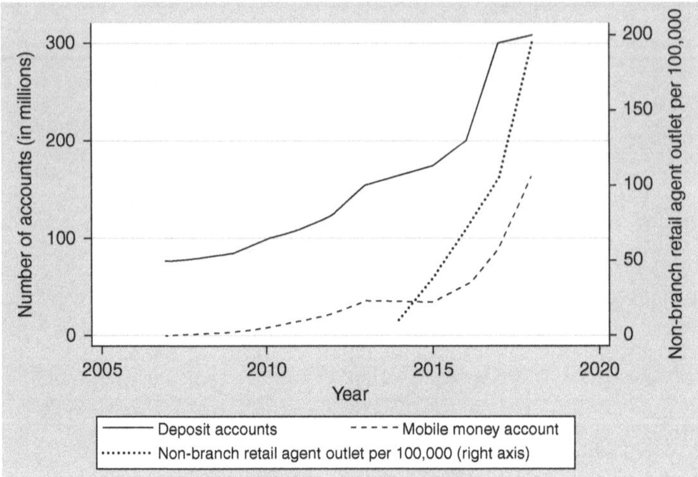

Figure 8.2 Expansion of banking in Indonesia.
Source: International Monetary Fund Financial Access Survey Statistics.

slow owing to regulatory hurdles, but its usage has expanded, according to the International Monetary Fund Financial Access Survey. Since the provision of branchless banking, both the number of deposits and mobile money accounts have increased rapidly (see Figure 8.2). Telkomsel's T-Cash and Go-Jek's Go-Pay are the most popular payment and money transfer services, which are well integrated with bank accounts. However, existing services are biased towards individuals who already have some degree of financial inclusion. For example, e-money regulations require providers to maintain a bank balance equivalent to the issued cash balance.

The provision of branchless banking received another boost with the launch of the service locally known as *Laku Pandai* in 2015 by four major commercial banks (Amianti, 2015). Under this programme, banks can provide (basic) savings, loan, and microinsurance services through their agents. In 2016, Bank Indonesia changed the regulation to make it easier for agents to sign up new customers for savings accounts (Diela, 2016).

The use of non-branch outlets is rising in Indonesia, with the number of non-bank retail outlets increasing exponentially from 10.75 per 100,000 adults in 2014 to 197 in 2018. In the Findex data, the proportion of respondents making or receiving digital payments[7] increased from 22% to 35% between 2014 and 2016 (Table 8.3). Although the rich–poor divide also exists in the use of digital payment services, progress is evident even amongst the poorest 40%, one-fifth of whom used digital payments in 2017. The service is equally available in rural areas, where one-third of respondents reported using digital payment services. Nonetheless, more effort is required to narrow the income and education gap in the use of digital payments.

Table 8.3 Percent of adults who made or received digital payments in the past year

Sample group	*2014*	*2017*
Overall	22.4	34.6
By subgroups		
Female (% age 15+)	23.1	35.5
In labour force (% age 15+)	25.1	38.5
Income, poorest 40% (% age 15+)	10.2	21.5
Income, richest 60% (% age 15+)	30.4	43.4
Male (% age 15+)	21.6	33.7
Older adults (% age 25+)	21.1	34.2
Out of labour force (% age 15+)	17.6	27.9
Primary education or less (% age 15+)	7.3	20.1
Rural (% age 15+)	15.7	33.4
Secondary education or more (% age 15+)	35.5	47.8
Young adults (% age 15–24)	26.6	36.0

Source: World Bank Financial Inclusion database.

8.3 Literature review – financial inclusion and savings

Given the concerted effort towards increasing financial inclusion, we conduct an original microdata analysis to understand its impact on households. We focus on savings ownership as our main outcome. Savings is one of the basic human activities and is seen as a universal indicator of financial inclusion. Economic theory suggests that most households would have a reason to save money. The life cycle hypothesis by Modigliani (1986) theorises the relationship between consumption, income, wealth, and savings of households. The main idea is that households would save part of their income to accumulate their wealth and use it in retirement. This hypothesis is supported by much evidence, especially in rich or developed countries (Karlan and Morduch, 2010).

However, the life cycle hypothesis requires some adjustments to be able to postulate savings behaviour in poor households. Rather than accumulate wealth, poor households tend to have a precautionary motive for savings to smoothen out their consumption (Deaton and Paxson, 1997; Karlan et al., 2010). Because many poor households have volatile income, they need to save in anticipation of lump-sum expenditure in the future. In this case, poor households need a mechanism to make deposits in small amounts and make occasional large withdrawals since most of their needs to cope with emergencies will require lump-sum money.

Adequate savings also allow households to accumulate assets that enable movement out of poverty and stable future income. Increased savings induce higher expenditure on health and education. Moreover, parents will save and make investments for their children's education and health outcomes, leading to intergenerational mobility (Becker and Tomes, 1979; Deaton and Paxson, 1997).

Despite this strong motive to save, many poor households do not save enough. Although lack of income is an obvious constraint, there are many additional reasons.

One of these is because they lack safe places to keep their money, indicating a lack of financial access (Banerjee and Duflo, 2007). This issue is exacerbated by their lack of trust in formal financial institutions and knowledge of financial products (Bachas et al., 2016). Therefore, even if banking institutions are available in their regions, they are still less likely to have accounts (Allen et al., 2012; Karlan and Morduch, 2010; Guiso et al., 2009). Recent research also highlights behavioural reasons for low savings. Households in rural areas tend to spend a significant part of their disposable income on festival expenses for sociocultural reasons (Banerjee and Duflo, 2007; Karlan and Morduch, 2010). Moreover, there may also be a commitment issue, where individuals or households have difficulty resisting impulsive consumption, or a lack of commitment to save a part of their income gradually (Banerjee and Duflo, 2007; Karlan and Morduch, 2010).

There is a large academic literature showing that improved financial inclusion can improve the welfare of poorer households. Bruhn and Love (2014) presented evidence that financial inclusion through increase in banking access in Mexico decreased poverty levels, with banking access positively impacting small businesses and households below median income levels. Burgess and Pande (2005) also showed similar evidence with bank openings in rural areas in India, where the government through its licensing policy strongly encouraged commercial banks to open branches in unbanked locations from the 1970s through the1990s. Therefore, reducing barriers to entry for bank branches could ease household and individual access to banking services, including account ownership (Beck et al., 2006).

While digital technology is changing the financial landscape, owning a bank account is one of the basic indicators of financial inclusion. Randomised control trials show that poor households take up savings accounts that have low costs and with banks that have branches nearby (e.g., Prina, 2015; Dupas et al., 2018). Distance to bank branches is an important barrier in Indonesia as well. The 2017 Findex data ask about the reason for not having a back account. The most common answer is lack of sufficient funds, which was chosen by 72% of the respondents, as shown in Table 8.4. However, one in three also indicated that financial institutions are too far away and financial services are too expensive.

Although the evidence of the positive effect from bank branches towards savings ownership increase is ubiquitous, the effectiveness of bank accounts to increase savings amounts is still debated. A recent study by Dupas et al. (2018) showed that simply having bank accounts does not necessarily translate into an increase in savings, even when the accounts are subsidised. One important reason is because poor households are simply not able to save or their necessities are not fulfilled with the current saving products. On the contrary, in their previous study, Dupas and Robinson (2013) found a positive effect of savings account ownership to savings amounts in rural Kenya, even with high withdrawal fees. This evidence is also supported by the finding of Ashraf et al. (2006), who surmised the increase in savings accounts also increased savings balances, although in this case the savings account was tied with individual commitment.

Table 8.4 Reason for not having bank account

FINDEX variable	*2017*
Financial institutions are too far away	33.0
Financial services are too expensive	31.7
Insufficient funds	72.1
Lack of necessary documentation	26.4
Lack of trust in financial institutions	8.0
No need for financial services ONLY	1.7
Religious reasons	5.2
Someone in the family has an account	29.2

Source: World Bank Financial Inclusion database.

8.4 Analysis of IFLS data

In our empirical analysis, we study how financial inclusion as determined by local bank branch density impacts household welfare. While the concept of household welfare is quite broad and depends on a multitude of factors, in a developing country context, arguably the most important measure of welfare is the ability to escape poverty in a sustained way. Although current consumption is a way of measuring welfare, it is subject to transitory shocks (positive or negative) that may provide a misleading picture. For a more permanent transition out of poverty, households must accumulate assets, which could include 'conventional, privately held productive and financial wealth, as well as social, geographic and market access positions that confer economic advantage' (Carter and Barrett, 2006, p. 179). In this regard, accumulation of savings is an important variable.

The main data for this analysis derive from the IFLS, which asks many relevant questions. The IFLS tracked the same 7,200 households (and their offshoots) since 1993. So far, five waves have been conducted in 1993, 1997, 2000, 2007, and 2014 (for details, see Strauss et al., 2009 and 2016). We use the 2007 and 2014 rounds (IFLS 4 and 5, respectively).

The survey asked households about possession of various types of assets, including savings or certificates of deposit. As in many developing countries, households tend to own various types of assets. In poor households especially, durable rather than financial assets are more common. We show ownership rates of various types of assets by the poorest 40% IFLS households in Table 8.5. House and land ownership is high at 80%, while ownership of additional land or houses is rare. Many poor households own livestock. Vehicle ownership is high, having increased significantly between 2007 and 2014, as did ownership of household appliances.

Some questions about financial inclusion were also available in the survey, although we do not use them in this study. Nonetheless, it is revealing to discuss some of them here as they cover aspects of financial literacy. Table 8.6 summarises several financial inclusion indicators of Indonesian households in 2007 and 2014.

Table 8.5 Asset ownership amongst poorest 40% of households

Type of asset	*2007*	*2014*
House and land occupied by this household	.8	.76
Other house/building (including land)	.063	.06
Land (not used for farm/non-farm)	.086	.085
Poultry	.35	.22
Livestock/fishpond	.082	.049
Hard stem plant that not used for farm or non-farm business	.2	.12
Vehicles (cars, boats, bicycles, motorbikes)	.49	.65
Household appliances	.8	.94
Savings/ certificate of deposit/ stocks	.13	.18
Receivables	.059	.073
Jewelry	.47	.38
Household Furniture and Utensils	.98	.98
Other assets	.08	.031

Source: Authors' compilation from IFLS 2007 and 2014.

Table 8.6 Household financial inclusion status in IFLS

Year	*2007*	*2014*	*Unit*
Known place to borrow money	88.08	82.29	%
Known financial institution (from known place)	87.01	83.56	%
Have Savings (overall)	26.09	30.42	%
Have Savings (bottom 20%)	9.2	15.4	%
Have Savings (top 20%)	47.8	46.8	%
Observations	12,987	15,178	

Source: Indonesia Family Life Survey (IFLS), calculated.

In general, Indonesian households knew how to get a loan from many sources. In addition, the majority (around 87% in 2007 and 83% in 2014) knew that they can get a loan from banks or other financial institutions. Savings rates increased slightly from 26% to 30% over the 7 years. Likewise, the average amount of savings in banks doubled since 2007, with around Rp17 million in 2014. Disaggregating the data by quintiles of per capita consumption, we find that lower expenditure group is less financially literate since fewer households could identify borrowing sources, or knew financial institutions, and they were more likely to be rejected when requesting loans. In addition, the lower expenditure group was also less likely to have savings and receivable accounts. Nonetheless, we do find that savings ownership increased by 6 percentage points amongst the poorest quintile of households, which shows gains at the bottom of the income distribution.

For our regression analysis, we focus specifically on savings ownership. For the dependent variable, we construct an indicator that takes value one if the household owned savings as well as a continuous variable that measures the value of the assets. It should be stressed that savings ownership is not the same as a savings account at a financial institution, as many Indonesians, especially those who are poor or living in rural areas, use informal savings arrangements. The Findex survey shows that, in 2017, almost 30% used savings clubs or saved with persons outside the family (see Table 8.1).

The measurement of financial inclusion at the household level is one of the key issues in the literature. Much of the literature has focused on developing national indicators (e.g., Sarma and Pais, 2011) and cross-country analysis of relationships to various development outcomes (e.g., Park and Mercado, 2015). For households, financial status, that is, whether the household owns a savings account, is the outcome rather than measure of financial inclusion. In a recent contribution, Zhang and Posso (2019) construct a multidimensional financial exclusion index by combining proxies for savings and credit and study the relationship between financial inclusion and household income.

In this chapter, financial inclusion is measured as a household's access to formal financial institutions in the form of a bank branch. The source of the data is the *Pendataan Potensi Desa* (Village Potential Survey – PODES) 2014. PODES is a census of over 60,000 villages in Indonesia that is conducted by the central statistical agency every 3 years. Starting in 2011, PODES queried the presence of commercial or rural bank branches in the village, and, if not present, the distance to the nearest one. In 2011, the median village had a bank within 7 km, but there was a wide variation across provinces, with those in eastern Indonesia having sparser banks (see Figure 8.3). In 2014, the survey asked about the existence of facilities but not the distance to the facility in case one does not exist in the village. The 2014 survey also distinguished between government and private commercial banks.

Figure 8.3 District-wise share of population living in villages with a bank branch.
Source: Authors' calculation from PODES 2014.

We use PODES to calculate a sub-national index of financial inclusion derived from the density of bank branches in the sub-district where households were located. For location j, S_j is the share of families living in villages with at least one bank branch. Then the financial inclusion index of location j,

$$FI_j = \frac{S_j - \underline{S}}{\overline{S} - \underline{S}}$$

where $\underline{S} = \min\{S_j\}\forall j$, $\overline{S} = \max\{S_j\}\forall j$. This mirrors the index constructed by Sarma and Pais (2011), but for sub-national locations. Figure 8.4 shows the distribution of financial inclusion indicators across sub-districts, which shows large variations. In many sub-districts, the availability of bank branches is quite low, with an index value below 0.4.

We conduct some robustness checks to ensure consistency of information provided by the IFLS community survey and indicators of financial inclusion. The IFLS community module asked about the presence of bank branches in the location. Out of the 311 IFLS communities, 181 (58%) had no banks in the village in 2007. By 2014, this number had reduced slightly to 171. Thus, within the dataset, there is no temporal variation in the availability of bank branches. We treat financial inclusion as a time-invariant explanatory variable.

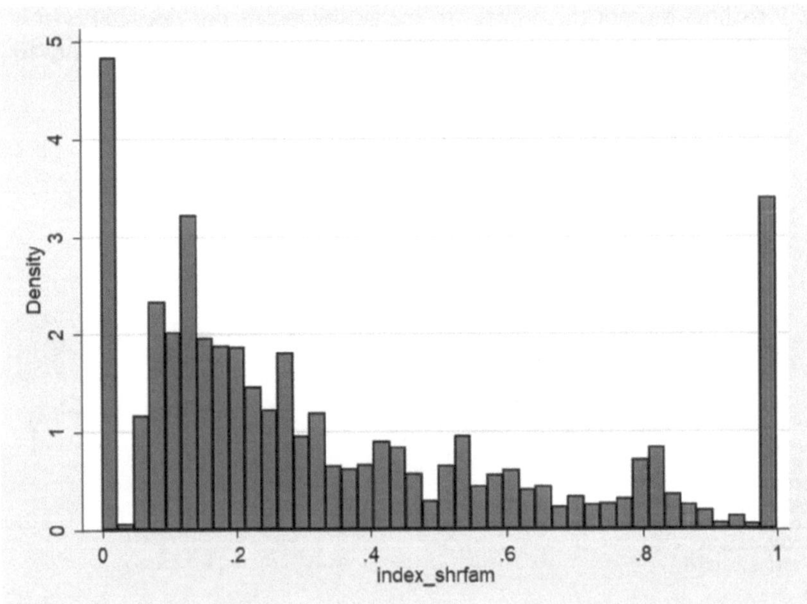

Figure 8.4 Distribution of sub-national financial inclusion index.
Source: Authors' calculation from PODES 2014.

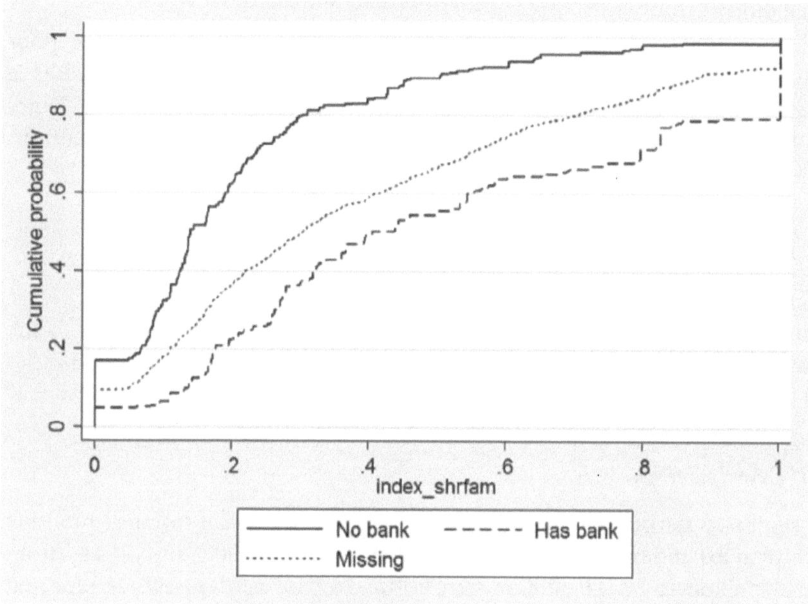

Figure 8.5 Financial inclusion index by bank presence in IFLS sub-district.

Note: Missing includes those households that had moved to non-IFLS locations where community data including bank facilities were not collected.

IFLS = Indonesian Family Life Survey

Source: Authors' calculation from IFLS 2014 and PODES 2014.

The difference in the two sources of information arises because the IFLS data pertain to the village where the household is located.[8] In Figure 8.5, we plot the distribution of the sub-national financial inclusion index derived from PODES separately for those IFLS communities that reported having a bank branch and those that did not. The financial inclusion index for locations with bank branches strongly dominates those without. In sub-districts with no bank present, 80% of the locations had a financial inclusion index below 0.35. On the contrary, over 60% of locations with banks also had 0.35 or higher financial inclusion index.

We estimate the following relationship between outcome Y_{ijt} of household i in location j at time t and financial inclusion F_{ijt}:

$$Y_{ijt} = \delta + \beta F_{ijt} + \alpha F_{ijt} \times T_{ijo} + \gamma X_{ijt} + \sigma_{ij} + e_{ijt}$$

where T_{ij0} denotes household characteristics at the baseline, X_{ijt} is a vector of time-variant household characteristics, σ_i indicates unobserved time-invariant household heterogeneity, and e_{ijt} is time-variant unobserved factors. The interaction between financial inclusion and baseline characteristics is to capture the heterogeneous impact across various types of households. A household-level fixed effects estimator is used to capture unobserved variation across households.

Baseline household characteristics include income level, presence of poor health for individuals (determines demand for health expenditure), and presence of school-age children (determines demand for education expenditure). Time-variant household characteristics include the number of family members, current income, and so on.

8.5 Results

In this section, we discuss the results of our econometric estimation. Before delving into the regression analysis, we provide some summary statistics of the household data and descriptive analysis of financial inclusion variables and household outcomes.

8.5.1 Descriptive analysis

The summary statistics are shown in Table 8.7. The median nominal monthly per capita expenditure more than doubled between 2007 and 2014, from Rp0.44 million to Rp0.9 million.[9] In 2007, 26% of the households reported that they had any savings; this increased slightly to 30% in 2014. The share of households residing in villages with any bank branch did not change during this period. For villages that did not have any bank branches, the closest bank branch was 6.5 km away.

The presence of bank branches is an important factor in owning savings, as shown in Table 8.8. Within each consumption quintile, the likelihood of owning a savings account is higher if the household lives in a community where a financial

Table 8.7 Summary statistics of selected variables in IFLS data

Variable (unit)	*2007*	*2014*
Number of households (N)	12,987	15,178
Household consumption per capita (Nominal Rp, median)	438,399	904,598
Has savings (% households)	26.1	30.4
Savings rate (% of household income, all households)		
HH education		
< 5 years	20.8	
6–8 years	23.2	
9–11 years	15.5	
12–15 years	27.8	
16 years	12.7	
Has bank branch in village (% households)	34.7	35.1
FI index (2014, median)	0.23	0.24

Source: Indonesia Family Life Survey (IFLS), calculated.

FI = financial inclusion; HH = household

Table 8.8 Savings ownership rate by consumption quintile and FI indicator

Consumption quintile	*(1)*	*(2)*	*(3)*	*(4)*
	2007, low FI	*2007, high FI*	*2014, low FI*	*2014, high FI*
1 (lowest)	0.09	0.10	0.14	0.19
2	0.15	0.18	0.20	0.24
3	0.19	0.26	0.25	0.30
4	0.29	0.37	0.31	0.41
5 (highest)	0.43	0.51	0.39	0.50
Total	0.19	0.30	0.24	0.36
N	5665	5548	7216	6964

Source: Indonesia Family Life Survey (IFLS), calculated.

FI = financial inclusion

inclusion indicator is above median. Over time, savings ownership has improved at each consumption quintile, with most improvement observed at the lowest three consumption quintiles. But the increase was larger in high financial inclusion locations. While savings ownership rate was about 10% amongst the lowest consumption quintile in 2007, it increased to 14% in low financial inclusion areas and 19% in high financial inclusion locations. We also note a slight decline in savings ownership amongst households in the highest consumption quintile in locations with a low financial index. This indicates that savings ownership could be more volatile amongst high income households in the absence of financial institutions.

Consistent with national economic growth, many households in the sample experienced growth in nominal per capita consumption between 2007 and 2014. However, this growth is uncorrelated with the financial inclusion index of the sub-district, as shown in Figure 8.6. This allows us to study the impact of living in areas with a high degree of financial inclusion on welfare outcomes.

8.5.2 *Impact on savings ownership*

We now report the results of a probit regression with savings ownership as the dependent variable and the financial inclusion index as the explanatory variable. We also report the coefficients on interactions between the financial inclusion index and key household characteristics. The marginal effects by categories of household characteristics are reported in Tables 8.9, 8.10, and 8.11 The regression coefficients are available from the author upon request.

In Table 8.9, the main explanatory variables are interactions between financial inclusion indicators and quintile of per capita household consumption. We find that greater financial inclusion enables poorer households to acquire savings. In the cross-sectional model, we find that financial inclusion has the largest impact on the lowest income quintile. Amongst the poorest households, the probability of owning a savings account increases by 29% for a 1-point increase in sub-district financial index value. At the average savings rate of 0.14 for this consumption

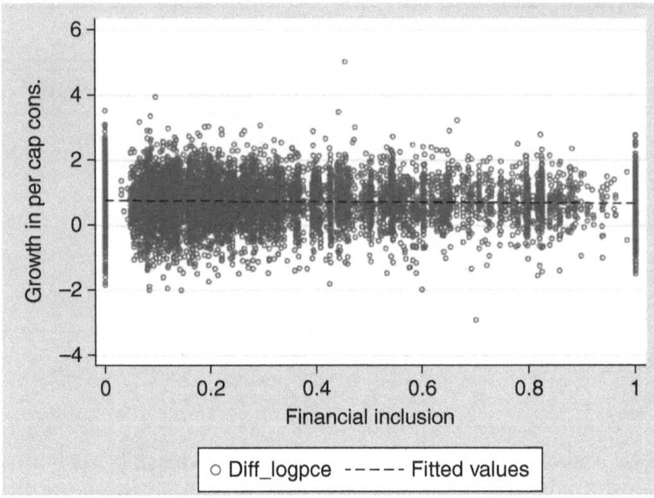

Figure 8.6 Correlation between consumption growth and financial inclusion index.

Source: Authors' calculation from Indonesian Family Life Survey 2007 and 2014. Only households observed in both years are included.

Table 8.9 Marginal effects of financial inclusion on savings ownership by 2014 consumption quintile

	2014		*2007*	
	Marginal effect	*Std. err.*	*Marginal effect*	*Std. err.*
Consumption quintile				
1st quintile	0.29	0.05	0.07	0.10
2nd quintile	0.13	0.05	0.16	0.07
3rd quintile	0.14	0.04	0.15	0.04
4th quintile	0.15	0.03	0.13	0.04
5th quintile	0.13	0.02	0.09	0.03
N	**14,177**		**11,211**	

Source: Authors' calculations.

Note: Table shows elasticity of probability of savings account with respect to financial inclusion index. It is based on a probit regression with an indicator for savings accounts as a dependent variable and interaction between the financial inclusion index and consumption quintile as main regressors. Classification into consumption quintile is based on 2014 household per capita consumption. Standard error is computed using delta method.

quintile, this implies an impact of just under 21% [= (2.9/14) × 100] for 0.1 higher financial inclusion index from the current average of 0.23. The estimated marginal effect on the upper four consumption quintiles is similar and about 0.14. Thus, the largest impact of financial inclusion is amongst the poorest segment of the population.

Table 8.10 Marginal effects of financial inclusion on savings ownership by 2007 and 2014 consumption quintile

	2007 definition		*2014 definition*	
	Marginal effect	*Std. err.*	*Marginal effect*	*Std. err.*
Consumption quintile				
1st quintile	0.21	0.07	0.30	0.07
2nd quintile	0.14	0.05	0.12	0.05
3rd quintile	0.17	0.04	0.16	0.05
4th quintile	0.11	0.03	0.14	0.03
5th quintile	0.11	0.02	0.13	0.03
N	**10,695**		**10,244**	

Source: Authors' calculations.

Note: Table shows elasticity of the probability of savings accounts with respect to the financial inclusion index by household education. It is based on a probit regression with indicator for savings accounts as a dependent variable and interaction between the financial inclusion index and household education categories as main regressors. Household education categories are based on the highest educational attainment of adults over 25 years in 2007. Standard error is computed using the delta method. We observe similar patterns when we use the 2007 consumption quintile definition instead of the 2014 consumption quintile definition.
FI = financial inclusion; HH = household.

Table 8.11 FI elasticity of savings probability by household education status

	Marginal effect	*Std. err.*
HH educ. Cat. (2007)		
< 6 years	0.25	0.08
6–8 years	0.16	0.05
9–11 years	0.15	0.04
12–15 years	0.05	0.03
16 years	0.07	0.02
N	**10,084**	

Source: Authors' calculations.

Note: Table shows elasticity of the probability of savings accounts with respect to the financial inclusion index by household education. It is based on a probit regression with indicator for savings accounts as a dependent variable and interaction between the financial inclusion index and household education categories as main regressors. Household education categories are based on the highest educational attainment of adults over 25 years in 2007. Standard error is computed using the delta method. We observe similar patterns when we use the 2007 consumption quintile definition instead of the 2014 consumption quintile definition.
FI = financial inclusion; HH = household.

For robustness check, we study the relationship between savings ownership in 2007 and financial inclusion index of 2014. The results are shown in the third and fourth columns of Table 8.9. We find that location's financial inclusion index in 2014 has no predictive power in 2007 for the savings probability of the poorest quintile. So, we can be assured that the 2014 results are not wholly driven by other location-specific factors. Furthermore, we can infer that the income growth experienced by Indonesian households since 2007 has translated into greater savings in areas with greater financial inclusion.

Next, since current per capita expenditure could be endogenous to current savings, we use information from the 2007 survey on the same household for classification into consumption quintiles. This means that we drop households in 2014 that did not appear in the 2007 survey.[10] The estimates of marginal effects by 2007 consumption quintiles are shown in Table 8.10, column (1), with standard errors in column (2). The financial inclusion elasticity of savings probability is slightly lower – 0.21 rather than 0.29 – when we divide households into consumption quintiles based on their 2007 per capita consumption. However, the general pattern holds: the strongest effect is found in the lowest quintile. Moreover, the 2014 results for this subsample shown in column (3) are the same as the full sample results from Table 8.8, assuring that sample selection issues are not driving the main results.

Instead of directly using consumption, we classify households based on determinants of consumption. On the basis of the highest educational attainment amongst adult household members older than 25 years, we find that households with the lowest education category (where the highest education level is 5 years) exhibit the greatest responsiveness to financial inclusion in their sub-district (Table 8.11). Thus, the households that are most likely to have lower economic status tend to benefit from being financially included.

8.5.3 Impact on quantity of savings

We also model the impact of financial inclusion on the quantity of savings using hurdle regression, which allows us to utilise information on households with no savings (see Cameron and Trivedi [2013] for exposition of hurdle regression analysis). The intuition behind this approach is that the values of the dependent variable are generated by two probability distributions: one that determines whether the dependent variable takes zero value (in our case, having no savings), and one that determines the actual value given that positive (the value of savings). In our analysis, we study how the financial inclusion index affects not only the probability of savings, but also the value of savings, which is used in the logarithmic form.

The results are reported in Table 8.12. Columns (1)–(3) report results from running the estimation on the full sample; column (4) reports the results when the sample is limited to the poorest three quintiles. The results indicate that financial inclusion affects whether or not a household owns savings, but not the amount of savings. The coefficient on the financial inclusion index is small and not statistically significant, nor economically meaningful for the savings model, but it does explain the ownership of the account. However, amongst the households with the poorest quintile, the financial inclusion index is significant in explaining not only selection into having savings, but also the amount of savings.

Table 8.12 Hurdle regression model for quantity of savings

	(1)	(2)	(3)	(4)
	logsavings	*logsavings*	*logsavings*	*logsavings*
logsavings				
Consumption				
2nd quintile	0.493***	0.492***	0.492***	0.435***
	(0.133)	(0.132)	(0.132)	(0.132)
3rd quintile	0.843***	0.838***	0.838***	0.739***
	(0.131)	(0.130)	(0.130)	(0.128)
4th quintile	1.155***	1.150***	1.150***	
	(0.131)	(0.131)	(0.131)	
5th quintile	1.850***	1.837***	1.837***	
	(0.145)	(0.144)	(0.144)	
HH educ cat				
6–8 years	–0.0902	–0.0941	–0.0941	–0.192
	(0.141)	(0.140)	(0.140)	(0.160)
9–11 years	0.199	0.192	0.192	0.212
	(0.164)	(0.163)	(0.163)	(0.177)
12–15 years	0.538***	0.522***	0.522***	0.436***
	(0.152)	(0.150)	(0.150)	(0.166)
16 years	1.131***	1.113***	1.113***	1.376***
	(0.178)	(0.176)	(0.176)	(0.230)
FI Index		0.170	0.170	0.457**
		(0.172)	(0.172)	(0.224)
_cons	13.60***	13.57***	13.57***	13.48***
	(0.178)	(0.185)	(0.185)	(0.206)
selection_ll				
FI Index	0.290***		0.290***	0.235**
	(0.0833)		(0.0833)	(0.117)
HH educ cat				
6–8 years	0.221***	0.228***	0.221***	0.240***
	(0.0541)	(0.0550)	(0.0541)	(0.0572)
9–11 years	0.386***	0.402***	0.386***	0.334***
	(0.0547)	(0.0553)	(0.0547)	(0.0684)
12–15 years	0.622***	0.658***	0.622***	0.485***
	(0.0556)	(0.0567)	(0.0556)	(0.0704)
16 years	1.145***	1.186***	1.145***	0.913***
	(0.0675)	(0.0690)	(0.0675)	(0.0975)
_cons	-1.253***	-1.212***	-1.253***	-1.318***
	(0.0751)	(0.0777)	(0.0751)	(0.0935)
lnsigma				
_cons	0.495***	0.494***	0.494***	0.461***
	(0.0153)	(0.0154)	(0.0154)	(0.0223)
N	9178	9178	9178	5929

Source: Authors' calculation.

FI = financial inclusion; HH = household.

Standard errors in parentheses. * p<.1, ** p<.05, *** p<.01

8.6 Discussion and conclusion

How might the recent efforts of governments in the developing world to expand access to formal financial institutions lead to better lives for citizens? The Indonesian government's expansion of financial inclusion has relied on various strategies. Recent data suggest that it is on its way to meeting the goal it set in 2015 of financially including 75% of its population. Bank branches remain the most common form of financial access, although awareness and usage of digital financial services is also growing. With the success and growing popularity of homegrown companies like Go-Jek, Indonesia is in a good position to leverage financial inclusion for sustainable growth.

Although much of the strategic push for greater financial inclusion in Indonesia took place after 2015, looking at available data still provides clues to the likely impact of this policy. Our results suggest that financial inclusion can be an effective pro-poor policy. It shows that having access to bank accounts increased savings ownership amongst the poor, which is the first step towards financial stability and long-term welfare.

However, our results are not adequate to assess some of the recent developments in the financial inclusion strategy. The advent of digital technology and recognition that true financial inclusion goes beyond access to encompass literacy and consumer protection gives rise to issues that are not salient with bank branches. Thus, further research is required to understand the impact of the recent push towards financial inclusion.

Notes

1 This is based on a US$1.9 per day poverty line. Data are available at http://povertydata.worldbank.org/poverty/country/IDN. This is different from the Indonesian Central Statistical Agency's estimation of poverty headcount rate based on the national poverty line, which was 12.52% in 2007 and 10% in 2016.

2 *Kecamatans* are the third-level sub-national administrative units in Indonesia, after provinces and districts. In 2014, there were 7,024 sub-districts, with the median sub-district comprising 6,500 families.

3 In the same year, Bank Indonesia's Household Balance Sheet Survey 2011 shows that 48% of households in Indonesia have accounts with banks and other formal financial institutions. So, financial inclusion at the household level is higher than amongst individuals as many families use a single account.

4 http://data.imf.org/?sk=E5DCAB7E-A5CA-4892-A6EA-598B5463A34C&sId=1390030341854

5 www.bi.go.id/id/perbankan/keuanganinklusif/edukasi/Contents/Booklet%20Financial%20Inclusion%20(English%20Version).pdf

6 In Indonesia, commercial banks provide a full range of banking products, while rural banks mostly work with microenterprises in rural and urban areas.

7 World Bank FINDEX defines digital services as 'using mobile money, a debit or credit card, or a mobile phone to make a payment from an account or using the internet to pay bills or to buy something online, in the past 12 months, [and] also includes … paying bills or sending remittances directly from a financial institution account or through a mobile money account in the past 12 months'.

8 While it is straightforward to merge PODES data with IFLS community locations at the sub-district level, we cannot do so at the village level.
9 As of August 2019, Rp1 million is equivalent to US$70.
10 Although the IFLS only tracks the same households over time, if a household member moves to a new household within an IFLS province, those households are also included in the new round.

References

Allen, F., A. Demirguc-Kunt, L. Klapper, and M.S. Peria (2012), 'The Foundations of Financial Inclusion: Understanding Ownership and Use of Formal Accounts', *World Bank Policy Research Working Paper*, No. 6290. Washington, DC: World Bank.

Amianti, G.D. (2015), 'Four Major Banks Launch Branchless Banking Program', *The Jakarta Post*, 27 March. www.thejakartapost.com/news/2015/03/27/four-major-banks-launch-branchless-banking-program.html (accessed 22 June 2020).

Ashraf, N., D. Karlan, and W. Yin (2006), 'Tying Odysseus to the Mast: Evidence from a Commitment Savings Product in The Philippines', *Quarterly Journal of Economics*, 121(2), pp.635–72.

Bachas, P., P. Gertler, and S. Higgins (2016), 'Banking on Trust: How Debit Cards Help the Poor to Save More', *NBER Working Paper Series*, No. 23252, Cambridge, MA: NBER.

Banerjee, A., and E. Duflo (2007), 'The Economic Lives of the Poor', *Journal of Economic Perspectives*, 21(1), pp.141–67.

Beck, T., A. Demirguc-Kunt, and M.S. Peria (2006), 'Banking Services for Everyone? Barriers to Bank Access and Use around the World', *World Bank Policy Research Working Paper*, No. 4079. Washington, DC: World Bank.

Beck, T., A. Demirguc-Kunt, and R. Levine (2007), 'Finance, Inequality and the Poor', *Journal of Economic Growth*, 12 (1), pp.27–49.

Becker, G. S., and N. Tomes (1979), 'An Equilibrium Theory of the Distribution of Income and Intergenerational Mobility', *Journal of Political Economy*, 87 (6), pp.1153–89.

Bruhn, M., and I. Love (2014), 'The Real Impact of Improved Access to Finance: Evidence from Mexico', *Journal of Finance*, 69(3), pp.1347–76.

Burgess, R., and R. Pande (2005), 'Do Rural Banks Matter? Evidence from the Indian Social Banking Experiment', *American Economic Review*, 95(3), pp.780–95.

Cameron, A.C., and P.K. Trivedi (2013), *Regression Analysis of Count Data* (2nd edition). New York: Cambridge University Press.

Carter, M.R., and C.B. Barrett, (2006), 'The Economics of Poverty Traps and Persistent Poverty: An Asset-Based Approach', *The Journal of Development Studies*, 42(2), pp.178–99.

Cole, S., T. Sampson, and B. Zia (2011), 'Prices or Knowledge? What Drives Demand for Financial Services in Emerging Markets?', *The Journal of Finance*, 66(6), pp.1933–67.

Deaton, A., and C. Paxson (1997), 'The Effects of Economic and Population Growth on National Saving and Inequality', *Demography*, 34(1), pp.97–114.

Demirguc-Kunt, A., L. Klapper, D. Singer, and P.V. Oudheusden (2015), 'The Global Findex Database 2014: Measuring Financial Inclusion around the World', *World Bank Policy Research Working Paper Series*, No. 7255. Washington, DC: World Bank.

Demirguc-Kunt, A., L. Klapper, D. Singer, S. Ansar, and J. Hess (2018), *The Global Findex Database 2017: Measuring Financial Inclusion and the Fintech Revolution*. Washington, DC: World Bank.

Diela, T. (2016), 'Bank Indonesia Relaxes Agent Regulation to Sign Up More First-Time Customers', *Jakarta Globe*, 10 September. https://jakartaglobe.id/context/bank-indonesia-relaxes-agent-regulation-sign-first-time-customers/ (accessed 22 June 2020).

Dupas, P., and J. Robinson (2013), 'Why Don't the Poor Save More? Evidence from Health Savings Experiments', *American Economic Review*, 103(4), pp.1138–71.

Dupas, P., D. Karlan, J. Robinson, and D. Ubfal (2018), 'Banking the Unbanked? Evidence from Three Countries', *American Economic Journal: Applied Economics*, 10(2), pp.257–97.

Greenwood, J., and B. Jovanovic (1990), 'Financial Development, Growth, and the Distribution of Income', *Journal of Political Economy*, 98(5), pp.1076–1107.

Guiso, L., P. Sapienza, and L. Zingales (2009), 'Cultural Biases in Economic Exchange?' *Quarterly Journal of Economics*, 124(3), pp.1095–1131.

Karlan, D., and J. Morduch (2010), 'Access to Finance', in D. Rodrik and M. Rosenzweig, *Handbook of Development Economics, Volume 5*. New York: Elsevier, pp.4703–84.

Kikkawa, K., and Y. Xing (2014), 'Financial Inclusion in Indonesia: A Poverty Alleviation Strategy', in *Financial Inclusion in Asia*. Tokyo: Asia-Pacific Finance and Development Center and Asian Development Bank Institute, pp.45–62.

Levine, R. (2005), 'Finance and Growth: Theory and Evidence', in P. Aghion and S. N. Durlauf, *Handbook of Economic Growth, Volume 1A*. New York: Elsevier, pp.865–934.

Modigliani, F. (1986), 'Life Cycle, Individual Thrift, and the Wealth of Nations', *American Economic Review*, 76(3), pp.297–313.

Otoritas Jasa Keuangan (2015), *Statistik Perbankan Indonesia [Indonesia Banking Statistics]*, (Vol. 14, No. 1). Jakarta: Otoritas Jasa Keuangan.

Otoritas Jasa Keuangan (2019), *Statistik Perbankan Indonesia [Indonesia Banking Statistics]*, (Vol. 17, No. 4). Jakarta: Otoritas Jasa Keuangan.

Park, C.-Y., and R. Mercado (2015), 'Financial Inclusion, Poverty, and Income Inequality in Developing Asia.' *Asian Development Bank Economics Working Paper Series No.* 426. Available at: https://papers.ssrn.com/sol3/papers.cfm?abstract_id=2558936

Prina, S. (2015), 'Banking the Poor Via Savings Accounts: Evidence from a Field Experiment', *Journal of Development Economics*, 115, pp.16–31.

Rosengard, J.K., and A. Prasetyantoko (2011), 'If the Banks Are Doing So Well, Why Can't I Get a Loan? Regulatory Constraints to Financial Inclusion in Indonesia', *Asian Economic Policy Review*, 6(2), pp.273–96.

Sarma, M., and J. Pais (2011), 'Financial Inclusion and Development', *Journal of International Development*, 23(5), pp.613–28.

Strauss, J., F. Witoelar, and B. Sikoki (2016), 'The Fifth Wave of the Indonesia Family Life Survey (IFLS5): Overview and Field Report', WR-1143/1-NIA/NICHD. California: RAND Corporation.

Strauss, J., F. Witoelar, B. Sikoki, and A.M. Wattie (2009), 'The Fourth Wave of the Indonesia Family Life Survey (IFLS4): Overview and Field Report', WR-675/1-NIA/NICHD. California: RAND Corporation.

Tim Nasional Percepatan Penanggulangan Kemiskinan (TNP2K) (2018), *The Future of the Social Protection System in Indonesia: Social Protection for All*. Jakarta: TNP2K.

World Bank (2010), *Improving Access to Financial Services in Indonesia*. Washington, DC: World Bank.

Zhang, Q., and A. Posso (2019), 'Thinking Inside the Box: A Closer Look at Financial Inclusion and Household Income', *The Journal of Development Studies*, 55(7), pp.1616–31.

9 Financial inclusion, active bank accounts, and poverty reduction in India

Tony Cavoli, Ilke Onur, and Patricia Sourdin

9.1 Introduction

Financial inclusion is defined as having access to useful and affordable financial products and services, delivered in a responsible and sustainable way (World Bank, 2020). There have been multiple studies showing access to financial services promoting growth, especially for developing countries. Similarly, there is a growing body of literature showing the positive role of financial inclusion on improving household well-being and economic growth. For example, Burgess and Pande (2005), Beck et al. (2007), and Bruhn and Love (2014) show that greater access to finance reduces income inequality and poverty. Similar positive effects on a myriad of outcome measures have also been presented in the literature.[1] However, the number of studies linking financial inclusion and reduction in poverty levels in a country are limited (Chibba, 2009; Jalilian and Kirkpatrick, 2005; Churchill and Marisetty, 2019).[2]

The focus of this chapter is financial inclusion and reducing poverty for India. To this end, we make use of a unique set of household-level data comprising more than 47,000 observations across India. India is an important case study, not just because of the size of the economy, but also because of the targeted efforts of the Reserve Bank of India (RBI) and the Government of India (GOI). Financial inclusion was in the RBI's 2005–2006 annual policy statement, and, in 2010, RBI required both private and public banks to submit a *3-year financial inclusion plan* (Menon, 2019). Furthermore, in August 2014, the Pradhan Mantri Jan Dhan Yojana (PMJDY) campaign was implemented with the aim of ensuring households have access to basic bank accounts, as well as combatting black money in the economy and making banking facilities (savings and deposit accounts, remittances, credit, insurance, and pension) available to the unbanked, especially by offering 0-balance accounts. More recently, in 2015, the Jan Dhan-Aadhar-Mobile (JAM) was introduced with the aim of integrating PMJDY with a biometric ID initiative and mobile technology.

In 2017, the GOI launched Cashless India, promoting cashless payment modes (banking cards, mobile wallets, digital banking, etc.). In addition to these targeted and direct efforts, financial inclusion in India benefitted from an indirect push through the deposit payments to bank accounts for the Mahatma Gandhi

National Rural Employment Guarantee scheme and the demonetisation programme that took place on 9 November 2016. These initiatives have helped to grow financial inclusion in India and encourage previously underbanked populations, such as women and rural and below-poverty-line individuals, to access formal financial institutions.

As a result of all these efforts by the RBI and the GOI, many of the disparities between previously unbanked populations have been reduced. Most Indians now own a bank account and have access to banking services. Our aim is to study the effect of this increase in financial inclusion on poverty alleviation in India. A few studies have previously focused on this question before, but from a range of different perspectives. Burgess and Pande (2005), for example, asked the same question using state-level panel data. More specifically, the authors studied the effect of rural bank branch expansion and showed that it helped with poverty reduction in rural India. They observed no significant effect on urban poverty. More recently, again using panel data for Indian states and union territories, Inoue (2019) utilised the numbers of bank branches and accounts (financial inclusion and financial deepening) to show the positive impact on poverty reduction. However, this effect is present only for public sector banks. Other studies using country, state, or district-level data to analyse similar research questions are Binswanger and Khandker (1995), Bell and Rousseau (2001), and Sehrawat and Giri (2016).

Only a few studies use micro-level data to focus on the poverty-reducing effect of financial inclusion in India. Using household survey data, Swamy (2014) focuses on gender differences, analysing the impact of financial inclusion programmes on income, expenditure, and food security. Ghosh and Vinod (2017) also emphasise the importance of gender, showing significant differences in both access to formal (and informal) finance, as well as the use of finance. Finally, a recent study by Churchill and Marisetty (2019) is closest to this chapter in terms of the data and the analysis. The authors make use of an earlier wave of the Financial Inclusion Insights (FII) survey (which will be utilised in this chapter) and construct a multidimensional indicator of financial inclusion to examine the effects of financial inclusion on poverty. Their findings show a strong poverty-reduction effect of financial inclusion in India. Moreover, similar to our chapter, the authors utilise instrumental variable techniques to correct for potential endogeneity bias in the regressions. Our chapter, however, uses the most recent wave of the FII survey and introduces new (and arguably better) variables to be used as exclusion restrictions. Methodologically, we also add to the current literature by using a two-stage residual inclusion technique, which has been mostly utilised in the health economics literature so far. Lastly, in addition to the standard financial inclusion variables, we focus on the active usage of bank accounts, due to the existence of many dormant bank accounts in India.

Our results show a considerable poverty-reduction effect of financial inclusion, as well as the active use of bank accounts. However, the effect is statistically significant only after the endogeneity is controlled for. As a result, one of the major implications of this chapter is the need for a careful empirical analysis before any policy decisions can be made. The real effect of financial inclusion on poverty could be masked by the bias due to endogeneity of the variable of interest.

The rest of the chapter is structured as follows. Section 9.2 provides an introduction to financial inclusion in India using multiple waves of the World Bank's Global Findex database. Section 9.3 introduces the data and the empirical model, and Section 9.4 presents the empirical results. In Section 9.5, we provide concluding remarks and possible policy implications.

9.2 Introduction to financial inclusion in India

We use the World Bank's Global Findex database to see how the concerted efforts in India have impacted financial inclusion.[3] We focus on three main indicators of financial inclusion: account ownership (formal account); savings in a formal financial institution (formal savings); and bank credit usage (formal credit). In Figure 9.1, we can observe a significant increase in the percentage of formal accounts held from 35% in 2011 to 80% in 2017 when all adults (aged 15 years or older) are considered. Similar success can be observed in closing the gender gap for account ownership. In 2017, we see no significant gender differences amongst Indian adults. We can observe whether access translates to the usage of these formal accounts for saving or borrowing. Figures 9.2 and 9.3 show the formal saving and credit behaviour for the same period and again for males and females. We observe a modest increase in the saving behaviour from 12% in 2011 to 20% in 2017. The gender gap, although narrowed, has not been eliminated, unlike the trend we have seen in account ownership. Formal credit percentages, on the contrary, have a slight decline over the same period. In 2011, 8% of Indian adults have been accessing formal credit while the same number in 2017 has been 7%. Moreover, the gender gap in formal credit has widened over time. In short, we see a considerable success in access (account ownership); however, this did not clearly translate into usage (formal saving and credit).

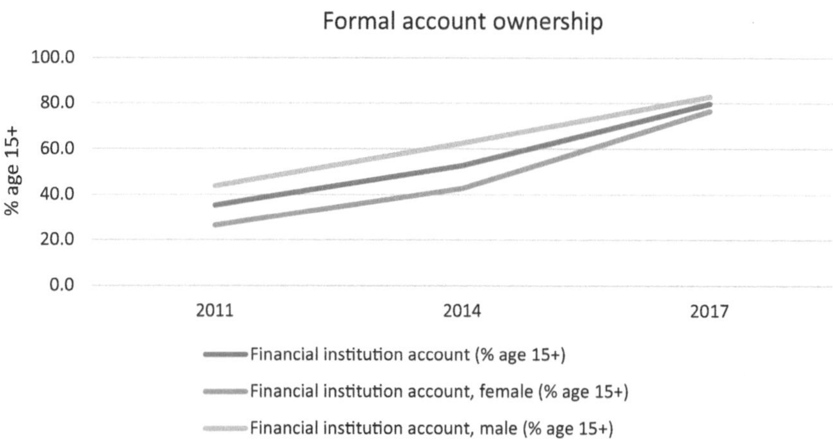

Figure 9.1 Formal account ownership in India.
Source: World Bank Global Findex data 2011–2017.

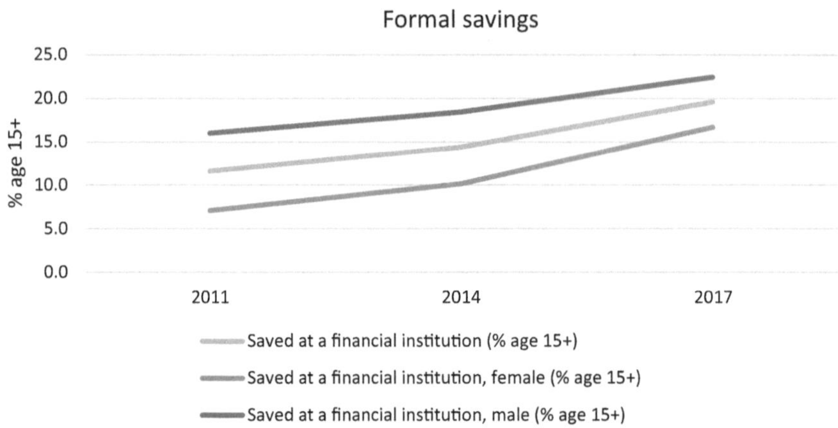

Figure 9.2 Formal savings in India.
Source: World Bank Global Findex data, 2011–2017.

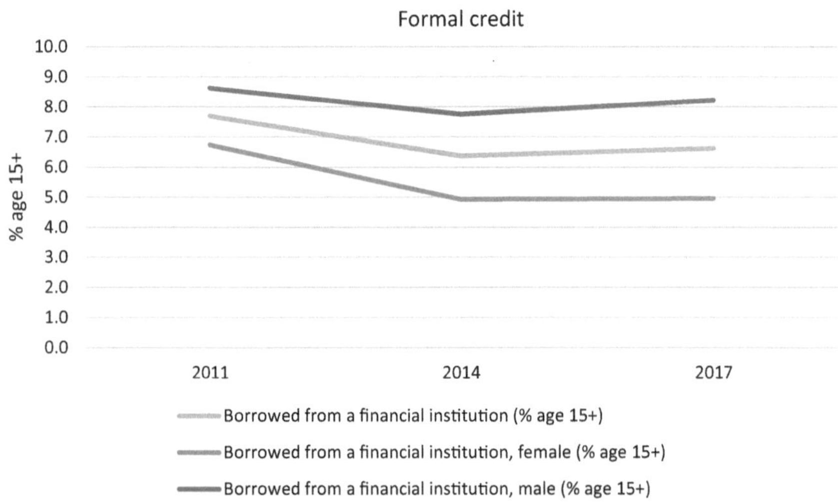

Figure 9.3 Formal credit in India.
Source: World Bank Global Findex data 2011–2017.

Further success of India's financial inclusion policies on account ownership can be observed in Figure 9.4. Focusing on the 2017 data, we see no significant difference in terms of age, education, income, being in or out of the labour force, and also no rural versus urban divide. It would appear, at least casually, that the policy objectives of the RBI and GOI have resulted in clear increases in bank account ownership.

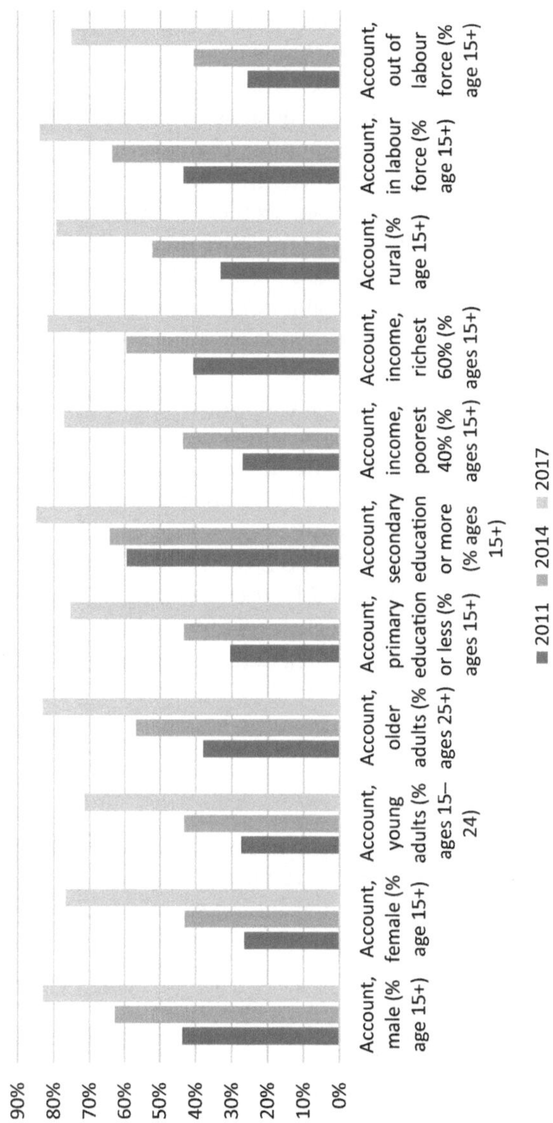

Figure 9.4 Account ownership in India for various sub-groups of the population.

Source: World Bank Global Findex data 2011–2017.

9.3 Data and empirical model

According to the World Bank, 'financial inclusion is a key enabler to reducing poverty and boosting prosperity'. It has also been shown in academic studies that financial inclusion has been found to reduce rural poverty (Burgess and Pande, 2005; Swamy, 2014).[4] Although we observe the success of financial inclusion, at least in terms of account ownership, in India, the lack of active usage of these accounts remains a concern. More recent data show 15% of the accounts having a 0 balance and 84% only being 'operative', with at least one transaction in the past 2 years (Abraham, 2019). Our study thus scrutinises whether basic financial inclusion, defined as account ownership, can alleviate poverty in India. Consequently, we consider the active users of these accounts, and see if usage is associated with households' propensity to be above the poverty level in India. In order to answer these questions, we make use of the FII survey database, which is more detailed and more frequently available compared to the World Bank Global Findex database.

We use the fifth wave of the FII surveys, which were collected in 2017.[5] The survey started in August 2017 and ended in December 2017. The data were gathered from a nationally representative sample of adults aged 15 and older.[6] The survey includes information on ownership and usage of banks, other financial institutions, and mobile phones as well as mobile financial services. Financial behaviours, poverty indicators, and socio-demographics, amongst other information, are also included in the data set. The 2017 FII survey was carried out on 47,132 adults. For the purpose of our study, after dropping the observations with missing information, the final sample includes 44,990 individuals.[7]

The main model for estimating the relationship between financial inclusion and poverty is the following:

$$Poverty_i = \alpha FI_i + \beta X_i + \delta_i + \varepsilon_i \tag{9.1}$$

where $Poverty_i$ is the main outcome variable, which is the measure of poverty for household i. As we discuss in detail, we make use of two distinct versions of the outcome variable. FI_i is the financial inclusion variable, which we measure in three different ways, as specified. X_i represents all the control variables in our analysis, including gender, age, location (rural or urban), marital status, number of people in the household, literacy, education, ownership of farmland, employment status, and religion. δ_i is the state-level dummy variable controlling for unobserved heterogeneity amongst the various states in India. Finally, ε_i is the error term, which we assume to be normally distributed.

We make use of two different measures of poverty in our analysis. First, we consider the Poverty Probability Index (PPI), which is already available in our data set. PPI is a continuous measure of poverty that provides a score for each household depending on the household characteristics and asset ownership. This score determines the likelihood of the household living below the poverty line.[8]

In our data set, the poverty line is set by the FII survey at US$2.50 per day. The PPI score ranges between 0 and 100, with 0 representing the most likely poor household and 100 with the least likely one.[9] Second, we make use of a dummy variable, *poor*, to represent a household that might or might not live in poverty. This variable takes the value 1 if the household lives below the poverty line of $2.50 per day, and 0 otherwise.

For the financial inclusion (*FI*) variable in our regression, we make use of three different measures. This first one is the *financial inclusion* measure introduced in the FII data set. Financially included are those who have an account in their name with a full-service institution.[10] Our second variable is a basic one. We use *bank account ownership* as a measure. It is a dummy variable that is equal to 1 if the respondent has a bank account under their name, and 0 otherwise. The last measure we consider is *active bank account*. Amongst those with a bank account, we identify the active ones as those who have used their bank account at least once in the previous 3 months. With this measure, we would like to see whether actively using the bank account, compared to having an unused one, matters for poverty alleviation.

Table 9.1 presents the summary statistics for all the variables in our study.[11] More than 60% of the households in our sample are classified as *poor*, while 78% are financially included. As mentioned earlier, due to the concerted efforts of the GOI, there is no gap in terms of *financial inclusion* between the poor and non-poor households. *Bank account ownership* average is very close to financial inclusion one since most of these efforts were focused on giving bank accounts and extending bank branches to rural areas of India. However, amongst those with a bank account, only 68% use their account actively. The majority of the households in our sample are in rural areas, with an average of four people in the household. Most of the respondents are married. While 32% do not have any formal education and 14% have less than 6 years of schooling, 72% of the respondents are literate. In terms of employment, almost half of the respondents are not working, with only 23% having a full-time job. And, 40% of households own farmland and majority of the respondents are Hindus, followed by 11% of the respondents being Muslim.

The last four variables in Table 9.1 are used as instrumental variables in our regression analysis: 22% of the respondents are financially literate, and 9% belong to an informal financial institution. Though 8% actively use a mobile phone, only 2% have an active mobile money account. These figures are low compared to some other countries, especially those in Africa, where mobile money services are highly prevalent.

9.4 Empirical results

Table 9.2 presents our linear regression results. The dependent variable is the poverty probability index. As for the variables of interest, column 1 uses the *financial inclusion* variable, while columns 2 and 3 have *bank account ownership* and *active bank account* variables. Amongst the three variables of interest, only the *bank account* variable is statistically significant, but at 10% level. Although

Table 9.1 Summary statistics

Variables	*Mean*	*Std. dev.*	*Min*	*Max*
Poverty Probability Index	0.51	0.22	0	1
Poor	0.61	0.49	0	1
Financial inclusion	0.78	0.41	0	1
Bank account ownership	0.76	0.43	0	1
Active bank account[a]	0.68	0.47	0	1
Male	0.52	0.5	0	1
Age				
15–24	0.21	0.41	0	1
25–34	0.26	0.44	0	1
35–44	0.21	0.41	0	1
45–54	0.15	0.35	0	1
55 and over	0.17	0.38	0	1
Rural	0.68	0.46	0	1
Married	0.73	0.44	0	1
Number of people	3.97	1.75	1	8
Education level				
No education	0.32	0.47	0	1
Less than 6 years	0.14	0.35	0	1
6–12 years	0.45	0.5	0	1
More than 12 years	0.09	0.29	0	1
Employment				
Full-time employed	0.23	0.42	0	1
Part-time employed	0.08	0.26	0	1
Self-employed	0.06	0.24	0	1
Occasionally employed	0.16	0.25	0	1
Not working	0.47	0.50	0	1
Religion				
Hinduism	0.85	0.36	0	1
Islam	0.11	0.32	0	1
Christianity	0.02	0.12	0	1
Sikhism	0.01	0.12	0	1
Buddhism	0.003	0.05	0	1
Literate	0.72	0.45	0	1
Farmland	0.4	0.49	0	1
Household head	0.39	0.49	0	1
Financial literacy	0.22	0.41	0	1
Active phone	0.08	0.26	0	1
Active mobile money	0.02	0.14	0	1
Belong to informal financial institution[b]	0.09	0.29	0	1
Num. of obs.	**47,132**			

Source: Authors' calculations using data from the Financial Inclusion Insights Program, InterMedia.

Note: All summary statistics have been weighted using the sampling weights provided in the 2017 Financial Inclusion Insights Survey – Wave 5.

a Summary statistics for the active bank account variable are based on a sub-sample of those with a bank account (n=37,165).

b Summary statistics for the informal financial institution variable are based on a reduced sample size due to missing values (n=39,400).

Table 9.2 Linear regression assuming exogeneity (dependent variable: PPI score)

Variables	*Financial inclusion*	*Bank account*	*Active bank account*
Financial inclusion	–0.002		
	(0.002)		
Bank account ownership		–0.003*	
		(0.002)	
Active bank account			0.000
			(0.002)
Male	0.004**	0.004**	0.001
	(0.002)	(0.002)	(0.002)
Age 15–24	0.036***	0.036***	0.036***
	(0.003)	(0.003)	(0.004)
Age 25–34	0.036***	0.036***	0.038***
	(0.003)	(0.003)	(0.003)
Age 35–44	0.022***	0.022***	0.022***
	(0.003)	(0.003)	(0.003)
Age 45–54	0.003	0.003	0.003
	(0.003)	(0.003)	(0.003)
Rural	0.029***	0.029***	0.026***
	(0.002)	(0.002)	(0.002)
Married	0.003	0.003	0.002
	(0.002)	(0.002)	(0.002)
Number of people	–0.068***	–0.068***	–0.068***
	(0.001)	(0.001)	(0.001)
Literate	–0.040***	–0.040***	–0.053***
	(0.004)	(0.004)	(0.005)
Less than 6 years	–0.002	–0.002	0.009
	(0.005)	(0.005)	(0.005)
6–12 years	0.004	0.004	0.020***
	(0.004)	(0.004)	(0.005)
More than 12 years	–0.018***	–0.017***	–0.003
	(0.005)	(0.005)	(0.006)
Farmland	–0.007***	–0.007***	–0.005**
	(0.002)	(0.002)	(0.002)
Part-time employed	–0.020***	–0.020***	–0.025***
	(0.004)	(0.004)	(0.004)
Occasionally employed	–0.013***	–0.013***	–0.012***
	(0.003)	(0.003)	(0.003)
Self-employed	–0.005	–0.005	–0.004
	(0.004)	(0.004)	(0.004)
Not working	–0.010***	–0.011***	–0.010***
	(0.003)	(0.003)	(0.003)
Hinduism	0.023	0.023	–0.007
	(0.054)	(0.055)	(0.076)
Islam	0.003	0.003	–0.026
	(0.055)	(0.055)	(0.077)
Christianity	–0.000	–0.000	–0.028
	(0.055)	(0.055)	(0.077)
Sikhism	–0.010	–0.010	–0.041
	(0.055)	(0.055)	(0.077)

(*continued*)

Table 9.2 Cont.

Variables	*Financial inclusion*	*Bank account*	*Active bank account*
Buddhism	−0.009	−0.009	−0.040
	(0.057)	(0.057)	(0.079)
Household head	0.009***	0.009***	0.013***
	(0.002)	(0.002)	(0.003)
R^2	0.43	0.43	0.43
N	44,990	44,990	35,671

Source: Authors' calculations.

Note: All models have been weighted using the sampling weights provided in the 2017 Financial Inclusion Insights Survey – Wave 5.
PPI = Poverty Probability Index.
Robust standard errors are reported in parenthesis.
*** significant at the 1% level; ** significant at the 5% level; * significant at the 10% level.

the sign is negative, the coefficient is relatively small. In other words, in our base regressions we find no notable effect of all three variables on poverty alleviation. For the explanatory variables, we see that gender, age, rural locale, number of people in the household, literacy and education, employment, having farmland, and the household head variables seem to have a significant effect. The two variables that are consistently insignificant for all three columns are the marital status and religion indicators.

Next, we focus on the results for probit regression. We now find statistically significant effects of the three variables of interest. Being financially included lowers the probability of being poor by 1.3%. Similarly, having a bank account lessens the likelihood by 1%. Finally, amongst those with a bank account, active usage of the account lowers the propensity to be poor by 1.4%. Although statistically significant, the magnitudes are quite small to make economic impact. Given all the work by the Indian government to financially include everyone, a decrease of 1%–1.4% might not economically justify the efforts. Most of the other variables in our regressions are statistically significant. Gender, age, rural, marital status, literacy, education variables, and employment status have significant effects on the likelihood of being poor, as expected. Only owning farmland, religion, and household head variables show no statistical significance.

Next, we conduct a robustness check for potential endogeneity between financial inclusion and the PPI index. The endogeneity might exist due to reverse causality and/or existence of factors that affect financial inclusion along with the poverty index.[12] If our concern of endogeneity is valid, the estimates presented in Tables 9.2 and 9.3 might be biased. In order to correct for potential endogeneity, instead of the linear regressions, we employ two-stage least squares (2SLS). Using two sets of instrumental variables, in the initial stage, we first obtain predicted values for financial inclusion variables using linear regression. The predicted values are then substituted into the poverty equation, where a linear regression is again used to obtain second-stage estimates.

Table 9.3 Probit regression assuming exogeneity (dependent variable: poor)

Variables	*Financial inclusion*	*Bank account*	*Active bank account*
Financial inclusion	–0.013** (0.005)		
Bank account ownership		–0.010** (0.005)	
Active bank account			–0.014*** (0.005)
Male	–0.016*** (0.005)	–0.016*** (0.005)	–0.009 (0.006)
Age 15–24	–0.072*** (0.008)	–0.072*** (0.008)	–0.073*** (0.009)
Age 25–34	–0.084*** (0.007)	–0.084*** (0.007)	–0.088*** (0.008)
Age 35–44	–0.057*** (0.007)	–0.057*** (0.007)	–0.060*** (0.007)
Age 45–54	–0.018** (0.007)	–0.018** (0.007)	–0.021*** (0.008)
Rural	–0.035*** (0.005)	–0.035*** (0.005)	–0.028*** (0.005)
Married	–0.015*** (0.005)	–0.015*** (0.005)	–0.010*** (0.006)
Number of people	0.116*** (0.001)	0.116*** (0.001)	0.115*** (0.001)
Literate	0.067*** (0.011)	0.067*** (0.011)	0.100*** (0.014)
Less than 6 years	0.003 (0.011)	0.003 (0.011)	–0.021 (0.014)
6–12 years	–0.019* (0.012)	–0.019* (0.012)	–0.057*** (0.014)
More than 12 years	–0.002 (0.013)	–0.003 (0.013)	–0.034** (0.015)
Farmland	0.005 (0.005)	0.005 (0.005)	0.003 (0.005)
Part-time employed	0.044*** (0.008)	0.044*** (0.008)	0.055*** (0.009)
Occasionally employed	0.034*** (0.007)	0.034*** (0.007)	0.036*** (0.007)
Self-employed	0.015* (0.009)	0.015* (0.009)	0.014 (0.010)
Not working	0.023*** (0.006)	0.023*** (0.006)	0.021*** (0.007)
Hinduism	0.034 (0.123)	0.033 (0.124)	–0.010 (0.163)
Islam	0.072 (0.124)	0.072 (0.124)	0.026 (0.164)
Christianity	0.093 (0.125)	0.092 (0.125)	0.051 (0.165)
Sikhism	0.064 (0.126)	0.064 (0.126)	0.031 (0.166)

(*continued*)

Table 9.3 Cont.

Variables	*Financial inclusion*	*Bank account*	*Active bank account*
Buddhism	0.111	0.111	0.077
	(0.129)	(0.129)	(0.168)
Household head	0.001	0.001	–0.010
	(0.006)	(0.006)	(0.006)
N	44,990	44,990	35,671

Source: Authors' calculations.

Note: All models have been weighted using the sampling weights provided in the 2017 Financial Inclusion Insights Survey – Wave 5. Marginal effects are reported, and they are measured at the mean of the corresponding control variable for continuous variables, and as the difference in predicted probability of switching from 0 to 1 for dummy variables. Robust standard errors are reported in parentheses.

*** significant at the 1% level; ** significant at the 5% level; * significant at the 10% level.

For the regressions where the variables of interest are *financial inclusion* and *own bank account*, we use *active phone* and *active mobile money* as the instruments. The first instrument is where the respondent owns a smartphone and has been using it for financial transactions in the past 90 days. Similarly, our second instrument represents those who have used a registered mobile money account within the past 90 days. We argue that these instruments are highly correlated with the financial inclusion variables in our data set. However, these instruments do not perform well when we restrict the analysis to those respondents with a bank account in the regression for the *active bank account*. Therefore, we use two other instrumental variables: *financial literacy* and *belonging to informal financial institution*. The informal financial institutions comprise informal societies or group saving schemes, and *financial literacy* is the dummy variable equal to 1 if the respondents answered three or more of the five financial literacy questions in the survey correctly.[13] Amongst those with a bank account, these two instruments are correlated with actively using a bank account.

Table 9.4 presents the endogeneity-corrected linear regression results.[14] Our variables of interest are now all positive and highly statistically significant. This substantial change is evidence of a sizeable downward endogeneity bias. After correcting for it, our estimates suggest being financially included increases the PPI value by 0.227 units. The effect of bank account ownership is even larger: 0.34 units. However, amongst those with a bank account, active usage of the account increases the PPI value only by 0.135 units. All three estimates are economically significant, hinting at the successful outcome of the efforts by the GOI to address the issue of poverty reduction by increasing bank accounts in households.

Next, in the mid-section of Table 9.4 we present the estimates of the instruments in the first-stage regression. We observe that they all have significant explanatory power. Moreover, at the bottom section of Table 9.4, we present tests for under-identification, weak identification, and over-identification of restrictions. The Kleibergen-Paap rk LM statistic indicates that our chosen

Table 9.4 Linear regression controlling for endogeneity (dependent variable: PPI score)

Variables	*Financial inclusion*	*Bank account*	*Active bank account*
Financial inclusion	0.227*** (0.037)		
Bank account ownership		0.340*** (0.062)	
Active bank account			0.135*** (0.039)
Other control variables	YES	YES	YES
R^2	0.26	0.03	0.33
N	44,990	44,990	30,165
Instrumental variables			
Active phone	0.052*** (0.007)	0.04*** (0.008)	–
Active mobile money	0.154*** (0.007)	0.093*** (0.011)	–
Financial literacy	–	–	0.026*** (0.006)
Belong to informal financial institution	–	–	0.082*** (0.008)
Tests			
Kleibergen-Paap rk LM statistic (p-value)	522.645 (0.0000)	140.81 (0.0000)	110.454 (0.0000)
Kleibergen-Paap rk Wald F statistic (10% maximal IV size)	502.706 (19.93)	78.33 (19.93)	56.189 (19.93)
Hansen J statistic (p-value)	0.039 (0.8438)	0.443 (0.5057)	0.818 (0.3658)

Source: Authors' calculations.

Note: All models have been weighted using the sampling weights provided in the 2017 Financial Inclusion Insights Survey – Wave 5.
PPI = Poverty Probability Index.
Robust standard errors are reported in parenthesis.
*** significant at the 1% level; ** significant at the 5% level; * significant at the 10% level.

set of instruments for all three columns is relevant and that the model is identified.[15] We also reject the null hypothesis of weak identification based on the Kleibergen-Paap rk Wald statistic.[16] Moreover, having multiple instruments lets us test the validity of the instruments. On the basis of the Hansen J statistic of overidentifying restrictions, we fail to reject the joint null hypothesis that the instruments are valid.

Earlier, when the dependent variable is *poor*, we used the probit model to identify the effects of financial inclusion variables on the household's likelihood of being poor. However, we did not control for possible endogeneity. In order to

Table 9.5 Linear probability model controlling for endogeneity (dependent variable: poor)

Variables	*Financial inclusion*	*Bank account*	*Active bank account*
Financial inclusion	–0.533***		
	(0.072)		
Bank account ownership		–0.797***	
		(0.109)	
Active bank account			–0.445***
			(0.090)
First-stage residual	0.522***	0.789***	0.429***
	(0.072)	(0.109)	(0.090)
Other control variables	YES	YES	YES
N	44,990	44,990	30,165
Instrumental variables			
Active phone	0.052***	0.04***	–
	(0.007)	(0.008)	
Active mobile money	0.154***	0.093***	–
	(0.007)	(0.011)	
Financial literacy	–	–	0.026***
			(0.006)
Belong to informal financial institution	–	–	0.082***
			(0.008)

Source: Authors' calculations

Note: All models have been weighted using the sampling weights provided in the 2017 Financial Inclusion Insights Survey – Wave 5. Marginal effects are reported, and they are measured at the mean of the corresponding control variable for continuous variables, and as the difference in predicted probability of switching from 0 to 1 for dummy variables. Robust standard errors are reported in parenthesis. *** significant at the 1% level; ** significant at the 5% level; * significant at the 10% level.

do that, we again need to implement a two-stage model, similar to 2SLS. Since *poor* is a dummy variable, implementing a linear two-stage least squares would not be appropriate. Thus, we use the two-stage residual inclusion (2SRI) method to address this concern.[17] To do this, in the first stage we estimate the financial inclusion variables using a linear probability model (LPM) and calculate the residual from this LPM estimation. We then include the residual as an additional regressor along with the financial inclusion variable in the probit model for the poverty regression.

Table 9.5 presents the endogeneity-corrected results. While the financial inclusion variables were all negative and significant in Table 9.3, the magnitudes of the estimates were minimal. Now, however, we observe the actual effect of these variables. Compared to not being financially included, those households that are financially included are 53.3% less likely to be poor. We observe an even larger effect for bank account ownership, which is consistent with our finding in Table 9.4. Having a bank account, compared to not having one, lowers the probability of being poor by 79.7%. Finally, having an active bank account, compared to having a dormant one, lowers the likelihood of being poor by 44.5%.

We report the estimates for the first-stage residual, which is added to the second-stage regression. This variable is statistically significant for all three columns, implying that the financial inclusion variables are indeed endogenous. Moreover, the bottom section of Table 9.5 presents the LPM estimates of the instruments for the first stage regression. All instrumental variables (IVs) are highly significant.

9.5 Conclusion

This chapter focuses on the effect of financial inclusion on poverty reduction in India. We first highlight the successful efforts by the RBI and the GOI in terms of extending access to banking services to the rural areas of the country. Using the World Bank's Global Findex data, we show that these efforts have been greatly successful; by 2017, a large majority of Indians had access to formal banking services. More impressively, the account ownership gaps in terms of gender, income, and location (rural/urban) have been eliminated.

We then scrutinise the poverty reduction effect of the financial inclusion success in India. We utilise various measures of poverty, as well as for financial inclusion. We also correct for possible endogeneity of the financial inclusion variables in our analysis. Our results show that financial inclusion has a positive and significant effect on reducing poverty in India. The findings are consistent across various measures. We also emphasise the importance of controlling for endogeneity bias. If the bias is not taken into consideration, we find potentially misleading results of no association between financial inclusion and poverty levels in India. Policymakers should be cautious about the significant level of bias while doing a similar analysis.

Finally, we focus on those with a bank account, and show that an active usage of the bank accounts would lead to *further* reductions in poverty levels in India. In other words, the RBI and the GOI, which have been quite successful in extending access to formal banking, should consider policies which would encourage the usage of these bank accounts. Targeted programmes, such as offering financial education both in and outside the schools, with the aim of improving financial literacy could lead to further poverty reduction in India.

Notes

1 See Allen et al. (2016) for an increase in savings, Prasad (2010) for employment, Mani et al. (2013) for better decision making, and Angelucci, Karlan, and Zinman (2013) for improvements in mental well-being.

2 In a recent study, Neaime and Gaysset (2018) show that while financial inclusion decreases income inequality, it has no significant effect on poverty in Middle East and North Africa (MENA) countries.

3 We use three waves of the Global Findex database (World Bank, 2020). The data can be accessed using the following link: https://globalfindex.worldbank.org/.

4 For a summary of empirical studies on financial inclusion and growth see Demirguc-Kunt, Leora, and Singer (2017).

5 The data are available at: http://finclusion.org/.

6 Sampling weights for the data are based on the probability of selection at each stage of sampling. They are then adjusted for non-response at the household and household member levels. The sampling weights are also normalised at the national level.

7 Note that in one part of our analysis we focus only on those respondents with a bank account. In this part of our study, our sample is reduced to 35,671 respondents.

8 For further details on PPI, see https://www.povertyindex.org/.

9 In our analysis, we rescale the PPI variable such that it is between 0 and 1.

10 FII considers an institution to be a full-service financial institution if it offers the following services: savings, credit, money transfers, insurance, and investment. According to the FII survey, these institutions are banks, mobile money service providers, and non-bank financial institutions, such as payments banks.

11 Detailed definitions of these variables are presented in Appendix 9.1.

12 See Churchill and Marisetty (2019) for a similar endogeneity correction analysis.

13 Our definition of *financial literacy* is similar to the one used by Lyons et al. (2019).

14 First-stage regression results, other than the estimates of the instrumental variables, are not presented in the chapter, but they are available upon request.

15 This is a rank test. Under the null hypothesis that the equation is under-identified, this statistic is distributed as χ^2 with (L1 – K1 + 1) degrees of freedom, where L1 is the number of excluded instruments and K1 is the number of endogenous regressors. A rejection of the null indicates that the matrix of reduced form coefficients is of full rank, meaning the model is identified (Baum, Schaffer, and Stillman, 2010).

16 The weak ID test critical values compiled by Stock and Yogo (2005) are:

10% maximal IV size – 19.93
15% maximal IV size – 11.59
20% maximal IV size – 8.75
25% maximal IV size – 7.25

17 The 2SRI method is a special case of the control function approach to address endogeneity. This approach has gained popularity recently, especially in applied health research. See, for instance, DeSimone (2002), Shea et al. (2007), Terza, Basu, and Rathouz (2008), Biro (2014), and Eldridge, Onur, and Velamuri (2017).

References

Abraham, N. (2019), 'Financial Inclusion Low Despite 356 Mn Jan Dhan Accounts', *Factchecker.in*, 17 May. www.factchecker.in/financial-inclusion-low-despite-356-mn-jan-dhan-accounts/ (accessed 25 June 2020).

Allen, F., A. Demirguc-Kunt, L. Klapper, and M.S.M. Peria (2016), 'The Foundations of Financial Inclusion: Understanding Ownership and Use of Formal Accounts', *Journal of Financial Intermediation*, 27(July), pp.1–30.

Angelucci, M., D. Karlan, and J. Zinman (2013), *Win Some Lose Some? Evidence from a Randomized Microcredit Program Placement Experiment by Compartamos Banco*. Cambridge, MA: National Bureau of Economic Research.

Baum, C., M. Schaffer, and S. Stillman (2010), 'IVREG29: Stata Module for Extending Instrumental Variables/2SLS, GMM and AC/HAC, LIML and K-Class Regression', http://ideas.repec.org/c/boc/bocode/s425401.html (accessed 17 March 2020).

Beck, T., A. Demirguc-Kunt, and R. Levine (2007), 'Finance, Inequality and the Poor', *Journal of Economic Growth*, 12(1), pp.27–49.

Bell, C., and P.L. Rousseau (2001), 'Post-independence India: A Case of Finance-Led Industrialization?', *Journal of Development Economics*, 65(1), pp.153–75.

Binswanger, H.P., and S.R. Khandker (1995), 'The Impact of Formal Finance on the Rural Economy of India', *The Journal of Development Studies,* 32(2), pp.234–62.

Biro, A. (2014), 'Supplementary Private Health Insurance and Health Care Utilization of People Aged 50+', *Empirical Economics*, 46(2), pp.501–24.

Bruhn, M., and I. Love (2014), 'The Real Impact of Improved Access to Finance: Evidence from Mexico', *Journal of Finance*, 69(3), pp.1347–76.

Burgess, R., and R. Pande (2005), 'Do Rural Banks Matter? Evidence from the Indian Social Banking Experiment', *American Economic Review*, 95(3), pp.780–95.

Chibba, M. (2009), 'Financial Inclusion, Poverty Reduction and the Millennium Development Goals', *The European Journal of Development Research*, 21(2), pp.213–30.

Churchill, S.A., and V.B, Marisetty (2019), 'Financial Inclusion and Poverty: A Tale of Forty- Five Thousand Households', *Applied Economics,* 52(16), pp. 1777–1788.

Demirguc-Kunt, A., S. Leora, and D. Singer (2017), 'Financial Inclusion and Inclusive Growth: A Review of Recent Empirical Evidence', *Policy Research Working Paper*, No. WPS. 8040. Washington, DC: World Bank Group. http://documents.worldbank.org/curated/en/403611493134249446/pdf/WPS8040.pdf (accessed 17 March 2020).

DeSimone, J. (2002), 'Illegal Drug Use and Employment', *Journal of Labor Economics,* 20(4), pp.952–77.

Eldridge, D., I. Onur, and M. Velamuri (2017), 'The Impact of Private Hospital Insurance on the Utilization of Hospital Care in Australia', *Applied Economics*, 49(1), pp.78–95.

Ghosh, S., and D. Vinod (2017), 'What Constrains Financial Inclusion for Women? Evidence from Micro Data', *World Development*, 92(April), pp.60–81.

Inoue, T. (2019), 'Financial Inclusion and Poverty Reduction in India', *Journal of Financial Economic Policy*, 11(1), pp.21–33.

Jalilian, H., and C. Kirkpatrick (2005), 'Does Financial Development Contribute to Poverty Reduction?', *Journal of Development Studies*, 41(4), pp.636–56.

Lyons, A.C., J. Kass-Hanna, F. Liu, A.J. Greenlee, and L. Zeng (2019), 'Building Financial Resilience through Financial and Digital Literacy in South Asia and Sub-Saharan Africa', *ADBI Working Paper Series.* Tokyo: Asian Development Bank Institute.

Mani, A., S. Mullainathan, E. Shafir, and J. Zhao (2013), 'Poverty Impedes Cognitive Function', *Science*, 341(6149), pp.976–80.

Menon, P. (2019), 'Financial Inclusion, Banking the Unbanked: Concepts, Issues, and Policies for India', *Journal of Public Affairs.* https://doi.org/10.1002/pa.1911 (accessed 17 March 2020).

Neaime, S., and I. Gaysset (2018), 'Financial Inclusion and Stability in MENA: Evidence from Poverty and Inequality', *Finance Research Letters*, 24(March), pp.230–37.

Prasad, E.S. (2010), *Financial Sector Regulation and Reforms in Emerging Markets: An Overview.*. Cambridge, MA: National Bureau of Economic Research.

Sehrawat, M., and A. Giri (2016), 'Financial Development and Poverty Reduction in India: An Empirical Investigation', *International Journal of Social Economics*, 43(2), pp.106–22.

Shea, D., J. Terza, B. Stuart, and B. Briesacher (2007), 'Estimating the Effects of Prescription Drug Coverage for Medicare Beneficiaries', *Health Services Research*, Part I, 42(3), pp.933–49.

Stock, J.H., and M. Yogo (2005), 'Testing for Weak Instruments in Linear IV Regression', in D.W.K. Andrews and J.H. Stock (eds.), *Identification and Inference for Econometric Models: Essays in Honor of Thomas of Thomas Rothenberg*. Cambridge, MA: Cambridge University Press, pp. 20–108.

Swamy, V. (2014), 'Financial Inclusion, Gender Dimension, and Economic Impact on Poor Households', *World Development*, 56(April), pp.1–15.

Terza, J., A. Basu, and P. Rathouz (2008), 'Two-Stage Residual Inclusion Estimation: Addressing Endogeneity in Health Econometric Modelling', *Journal of Health Economics*, 27(3), pp.531–43.

World Bank (2020), *Financial Inclusion*. Washington, DC: World Bank. www.worldbank.org/en/topic/financialinclusion (accessed 25 June 2020).

Appendix 9.1 Variable definitions

Variable	*Definition*
PPI score	A continuous score between 0 and 1 measuring the likelihood of a household living below the $2.50/day (2005 PPP) poverty line.
Poor	Equals 1 if the household is living below the $2.50/day (2005 PPP) poverty line, and 0 otherwise.
Bank account ownership	Equals 1 if the respondent has a bank account registered in their name, and 0 otherwise.
Active bank account	Equals 1 if account is used for withdrawal/deposit or other financial activity in the past 90 days, and 0 otherwise.
Male	Equals 1 if the respondent is male, and 0 otherwise.
Age	Age of the respondent.
Rural	Equals 1 if the respondent lives in a rural area, and 0 otherwise.
Married	Equals 1 if the respondent is married, and 0 otherwise.
Number of people	Number of people in the household.
Education	Variable that shows the education level of the respondent being no education, 1–6 years, 6–12 years, or more than 12 years.
Literate	Equals 1 if the respondent is literate, and 0 otherwise.
Farmland	Equals 1 if the household owns farmland, and 0 otherwise.
Employment	Variable that shows if a person is full-time, part-time, occasionally employed, self-employed, or not employed.
Religion	Variable representing the religion of the respondent being Hinduism, Islam, Christianity, Sikhism, or Buddhism.
Household head	Equals 1 if the respondent is the head of the household, and 0 otherwise.
Financial literacy	Equals 1 if the respondent answered three or more of the five financial literacy questions in the survey correctly, and 0 otherwise.
Active phone	Equals 1 if the respondent owns a smartphone and has been using it for financial transactions in the past 90 days, and 0 otherwise.
Active mobile money	Equals 1 if the respondent has used a registered mobile money account in the past 90 days, and 0 otherwise.
Belong to informal financial institution	Equals 1 if the respondent belongs to an informal financial institution such as informal societies or group saving schemes, and 0 otherwise.

Source: The Financial Inclusion Insights Program, InterMedia.

Note: Five financial literacy questions assess the respondent's knowledge of interest rates, compounding interest (two questions), inflation, and risk diversification.
PPI = Poverty Probability Index; PPP = Purchasing Power Parity.

Index